A·N·N·U·A·L E·D·I

MW00826327

Western Civilization
Volume II

12th Edition

Early Modern Through the 20th Century

EDITOR

Robert L. Lembright

James Madison University

Robert L. Lembright teaches World Civilization, Ancient Near East, Byzantine, Islamic, and Greek/Roman history at James Madison University. He received his B.A. from Miami University and his M.A. and Ph.D from The Ohio State University. Dr. Lembright has been a participant in many National Endowment for the Humanities Summer Seminars and Institutes on Egyptology, the Ancient Near East, Byzantine History, and the Ottoman Empire. He has written several articles in the four editions of *The Global Experience*, as well as articles in the *James Madison Journal* and *Western Views of China and the Far East*. His research has concentrated on the French Renaissance of the sixteenth century, and he has published reports in the *Bulletins et memoires, Société archéologique et historique de la Charente*. In addition, Dr. Lembright has written many book reviews on the ancient world and Byzantine and Islamic history for *History: Reviews of New Books*.

McGraw-Hill/Dushkin

530 Old Whitfield Street, Guilford, Connecticut 06437

Visit us on the Internet
http://www.dushkin.com

Credits

1. **The Age of Power**
   Unit photo—National Gallery of Art, Washington, DC.
2. **Rationalism, Enlightenment, and Revolution**
   Unit photo—National Archives photo.
3. **Industry, Ideology, Nationalism, and Imperialism: The Nineteenth Century**
   Unit photo—Library of Congress photo.
4. **Modernism, Statism, and Total War: The Twentieth Century**
   Unit photo—National Gallery of Art, Washington, DC.
5. **Conclusion: The New Millennium and the Human Perspective**
   Unit photo—United Nations photo by John Isaac.

Copyright

Cataloging in Publication Data
Main entry under title: Annual Editions: Western Civilization, Vol. II: Early Modern Through the 20th Century.
    1. Civilization—Periodicals. 2. World history—Periodicals. I. Lembright, Robert L. *comp.* II. Title: Western Civilization, Vol. II.
ISBN 0–07–254827–4   901.9'05   82–645823   ISSN 0735-0392

Twelfth Edition

Cover image © 2003 PhotoDisc, Inc.
Printed in the United States of America   1234567890BAHBAH543   Printed on Recycled Paper

To the Reader

What does it mean to say that we are attempting to study the history of Western civilizations?

A traditional course in Western civilization was often a chronological survey in the development of European institutions and ideas, with a slight reference to the Near East and the Americas and other places where Westernization has occurred. Typically it began with the Greeks, then the Romans, and on to the medieval period, and finally to the modern era, depicting the distinctive characteristics of each stage, as well as each period's relation to the preceding and succeeding events. Of course, in a survey so broad, from Adam to the atomic age in two semesters, a certain superficiality was inevitable. Main characters and events galloped by; often there was little opportunity to absorb and digest complex ideas that have shaped Western culture.

It is tempting to excuse these shortcomings as unavoidable. However, to present a course in Western civilization which leaves students with only a scrambled series of events, names, dates, and places, is to miss a great opportunity. For the promise of such a broad course of study is that it enables students to explore great turning points or shifts in the development of Western culture. Close analysis of these moments enables students to understand the dynamics of continuity and change over time. At best, the course can give a coherent view of the Western tradition and its interplay with non-Western cultures. It can offer opportunities for students to compare various historical forms of authority, religion, and economic organization, to assess the great struggles over the meaning of truth and reality that have sometimes divided Western culture, and even to reflect on the price of progress.

Yet, to focus exclusively on Western civilization can lead us to ignore non-Western peoples and cultures or else to perceive them in ways that some label as "Eurocentric." But contemporary courses in Western history are rarely, if ever, mere exercises in European tribalism. Indeed, they offer an opportunity to subject the Western tradition to critical scrutiny, to asses its accomplishments and its shortfalls. Few of us who teach these courses would argue that Western history is the only history which contemporary students should know. Yet it should be an essential part of what they learn, for it is impossible to understand the modern world without some specific knowledge of the basic tenets of the Western tradition.

When students learn the distinctive traits of the West, they can develop a sense of the dynamism of history. They can begin to understand how ideas relate to social structures and social forces. They will come to appreciate the nature and significance of innovation and recognize how values often influence events. More specifically, they can trace the evolution of Western ideas about such essential matters as nature, humans, authority, the gods, even history itself; that is, they learn how the West developed its distinctive character. And, as historian Reed Dasenbrock has observed, in an age that seeks multicultural understanding there is much to be learned from "the fundamental multiculturalism of Western culture, the fact that it has been constructed out of a fusion of disparate and often conflicting cultural tradition." Of course, the articles collected in this volume cannot deal with all these matters, but by providing an alternative to the summaries of most textbooks, they can help students better understand the diverse traditions and processes that we call Western civilization. As with the last publication of Annual Editions: Western Civilization, Volumes I and II, have World Wide Web sites that can be used to further explore topics that are addressed in the essays. These sites can be hot-linked through the Annual Editions home page: http://www.dushkin.com/annualeditions.

This book is like our history—unfinished, always in process. It will be revised biennially. Comments and criticisms are welcome from all who use the book. For that a postpaid article rating form is included at the back of this volume. Please feel free to recommend articles that might improve the next edition. With your assistance, this anthology will continue to improve.

Robert Lembright
Editor

Contents

To the Reader   iv
Topic Guide   xi
Selected World Wide Web Sites   xiii

UNIT 1
The Age of Power

Five selections trace the evolution of political power in early modern times. Topics include the European state system, the emergence of British power, and the introduction of new cultures in developing areas.

Unit Overview   xvi

1. **The Emergence of the Great Powers,** Gordon A. Craig and Alexander L. George, from *Force and Statecraft: Diplomatic Problems of Our Times,* Oxford University Press, 1983
In 1600 Europe's greatest power complex was the Holy Roman Empire, which was in league with Spain. By the eighteenth century, however, the **European state system** was transformed so drastically that the **great powers** were Great Britain, France, Austria, Prussia, and Russia. This essay traces this significant shift in the balance of power.   2

2. **From Mercantilism to 'The Wealth of Nations',** Michael Marshall, *The World & I,* May 1999
Mercantilism was the practice of measuring a country's wealth by how much gold and silver bullion it could amass. This theory was challenged by Adam Smith in his **Wealth of Nations,** who belived that economies worked best when they had the least government interference.   8

3. **The Poisons Affair,** Reggie Oliver, *History Today,* March 2001
A **poison scandal** erupted in 1679 at the court of **Louis XIV,** which touched the king, his mistress Madame de Montespan, and several ministers of the court. Reggie Oliver investigates the scandal and its results.   14

4. **400 Years of the East India Company,** Huw V. Bowen, *History Today,* July 2000
The East India Company proved to be one of the longest commercial enterprises ever undertaken in Britain. It was chartered in 1600 and finally dissolved after 1857. It was charged with the commercial **exploitation and defense** in a large part of India. What brought about its demise was excessive administrative costs and charges of misrule.   18

5. **"Thus in the Beginning All the World Was America",** Edward Cline, *Colonial Williamsburg,* April/May 1999
John Locke's influence in both England and colonial America is detailed by Edward Cline. Locke's essays contained ideas on **constitutional government** and laid the groundwork for the **separation of state and religion.**   23

The concepts in bold italics are developed in the article. For further expansion, please refer to the Topic Guide and the Index.

UNIT 2
Rationalism, Enlightenment, and Revolution

Nine articles discuss the impact of science, politics, changing social attitudes, and the rights of women in the Age of Enlightenment.

Unit Overview   **30**

6. **Descartes the Dreamer,** Anthony Grafton, *The Wilson Quarterly,* Autumn 1996
   Descartes advanced, even epitomized, *rationalism.* Anthony Grafton explains why this seventeenth-century thinker seems *modern* three and one-half centuries after his death.   **32**

7. **Benjamin Franklin: An American in London,** Esmond Wright, *History Today,* March 2000
   Esmond Wright details how the *philosopher-scientist* Benjamin Franklin spent 17 years in London and had respect and admiration for everything British and hoped for a colonial or governmental post. Yet, when the *American Revolution* occurred, Franklin wrote with pride about the possibilities of America.   **39**

8. **A New Light on Alchemy,** Zbigniew Szydlo and Richard Brzezinski, *History Today,* January 1997
   Were the earliest alchemists complete *charlatans* or the forerunners of *modern chemistry*? The authors state that the alchemists' goal was to find the Philosopher's Stone, a mysterious substance through which gold traveled to Earth's surface. They also searched for a universal solvent *(alkabest),* which could dissolve all substances, and an elixir of life, which would cure all diseases.   **44**

9. **Matrix of Modernity,** Roy Porter, *History Today,* April 2001
   A belief that *progress* was developing in economics, science, and manufacturing became the byword for the eighteenth-century English Englightenment writers. None was more prominent than Erasmus Darwin's poem, *Zoonomia,* which united the arts, sciences, medicine, and technology in praise of enlightened values.   **50**

10. **Witchcraft: The Spell That Didn't Break,** Owen Davies, *History Today,* August 1999
    Although the Enlightenment was supposed to eliminate all superstition, Owen Davies reports that many still believed in *witches* well into the nineteenth century. Illnesses, famines, jealousy, and gossip still provided sources of accusations.   **56**

11. **The Passion of Antoine Lavoisier,** Stephen Jay Gould, *Natural History,* June 1989
    Many people paid the price for the *French Revolution.* One was France's greatest scientist, Antoine Lavoisier. A proponent of some of the Revolution's early accomplishments, the famous chemist ran afoul of the *Committee of Public Safety* and its revolutionary tribunals. Stephen Jay Gould cites Lavoisier's accomplishments and ponders why in revolutionary times even a brilliant scientist was not immune from political extremists.   **62**

12. **The First Feminist,** Shirley Tomkievicz, *Horizon,* Spring 1972
    Mary Wollstonecraft, author of *Vindication of the Rights of Women* (1792), cogently argued that the *ideals of the Enlightenment* and of the *French Revolution* should be extended to *women.* This is her story.   **67**

13. **Catherine the Great: A Personal View,** Isabel de Madariaga, *History Today,* November 2001
    Catherine the Great has been seen as a usurper of the Russian throne, murderer of her husband, Peter III, and promiscuous in her lovers. Isabel de Madariaga says that Catherine was a very hard-working monarch, greatly interested in a *well-organized government* and the *welfare of her subjects.*   **72**

The concepts in bold italics are developed in the article. For further expansion, please refer to the Topic Guide and the Index.

14. **Napoleon the Kingmaker,** Philip Mansel, *History Today,* March 1998
    When **Napoleon** seized power in 1799 and established his empire in 1804, he swept away many ideas of the **French Revolution** and reverted to the ideas, manners, and costumes of the Old Regime. Philip Mansel contends that most monarchs feared rather than applauded Napoleon as a fellow ruler. **77**

UNIT 3
Industry, Ideology, Nationalism, and Imperialism: The Nineteenth Century

Nine articles focus on the nineteenth century in the Western world. Topics include the Industrial Revolution, role models, social issues, and the expansion of Europe.

Unit Overview **82**

15. **Arkwright: Cotton King or Spin Doctor?,** Karen Fisk, *History Today,* March 1998
    Richard Arkwright (1732–1792), inventor and entrepreneur, is given much of the credit for Britain's leadership in the **Industrial Revolution** during the late eighteenth and early nineteenth centuries. Author Karen Fisk raises questions about his accomplishments. **84**

16. **The Origins of Prussian Militarism,** Peter H. Wilson, *History Today,* May 2001
    Eighteenth-century contemporaries wrote that it was the **determination and skills** of the Prussian kings who militarized the Prussian state and society. With new German archives at his disposal, Peter Wilson says that it was the **successful wars of German unification** in 1866 and 1871 that brought about militarism. **89**

17. **Slavery and the British,** James Walvin, *History Today,* March 2002
    Although the British were not its originators, by the mid-eighteenth century they dominated the **Atlantic slave trade.** This trade was part of the global exchange of goods that added to the "greatness" of England. James Walvin examines the **economic and social consequences** of this trade. **93**

18. **Scrooge and Albert: Christmas in the 1840s,** Christine Lalumia, *History Today,* December 2001
    As Christine Lalumia points out, most of our Christmas traditions, such as carols and trees, have been around for centuries. It was **Queen Victoria and Prince Albert** who stressed family values and **Charles Dickens's** emphasis on sharing with the less fortunate that made Christmas one of the biggest yearly celebrations in Britain. **97**

19. **Nation-Building in 19th-Century Italy: The Case of Francesco Crispi,** Christopher Duggan, *History Today,* February 2002
    As **Prime Minister** Francesco Crispi introduced public health and welfare services, he felt that involving Italy in a great war would create a great feeling of partriotism. His ideas were later taken over by the **Italian Fascists.** **103**

20. **Not So Saintly?,** David van Biema, *Time,* September 4, 2000
    David van Biema details the controversy that arose when the Roman Catholic Church decided to beatify, or recognize **Pope Pius IX** as a candidate for sainthood. **108**

21. **Sweep Them Off the Streets,** John Marriott, *History Today,* August 2000
    John Marriott examines how writers viewed the **poor,** from the seventeenth century through the Victorian era, and how they described the poor as a race apart. **111**

22. **The Hunt for Jack the Ripper,** William D. Rubinstein, *History Today,* May 2000
    The most sensational murder cases of the nineteenth century occurred in London in 1888: five working-class **prostitutes** were gruesomely slashed to death. William Rubinstein discusses the possible identity of the first serial murderer, **Jack the Ripper.** **115**

The concepts in bold italics are developed in the article. For further expansion, please refer to the Topic Guide and the Index.

23. **Destroyers and Preservers: Big Game in the Victorian Empire,** Harriet Ritvo, *History Today,* January 2002

In Victorian England, ***hunting of exotic game*** came to symbolize ***imperialism*** in the nineenth century. But as wild game disappeared, the view that they were to be exploited as rewards of imperialism was replaced by one that viewed game as a ***valuable resource to be protected.***   **123**

UNIT 4
Modernism, Statism, and Total War: The Twentieth Century

Eight selections discuss the evolution of the modern Western world, the world wars, the Nazi state, and the status of U.S. economic and political dominance in world affairs.

Unit Overview   **128**

24. **The Divine Sarah,** Joseph A. Harriss, *Smithsonian,* August 2001

Born in 1844, Sarah Bernhardt was a sickly child and not expected to live. But live she did, and she grew to become the first worldwide ***"superstar diva,"*** making her reputation as a great tragedienne, mistress of nobles, and political activist.   **130**

25. **Art Nouveau,** Stanley Meisler, *Smithsonian,* October 2000

Drawing inspiration from many sources—Japanese, Islamic, femmes fatales, and the Arts and Crafts movement—Art Nouveau used ***botanicals, arabesques, and curves.*** Its influence spread from Europe to America where architects such as ***Frank Lloyd Wright*** and artists such as ***Louis Comfort Tiffany*** employed the style. Yet, the vogue was over by the first decade of the twentieth century when artists such as Picasso declared that it was not modern enough.   **136**

26. **Searching for Gavrilo Princip,** David DeVoss, *Smithsonian,* August 2000

When the Bosnian Serb ***Gavrilo Princip*** shot Archduke Franz Ferdinand and his wife on June 28, 1914, no one knew that it would precipitate ***World War I.*** David DeVoss discusses the details of the assassination and how Princip is remembered today.   **141**

27. **How the Modern Middle East Map Came to Be Drawn,** David Fromkin, *Smithsonian,* May 1991

The long-awaited collapse of the ***Ottoman Empire*** finally occurred in 1918. ***World War I*** and the ***Arab uprising*** paved the way for a new era in the Middle East. But it was the British, not the Arabs, who played the central role in the reshaping of the ***geopolitics*** of the region.   **147**

28. **Nazism in the Classroom,** Lisa Pine, *History Today,* April 1997

Lisa Pine explains how Germany's ***National Socialist dictatorship*** brought political correctness—Nazi-style—to German schoolchildren. The new curriculum featured pseudoscience, racial and gender ***stereotypes,*** distorted history, Aryan pride, and political arithmetic.   **155**

29. **Pearl Harbor: The First Energy War,** Charles Maechling, *History Today,* December 2000

Before World War II, the United States was the ***major oil*** supplier to Japan. When Japan and Russia signed the nonaggression Pact of 1941 and the Japanese moved into ***French Indochina,*** President Franklin Roosevelt ordered all Japanese assets frozen and embargoed oil exports. Charles Maechling details the actions and reactions of each government in the move to war.   **159**

30. **His Finest Hour,** John Keegan, *U.S. News & World Report,* May 29, 2000

When Adolf Hitler overpowered Western Europe, he expected Britain to submit, but one man, Prime Minister ***Winston Churchill,*** arose to reject surrender and eventually lead his country to victory. John Keegan details Churchill's life as a ***politician, war leader,*** and ***Noble Prize–winning author.***   **166**

The concepts in bold italics are developed in the article. For further expansion, please refer to the Topic Guide and the Index.

31. **Mutable Destiny: The End of the American Century?,** Donald W. White, *Harvard International Review,* Winter 1997–1998
For much of the twentieth century, the **United States** was a great **hegemonic power** with global military commitments—an economic dynamo, a magnet for immigration, and an unparalled cultural force. But now with the start of the new **millennium,** historians and other social analysts suggest that the nation may be in decline. Donald White considers recent assessments of America's condition. **171**

UNIT 5
Conclusion: The New Millennium and the Human Perspective

Nine articles examine how politics, war, economics, and culture affect the prospects of humankind.

Unit Overview   176

32. **A Brief History of Relativity,** Stephen Hawking, *Time,* December 31, 1999
Albert Einstein was chosen as **Time**'s "Man of the Twentieth Century" because of his **theory of relativity.** Stephen Hawking summarizes Einstein's contributions, which challenged Issac Newton's universe and transformed physics forever. **178**

33. **Malaria Kills One Child Every 30 Seconds,** Donovan Webster, *Smithsonian,* September 2000
Donovan Webster says that until recently the affluent countries of the world paid little attention to **malaria,** which affects 40 percent of the world's population. With cases now appearing in the United States, the West should revaluate the danger and take steps to prevent the disease from spreading. **183**

34. **The Big Meltdown,** Eugene Linden, *Time,* September 4, 2000
Scientists have observed a **warming** trend in the Arctic region. The difference in temperatures between the tropics and the Arctic drives the global climate system. If glacial ice melts quickly, it could cover the denser sea water and that might drastically drop temperatures, plunging Europe and North America into an **Ice Age.** **188**

35. **Jungles of the Mind: The Invention of the 'Tropical Rain Forest',** Philip Stott, *History Today,* May 2001
The idea of a **tropical rain forest** is a twentieth-century development, derived from the German romantic myth that sees the Earth as the last Eden, only vulnerable to human greed. Most would be shocked to learn that **forests are the exception** in the world and that rain forests are less than 12,000 years old. **191**

36. **Why Don't They Like Us?,** Stanley Hoffmann, *The American Prospect,* November 19, 2001
In the wake of September 11, 2001, Stanley Hoffmann explores the factors that have led to various strands of **anti-Americanism** around the globe. He also suggests ways of addressing legitimate grievances against the contemporary world's sole **superpower.** **197**

37. **Folly & Failure in the Balkans,** Tom Gallagher, *History Today,* September 1999
Although Otto von Bismarck said that the Balkans were not worth the bones of a single Pomeranian grenadier, for 200 years the major European powers have intervened in the region. The results of this interference created small, weak states while **neglecting differing religions, ethnic identities, and rising nationalism.** This has led to the difficult situations that now confront the West. **201**

38. **The Poor and the Rich,** *The Economist,* May 25, 1996
Why are some countries richer than others? The issues of **economic growth** and **national development** are attracting the attention of contemporary economists. Here is a survey of their findings. **206**

The concepts in bold italics are developed in the article. For further expansion, please refer to the Topic Guide and the Index.

39. Reform for Russia: Forging a New Domestic Policy, Boris Nemtsov, *Harvard International Review,* Summer 2000

Boris Nemtsov surveys the various reforms in Russia and writes that, while some *political, economic, and legal rights* might be curtailed in the short term, in the long term Russia needs time to develop.   **210**

40. 'The Barbarians Have Not Come', Peter Waldron, *History Today,* June 2000

Peter Waldron explains that while Europe in the twentieth century had *terrible wars, massive civilian deaths,* and violent *dictatorships,* there were many signs of progress. Public health, social insurance, literacy, and the transformation of women's lives were all a part of this progress.   **215**

Index   **219**

Test Your Knowledge Form   **222**

Article Rating Form   **223**

The concepts in bold italics are developed in the article. For further expansion, please refer to the Topic Guide and the Index.

Topic Guide

This topic guide suggests how the selections in this book relate to the subjects covered in your course. You may want to use the topics listed on these pages to search the Web more easily.

On the following pages a number of Web sites have been gathered specifically for this book. They are arranged to reflect the units of this *Annual Edition.* You can link to these sites by going to the DUSHKIN ONLINE support site at *http://www.dushkin.com/online/.*

ALL THE ARTICLES THAT RELATE TO EACH TOPIC ARE LISTED BELOW THE BOLD-FACED TERM.

Archaeology
25. Art Nouveau

Art
25. Art Nouveau

Asia
4. 400 Years of the East India Company

Authority
1. The Emergence of the Great Powers
5. "Thus in the Beginning All the World Was America"
9. Matrix of Modernity
13. Catherine the Great: A Personal View
14. Napoleon the Kingmaker
31. Mutable Destiny: The End of the American Century?
39. Reform for Russia: Forging a New Domestic Policy

Business nations
2. From Mercantilism to 'The Wealth of Nations'
4. 400 Years of the East India Company
15. Arkwright: Cotton King or Spin Doctor?

Cities
22. The Hunt for Jack the Ripper

Cold war
39. Reform for Russia: Forging a New Domestic Policy

Colonialism
4. 400 Years of the East India Company
27. How the Modern Middle East Map Came to Be Drawn

Culture
3. The Poisons Affair
9. Matrix of Modernity
10. Witchcraft: The Spell That Didn't Break
12. The First Feminist
18. Scrooge and Albert: Christmas in the 1840s
24. The Divine Sarah
28. Nazism in the Classroom
31. Mutable Destiny: The End of the American Century?
37. Folly & Failure in the Balkans

Democracy
39. Reform for Russia: Forging a New Domestic Policy

Descartes, Rene
6. Descartes the Dreamer

Ecology
23. Destroyers and Preservers: Big Game in the Victorian Empire
34. The Big Meltdown
35. Jungles of the Mind: The Invention of the 'Tropical Rain Forest'

Economics
1. The Emergence of the Great Powers
2. From Mercantilism to 'The Wealth of Nations'
4. 400 Years of the East India Company
15. Arkwright: Cotton King or Spin Doctor?
17. Slavery and the British
21. Sweep Them Off the Streets
29. Pearl Harbor: The First Energy War
38. The Poor and the Rich

Einstein, Albert
32. A Brief History of Relativity

Enlightenment
6. Descartes the Dreamer
7. Benjamin Franklin: An American in London
9. Matrix of Modernity
10. Witchcraft: The Spell That Didn't Break
11. The Passion of Antoine Lavoisier
12. The First Feminist
13. Catherine the Great: A Personal View

Ethnic issues
26. Searching for Gavrilo Princip
27. How the Modern Middle East Map Came to Be Drawn
28. Nazism in the Classroom
37. Folly & Failure in the Balkans

Fascism
28. Nazism in the Classroom

Hawking, Stephen
32. A Brief History of Relativity

Ideology
6. Descartes the Dreamer
12. The First Feminist
28. Nazism in the Classroom

Labor
17. Slavery and the British

Lavoisier, Antoine
11. The Passion of Antoine Lavoisier

Liberalism
5. "Thus in the Beginning All the World Was America"
9. Matrix of Modernity

Middle class
18. Scrooge and Albert: Christmas in the 1840s

Middle East
27. How the Modern Middle East Map Came to Be Drawn

Modernization

39. Reform for Russia: Forging a New Domestic Policy

Napoleon

14. Napoleon the Kingmaker

Nation-state

1. The Emergence of the Great Powers
7. Benjamin Franklin: An American in London
19. Nation-Building in 19th-Century Italy: The Case of Francesco Crispi

Nationalism

14. Napoleon the Kingmaker
16. The Origins of Prussian Militarism
26. Searching for Gavrilo Princip
27. How the Modern Middle East Map Came to Be Drawn
37. Folly & Failure in the Balkans

Newton, Isaac

32. A Brief History of Relativity

Philosophy

5. "Thus in the Beginning All the World Was America"
6. Descartes the Dreamer

Politics

1. The Emergence of the Great Powers
4. 400 Years of the East India Company
5. "Thus in the Beginning All the World Was America"
9. Matrix of Modernity
11. The Passion of Antoine Lavoisier
13. Catherine the Great: A Personal View
14. Napoleon the Kingmaker
27. How the Modern Middle East Map Came to Be Drawn
30. His Finest Hour
31. Mutable Destiny: The End of the American Century?
39. Reform for Russia: Forging a New Domestic Policy

Religion

10. Witchcraft: The Spell That Didn't Break
20. Not So Saintly?
35. Jungles of the Mind: The Invention of the 'Tropical Rain Forest'
37. Folly & Failure in the Balkans

Revolution

7. Benjamin Franklin: An American in London
11. The Passion of Antoine Lavoisier
14. Napoleon the Kingmaker
19. Nation-Building in 19th-Century Italy: The Case of Francesco Crispi

Science

8. A New Light on Alchemy
11. The Passion of Antoine Lavoisier
32. A Brief History of Relativity
33. Malaria Kills One Child Every 30 Seconds

Slavery

17. Slavery and the British

Society

3. The Poisons Affair
10. Witchcraft: The Spell That Didn't Break
18. Scrooge and Albert: Christmas in the 1840s
21. Sweep Them Off the Streets
22. The Hunt for Jack the Ripper
24. The Divine Sarah
25. Art Nouveau

Technology

15. Arkwright: Cotton King or Spin Doctor?

Totalitarianism

28. Nazism in the Classroom

Values

36. Why Don't They Like Us?

War

1. The Emergence of the Great Powers
14. Napoleon the Kingmaker
26. Searching for Gavrilo Princip
29. Pearl Harbor: The First Energy War
30. His Finest Hour
37. Folly & Failure in the Balkans

Warfare

4. 400 Years of the East India Company
30. His Finest Hour

Westernization

39. Reform for Russia: Forging a New Domestic Policy

Women

10. Witchcraft: The Spell That Didn't Break
12. The First Feminist
13. Catherine the Great: A Personal View
24. The Divine Sarah

World War I

27. How the Modern Middle East Map Came to Be Drawn

World War II

30. His Finest Hour

38. The Poor and the Rich
40. 'The Barbarians Have Not Come'

World Wide Web Sites

The following World Wide Web sites have been carefully researched and selected to support the articles found in this reader. The easiest way to access these selected sites is to go to our DUSHKIN ONLINE support site at *http://www.dushkin.com/online/*.

AE: Western Civilization, Volume 2

The following sites were available at the time of publication. Visit our Web site—we update DUSHKIN ONLINE regularly to reflect any changes.

General Sources

Archaeological Institute of America (AIA)
http://www.archaeological.org

Review this site of the AIA for information about various eras in Western civilization.

Archive of Texts and Documents—Hanover College
http://history.hanover.edu/texts.html

This Hanover College historical texts project is very creative. Sources are available on Europe and East Asia.

Biographies; The Philosophers
http://www.blupete.com/Literature/Biographies/ Philosophy?BiosPhil.htm

At this site, find biographies and works of René Descartes, John Locke, and many other philosophers whose ideas affected Western civilization.

Discover's Web
http://www.win.tue.nl/~engels/discovery/index.html

Data on historical voyages of discovery and exploration from ancient to modern times are available from this Web site.

Facets of Religion/Caspar Voogt
http://bounty.bcca.org/~cvoogt/Religion/mainpage.html

Caspar Voogt offers this virtual library of links to information on major world religions, including Islam, Judaism, Zoroastrianism, Baha'ism, and Christianity. Various links in comparative religion are provided.

The History of Costumes
http://www.siue.edu/COSTUMES/history.html

This distinctive site illustrates garments worn by people in various historical eras. Clothing of common people is presented along with that worn by nobility. The site is based on a history of costumes through the ages that was originally printed between 1861 and 1880.

Key Religious and Philosophical Figures and Ideas and Personalities
http://www.sonoma.edu/history/reason/religious.html.htm

This list contains significant philosophical and/or religious works that were written during the time frame of 1605 through 1799 as well as the lifespan of those born during this time. Descartes, Locke, and Spinoza are just a few of the people whose works you can find here.

Library of Congress
http://www.loc.gov/

Examine this Web site to learn about the extensive resource tools, library services/resources, exhibitions, and databases available through the Library of Congress in many different subfields of historical studies.

Michigan Electronic Library
http://mel.lib.mi.us/humanities/history/

Browse through this enormous history site for an array of resources on the study of Western civilization, which are broken down by historical era, geographical area, and more.

Smithsonian Institution
http://www.si.edu/

This site provides access to the enormous resources of the Smithsonian, which holds some 140 million artifacts and specimens in its trust for "the increase and diffusion of knowledge." Here you can learn about social, cultural, economic, and political history, particularly about the United States, from a variety of viewpoints.

Western Civilization: Act 3
http://www.omnibusol.com/westernciv.html

An Interesting mix of information can be found at this eclectic site whose span is from the French Revolution to the present day. Thirty-seven pages lead to many other Internet sites.

UNIT 1: The Age of Power

EuroDocs: Primary Historical Documents from Western Europe
http://www.lib.byu.edu/~rdh/eurodocs/

This collection from the Brigham Young University Library is a high-quality set of historical documents from Western Europe. Facsimiles, translations, and even selected transcriptions are included. Click on the links to materials related to "Europe as a Supernational Region" and individual countries.

1492: An Ongoing Voyage/Library of Congress
http://lcweb.loc.gov/exhibits/1492/

Displays examining the causes and effects of Columbus's voyages to the Americas are provided on this site. "An Ongoing Voyage" explores the rich mixture of societies coexisting in five areas of the Western Hemisphere before European arrival. It also surveys the polyglot Mediterranean world at a dynamic turning point in its development.

Medieval Maps/University of Kansas
http://www.ukans.edu/kansas/medieval/graphics/maps/

Check out this unusual site for access to interesting, full-color maps of Europe. Each map is keyed to a specific date, and some pertain to the Age of Power.

World Wide Web Virtual Library/Latin American Studies
http://lanic.utexas.edu/las.html

Maintained by the University of Texas, this is the site of first resort for the exploration of a topic dealing with Latin America. It lists resources available on the Web for historical topics and related cultural subjects.

www.dushkin.com/online/

UNIT 2: Rationalism, Enlightenment, and Revolution

Adam Smith

http://cepa.newschool.edu/het/profiles/smith.htm

AQt this site there are links to the major works of Adam Smith, including the *Wealth of Nations,*and a list of additional resources.

Eighteenth-Century Resources/JackLynch

http://andromeda.rutgers.edu/~jlynch/18th/

Open this page to find links in eighteenth-century studies, including History, Literature, Religion and Theology, Science and Mathematics, and Art. Click on History, for example, for a number of resources for study of topics from Napoleon, to piracy and gambling, to a discussion of Catalonia in the eighteenth century.

Napoleon Bonaparte

http://www.napoleonbonaparte.nl

According to this site, you will find the best Napoleonic Internet sites in the world right here. Inaddition to many articles, there are many links to other sites as well as newspaper articles edited by Beryl Bernardi, called "News From the Front."

Western European Specialists Section/Association of College and Research Libraries

http://www.lib.virginia.edu/wess/

WESS provides links in regional and historical resources in European studies, as well as materials on contemporary Europe. Visit this site for texts and text collections, guides to library resources, book reviews, and WESS publications.

Women and Philosophy Website

http://www.nd.edu/~colldev/subjects/wss.html

Explore the many materials available through this site. It provides Internet collections of resources, ethics updates, bibliographies, information on organizations, and access to newsletters and journals.

UNIT 3: Industry, Ideology, Nationalism, and Imperialism: The Nineteenth Century

The Victorian Web

http://www.victorianweb.org/victorian/victov.html

The Victorian Web offers a complete examination into all aspects of Victorian life.

Historical U.S. Census Data Browser

http://fisher.lib.virginia.edu/census/

At this site, the interuniversity Consortium for Political and Social Research offers materials in various categories of historical social, economic, and demographic data. Access here a statistical overview of the United States, beginning in the late eighteenth century.

Society for Economic Anthropology Homepage

http://nautarch.tamu.edu/anth/sea/

This is the home page of the Society for Economic Anthropology, an association that strives to understand diversity and change in the economic systems of the world, and hence, in the organization of society and culture.

UNIT 4: Modernism, Statism, and Total War: The Twentieth Century

History Net

http://www.thehistorynet.com/THNarchives/AmericanHistory/

This National Historical Society site provides information on a wide range of topics, with emphasis on American history, book reviews, and special interviews.

Inter-American Dialogue (IAD)

http://www.iadialog.org/

This is the Web site for IAD, a premier U.S. center for policy analysis, communication, and exchange in Western Hemisphere affairs. The organization has helped to shape the agenda of issues and choices in hemispheric relations.

ISN International Relations and Security Network

http://www.isn.ethz.ch/

This site, maintained by the Center for Security Studies and Conflict Research, is a clearinghouse for extensive information on international relations and security policy. The many topics are listed by category (Traditional Dimensions of Security, New Dimensions of Security) and by major world regions.

Russian and East European Network Information Center/ University of Texas at Austin

http://reenic.utexas.edu/reenic.html

This is *the* Web site for exhaustive information on Russia and other republics of the former Soviet Union and Central/Eastern Europe on a large range of topics.

Terrorism Research Center

http://www.terrorism.com/

The Terrorism Research Center features original research on terrorism, counterterrorism documents, a comprehensive list of Web links, and monthly profiles of terrorist and counterterrorist groups.

World History Review/Scott Danford and Jon Larr

http://members.aol.com/sniper43/index.html

Associated with a college course, this site will lead you to information and links on a number of major topics of interest when studying Western civilization in the twentieth century: Imperialism, the Russian Revolution, World War I, World War II, the cold war, the Korean War, and Vietnam.

UNIT 5: Conclusion: The New Millennium and the Human Perspective

Center for Middle Eastern Students/University of Texas/

http://menic.utexas.edu/menic/religion.html

This site provides links to Web sites on Islam and the Islamic world. Information on Judaism and Christianity is also available through this Middle East Network Information Center.

Europa: European Union

http://europa.eu.int/

This site leads you to the history of the European Union (and its predecessors such as the European Community and European Common Market); descriptions of the increasingly powerful regional organization's policies, institutions, and goals; and documentation of treaties and other materials.

www.dushkin.com/online/

InterAction

http://www.interaction.pair.com/advocacy/

InterAction encourages grassroots action and engages government bodies and policymakers on various advocacy issues. Its Advocacy Committee provides this site to inform people on its initiatives to expand international humanitarian relief, refugee, and development-assistance programs.

The North-South Institute

http://www.nsi-ins.ca/ensi/index.html

Searching this site of the North-South Institute—which works to strengthen international development cooperation and enhance gender and social equity—will help you find information and debates on a variety of global issues.

Organization for Economic Co-operation and Development/ FDI Statistics

http://www.oecd.org/daf/statistics.htm

Explore world trade and investment trends and statistics on this site that provides links to related topics and addresses global economic issues on a country-by-country basis.

U.S. Agency for International Development

http://www.info.usaid.gov/

This Web site covers such issues as democracy, population and health, economic growth, and development. It provides specific information about different regions and countries.

Virtual Seminar in Global Political Economy/Global Cities & Social Movements

http://csf.colorado.edu/gpe/gpe95b/resources.html

This site of Internet resources is rich in links to subjects of interest in assessing the human condition today and in the future, covering topics such as sustainable cities, megacities, and urban planning.

World Bank

http://www.worldbank.org/

Review this site and its links for information on immigration and development now and in the future. News (press releases, summaries of new projects, speeches), publications, and coverage of numerous topics regarding development, countries, and regions are provided here.

World Wide Web Virtual Library: International Affairs Resources

http://www.etown.edu/vl/

Surf this site and its extensive links to learn about specific countries and regions, to research various think tanks and international organizations, and to study such vital topics as international law, human rights, and peacekeeping.

We highly recommend that you review our Web site for expanded information and our other product lines. We are continually updating and adding links to our Web site in order to offer you the most usable and useful information that will support and expand the value of your Annual Editions. You can reach us at: *http://www.dushkin.com/annualeditions/*.

UNIT 1

The Age of Power

Unit Selections

1. **The Emergence of the Great Powers**, Gordon A. Craig and Alexander L. George
2. **From Mercantilism to 'The Wealth of Nations'**, Michael Marshall
3. **The Poisons Affair**, Reggie Oliver
4. **400 Years of the East India Company**, Huw V. Bowen
5. **"Thus in the Beginning All the World Was America"**, Edward Cline

Key Points to Consider

- How did the European nations change in the 17th century?

- How did Adam Smith's economic theories challenge European thought?

- Who was involved in the poisoning scandal? Why did it happen?

- How did the East India Company evolve from a business enterprise into a governing body? Why was it abolished?

- How did John Locke influence constitutional government? What were some of the results of his influence?

 **Links: www.dushkin.com/online/**
These sites are annotated in the World Wide Web pages.

EuroDocs: Primary Historical Documents from Western Europe
http://www.lib.byu.edu/~rdh/eurodocs/

1492: An Ongoing Voyage/Library of Congress
http://lcweb.loc.gov/exhibits/1492/

Medieval Maps/University of Kansas
http://www.ukans.edu/kansas/medieval/graphics/maps/

World Wide Web Virtual Library/Latin American Studies
http://lanic.utexas.edu/las.html

The early modern period (c. 1450–c.1700) was a time of profound change for Western civilization. During this epoch the medieval frame of reference gave way to a modern orientation. The old order had been simply, but rigidly, structured. There was little social or geographical mobility. Europe was relatively backward and isolated from much of the world. The economy was dominated by self-sufficient agriculture in which trade and cities did not flourish. There were few rewards for technological innovation. A person's life seemed more attuned to revelation than to reason and science. The Church both inspired and limited intellectual and artistic expression. Most people were prepared to suppress their concerns to a higher order—whether religious or social.

This narrow world gradually gave way to the modern world. There is no absolute date that marks the separation, but elements of modernity were evident throughout Western civilization by the eighteenth century. In this context the late Medieval, Renaissance, and Reformation periods were transitional. They linked the medieval to the modern. But what were the facets of this emerging modernity? Beginning with the economic foundation, an economy based on money and commerce overlaid the old agrarian system, thus creating a new and important middle class in society. Urban life became increasingly important, allowing greater scope for personal expression. Modernity involved a state of mind as well. Europeans of the early modern period were conscious that their way of life was different from that of their ancestors. In addition, these moderns developed a different sense of time—for urban people, clock time superseded the natural rhythms of the changing season and the familiar cycles of planting and harvesting. As for the intellect, humanism, rationalism, and science began to take precedence over tradition—though not without a struggle. Protestantism presented yet another challenge to orthodoxy. And, as economic and political institutions evolved, new attitudes about power and authority emerged.

The early modern period is often called the Age of Power, because the modern state, with its power to tax, conscript, subsidize, and coerce, was taking shape. Its growth was facilitated by the changing economic order, which made it possible for governments to acquire money in unprecedented amounts—to hire civil servants, raise armies, protect and encourage national enterprise, and expand their power to the national boundaries and beyond.

Power, in various early modern manifestations, is the subject of the articles assembled in this unit. The first essay, "The Emergence of the Great Powers," surveys the shifting international balance of power during the seventeenth and eighteenth centuries. The second essay "From Mercantilism to the 'Wealth of Nations'" describes the new economic ideas that revolutionized Europe. While "400 Years of the East India Company" shows how one business venture used economic power to become a government agency. While the article "The Poisons Affair" shows the lengths to which some would go to have personal power. The last article deals with John Locke and his influence on constitutional power in England and America as seen in "'Thus in the Beginning All the World Was America.'"

The Emergence of the Great Powers

Gordon A. Craig and Alexander L. George

I

Although the term *great power* was used in a treaty for the first time only in 1815, it had been part of the general political vocabulary since the middle of the eighteenth century and was generally understood to mean Great Britain, France, Austria, Prussia, and Russia. This would not have been true in the year 1600, when the term itself would have meant nothing and a ranking of the European states in terms of political weight and influence would not have included three of the countries just mentioned. In 1600, Russia, for instance, was a remote and ineffectual land, separated from Europe by the large territory that was called Poland-Lithuania with whose rulers it waged periodic territorial conflicts, as it did with the Ottoman Turks to the south; Prussia did not exist in its later sense but, as the Electorate of Brandenburg, lived a purely German existence, like Bavaria or Wurttemberg, with no European significance; and Great Britain, a country of some commercial importance, was not accorded primary political significance, although it had, in 1588, demonstrated its will and its capacity for self-defense in repelling the Spanish Armada. In 1600, it is fair to say that, politically, the strongest center in Europe was the old Holy Roman Empire, with its capital in Vienna and its alliances with Spain (one of the most formidable military powers in Europe) and the Catholic states of southern Germany—an empire inspired by a militant Catholicism that dreamed

of restoring Charles V's claims of universal dominion. In comparison with Austria and Spain, France seemed destined to play a minor role in European politics, because of the state of internal anarchy and religious strife that followed the murder of Henri IV in 1610.

Why did this situation not persist? Or, to put it another way, why was the European system transformed so radically that the empire became an insignificant political force and the continent came in the eighteenth century to be dominated by Great Britain, France, Austria, Prussia, and Russia? The answer, of course, is war, or, rather more precisely, wars— a long series of religious and dynastic conflicts which raged intermittently from 1618 until 1721 and changed the rank order of European states by exhausting some and exalting others. As if bent upon supplying materials for the nineteenth-century Darwinians, the states mentioned above proved themselves in the grinding struggle of the seventeenth century to be the fittest, the ones best organized to meet the demands of protracted international competition.

The process of transformation began with the Thirty Years War, which stretched from 1618 to 1648. It is sometimes called the last of the religious wars, a description that is justified by the fact that it was motivated originally by the desire of the House of Habsburg and its Jesuit advisers to restore the Protestant parts of the empire to the true faith and because, in thirty years of fighting, the

religious motive gave way to political considerations and, in the spreading of the conflict from its German center to embrace all of Europe, some governments, notably France, waged war against their own coreligionists for material reasons. For the states that initiated this wasting conflict, which before it was over had reduced the population of central Europe by at least a third, the war was an unmitigated disaster. The House of Habsburg was so debilitated by it that it lost the control it had formerly possessed over the German states, which meant that they became sovereign in their own right and that the empire now became a mere adjunct of the Austrian crown lands. Austria was, moreover, so weakened by the exertions and losses of that war that in the period after 1648 it had the greatest difficulty in protecting its eastern possessions from the depredations of the Turks and in 1683 was threatened with capture of Vienna by a Turkish army. Until this threat was contained, Austria ceased to be a potent factor in European affairs. At the same time, its strongest ally, Spain, had thrown away an infantry once judged to be the best in Europe in battles like that at Nordlingen in 1634, one of those victories that bleed a nation white. Spain's decline began not with the failure of the Armada, but with the terrible losses suffered in Germany and the Netherlands during the Thirty Years War.

In contrast, the states that profited from the war were the Netherlands, which completed the winning of its independence from Spain in the course of the war and became a commercial and financial center of major importance; the kingdom of Sweden, which under the leadership of Gustavus Adolphus, the Lion of the North, plunged into the conflict in 1630 and emerged as the strongest power in the Baltic region; and France, which entered the war formally in 1635 and came out of it as the most powerful state in western Europe.

It is perhaps no accident that these particular states were so successful, for they were excellent examples of the process that historians have described as the emergence of the modern state, the three principal characteristics of which were effective armed forces, an able bureaucracy, and a theory of state that restrained dynastic exuberance and defined political interest in practical terms. The seventeenth century saw the emergence of what came to be called *raison d'état* or *ragione di stato*—the idea that the state was more than its ruler and more than the expression of his wishes; that it transcended crown and land, prince and people; that it had its particular set of interests and a particular set of necessities based upon them; and that the art of government lay in recognizing those interests and necessities and acting in accordance with them, even if this might violate ordinary religious or ethical standards. The effective state must have the kind of servants who would interpret *raison d'état* wisely and the kind of material and physical resources necessary to implement it. In the first part of the seventeenth century, the Dutch, under leaders like Maurice of Nassau and Jan de Witt, the Swedes, under Gustavus Adolphus and Oxenstierna, and the French, under the inspired ministry of Richelieu, developed the administration and the forces and theoretical skills that exemplify this ideal of modern statehood. That they survived the rigors of the Thirty Years War was not an accident, but rather the result of the fact that they never lost sight of their objectives and never sought objectives that were in excess of their capabilities. Gustavus Adolphus doubtless brought his country into the Thirty Years War to save the cause of Protestantism when it was at a low ebb,

but he never for a moment forgot the imperatives of national interest that impelled him to see the war also as a means of winning Swedish supremacy along the shore of the Baltic Sea. Cardinal Richelieu has been called the greatest public servant France ever had, but that title, as Sir George Clark has drily remarked, "was not achieved without many acts little fitting the character of a churchman." It was his clear recognition of France's needs and his absolute unconditionality in pursuing them that made him the most respected statesman of his age.

The Thirty Years War, then, brought a sensible change in the balance of forces in Europe, gravely weakening Austria, starting the irreversible decline of Spain, and bringing to the fore the most modern, best organized, and, if you will, most rationally motivated states: the Netherlands, Sweden, and France. This, however, was a somewhat misleading result, and the Netherlands was soon to yield its commercial and naval primacy to Great Britain (which had been paralyzed by civil conflict during the Thirty Years War), while Sweden, under a less rational ruler, was to throw its great gains away.

The gains made by France were more substantial, so much so that in the second half of the century, in the heyday of Louis XIV, they became oppressive. For that ruler was intoxicated by the power that Richelieu and his successor Mazarin had brought to France, and he wished to enhance it. As he wrote in his memoirs:

> The love of glory assuredly takes precedence over all other [passions] in my soul…. The hot blood of my youth and the violent desire I had to heighten my reputation instilled in me a strong passion for action…. *La Gloire*, when all is said and done, is not a mistress that one can ever neglect; nor can one be ever worthy of her slightest favors if one does not constantly long for fresh ones.

No one can say that Louis XIV was a man of small ambition. He dreamed in universal terms and sought to realize those dreams by a combination of diplo-

matic and military means. He maintained alliances with the Swedes in the north and the Turks in the south and thus prevented Russian interference while he placed his own candidate, Jan Sobieski, on the throne of Poland. His Turkish connection he used also to harry the eastern frontiers of Austria, and if he did not incite Kara Mustafa's expedition against Vienna in 1683, he knew of it. Austria's distractions enabled him to dabble freely in German politics. Bavaria and the Palatinate were bound to the French court by marriage, and almost all of the other German princes accepted subsidies at one time or another from France. It did not seem unlikely on one occasion that Louis would put himself or his son forward as candidate for Holy Roman emperor. The same method of infiltration was practiced in Italy, Portugal, and Spain, where the young king married a French princess and French ambassadors exerted so much influence in internal affairs that they succeeded in discrediting the strongest antagonist to French influence, Don Juan of Austria, the victor over the Turks at the battle of Lepanto. In addition to all of this, Louis sought to undermine the independence of the Netherlands and gave the English king Charles II a pension in order to reduce the possibility of British interference as he did so.

French influence was so great in Europe in the second half of the seventeenth century that it threatened the independent development of other nations. This was particularly true, the German historian Leopold von Ranke was to write in the nineteenth century, because it

> was supported by a preeminence in literature. Italian literature had already run its course, English literature had not yet risen to general significance, and German literature did not exist at that time. French literature, light, brilliant and animated, in strictly regulated but charming form, intelligible to everyone and yet of individual, national character was beginning to dominate Europe….[It] completely corresponded to the state and helped the latter to attain its supremacy[.] Paris was the capital of Europe. She wielded a domin-

ion as did no other city, over language, over custom, and particularly over the world of fashion and the ruling classes. Here was the center of the community of Europe.

The effect upon the cultural independence of other parts of Europe—and one cannot separate cultural independence from political will—was devastating. In Germany, the dependence upon French example was almost abject, and the writer Moscherosch commented bitterly about "our little Germans who trot to the French and have no heart of their own, no speech of their own; but French opinion is their opinion, French speech, food, drink, morals and deportment their speech, food, drink, morals and deportment whether they are good or bad."

But this kind of dominance was bound to invite resistance on the part of others, and out of that resistance combinations and alliances were bound to take place. And this indeed happened. In Ranke's words, "The concept of the European balance of power was developed in order that the union of many other states might resist the pretensions of the 'exorbitant' court, as it was called." This is a statement worth noting. The principle of the balance of power had been practiced in Machiavelli's time in the intermittent warfare between the city states of the Italian peninsula. Now it was being deliberately invoked as a principle of European statecraft, as a safeguard against universal domination. We shall have occasion to note the evolution and elaboration of this term in the eighteenth century and in the nineteenth, when it became one of the basic principles of the European system.

Opposition to France's universal pretensions centered first upon the Dutch, who were threatened most directly in a territorial sense by the French, and their gifted ruler, William III. But for their opposition to be successful, the Dutch needed strong allies, and they did not get them until the English had severed the connection that had existed between England and France under the later Stuarts and until Austria had modernized its administration and armed forces, contained the threat from the east, and regained the ability to play a role in the politics of central and western Europe. The Glorious Revolution of 1688 and the assumption of the English throne by the Dutch king moved England solidly into the anti-French camp. The repulse of the Turks at the gates of Vienna in 1683 marked the turning point in Austrian fortunes, and the brilliant campaigns of Eugene of Savoy in the subsequent period, which culminated in the smashing victory over the Turks at Zenta and the suppression of the Rakoczi revolt in Hungary, freed Austrian energies for collaboration in the containment of France. The last years of Louis XIV, therefore, were the years of the brilliant partnership of Henry Churchill, Duke of Marlborough, and Eugene of Savoy, a team that defeated a supposedly invulnerable French army at Blenheim in 1704, Ramillies in 1706, Oudenarde in 1708, and the bloody confrontation of Malplaquet in 1709.

These battles laid the basis for the Peace of Utrecht of 1713–1715, by which France was forced to recognize the results of the revolution in England, renounce the idea of a union of the French and Spanish thrones, surrender the Spanish Netherlands to Austria, raze the fortifications at Dunkirk, and hand important territories in America over to Great Britain. The broader significance of the settlement was that it restored an equilibrium of forces to western Europe and marked the return of Austria and the emergence of Britain as its supports. Indeed, the Peace of Utrecht was the first European treaty that specifically mentioned the balance of power. In the letters patent that accompanied Article VI of the treaty between Queen Anne and King Louis XIV, the French ruler noted that the Spanish renunciation of all rights to the throne of France was actuated by the hope of "obtaining a general Peace and securing the Tranquillity of *Europe* by a Ballance of Power," and the king of Spain acknowledged the importance of "the Maxim of securing for ever the universal Good and Quiet of Europe, by an equal Weight of Power, so that many being united in one, the Ballance of the Equality desired, might not turn to the Advantage of one, and the Danger and Hazard of the rest."

Meanwhile, in northern Europe, France's ally Sweden was forced to yield its primacy to the rising powers of Russia and Prussia. This was due in part to the drain on Swedish resources caused by its participation in France's wars against the Dutch; but essentially the decline was caused, in the first instance, by the fact that Sweden had too many rivals for the position of supremacy in the Baltic area and, in the second, by the lack of perspective and restraint that characterized the policy of Gustavus Adolphus's most gifted successor, Charles XII. Sweden's most formidable rivals were Denmark, Poland, which in 1699 acquired an ambitious and unscrupulous new king in the person of Augustus the Strong of Saxony, and Russia, ruled since 1683 by a young and vigorous leader who was to gain the name Peter the Great. In 1700, Peter and Augustus made a pact to attack and despoil Sweden and persuaded Frederick of Denmark to join them in this enterprise. The Danes and the Saxons immediately invaded Sweden and to their considerable dismay were routed and driven from the country by armies led by the eighteen-year-old ruler, Charles XII. The Danes capitulated at once, and Charles without pause threw his army across the Baltic, fell upon Russian forces that were advancing on Narva, and, although his own forces were outnumbered five to one, dispersed, captured, or killed an army of forty thousand Russians. But brilliant victories are often the foundation of greater defeats. Charles now resolved to punish Augustus and plunged into the morass of Polish politics. It was his undoing. While he strove to control an intractable situation, an undertaking that occupied him for seven years, Peter was carrying through the reforms that were to bring Russia from its oriental past into the modern world. When his army was reorganized, he began a systematic conquest of the Swedish Baltic possessions. Charles responded, not with an attempt to retake those areas, but with an invasion of Russia—and this, like other later invasions, was defeated by winter and famine and ultimately by a lost battle, that of Pultawa in 1709, which broke the power of Sweden and marked the emergence of Russia as its successor.

Sweden had another rival which was also gathering its forces in these years.

This was Prussia. At the beginning of the seventeenth century, it had, as the Electorate of Brandenburg, been a mere collection of territories, mostly centered upon Berlin, but with bits and pieces on the Rhine and in East Prussia, and was rich neither in population nor resources. Its rulers, the Hohenzollerns, found it difficult to administer these lands or, in time of trouble, defend them; and during the Thirty Years War, Brandenburg was overrun with foreign armies and its population and substance depleted by famine and pestilence. Things did not begin to change until 1640, when Frederick William, the so-called Great Elector, assumed the throne. An uncompromising realist, he saw that if he was to have security in a dangerous world, he would have to create what he considered to be the sinews of independence: a centralized state with an efficient bureaucracy and a strong army. The last was the key to the whole. As he wrote in his political testament, "A ruler is treated with no consideration if he does not have troops of his own. It is these, thank God! that have made me *considerable* since the time I began to have them"—and in the course of his reign, after purging his force of unruly and incompetent elements, Frederick William rapidly built an efficient force of thirty thousand men, so efficient indeed that in 1675, during the Franco-Swedish war against the Dutch, it came to the aid of the Dutch by defeating the Swedes at Fehrbellin and subsequently driving them out of Pomerania. It was to administer this army that Frederick William laid the foundations of the soon famous Prussian bureaucracy; it was to support it that he encouraged the growth of a native textile industry; it was with its aid that he smashed the recalcitrant provincial diets and centralized the state. And finally it was this army that, by its participation after the Great Elector's death in the wars against Louis XIV and its steadiness under fire at Ramillies and Malplaquet, induced the European powers to recognize his successor Frederick I as king of Prussia.

Under Frederick, an extravagant and thoughtless man, the new kingdom threatened to outrun its resources. But the ruler who assumed the throne in 1715, Frederick William I, resumed the work begun by the Great Elector, restored Prussia's financial stability, and completed the centralization and modernization of the state apparatus by elaborating a body of law and statute that clarified rights and responsibilities for all subjects. He nationalized the officer corps of the army, improved its dress and weapons, wrote its first handbook of field regulations, prescribing manual exercises and tactical evolutions, and rapidly increased its size. When Frederick William took the throne after the lax rule of his predecessor, there were rumors of an impending coup by his neighbors, like that attempted against Sweden in 1700. That kind of talk soon died away as the king's work proceeded, and it is easy to see why. In the course of his reign, he increased the size of his military establishment to eighty-three thousand men, a figure that made Prussia's army the fourth largest in Europe, although the state ranked only tenth from the standpoint of territory and thirteenth in population.

Before the eighteenth century was far advanced, then, the threat of French universal dominance had been defeated, a balance of power existed in western Europe, and two new powers had emerged as partners of the older established ones. It was generally recognized that in terms of power and influence, the leading states in Europe were Britain, France, Austria, Russia, and probably Prussia. The doubts on the last score were soon to be removed; and these five powers were to be the ones that dominated European and world politics until 1914.

II

Something should be said at this point about diplomacy, for it was in the seventeenth and eighteenth centuries that it assumed its modern form. The use of envoys and emissaries to convey messages from one ruler to another probably goes back to the beginning of history; there are heralds in the *Iliad* and, in the second letter to the Church of Corinth, the Apostle Paul describes himself as an ambassador. But modern diplomacy as we know it had its origins in the Italian city states of the Renaissance period, and particularly in the republic of Venice and the states of Milan and Tuscany. In the fourteenth and fifteenth centuries, Venice was a great commercial power whose prosperity depended upon shrewd calculation of risks, accurate reports upon conditions in foreign markets, and effective negotiation. Because it did so, Venice developed the first systemized diplomatic service known to history, a network of agents who pursued the interests of the republic with fidelity, with a realistic appraisal of risks, with freedom from sentimentality and illusion.

From Venice the new practice of systematic diplomacy was passed on to the states of central Italy which, because they were situated in a political arena that was characterized by incessant rivalry and coalition warfare, were always vulnerable to external threats and consequently put an even greater premium than the Venetians upon accurate information and skillful negotiation. The mainland cities soon considered diplomacy so useful that they began to establish permanent embassies abroad, a practice instituted by Milan and Mantua in the fifteenth century, while their political thinkers (like the Florentine Machiavelli) reflected upon the principles best calculated to make diplomacy effective and tried to codify rules of procedure and diplomatic immunity. This last development facilitated the transmission of the shared experience of the Italian cities to the rising nation states of the west that soon dwarfed Florence and Venice in magnitude and strength. Thus, when the great powers emerged in the seventeenth century, they already possessed a highly developed system of diplomacy based upon long experience. The employment of occasional missions to foreign courts had given way to the practice of maintaining permanent missions. While the ambassadors abroad represented their princes and communicated with them directly, their reports were studied in, and they received their instructions from, permanent, organized bureaus which were the first foreign offices. France led the way in this and was followed by most other states, and the establishment of a foreign Ministry on the French model was one of Peter the Great's important reforms. The emergence of a single individual who was charged with the coordination of all foreign business and who represented his sovereign in the conduct of foreign affairs came a bit later, but by the beginning of the eighteenth century, the major powers all had such officials, who came to be known as foreign ministers or secretaries of state for foreign affairs.

From earliest times, an aura of intrigue, conspiracy, and disingenuousness surrounded the person of the diplomat, and we have all heard the famous quip of Sir Henry Wotton, ambassador of James I to the court of Venice, who said that an ambassador was "an honest man sent to lie abroad for the good of his country." Moralists were always worried by this unsavory reputation, which they feared was deserved, and they sought to reform it by exhortation. In the fifteenth century, Bernard du Rosier, provost and later archbishop of Toulouse, wrote a treatise in which he argued that the business of an ambassador is peace, that ambassadors must labor for the common good, and that they should never be sent to stir up wars or internal dissensions; and in the nineteenth century, Sir Robert Peel the younger was to define diplomacy in general as "the great engine used by civilized society for the purpose of maintaining peace."

The realists always opposed this ethical emphasis. In the fifteenth century, in one of the first treatises on ambassadorial functions, Ermalao Barbaro wrote: "The first duty of an ambassador is exactly the same as that of any other servant of government: that is, to do, say, advise and think whatever may best serve the preservation and aggrandizement of his own state."

Seventeenth-century theorists were inclined to Barbaro's view. This was certainly the position of Abram de Wicquefort, who coined the definition of the diplomat as "an honorable spy," and who, in his own career, demonstrated that he did not take the adjectival qualification very seriously. A subject of Holland by birth, Wicquefort at various times in his checkered career performed diplomatic services for the courts of Brandenburg, Luneburg, and France as well as for his own country, and he had no scruples about serving as a double agent, a practice that eventually led to his imprisonment in a Dutch jail. It was here that he wrote his treatise *L'Ambassadeur et ses fonctions*, a work that was both an amusing commentary on the political morals of the baroque age and an incisive analysis of the art and practice of diplomacy.

Wicquefort was not abashed by the peccadilloes of his colleagues, which varied from financial peculation and sins of the flesh to crimes of violence. He took the line that in a corrupt age, one could not expect that embassies would be oases of virtue. Morality was, in any case, an irrelevant consideration in diplomacy; a country could afford to be served by bad men, but not by incompetent ones. Competence began with a clear understanding on the diplomat's part of the nature of his job and a willingness to accept the fact that it had nothing to do with personal gratification or self-aggrandizement. The ambassador's principal function, Wicquefort wrote, "consisted in maintaining effective communication between the two princes, in delivering letters that his master writes to the Prince at whose court he resides, in soliciting answers to them,… in protecting his Master's subjects and conserving his interests." He must have the charm and cultivation that would enable him to ingratiate himself at the court to which he was accredited and the adroitness needed to ferret out information that would reveal threats to his master's interests or opportunities for advancing them. He must possess the ability to gauge the temperament and intelligence of those with whom he had to deal and to use this knowledge profitably in negotiation. "Ministers are but men and as such have their weaknesses, that is to say, their passions and interests, which the ambassador ought to know if he wishes to do honor to himself and his Master."

In pursuing this intelligence, the qualities he should cultivate most assiduously were *prudence* and *modération*. The former Wicquefort equated with caution and reflection, and also with the gifts of silence and indirection, the art of "making it appear that one is not interested in the things one desires the most." The diplomat who possessed prudence did not have to resort to mendacity or deceit or to *tromperies* or *artifices*, which were usually, in any case, counterproductive. *Modération* was the ability to curb one's temper and remain cool and phlegmatic in moments of tension. "Those spirits who are compounded of sulphur and saltpeter, whom the slightest spark can set afire, are easily capable of compromising affairs by their excitability, because it is so easy to put them in a rage or drive them to a fury, so that they don't know what they are doing." Diplomacy is a cold and rational business, in short, not to be practiced by the moralist, or the enthusiast, or the man with a low boiling point.

The same point was made in the most famous of the eighteenth-century essays on diplomacy, Francois de Callières's *On the Manner of Negotiating with Princes* (1716), in which persons interested in the career of diplomacy were advised to consider whether they were born with "the qualities necessary for success." These, the author wrote, included an observant mind, a spirit of application which refused to be distracted by pleasures or frivolous amusements, a sound judgment which takes the measure of things, as they are, and which goes straight to its goal by the shortest and most neutral paths without wandering into useless refinements and subtleties which as a rule only succeed in repelling those with whom one is dealing.

Important also were the kind of penetration that is useful in discovering the thoughts of men, a fertility in expedients when difficulties arise, an equable humor and a patient temperament, and easy and agreeable manners. Above, all, Callières observed, in a probably not unconscious echo of Wicquefort's insistence upon moderation, the diplomat must

have sufficient control over himself to resist the longing to speak before he has really thought what he shall say. He should not endeavour to gain the reputation of being able to reply immediately and without premeditation to every proposition which is made, and he should take a special care not to fall into the error of one famous foreign ambassador of our time who so loved an argument that each time he warmed up in controversy he revealed important secrets in order to support his opinion.

In his treatment of the art of negotiation, Callières drew from a wealth of experience to which Wicquefort could not pretend, for he was one of Louis XIV's most gifted diplomats and ended his career as head of the French delegation during the negotiations at Ryswick in 1697. It is interesting, in light of the heavy reliance upon lawyers in contemporary United States diplomacy (one thinks of President Eisenhower's secretary of state and President Reagan's national security adviser) and of the modern practice of negotiating in large gatherings, that Callières had no confidence in either of these preferences. The legal mind, he felt, was at once too narrow, too intent upon hair-splitting, and too contentious to be useful in a field where success, in the last analysis, was best assured by agreements that provided mutuality of advantage. As for large conferences—"vast concourses of ambassadors and envoys"—his view was that they were generally too clumsy to achieve anything very useful. Most successful conferences were the result of careful preliminary work by small groups of negotiators who hammered out the essential bases of agreement and secured approval for them from their governments before handing them over, for formal purposes, to the *omnium-gatherums* that were later celebrated in the history books.

Perhaps the most distinctive feature of Callières's treatise was the passion with which he argued that a nation's foreign relations should be conducted by persons trained for the task.

Diplomacy is a profession by itself which deserves the same preparation and assiduity of attention that men give to other recognized professions .... The diplomatic genius is born, not made. But there are many qualities which may be developed with practice, and the greatest part of the necessary knowledge can only be acquired, by constant application to the subject. In this sense, diplomacy is certainly a profession itself capable of occupying a man's whole career, and those who think to embark upon a diplomatic mission as a pleasant diversion from their common task only prepare disappointment for themselves and disaster for the cause which they serve.

These words represented not only a personal view but an acknowledgment of the requirements of the age. The states that emerged as recognizedly great powers in the course of the seventeenth and eighteenth centuries were the states that had modernized their governmental structure, mobilized their economic and other resources in a rational manner, built up effective and disciplined military establishments, and elaborated a professional civil service that administered state business in accordance with the principles of *raison d'état*. An indispensable part of that civil service was the Foreign Office and the diplomatic corps, which had the important task of formulating the foreign policy that protected and advanced the state's vital interests and of seeing that it was carried out.

BIBLIOGRAPHICAL ESSAY

For the general state of international relations before the eighteenth century, the following are useful: Marvin R. O'Connell, *The Counter-Reformation, 1559–1610* (New York, 1974); Carl J. Friedrich, *The Age of the Baroque, 1610–1660* (New York, 1952), a brilliant volume; C. V. Wedgwood, The *Thirty Years War* (London, 1938, and later editions); Frederick L. Nussbaum, *The Triumph of Science and Reason, 1660–1685* (New York, 1953); and John B. Wolf, *The Emergence of the Great Powers, 1685–1715* (New York, 1951). On Austrian policy in the seventeenth century, see especially Max Braubach, *Prinz Eugen von Savoyen*, 5 vols. (Vienna, 1963–1965); on Prussian, Otto Hintze, *Die Hohenzollern und ihr Werk* (Berlin, 1915) and, brief but useful, Sidney B. Fay, *The Rise of Brandenburg-Prussia* (New York, 1937). A classical essay on great-power politics in the early modern period is Leopold von Ranke, *Die grossen Mächte*, which can be found in English translation in the appendix of Theodore von Laue, *Leopold Ranke: The Formative Years* (Princeton, 1950). The standard work on *raison d'état* is Friedrich Meinecke, *Die Idee der Staatsräsan*, 3rd ed. (Munich, 1963), translated by Douglas Scoff as *Machiavellianism* (New Haven, 1957). On the origins and development of diplomacy, see D. P. Heatley, *Diplomacy and the Study of International Relations* (Oxford, 1919); Leon van der Essen, *La Diplomatie: Ses origines et son organisation* (Brussels, 1953); Ragnar Numelin, *Les origines de la diplomatie*, trans. from the Swedish by Jean-Louis Perret (Paris, 1943); and especially Heinrich Wildner, *Die Technik der Diplomatie: L'Art de négocier* (Vienna, 1959). Highly readable is Harold Nicolson, *Diplomacy*, 2nd ed. (London, 1950). An interesting comparative study is Adda B. Bozeman, *Politics and Culture in International History* (Princeton, 1960).

There is no modern edition of *L'ambassadeur et ses fonctions par Monsieur de Wicquefort* (College, 1690); but Callières's classic of 1776 can be found: Francois de Callières, *On the Manner of Negotiating with Princes*, trans. A. F. Whyte (London, 1919, and later editions).

From Mercantilism to 'The Wealth of Nations'

The Age of Discovery gave rise to an era of international trade and to arguments over economic strategies that still influence the policies of commerce.

By Michael Marshall

We live in an era when continual economic growth is almost considered a birthright, at least in the developed world. It has become the benchmark of the health of a society, guaranteeing an ever-expanding prosperity. The current president of the United States even finds that his extensive misbehavior is overlooked by a majority of Americans because he happens to be presiding over an extended period of economic growth and optimism.

If annual growth drops below about 2 percent, planners and politicians start to get nervous, while a recession (negative growth) is considered a serious crisis. Where will it all end? Can such growth continue—with periodic setbacks, of course—indefinitely? We do not know and usually do not care to ask.

One thing is clear, however. It was not always so. For most of human history it has not been so. In western Europe in the period 1500–1750, output increased by a mere 65 percent, by one estimate, or an average of 0.26 percent a year, even though the population grew about 60 percent. For most of this period, 80 percent or more of the population worked the land. Studies of wage rates in England and France suggest that the working poor had to spend a full four-fifths of their income on food alone.

So this was not an economically dynamic society. There was relatively little disposable income, that being enjoyed by the prosperous elite of landed aristocracy and, increasingly in this period, merchants. Consequently, there was no prospect of creating a mass domestic market for new products. Most wealth was still tied up in the relatively static commodity of land, and agriculture was the major measure of a country's wealth.

Yet in the period from the voyages of discovery in the late fifteenth and early sixteenth centuries [see "Columbus and the Age of Exploration," THE WORLD & I, November 1998, p. 16] up till the Industrial Revolution there occurred what has been called a "commercial revolution."

The story of that revolution, which I will tell here, weaves together a number of significant themes. The upshot of the Age of Discovery was the emergence of a network of global trade. The consequences of that trade, and the measures taken by increasingly centralized European governments [see "The Ascent of the Nation-State," THE WORLD & I, March 1999, p. 18] to control and direct it, produced the system later labeled, most notably by Adam Smith, mercantilism. This was the practice of imperial rivalry between European powers over global trade, and it gave impetus to the disagreements between Britain and its American colonists that led to the American Revolution. Critical consideration of these issues gave birth to Smith's theoretical study of economics, which culminated in the publication of his masterwork *The Wealth of Nations*.

PROTECTING BULLION RESERVES

Smith wrote: "The discovery of America and that of a passage to the East Indies are the two greatest and most important events recorded in the history of mankind." No doubt he exaggerated,

The Commercial Revolution

Voyages of discovery in the fifteenth and sixteenth centuries resulted in a growing network of international trade.

Silver from the New World became the lubricant for the machinery of an emerging global economy.

Fearing the success of their rivals, European governments imposed trade restrictions to protect their national interests.

Viewing commerce as an arena of conflicting national interests at times thrust competing European powers into war.

Advocates of free trade criticized mercantilist policies, suggesting peace could arise from mutually beneficial terms of trade.

Clashes over trade were significant factors in the antagonisms that led to the American Declaration of Independence.

The growth of economic relations between America and Britain after the Revolutionary War suggests that the free traders werc right.

but nothing was more important in the unfolding of this story. The Spanish conquistadores went to the New World in search of El Dorado. They found little gold but plenty of silver at Potosi in Peru and in northern Mexico. This silver became the lubricant of the machinery of an emerging global economy.

It flowed into Spain, from where much of it went to the rest of Europe, especially Holland, to pay the debts the Hapsburg rulers had incurred through the religious and dynastic struggles in their German possessions and in the Spanish Netherlands. Some of it then flowed to the Baltic to pay for the timber, rope, and other shipbuilding materials that the region supplied, especially to Holland and Britain. The bulk of it, though, went to Asia to satisfy the growing European demand for spices, silk, Indian calico, and later, Chinese tea.

Without the silver that demand could not have been satisfied: Europe had nothing that Asia wanted to import in exchange. That situation would not change until after the Industrial Revolution, when clothing from the Lancashire cotton industry in the north of England found a market in Asia. Even then problems remained. The economic reason for the shameful opium trade in the early and mid-nineteenth century, when opium grown in India was exported illegally to China, was to earn exchange to pay for tea without having to export silver.

Silver was not without problems. So much of it flowed into Europe in the sixteenth century that it caused serious price inflation. The Spanish economy, in particular, was considerably disrupted, a significant factor in Spain's gradual decline. During the seventeenth century, from a peak around 1600, the

supply of silver began to decrease. The demand for goods from Asia, however, did not. The result was a net outflow of silver bullion from Europe, a shrinkage of the money supply, and as a result, economic recession.

No economic theory existed at the time, and no contemporary thought argued that governments should not regulate such matters affecting national wealth in the national interest. So they did. The ad hoc system of tariffs and other measures influencing trade and manufactures that came to be known as mercantilism began to emerge.

The context in which this happened was one of increasingly centralized emerging nation-states that were spending a greater portion of the total national income than in the past, especially in the frequent times of war. They exercised closer control over more aspects of life in pursuit of national policy than in the past, especially through the taxation needed to fund wars. Trade with the New World nurtured the idea that commerce could be a source of national wealth and strength just as much as agriculture and should be developed to that end.

Spain, Britain, and France all banned the export of gold or silver bullion, but this proved to be like trying to stop water from running downhill. The belief was that bullion represented the national wealth or treasure, and that trade should be conducted so as to amass a surplus of it. A country would then have a reserve to cushion itself from the economic effects of adverse fluctuations in the supply of gold and, especially, silver.

Underlying this thinking was the assumption that markets and the amount of trade were relatively fixed, and that gaining a larger share of the pie necessarily meant depriving another country of part of its share. Trade was thus conceived as an arena of national competition and even conflict, a form of war by other means.

COLBERT AND FRENCH MERCANTILISM

Advocates of free trade in the late eighteenth and the nineteenth centuries strongly criticized this aspect of mercantilist policy. They proposed that peace was one of the benefits of free trade, since it tied trading partners in mutually beneficial exchanges that could only be lost through war. Neither side was totally right. Circumstances always affect cases, and the mercantilist policymakers were pragmatists who reacted to the situation before them.

The most systematic practitioner of mercantilist policies was undoubtedly Jean-Baptiste Colbert, finance minister for France's Louis XIV in the later seventeenth century. Colbert used the considerable power of the Sun King's state to increase its wealth through the promotion of French trade and manufactures. He certainly banned the export of bullion, but his policy was aimed at replacing bullion as the means of payment for necessary imports with the earnings from the export of French manufactures.

To that end he developed selected industries by state subsidies and bringing in skilled foreign artisans. He particularly encouraged high-value products such as quality furniture, glass, and tapestries, and the quality of French workmanship in these areas became legendary throughout Europe. He used tariff barriers to protect industries that faced serious foreign competition. Wanting to develop the French cloth industry in the face of the well-established British cloth trade, he doubled the duty on imports.

Thus emerged the classic mercantilist pattern that, because it came about in a piecemeal, pragmatic manner, has only existed in its complete form in the writings of historians. The export of domestic raw materials was largely discouraged, so that domestic manufacturers could enjoy their use. The export of sheep and raw wool from Britain, for example, was heavily regulated for the benefit of the domestic textile industry. The export of manufactures was encouraged as the means to a favorable balance of trade and the bullion inflows that came with it.

The import of foreign manufactures was restricted since this adversely affected the balance of trade. Raw material imports were looked on favorably to the degree that they could be used in or support domestic manufactures, although a large agricultural country like France, under Colbert, aimed at as much self-sufficiency as possible.

Colbert realized that encouraging French industry had little point if its products could not then be exported. That meant commercial shipping and a navy to protect it. Colbert had before him the example of the Dutch. They were the dominant economic power in Europe in the early and mid-sixteenth century through their skills in trade and shipping.

The Dutch dominated North Sea fishing, annoying the British by taking huge catches of herring from Britain's east coast, developing a factory-style industry for salting the catch, and then exporting it throughout Europe. They dominated the carrying trade from the Baltic to western Europe, were major carriers of imports to Europe from the Americas and from the East, and grew rich through their control of the lucrative reexport of those imports throughout Europe from their initial port of entry in Amsterdam.

To support these efforts the Dutch dredged and improved their rather shallow harbors and developed specialized forms of shipping, both for fishing and for moving bulk materials. They also developed financial instruments to ease the flow of trade and extend the use of credit. Most notably, they established the Bank of Amsterdam, a public bank that offered a source of capital very different from the government funding of chartered companies that had marked the enterprise of discovery and trade in the sixteenth century.

Colbert built up a merchant marine to rival that of the Dutch and ensure that French trade was carried in French ships. Under his direction the merchant fleet grew from a mere 60 ships of 300 tons or more to over 700 ships of that size. He provided for the protection of French maritime commerce by building up the French navy from 20 ships to 250 by the time of his death in 1683.

He always viewed commerce as an instrument of national policy, and merchants had little say in his decisions. This was unlike the situation in England, where various merchant groups formed influential lobbies on the Crown's commercial policies. The prizes of commerce remained for him a zero-sum game: France's gain must be someone else's loss. He created a successful glass industry in Paris by inviting Venetian glass-blowers to teach their skills. He later boasted that the successful royal mirror factory that resulted was depriving Venice of one million livres a year.

COMMERCE AND CONFLICT

Colbert's attitude was much derided by the later free-trade economists, most notably Smith. The Scottish philosopher David Hume, a contemporary and good friend of Smith's, wrote on the subject: "I shall therefore venture to acknowledge that, not only as a man, but as a British subject, I pray for the flourishing commerce of Germany, Spain, Italy and even France itself."

It was an irony, too, and one that later critics did not fail to point out, that a considerable contribution was made to the growth of French transatlantic exports by industries that did not receive Colbert's nurturing support. Iron and coal, hardware, and the cheaper cloths produced by the textile industry in Normandy all developed through their own enterprise.

Nevertheless, Colbert's legacy was a foundation for rapid and successful French commercial development in the eighteenth century. Between 1715 and 1771 the total value of French foreign trade grew eightfold until it almost matched British trade. The value of French exports multiplied more than four times between 1716 and 1789. Colbert must have been doing something right.

Advocates of free trade proposed that peace was one of its benefits.

Nor were the policymakers of the time completely wrong in their view of commerce as conflict to gain the largest share of a fixed prize. It is certainly true that bilateral trade is mutually beneficial. If a country wants to export its goods, its potential trading partners must have the means to pay for those goods. So it is in the exporter's interest that partners have their own successful export markets, perhaps in the original country's own home market, to generate the revenue needed to buy its exports.

This is not true of the carrying and reexport trade, however. The Dutch had grown rich on this trade, and the British and French set out to take it away from them. Both ended up fighting trade wars with the Dutch over the issue. In the second half of the seventeenth century, Britain passed a series of Navigation Acts, which required that goods shipped in and out of British ports, and to and from British colonies, had to be carried in British ships.

This struck at the heart of the Dutch trade, hence the tensions that led to war. At issue was who would distribute the new colonial imports throughout the rest of Europe. The Dutch gradually lost out to the French and British. Between the 1660s and 1700 British exports grew by 50 percent. Half of that increase came from the reexport of colonial imports, mostly to Europe.

As a result, the eighteenth century was the Anglo-French century in terms of commerce. I have already mentioned the spectacular growth in French trade. The value of British trade grew threefold between 1702 and 1772, and British shipping grew at a similar rate, reaching over one million tons by 1788. This phenomenal growth represented a tremendous amount of new wealth, most of it associated with colonial trade, especially that of the New World.

The bulk of British trade in 1700 was still with Europe, but by 1776 two-thirds of its overseas trade was outside Europe. Between 1700 and 1763 the value of British exports to America and the West Indies multiplied fivefold, while the value of imports from those areas grew fourfold. Anglo-French rivalry resulted in a number of wars throughout the century. It is small wonder, given the importance of colonial trade, that parts of those wars were fought in North America and in India, over strategic control of its sources.

'BADGES OF SLAVERY'

The Atlantic trade not only was the most substantial but it also formed an interlocking network. From the plantations of the southern colonies of America, the Caribbean, and the Brazilian coast, tropical staples—tobacco, cotton, sugar, coffee, cocoa, rice—flowed to Europe. European manufactures flowed back west, supplying the plantation economies with necessities they did not produce themselves. European cities, especially those on the Atlantic, grew and prospered on this trade. From Cadiz and Lisbon in the south, through Bordeaux and Nantes in France, to Bristol, Liverpool, Glasgow, and the burgeoning entrepôt of London in England, they all became part of the Atlantic economy.

A city like Liverpool benefited from importing, refining, and reexporting sugar and tobacco. It also benefited from a new and increasingly significant part of the Atlantic economy—slavery. Plantation agriculture is labor intensive, and the plantations of the Americas looked to West Africa to supply that need. Ships from Liverpool or Bristol, or Lisbon for that matter, would sail to West Africa and trade cheap manufactured items to local chiefs in return for live bodies.

These were then shipped across the Atlantic—the Middle Passage—to the Caribbean or the American South, where those still alive after the horrors of the voyage were sold. The ships then returned home laden with cotton, tobacco, or sugar. In the case of Portuguese ships, they would sail to Brazil and return with Brazilian produce.

European manufactures were also exported to the settler societies of the Americas. The half million Spanish settlers in Mexico and Peru paid for these with silver. As the supply of silver slackened and Latin American society became increasingly self-sufficient, this trade became less important.

The North American trade continued to burgeon. European manufactures were paid for by the products of the region. The question arose as to what those products were to be, and who should determine that: the colonists or the government in London? At this point, questions of mercantilist policy become questions about the future of the American colonies, in other words questions about independence. Adam Smith addressed both sets of questions in *The Wealth of Nations*.

LIBRARY OF CONGRESS

Slaves on the deck of the bark *Wildfire*, brought into Key West, Florida, on April 30, 1860. Carrying 510 slaves, the ship violated the 1809 slave trade law that prohibited slave importation. This engraving was made from a daguerreotype for *Harper's Weekly*, June 2, 1860. Blacks were rarely allowed on deck except for occasional "exercise."

He described the regulations by which London sought to control the American economy as "impertinent badges of slavery." They were intended to ensure that the American economy would complement the British economy, but that, of course, also meant subordinating the one to the other. The American colonies were viewed as a supplier of those staples mentioned above and a protected market for British manufactures.

The colonies were by no means expected to develop industries that might compete with those in Britain. In 1699, Britain sought to ban the woolen industry in America and prevent any intercolony trade in woolen goods. In 1750 a similar ban was applied to steelmaking and the manufacture of finished products from iron.

The role of the New England colonies was to reduce British reliance on the Baltic region for naval materials and certain types of shipbuilding timber. Thus, these strategically sensitive materials—essential for building the ships of the Royal Navy that protected British commerce—would be under British political control. These products were allowed into Britain duty-free, as was pig iron, in that case to reduce British reliance on Swedish and Russian sources. But the pig iron was not to be any further refined in the colonies, lest it compete with the British iron industry.

Being true Englishmen jealous of their liberties, the colonists chafed under these restrictions. Political conflict inevitably resulted, and many commentators in Britain considered that the costs of that conflict outweighed any economic benefit from trying to restrict the natural economic development of the colonies. Matters came to a head in 1776, the year in which both the Declaration of Independence and *The Wealth of Nations* were published.

NEW ECONOMIC DIRECTIONS

Smith had definite views on the American economy and on the system of tariffs and trade regulations that had helped produce the conflict. Unlike the views advocated by other contributors to the debate, however, his arose from the context of an extensive theoretical consideration of how wealth is created. It is only a slight exaggeration to say that he invented economic theory.

He can certainly be considered the originator of classical economics. It was his ideas that were first developed and interpreted by David Ricardo and then by John Stuart Mill in *Principles of Political Economy*. At the end of the nineteenth century they were revived and revised as "neoclassical" economics by Alfred Marshall. Even the economic ideas of Karl Marx and, in this century, John Maynard Keynes, started from the principles first enunciated by Smith, although they then moved in very different directions.

His book discusses systematically the basic economic questions: a theory of price or value; wages, profits, and rents; the role of labor; how wealth is distributed among owners of the different factors of production; the role of capital, money, and the banking system; and taxation and the national debt. He famously introduced the concept of the division of labor, explaining how it increases productivity and also is limited by the extent of the market.

He held a dynamic view of the economy. National wealth resulted from the flow of income over time rather than from the size of the stock of capital held. His theory anticipated the actuality of burgeoning economic growth produced by the Industrial Revolution. It differed significantly from the assumptions that lay behind mercantilist policies.

Smith and his good friend Hume refuted the argument that trade should be managed in such a way as to maintain a positive balance so as to earn bullion. Hume pointed out that if bullion flowed out of a country its prices would fall, which would render its exports more competitive, thus increasing the flow of export earnings into the country until balance was restored. In other words, Hume and Smith thought of the economy as a dynamic self-regulating system. In Smith's most famous phrase, it was as if an "invisible hand" harmonized individual economic actions pursued out of self-interest into an overall balance that served the public good. It worked best without government interference.

Economic historian Peter Mathias sums up Smith's arguments on this topic admirably, saying that

> a system of freely operating market prices, under naturally competitive conditions, would ensure the lowest effective prices to the consumer and produce the most efficient allocation of resources between the different branches of economic activity. The ultimate test of efficiency and welfare thus became a freely moving price level not distorted by legislative interference.

On the basis of this argument, Smith launched into a critique of tariffs, subsidies, and monopolies, all the tools of the commercial policy of the era that he dubbed mercantilism. "Consumption," he argued, "is the sole end and purpose of all production," yet under the mercantilist system the consumers' interest was sacrificed to that of producers, who sought special favors from the government for their particular industries.

With such views he could not help but be critical of contemporary British policy toward the American colonies. He thought that Britain could rightly impose its own taxation system on the colonies but only in the context of colonist representation at Westminster. (He was, incidentally, a friend of Benjamin Franklin's, and the two discussed these issues when Franklin was in London.) He thought, too, that Britain could extend its customs laws to America provided that *all* internal barriers to trade were abolished.

Smith thus conceived of the British Empire as a vast and free internal market for each and all of its component regions. He even envisaged that the seat of the empire should not remain fixed in London but should move "to that part of the Empire which contributed most to the general defense and support of the whole."

THE DISCUSSION CONTINUES

Economic relations between Britain and America after the Revolutionary War suggested that the free-trade arguments promoted by Smith and his fellow critics of the system of colonial regulation were right. After 1782, British exports to the United States began to grow more rapidly than those to any other region. By 1836 about a quarter of Britain's total exports went there, while the United States provided 80 percent of Lancashire's cotton.

Such evidence boosted free-trade ideas, which became increasingly influential in the nineteenth century, especially in Britain—whose manufacturers, of course, stood to gain the most by them. But the argument that Smith first articulated against mercantilist policy is still going on today. Countries still remain very sensitive about their balance of trade. In the United States, a Republican presidential candidate, Pat Buchanan, argues for greater protection for American industry, in the face of widespread free-trade thinking in both parties.

Back in the 1970s, the Carter administration bailed out Lee Iacocca's Chrysler Corporation because it was thought that the damage to the economy as a whole and the social cost of the resulting unemployment were worse than paying the cost of a bailout. Right now the United States is entering into a tariff war with western Europe over Caribbean bananas. The Europeans want to reserve 25 percent of their banana market for producers in their former colonies. Without that guaranteed market those producers probably could not survive. The United States is arguing for unrestricted free trade in bananas, which would benefit the mighty Dole Corporation. Whoever is right in the argument, its roots lie in the system of Atlantic trade and colonies that developed in the seventeenth and eighteenth centuries.

The "commercial revolution" of the eighteenth century generated a huge increase in trade and wealth. This all happened under a system of mercantilist policy. Whether that policy nurtured the development or, as Smith argued, it took place despite the policy is a question that can probably never be resolved.

What can be said is that the commercial revolution was an important prelude to the Industrial Revolution. Some of the capital generated from trade found its way into the new manufacturing industries. Perhaps more important was the development of extensive new global markets, for it is questionable whether in the absence of those markets European domestic demand could have grown enough to sustain the rapid growth of the new industries. As it was, those industries found an already established international network of markets through which their new products could flow.

Michael Marshall is executive editor of THE WORLD & I.

The Poisons Affair

Reggie Oliver looks at the links between some of the highest-placed women in Louis XIV's court and some notorious Parisian dealers in drugs, death and the dark arts.

IN THE ARCHIVES OF THE Bastille there is a scrap of paper simply dated 1673 which marks the beginning of a scandal which was to reverberate widely touching Louis XIV himself. It reads:

> The confessors of Notre Dame have given notice, without disclosing any name, that for some time a great proportion of those who confessed to them accused themselves of having poisoned someone. It is thought that Monsieur, the Lieutenant of Police, should regulate the ease with which poisons are sold and bought.

Most murders are acts of unpremeditated violence; poisoning requires calculation and forethought. History records only one time and place at which poisoning became the preferred means of despatch and in which its practice reached epidemic proportions. This was France—more particularly, Paris—in the last quarter of the seventeenth century.

There were a number of sociological and scientific reasons for this. In the first place, forensic pathology was virtually non-existent. The Marsh Test (for arsenic) was not discovered until 1838. Death came naturally in many unknown guises, so that poison, though often suspected, could rarely be proved. At the same time poisoning may on occasion have been erroneously suspected, as was the case with 'Madame', Louis XIV's beloved sister-in-law, Henrietta of England, who died in 1670 almost certainly of natural causes.

Chemistry was beginning to emerge from the dark ages of alchemy. It became a fashionable pursuit for the rich, and a lucrative one for some of the more disreputable elements of society. Small laboratories began to spring up everywhere, attracting the gullible and ill-intentioned in equal numbers. In these dens coining was practised, while quack nostrums, love philtres and poisons—wittily dubbed 'Succession Powders'—were manufactured.

Arsenic, sometimes called *mortaux-rats*, was the principal poison used. It was available usually in the form of white arsenic (arsenic trioxide), which had the advantage of being tasteless, and the poisoner could further allay suspicions by administering it in small doses, thus inducing a slow, lingering death, similar to one brought about by natural causes.

Other poisons, more repulsive in their composition, were more dubious in their effects. There were powders compounded from bats, moles, horsehair, the urine and slime from a toad (only the latter possessing some genuinely venomous properties). Of vegetable poisons there was opium, aconite, hemlock, broom, the black morel and mandrake root. Cantharides, or powdered Spanish Fly (a kind of beetle), powdered bluebottles and groundsel were regarded as love philtres but were far from safe. An infusion of peach blossom was used to poison gloves and clothing. Nail clippings, blood, semen and excrement were also used. For the dispensers of these wares there was no clear demarcation between

sorcery and toxicology, but the empirical science of poison was sufficiently advanced to sustain a considerable underground industry together with its large and generally satisfied clientele.

In the year that the confessors of Notre Dame made their disturbing report, another significant event occurred. The Comte de Soissons (1633–73), husband of Olympe Mancini (1639–1708), a former favourite of Louis XIV and niece of Cardinal Mazarin, died in circumstances that suggested poisoning. The Comtesse was later accused of causing his death. Meanwhile Paris was agog with a case which serves as a sort of prelude to the main event. The Marquise de Brinvilliers (1630–76) had been found to have poisoned her father and brothers and to have made attempts on other members of her family including her husband. The crimes were revealed when her lover Godin de Sainte-Croix died in 1672 leaving behind evidence incriminating both of them. Not only had the Marquise killed her relations but also several inmates of charity hospitals. Wishing to perfect her deadly arts she had toured these institutions in the guise of an angel of mercy, dispensing patés and tartlets spiked with arsenic.

In many ways Brinvilliers was typical of the poisoners thrown up by the affair. She was sophisticated, aristocratic and a woman, aware of the possibilities of the new age, frustrated by the restrictions it still imposed on her sex and status. She killed her father and brothers to gain and then increase her inheritance; poison was the only way by which she thought she could achieve independence, indulge her lover and pay off her gambling debts.

In 1672 Brinvilliers had fled to England, but she later returned to mainland Europe. Justice caught up with her in 1676 when she was apprehended at a convent in Lille and brought back to Paris. A search of her cell had yielded a written confession which she subsequently retracted. Her trial and execution aroused great interest, and was vividly described by Madame de Sévigné (1626–96) in her letters. The death of the Marquise de Brinvilliers was so exemplary in its piety that the crowds regarded her as a saint and scrambled for relics in the ashes of her pyre. Shortly before her execution she had said: 'Half the nobility are at it as well. If I wanted to speak out I could destroy them.'

The following year, 1677, a plot was discovered to kill the King, needless to say by poison. It was believed to have been hatched by supporters of Louis' disgraced minister Fouquet. A number of significant arrests were made in the Paris underworld.

It was in the year 1679 that the Poisons Affair erupted into a public scandal. A lawyer, Maitre Perrin, had been dining with his wife's dressmaker, a Madame Vigoureux. (Why he should have been at the table of such a lowly member of society is a mystery.) At the table was a lodger of Vigoureux, Marie Bosse, whose tongue became loosened by drink. Perrin heard Bosse say: 'What a marvellous job I have! What a superb clientele. Only duchesses, marquises, princes and lords. Three more poisonings and I retire, my fortune made.' Perrin deduced from Vigoureux's alarmed reaction that Bosse was not joking but had made a genuinely damaging admission.

Perrin reported the matter to Desgrez, the police officer who had been responsible for the arrest of Brinvilliers. Wishing to be absolutely certain of Bosse's guilt, Desgrez sent the wife of one of his policemen (called 'archers') to Bosse, with the story that she had a troublesome husband whom she wished to eliminate. Bosse duly obliged by offering to sell her poison and on January 4th, 1679, by the order of Nicholas de La Reynie, Paris's first Lieutenant General of Police, Desgrez and his men swooped on Vigoureux's house. They arrested both her and Bosse whom they found sleeping in the same bed, together with Bosse's son and two daughters.

Almost at once Bosse and Vigoureux began to incriminate others. The first arrest to be made among the upper echelons of society occurred on February 11th, 1679. This was Madame de Poulaillon, who had attempted to murder her rich elderly husband with a poisoned chemise supplied by Marie Bosse. Bosse and Vigoureux also informed on their own class, in particular naming a Catherine Monvoisin, known as 'La Voisin', a fashionable fortune teller. La Voisin was living with a man called Lesage (alias Du Coeuret and Dubuisson), a shady character already 'known to the authorities'. On March 12th, 1679, La Voisin was arrested coming out of Mass.

Three days later, Louis XIV's mistress, the superb Athenais de Montespan (1641–1707), suddenly left the court at Saint Germain for Paris without giving any explanation for her departure. Could it have been connected with the arrest of La Voisin?

By this time La Reynie must have known that the case had serious implications because La Voisin enjoyed the patronage—ostensibly in her capacity as a fortune teller—of some of the most illustrious names in France. She was discovered to be not only a poisoner but an abortionist (an 'angel-maker' in the euphemistic cant of the day) and a sorceress who could provide a renegade priest to celebrate a black mass for you.

Allegation and counter-allegation flew between Bosse, Vigoureux and Voisin. Others were arrested and also began to talk. Some very important names were being mentioned, among them the Duchesse de Bouillon, the Marechal de Luxembourg and the Marquise de Montespan's sister-in-law, the Duchesse de Vivonne. From the start there were two distinct categories of accused: members of the criminal underworld such as Voisin and Bosse, and their clients, most of whom belonged to the nobility.

By this time the Marquis de Louvois (1641–91), Louis' Secretary for War and, after Colbert (1619–83), his most powerful minister, had stepped in. He saw the scandal that would be caused if all these great names were to face accusations of poisoning and sorcery in open court. Four days before Voisin's arrest he had proposed that a secret investigative tribunal be set up to look into the affair. This was the Commission of the Arsenal, better known as the 'Chambre Ardente' after the old inquisitorial chambers which were hung with black drapes and lit only by candles. Louis approved and the first session of the Chambre Ardente took place on April 10th, 1679.

The reason for its establishment was not only to preserve discretion, but to prevent the guilty escaping justice, for many of the accused were closely connected—some even married—to members of the main judicial body of the Parlement. In the event, the Chambre Ardente proved to be just as indulgent towards aristocratic defendants as the Parlement might have been. (Poulaillon, for example, was banished while her lowly suppliers were condemned to death.) At the time, however, its setting up aroused much indignation among the privileged classes.

By September 1679 Madame de Montespan was being mentioned in connection with the Poisons Affair. At first she was only obliquely implicated through her maid, Cato, and her lady in waiting Mademoiselle des Œillets who had bought love potions from La Voisin. (It was suggested that they had been bought for Montespan to retain the favours of the King, though des Œillets herself had also enjoyed the royal favours and borne Louis a daughter.) The situation had sufficiently alarmed Louis that on September 21st he wrote to La Reynie requesting that records of interrogations be written on separate sheets rather than in ledgers, presumably so that embarrassing items could be destroyed at a later date.

The passionate liaison between the King and Madame de Montespan was over. The King, now forty-one, had begun to show interest in the exquisite, empty-headed eighteen-year-old Mademoiselle de Fontanges (1661–81). But Montespan was still a very important figure at court since she had given birth to seven children by the King. The six that survived beyond infancy Louis had legitimised as his own. In April 1679 Montespan was made Superintendent of the Queen's Household, the most important job for a woman at court. Her predecessor in the post had been the same Comtesse de Soissons who was suspected of poisoning her husband. The latter had fled to Brussels in January 1680. She had been about to be arrested when she was tipped off just in time, almost certainly by Louis himself.

In February the following month, La Voisin was interrogated under torture and then burned to death in public. Contrary to the evidence of Lesage, a criminal associate and former lover, she denied all connection with Montespan, though, according to one memoirist, 'she promised Louvois sensational revelations if her life was spared'. Then, in June of that year, a still more sinister figure made his appearance on the scene. This was the hideous old priest, the Abbe Guibourg, who had celebrated black masses in the course of which children had been sacrificed. When interrogated he, together with La Voisin's daughter, Marguerite Monvoisin and another woman, Madame Filastre, began to implicate Montespan in their dark doings.

The allegations against Montespan were fourfold: that she had bought love potions to retain her hold over the King; that she had allowed Guibourg to cut the throats of children at a black mass using her naked belly as an altar with the same purpose of retaining the King's favour; that she had attempted to kill her rival Mademoiselle de Fontanges using a pair of poisoned gloves (or, according to other reports, with poisoned milk); that she had attempted to have the King himself killed by means of a poisoned letter.

It is now generally believed that these allegations were cooked up by Guibourg, Marguerite Monvoisin and Lesage to save their own skins, calculating—accurately as it turned out—that because the King would not bring the full rigour of the law to bear on the mother of his legitimised children, he could not bring it to bear on her guilty accusers. (Though, in the event, their fate of life imprisonment was scarcely more desirable than the death penalty.) That the statements of these three (which survive to this day in the Bastille archives) were full of self-serving exaggerations is clear; what

seems to be equally certain is that there must have been enough substance to at least two of the charges for them to be taken seriously. The smearing of Montespan was a risky strategy, but it would have been utterly foolhardy had there been no facts whatever to back it up.

Indeed it appeared there were. In the Bastille archives there is a résumé by La Reynie of an earlier interview with two acquaintances of La Voisin, the Abbé Mariette and the same Lesage, dated September 1668. It refers to various 'ceremonies' and 'conjurations' which they performed for Montespan 'for the purpose of causing the death of Madame de La Valliere.' This was at the time when Montespan was bidding to take over as the King's chief mistress from Louise de La Vallière. Following the interview the Abbé Mariette was banished and Lesage condemned to the galleys, though Voisin used her influence to obtain his release in 1672. It is odd that nothing was done about Montespan at the time, but there is no reason to doubt that the Abbé Mariette and Lesage were telling the truth. Montespan was not a power in the land, as she was in 1680, and mentioning her did not benefit them.

On October 1st, 1680, following the execution of Madame Filastre, Louis decided to suspend sessions of the Chambre Ardente. This course was taken, according to clerk of the court Sagot, on the specious grounds that a continuation of the enquiry 'would denigrate the nation in the eyes of foreigners'. The real reason was that, under torture, Filastre had made damaging allegations against Montespan. La Reynie tried to insist on continuing the work of La Chambre Ardente, but more powerful counsels prevailed. As a result Guibourg, Lesage and Marguerite Monvoisin among others escaped trial and condemnation.

Between May and July 1681 the process wound down. Some of the minor players were condemned to death or sent to the galleys. It seems peculiarly unjust that Jeanne Chanfrain, Guibourg's mistress and surely more victim than culprit, should have been tortured and condemned to death in June 1681, while the odious Abbé lived on in solitary confinement at Besancon until January 1686. In April 1682 the Chambre Ardente was of-

ficially disbanded and in December Louis ordered fourteen people (including Marguerite Voisin, and Guibourg) to perpetual imprisonment in various castles and convents. The end of the affair was more whimper than bang. In the three years of its existence the Chambre Ardente had passed judgement on 104 cases. Thirty-four of the accused were executed; two condemned *in absentia* and four sent to the galleys; thirty-four sentences involved banishment or financial amends and thirty were acquitted. But many more had been involved in some way or other.

There were at least some beneficial consequences to the Poisons Affair in that it led on August 31st, 1682, by a special decree of the Parlement, to the first legal restrictions on the sale of poisons. This decree still forms the basis of present day French legislation on poisons. A ban was also placed on private laboratories and stills.

What are we to make of the Affair as a whole? Some historians have alleged that Louvois exploited the Poisons Affair to discredit his great rival Colbert, but while it is true that some of the accused (such as Soissons) were enemies of Louvois and friends of Colbert, it is not true of Montespan, who was on good terms with both. Besides, La Reynie, the man in charge of the day to day conduct of the enquiry, was once a protégé of Colbert's and all the evidence shows him to have been both astute and incorruptible.

The most conclusive proof that the affair was not pumped up for political purposes comes from La Reynie's own surviving memoranda. He was aware of the extreme sensitivity of the case where Montespan was concerned and was constantly wracked by doubts. In a surviving memorandum he agonises:

I have done all I can... to convince myself that these acts [i.e. crimes attributed to Montespan] were committed, but have not reached a conclusion. By contrast, I searched for everything that could persuade me that they were not done, and this proved equally impossible.

Nicholas de La Reynie, father of the Paris police, retired in 1697 and died on June 13th, 1709. One month later, almost to the day, Louis had all the papers in his possession relating to 'L'Affaire *des Poisons'* burnt. What these papers contained no one can say for certain, but unknown to Louis, La Reynie's memoranda on the affair survived. The attempt at a cover-up, if such it was, failed. The period of the Poisons Affair marked a change in Louis' character from the sensual amoralist of the Montespan era to the more strait-laced, pious character he became after he married Madame de Maintenon secretly in 1684. It would be an exaggeration to say that the Affair was what made him the austere figure of his later years, but it surely hastened the transition. It must also have strengthened his suspicions of the aristocracy and his inclination to rule absolutely without their mediation. His high-born mistress had been implicated in acts of monstrous impiety, even of attempted regicide. He had seen the consequences of license and toleration.

Throughout this period the Huguenots of France were being put under increasing pressure to convert to Catholicism. 1682 saw the height of the notorious *'dragonnades'* in which, on the orders of Louvois, dragoons were billeted on obdurately Protestant families. Finally on October 18th, 1685, the Edict of Nantes was revoked and with it the last vestiges of religious toleration. Heresy was suppressed and uniformity was imposed. Catholics rejoiced in the religious zeal of a reformed character; only a few saw the Revocation as a moral and political blunder.

But how guilty was Montespan? The general consensus these days is that she did little more than perhaps have La Voisin tell her fortune. Certainly the chief witnesses against her—Marguerite Voisin, Guibourg, Lesage, Filastre—were

tainted, but there is no reason to believe that everything they said was untrue.

Did she poison Fontanges and attempt to kill Louis? No. She had no compelling motive to do either. She had nothing to gain by killing the King and, angry as she was at Fontanges' arrival on the scene, Montespan had every reason to believe that her rival's ascendancy would not last long. This proved to be the case. Fontanges fell from grace in June 1680 and died the following year. The autopsy showed death to be due to natural causes.

Did she buy love philtres either directly or through des Œillets to preserve the King's ardour? Almost certainly. La Reynie in a memorandum conjectured that others may have attempted to kill the King through Montespan by supplying her with poisoned aphrodisiacs.

Did she take part in infanticidal black masses to retain the King's favour? The evidence for this is more doubtful, but I would say, on balance, yes. It is incontestable that she knew La Voisin from 1667 and that she was a party to sacrilegious ceremonies conducted by the Abbé Mariette at that time. Marguerite Voisin's and Guibourg's mutually corroborating accounts of the Montespan black masses convinced La Reynie.

Those who believe Montespan innocent of the black masses point to the fact that she remained at court until 1691, no longer Louis' mistress, but still an important and influential figure. Did Louis then believe her innocent? I think he believed what it was in his interests to believe. It did not suit him for the mother of his legitimised children, of whom, especially in the case of the Duc du Maine, he was extremely fond, to be openly disgraced.

Psychologically, Montespan was capable of it. She was a haughty, reckless character who played for high stakes. She was pious, yes, but still committed the mortal sin of adultery with Louis. Her faith may have been like that of La Voisin who would recommend her clients say an ordinary mass to obtain their ends, and only proposed the black variety if that failed.

Montespan's penitential piety towards the end of her life was extreme to the point of morbidity. According to Saint-Simon, she became afraid of the dark and slept with two women in her room who had always to be playing cards or eating or enjoying themselves if she happened to wake up in the middle of the night. She was terrified of death, though she faced it serenely at the end which came in 1707. All this suggests that she was atoning for a more sinister crime than adultery.

Finally, if there were no substance to the allegations made against his former mistress and mother of his children, why did Louis take personal charge of all the papers relating to the Affair, and burn them, in 1709?

FOR FURTHER READING:

Ian Dunlop, *Louis XIV* (Chatto & Windus, 1999); Nancy Mitford, *The Sun King* (Sphere Books, 1966); Madame de Sévigné, *Selected Letters* (Penguin Classics, 1982); Georges Mongrédien. *Mme de Montespan et L'Affaire des Poisons* (Paris 1953); Frances Mossiker *The Affair of the Poisons* (Gollancz, 1970).

Reggie Oliver is a translator and writer. He is the author of *Out of the Woodshed,* a life of Stella Gibbons (Bloomsbury, 1998).

This article first appeared in *History Today*, March 2001, pp. 28-34. © 2001 by History Today, Ltd. Reprinted by permission.

400 Years of the East India Company

Huw V. Bowen asks whether the East India Company was one of the 'most powerful engines' of state and empire in British history.

The year 2000 marks the 400th anniversary of the founding of the English East India Company, the trading organisation that acted as the vehicle for British commercial and imperial expansion in Asia. For over two hundred years, the Company stood like a colossus over trade, commerce and empire, and contemporaries could only marvel at its influence, resources, strength and wealth. Writing at the beginning of the nineteenth century, the political economist David Macpherson was unequivocal in his assessment that the Company was 'the most illustrious and most flourishing commercial association that ever existed in any age or country.'

Today even the most powerful firm pales by comparison in terms of longevity and wide-ranging economic, political and cultural influence. In an era before fast travel and instant communication, the East India Company established a far-flung empire and then set about governing, controlling and exploiting it from a great distance in London. It managed to do this until it was finally rendered obsolete by the tumultuous events surrounding the Indian Mutiny in 1857.

The Company was granted its first charter by Elizabeth I on the last day of 1600, and it had to survive an uncertain first century or so as it sought access to Asian markets and commodities. At

HT ARCHIVES

The frontispiece of Isaac Pike's Journal of the Stringer (1713) showed the Company robustly defending its trading position.

home, it was restructured several times, notably between 1698 and 1708 when an 'old' and 'new' East India Company

co-existed before merging to form the United Company of Merchants Trading to the East Indies. In the East, the Company came under such pressure from its Dutch rivals during the mid-seventeenth century that it was obliged to shift the main focus of its activities from the Malay archipelago and the Spice Islands to South Asia. Over time, it managed to establish a commercial presence in India centred upon three 'presidencies' established at Madras, Bombay and Calcutta. These tenuous footholds were fortified and defended by the Company as it sought to consolidate its position in an often hostile commercial and political world. This in turn gave rise to the growth of a small private army that was eventually to rival the regular British army in terms of size and manpower. The Company's role in India was thus defined by both commercial activity and a military presence: it was considered legitimate to use force in support of trade, and the overseas personnel were organised and deployed accordingly. In the words of one contemporary, it was a 'fighting company'.

By the mid-eighteenth century, the Company had begun to assert itself over rival European companies and Indian powers alike, and this placed it in a position from which it could begin to carve out an extended territorial and commercial empire for itself. The actions of men such as Robert Clive (1725–74), Warren Hastings (1732–1818) and Charles Cornwallis (1738–1805) helped to transform the Company from trader to sovereign, so that during the second half of the eighteenth century millions of Indians were brought under British rule. As William Playfair put it in 1799:

From a limited body of merchants, the India Company have become the Arbiters of the East.

The Company created the British Raj, and as such it has left a deep and permanent imprint on the history and historiography of India. The story, once almost universally described as the 'rise of British India', not so long ago formed part of the staple reading diet of British schoolchildren and students. In the post-colonial era, when imperial history has ceased to be fashionable, the legacies of British India are still hotly debated and contested. It is within this context that the history of the East India Company remains to the fore.

Today's casual observer finds few signs of the leading role the Company once played in the life of the nation.

Rather less obvious, perhaps, is the part played by the East India Company in the domestic development of Britain. Indeed, today's casual observer finds few signs of the leading role it once played in the nation's business, commercial, cultural and political life. In terms of architecture, for example, there is little surviving evidence in London of the Company's once-extensive property empire. The London docklands, home to the East India dock complex, has been reshaped. Although Commercial Road and East India Dock Road—the purpose-built link with the City—survive, the docks themselves have been filled in and redeveloped, leaving only a few poignant reminders of the Company's once

formidable presence in the area. To the West, the great fortress-like warehouses built by the Company at Cutler Street were partially demolished and refurbished in controversial circumstances during the late 1970s. There is no trace remaining whatsoever of the Company's headquarters in Leadenhall Street. Charles Dickens once described the 'rich' East India House 'teeming with suggestions' of eastern delights, but it was unceremoniously pulled down in the 1860s, and in its place today stands the new Lloyd's Building, also a monument to commercial capitalism, but displaying rather different architectural qualities. In recent years, the only obvious local clue to the Indian connection was provided by the East India Arms, a tavern in nearby Lime Street, but that too has now fallen victim to the modern re-naming and re-branding process. As a result, the East India Company is now out of sight and out of mind.

It was not always like this. During the late eighteenth century, the Company played a key role in London's economy, employing several thousand labourers, warehousemen and clerks. Returning fleets of East Indiamen moored in Blackwall Reach, before their Indian and Chinese cargoes were transferred via hoys and carts to enormous warehouses where they awaited distribution and sale in Britain's burgeoning consumer markets. The profile of the Company in London was always high and the eyes of many were on Leadenhall Street. Political infighting at East India House regularly captured the attention of the metropolitan chattering classes. The Company itself was repeatedly subjected to inquiry by a Parliament uneasy about the turn being taken by events in the East.

The Company's domestic tentacles extended well beyond London, however, and its influences were widely felt across the south of England. Provincial outposts were established in the form of the agencies in ports such as Deal, Falmouth, Plymouth and Portsmouth. Over the years the Company maintained camps for its military recruits at Newport in the Isle of White, Warley in Essex and at Chatham in Kent. Educational establishments were set up for the purpose of preparing those destined for service overseas. During the first half of the nineteenth century, the

East India College at Haileybury in Hertfordshire educated boys for the civil service, while Addiscombe Military Seminary near Croydon trained military cadets.

More generally, the Company touched many sectors of British society and the economy, as some contemporaries acknowledged. In 1813, for example, a friend to the Company, Thomas William Plummer, set about identifying what 'proportion of the community' had a connection with the Company. Without mentioning several million purchasers of tea, spices, silks, muslins and other Asian commodities, he listed investors, Company employees of many types, tradesmen, manufacturers, shipbuilders, dealers, private merchants, military personnel and ship crews, before concluding that:

Scarcely any part of the British community is distinct from some personal or collateral interest in the welfare of the East India Company.

There was more than a grain of truth in what Plummer wrote, and by the beginning of the nineteenth century many interests across the country had been tied closely to the Company. This was particularly the case with the several thousand or so well-to-do individuals who chose to invest in Company stocks and bonds. For much of the eighteenth century East India stock was the most attractive investment available in the nascent stock market, not least because it always paid out an annual dividend of more than 5 per cent. The India bonds that provided the Company with its short-term working capital were also highly prized, with one early stock market analyst describing them as 'the most convenient and profitable security a person can be possessed of'.

The fortunes of Company and nation had become so tightly intertwined that they had begun to move in tandem with one another as those who took a broad view of political and economic matters were able to see. When the Company flourished, the nation flourished. Equally, as Edmund Burke put it, 'to say the Company was in a state of distress was neither more nor less than to say the country was in a state of distress'. Such logic dictated that the effects of any crisis or catastrophe experienced by the Company in India would be deeply felt in Britain and the wider British Empire, and this was well understood by close observers of the imperial scene. One pamphleteer wrote in 1773 that the loss of India would occasion a 'national bankruptcy' while the imperial theorist Thomas Pownall suggested that such an event would cause 'the ruin of the whole edifice of the British Empire'. These concerns lay behind the increased levels of government anxiety about Company adventurism, misrule, and mismanagement in India that became evident after 1760.

> *By the 1770's the Company was akin to a semi-privatised imperial wing of the Hanoverian state.*

Late eighteenth-century concerns about events in the East reflected the fact that the East India Company was no longer an ordinary trading company. It had evolved into an immensely powerful hybrid commercial and imperial agency, and after the conquest of Bengal it fundamentally reshaped its traditional commercial policy based upon the exchange of exported British goods and bullion for Asian commodities. Instead, the Company concentrated its efforts on the collection of territorial and customs revenues in northeast India. The right to collect these revenues had been granted by the Mughal Emperor Shah Alam II in 1765, an event which both confirmed British military supremacy in the region and served to elevate the Company to the position of *de facto* sovereign in Bengal and the neighbouring provinces of Bihar and Orissa. Thereafter, trade was used to facilitate the transfer of 'tribute' from Asia to London as surplus revenue was ploughed into the purchase of Indian and Chinese commodities for export to Britain. As Edmund Burke later remarked, this marked a 'revolution' in the Company's commercial affairs.

The Company's empire had now become self-financing to the point that further military expansion could be sustained, but it was also believed that generous payments could be made to domestic stockholders and the British government alike. This proved to be a vain hope, but the transfer of tribute helped to define the essential characteristics of the late-eighteenth-century state-Company relationship. Successive ministers declared the state's 'right' to a share of the Bengal revenues, but in return for the promise of annual payments into the public treasury they allowed the Company to continue in its role as the administrator, defender and revenue collector of Bengal. This brought the British government the benefits of empire without any expensive administrative or military responsibilities. It was a welcome and convenient arrangement at a time when the national debt was spiralling ever-upwards and parts of the Empire, most notably North America, were proving increasingly difficult to control and subdue.

By the 1770s the Company thus found itself as something akin to a semi-privatised imperial wing of the Hanoverian state, with its operations being defined by the dual pursuit of both private and public interest. It was charged with the protection, cultivation, and exploitation of one of Britain's most important national assets, and contemporary observers described its new role accordingly. In 1773 the prime minister, Lord North, declared that the Company was acting as '[tax] farmers to the publick', while a late-century pamphleteer suggested that the Company had become 'stewards to the state'. In this scheme of things, there was a greater need for the Company to become more accountable, efficient, and reliable, and this desire lay behind the reforms embodied in North's Regulating Act of 1773 and Pitt's India Act of 1784.

The Company's importance to the British state was not, however, simply to be assessed in terms of its role as the licensed agent through which metropolitan administrative, fiscal and military influences were brought to bear upon the Indian empire. The Company had been present at the birth of the eighteenth-century state during the troubled period following the 'Glorious Revolution' of 1688–89. As a hard-pressed nation struggled to cope with the demands of the Nine Years' War, ministers had drawn heavily on the financial resources of the 'new' East India Company that had received its charter in 1698. This meant that when the United Company was established in 1709 it was already deeply embedded in both the public finances and the City of London where, together with the Bank of England, it formed part of the 'monied interest'.

The financial relationship between state and Company took several different forms, all of which were a variation on a theme that saw the Company's monopoly privileges periodically confirmed or extended by the Crown in return for loans or payments made to the public purse. Indeed, by the 1720s the entire paid-up share capital of the Company, almost £3.2 million, was on longterm loan to the state at 5 per cent interest. This sizeable advance was extended to £4.2 million before prime minister and chancellor Henry Pelham's restructuring of the national debt in 1749–50 saw the reduction of interest payments to 3 per cent and the creation of the East India annuities. This extensive underwriting of the post-settlement regime was such that a Chairman of the Company, Jacob Bosanquet, was later to borrow a phrase from Adam Smith and declare that the Company, together with the Bank of England, had become one of the 'most powerful engines of the state'. As Chairman of a company under great pressure from critics by 1799, Bosanquet was hardly likely to say anything else, but his comments were not altogether inaccurate. His organisation had established itself as a cornerstone of the City of London, and as such it had played a key role in supporting the state and public credit.

By the end of the eighteenth century, apologists were thus arguing that the Company formed part of the very foundations of Britain's state and empire, yet within sixty years it had ceased to exist at all. What happened to make the great 'engine' run out of steam so rapidly?

There are a great many answers to this question but the most basic one is undoubtedly the most important. Quite simply, in economic terms the Company failed to deliver what it had promised since the 1760s. As the military and administrative costs of empire multiplied, the Company proved itself unable to generate a revenue surplus for transfer to Britain. A great many attempts were made to remodel the Company's fiscal and commercial operations but successes in one area were always offset by failures and setbacks elsewhere. Only the striking growth of the China tea trade offered the Company any prospect of success, but that in itself was not enough to satisfy the demands of profit-hungry stockholders and ministers. Indeed, the annual flow of 'tribute' to the state Treasury promised by the Company in 1767 had dried up almost at once. By 1772 the Company was teetering on the edge of bankruptcy, having failed to master the complexities of its new role in India, and a degree of desperation forced it into the measures that ultimately led to the Boston Tea Party the following year. Thereafter, the Company staggered from crisis to crisis, requiring government loans to enable it to continue functioning. In effect, this meant that roles had been reversed, and the Company had become dependent upon the state for financial support.

The Company failed to argue convincingly that it offered the best way forward for the Anglo-Asian connection.

A dose of economic reality, coupled with widespread metropolitan unease about 'despotic' Company government in India, caused many commentators rapidly to reassess their views of Britain's eastern empire. Nowhere was this more evident than with Edmund Burke who became one of the Company's harshest critics and campaigned long and hard for reform and the punishment of British misdemeanours in India. Initially, though, Burke had been as captivated as any observer by the prospect of Britain gaining very real material advantage from the Company's successes in Bengal. He had outlined the economic potential of India to the House of Commons in 1769 before concluding that 'The Orient sun never laid more glorious expectations before us.' This type of view was commonplace during the 1760s, but it was replaced by much gloomier assessments of the situation in the decades that followed. Commentators soon tired of hearing about the promise of Indian wealth being used to the advantage of the metropolis, and began instead to expose the flaws that were evident in the Company's calculations and methods. The figures did not seem to add up, leaving one MP, George Tierney, to complain that 'Our Indian prosperity is always in the future tense'.

Criticism such as this only strengthened the case of those in Britain who were campaigning vigorously for the East India trade to be opened up to free competition. Just as the utility of the Company to the nation began to be discussed, old mercantilist assumptions about the organisation of trade were being called into question. Taking a lead from Adam Smith, who had condemned chartered companies as being 'nuisances in every respect', critics exposed the Company to searching analyses of its methods and practices.

Under such attack, the Company proved unable, indeed almost unwilling, to answer the charges levelled against it. Although it began to emphasise the contribution it made to intellectual and scientific life in Britain, it failed to argue convincingly that it alone offered the best way forward for the further development of the Anglo-Asian connection. Part of the reason for this was that the Company believed it had already taken the organisation of its commercial and financial affairs to the highest possible level. It proved to be remarkably complacent and, together with a deep-rooted institutional conservatism, this meant that any change was regarded with the deepest suspicion. As one director of the Company put it, 'Innovations in an established system are at all times dangerous'. Few friends of the Company could see any need to alter an organisation that was thought to be beyond improvement, and this case was restated time and again. Most would have agreed with Thomas Mortimer who argued during the 1760s that the Company had 'brought the commerce and mercantile credit of Great Britain to such a degree of perfection, as no age or country can equal.' To alter anything would be to invite trouble. Sustained failure and disappointing performance, however, flew in the face of such opinion, and this ensured that pressure for change continued to grow from outside the Company.

In the end, the Company's failure was essentially two-fold as far as many of those in the metropolis were concerned. It failed to deliver to Britain the great financial windfall that had been anticipated after the conquest of Bengal; and because of this it was unable to sustain much beyond 1760 its position as one of the major institutional and financial props of the Hanoverian state. When charges related to misrule, despotism, unfair monopoly practices and a host of other complaints were added to the scales, they served eventually to tip the balance of political opinion.

The immediate and outright abolition of the Company, however, was never an option because the state did not possess the resources, skills or will necessary to govern a large empire in India. Instead, successive breaches were made in the Company's commercial position. Trade with the East was opened up to a limited degree in 1793; the Indian monopoly was ended in 1813; and the exclusive trade with China was abolished in 1833. The Company survived for another twenty-five years as Britain's administrative and military representative in India, but by then it was a trading company in name only. The Company had achieved the full transition from trader to sovereign, amply fulfilling Adam Smith's prediction that trade and government were incompatible within a 'company of merchants'.

The Company ended its days in the aftermath of the Indian Mutiny when no case at all could be advanced for its survival in any form. Its powerful legacy endured in India for many more years in the form of the Indian army and civil service, but sight was soon lost of the importance of its contribution to the development of the metropolitan state and to imperial Britain itself. Today the Company has been almost entirely removed from the geographical and historical landscape and it has been more or less erased from our national consciousness. As the 400th anniversary of the founding of the Company approaches, this makes it all the more necessary for us to reflect on the deep, but now hidden, impression left on British history by this quite extraordinary institution.

FOR FURTHER READING

H.V. Bowen, 'Investment and Empire in the Later Eighteenth Century: East India Stockholding, 1756–1791', *Economic History Review* (1989); K.N. Chaudhuri, *The English East India Company: The Study of an Early Joint-Stock Company* (Cass, 1965); John Keay, *The Honourable Company: The History of the English East India Company* (Harper Collins, 1991); Philip Lawson, *The East India Company: A History* (Macmillan, 1993); Martin Moir, *A General Guide to the India Office Records* (British Library, 1996); Jean Sutton, *Lords of the East: The East India Company and its Ships* (Conway Maritime Press, 1981). Information about the records of the East India Company can be found on the British Library's website http://www.bl.uk/ (follow the links to the Oriental and India Office collections).

Huw Bowen is Senior Lecturer in Economic and Social History at the University of Leicester and the author of War and British Society 1688–1815 **(Cambridge UP, 1998)**.

This article first appeared in *History Today*, July 2000, pp. 47-53. © 2000 by History Today, Ltd. Reprinted by permission.

"Thus in the beginning all the world was America"

—*John Locke, Second Treatise of Government*

by Edward Cline

THE TWO MEN most responsible for the founding of the United States never set foot in it, though their intellectual signatures are stamped on the Declaration of Independence as indelibly as any of the signers' flourishes: Aristotle and John Locke. It was the Greek philosopher who bequeathed to the West—via Thomas Acquinas—the fundamental rules of reason and logic and the means for men to determine their purpose for living on earth. It was Locke who applied reason to politics more thoroughly and convincingly than had any political thinker before him. And it was to Locke that the Founders turned for their most trenchant arguments in the conflict with Britain. As Dr. Harry Binswanger, a lecturer on Locke's importance in the history of ideas, has said, "As far as I can determine, Locke is the originator of individual rights."

Locke may even be granted indirect credit for the naming of Williamsburg—and even for its founding. It was during the reigns of Charles II and James II (the Restoration) that he wrote his most important works in response to the struggles between Parliament and the Stuarts, which culminated in 1688 with the abdication and flight of James II and with the Convention Parliament's welcome of William and Mary as regents of England, Scotland, Ireland, and France in 1689. The College of William and Mary, founded in 1693, was named in their honor. (Mary died in 1694, thus sparing

the town fathers, in 1699, the task of devising what could only have been an awkward compound name for the new capital.) Locke's *Two Treatises of Government* and *A Letter concerning Toleration*, written between 1680 and 1685, contributed at least part of the intellectual basis for that "Glorious Revolution." They were to have a more profound influence on the thinking of another generation of revolutionaries.

Almost 100 years later, Samuel Adams wrote to a friend: "Mr. Locke has often been quoted in the present dispute between Britain and her colonies, and very much to our purpose. His reasoning is so forcible, that no one has even attempted to confute it." Thomas Jefferson displayed the portraits of Isaac Newton, Francis Bacon, and Locke on the walls of his Monticello home. In a letter to Benjamin Rush, he wrote that these "were my trinity of the three greatest men the world had ever produced." Lockean phraseology and style of expression color many of the most eloquent statements in the Declaration, which Jefferson composed.

POLITICS HAS DOMINATED history books and commanded men's first concerns because it is the most immediate, tangible application of philosophical inquiry; the effect of a tax, a law, or an injustice is more obvious and personal than that of a proposition, a syllogism, or an

abstract deduction in metaphysics or epistemology, even though the latter two fields can determine the ultimate efficacy or tragedy of any political system. Locke lived, thought, and wrote in the tempestuous world of 17th-century England and formulated a political philosophy that would accelerate the pace of men's progress from abject deference and servility to kings and bishops to valuing life, liberty, and property as norms to be championed and defended. Locke began his thinking life as a "conservative" and ended it as a "radical," in both political theory and epistemology, thanks to his commitment to truth, which made possible his intellectual honesty. "[He] who has raised himself above the Alms-Basket, and not content to live lazily on scraps of begg'd Opinions, sets his own Thoughts on work, to find and follow Truth," he observed in "The Epistle to the Reader" of *An Essay concerning Human Understanding*.

Locke did not regard himself as a formal philosopher nor even much of an innovator in the realm of ideas. This was not false modesty but an integral part of his character. "There was an introverted, valetudinarian component in Locke's nature," writes Peter H. Nidditch, editor of one edition of the *Essay*. "He was a careful, cautious man possessed of a good sense of business and method." Carefulness and caution were Locke's bywords, inculcated in him in the often perilous times of the Civil War, Cromwell's

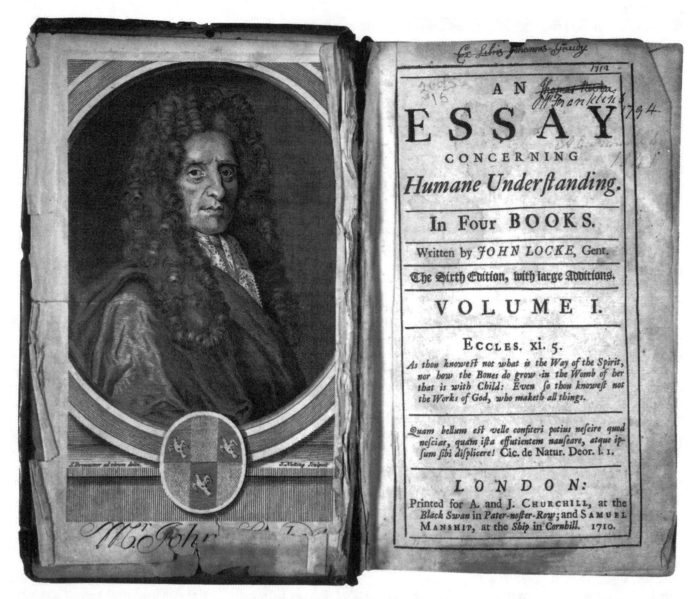

In his lifetime, Locke was prudently wary of admitting authorship of the *Two Treatises* and his *Letter concerning Toleration*. Philosophical speculation, however, was safe enough.

Commonwealth and Protectorate, and the Restoration.

LOCKE WAS, if not a philosopher, then an intellectual. As Adam Smith did in the field of economics nearly a century later, he drew together all the disparate threads of thought on rights, liberty, and property that preceded him—by a legion of thinkers who included James Harrington, John Milton, Henry Neville, John Hampden, to name but a few—and weaved the best of them into a single, comprehensible fabric in the *Two Trea-* tises. Like the Founders, he held that reason or rationality was men's only means of living alone or in society, and that this attribute of men was as much "endowed by their creator" as were certain unalienable rights. The attempt by a criminal or a magistrate to force man to think or act against his own reason was a violation of the "law of nature." Reason was the antithesis of "innate" ideas, which Locke argued in his *Essay* could not exist, thus robbing the advocates of absolute monarchy of a key tenet of their arguments. It could be argued that the *Essay* and the *Two Treatises* are affirmations of and companions to each other. By the time the Founders were impelled to compose thoughtful rebuttals to king and Parliament, Locke's works were near-gospel in the colonies. Hardly a library existed—private or college—in 18th-century colonial America that did not boast at least one title by Locke. He had made nearly everything "self-evident."

LOCKE'S IMPORTANCE to the Founders cannot be appreciated without first painting a miniature of his times. As the sun of the Enlightenment slowly burned off the heavy, clinging fog of the Medieval Age, men began to see the possible in all realms of human thought and action, particularly in politics. They were emerging from the miasma of edict- and sword-enforced ignorance, and they were dazzled. Obstructing their way, or waiting in doctrinal ambushes to pounce on the least hint of blasphemy or treason, were the forces of the Medievalists—or their royalist or secular descendants, whose notion of a stable polity was a monarch wielding absolute, unquestioned dominion over his realm, with a bishop on his right hand ready to field any questions he himself could not answer.

The political fact of Locke's time was that religion was inextricably tied to politics. Locke did not separate the two realms, but he laid the groundwork for it to be accomplished later. To question the political status quo, however, was to question religious orthodoxy—and vice versa.

The genesis of this alliance in Britain was the English Reformation, precipitated by Henry VIII's break with the Roman Catholic Church over his marriage to Anne Boleyn and the establishment of the Church of England in 1534. Leap ahead over nearly a hundred years of roiling English history to the abrupt transition from the Tudor era to that of the Stuarts, marked by the machinations of James I and Charles I to amass more money, power, and influence than Parliament wished to grant them.

There were two civil wars, the first between the Roundheads and Cavaliers, the second between a Presbyterian Parliament and the Independent army of Oliver Cromwell. Cromwell's own brand of "republicanism" began with Pride's Purge of Presbyterians from Parliament by the army (Algernon Sidney refused to vacate his seat, until a soldier put a hand on his shoulder) and the gradual establishment of a dictatorship that nominated and controlled a complaisant "Barebones" Parliament. It was Cromwell's Rump Parliament that passed the first Navigation Act in October 1651.

Religious passions moved most of these events. Royal or parliamentary toleration of Catholics, Nonconformists—this time the outlawed Anglicans or Episcopalians—Jews, or Dissenters was viewed as a political act fraught with danger. Catholicism in particular was anathema to most Protestant Englishmen, whatever their sectarian suasion, whether they were well-read lords or gentry, or illiterate publicans or chimney sweeps; they had only to nod across the Channel to France or Spain to prove the consequences of a Catholic monarchy. Papist sympathies from any quarter were regarded as cryptic designs on the liberties and privileges of Englishmen and Parliament. This animus, based partly on bigotry but mostly on demonstrable fact in England's own history and on events on the Continent, would survive well into the 19th century.

Before Locke published his *Two Treatises*, those who championed rights—to life, liberty, and property—floundered on the shoals of custom, precedent, tradition, or convention. Or on Scripture, which the enemies of liberty were as adept in employing as their opponents. Some of the most eloquent and incisive statements in favor of liberty were recorded in the Army Debates of 1647–49, conducted while a Puritan Parliament negotiated with a stubborn Charles I. Both sides of the issues—which included toleration, freedom of conscience, and security of property—brandished their Bibles (ironically, the King James Version, completed in 1611) and assailed each other with book, chapter, and verse in support of myriad positions, accusations, and compromises.

But the revolutionaries had no Locke to show them the way out of the intractable dilemma. When Cromwell died in 1658, the "republic" collapsed tiredly on its own contradictions and for lack of a common moral base. The Rump Parliament invited Charles II—whose father had been beheaded in 1649—to resume the throne. Countless Puritans rushed to conform to the Anglican Church. If they could not agree on a moral base, at least England would have a moral authority.

But history was to repeat itself less than 30 years later.

ENTER JOHN LOCKE, philosopher. Most portraits of him stare intensely back at the viewer, challenging one to be as thoughtful or serious as he, or daring one to be fatuous or insincere. In the first instance, one would gain a friend, even if he disagreed with you; in the second, one would gain a disdainful enemy or, worse, an enemy who would dismiss you and never think of you again. Locke was a retiring man who grew to believe that ideas had a more profound effect on men's actions, lives, and fates than bullets. He was a dark, thin, plainly-dressed man who preferred quiet, civil conversation to boisterous company. Once he broke up a card game by taking out his notebook and proposing to record the verities of the players.

Locke was a shrewd manager of his money and died a rich man. Even in the most unsettling periods of his life, he kept exact accounts of his financial dealings. He preferred country life to life in London, chiefly because prolonged stays in the city aggravated his asthmatic cough—as did the stress of political crises. Travel for his health, coinciding often with Restoration turmoil, more than once saved his life.

Locke was born in August 1632 and raised in the bucolic setting of rural Somerset near Bristol. He was the son of John Locke, Senior, clerk to the justice of the peace in the parish of Chew Magna. The father served in the Civil War as captain of a troop of horse with the Parliamentarians, and he was also an attorney for the commander of that unit, Alexander Popham. An influential Presbyterian, Popham later arranged to send young Locke to Westminster School in London in 1646.

Raised in a Calvinist household, Locke spent the next six years in this royalist and largely high-church school, mastering Greek and Latin by way of Cicero, Livy, Plutarch, and other classical authors. Charles I was executed in Whitehall Palace Yard, a stone's throw from the school. It is tempting to imagine that Locke witnessed the event. But the school's headmaster was a staunch royalist and opponent of Cromwell. On that somber January 30, the student body was made to pray all day for the tried and convicted king's soul, and it is doubtful that any student was permitted to venture outside Westminster Abbey's enclosure.

It was not until Locke went to Christ Church at Oxford in 1652 that his reading began to venture beyond the college's scholastic curriculum of rhetoric, logic, grammar, moral philosophy, and more classical studies. Oxford had been purged of its royalist faculty and was under firm Calvinist control. As an undergraduate, Locke was obliged to attend two sermons a day and to pray every night with his tutor. His first published work was an ode to Cromwell included in a book of poems issued by the college in 1655. Five years later he would pen, in a similar volume, a poem praising Charles II on the occasion of the restored Stuart's entrance into London.

Locke was made a Fellow of Christ Church the year Cromwell died and would continue his Oxford association until he was ordered expelled in 1684 by Charles II for his suspected role in the Rye House Plot to assassinate the king. Locke had welcomed the Stuart's return, if only because it brought an end to the dour, stifling regime of the Puritans. When a lecturer in Greek, rhetoric, and moral philosophy, he wrote the *Two Tracts on Government*, in which he asserted that a "magistrate"—or a sovereign—had every right to impose conformity on his subjects; since the rituals and times and places of worship were "indifferent," there was no good reason for a subject to resist conformity, as the object of worship was universal. Locke did not believe, at that time, that civil upheaval was justified over what he asserted were picayune differences in the style and content of religious services.

In his future *Two Treatises* and *A Letter concerning Toleration*, Locke was to advance the opposite of this position: That a magistrate's power to impose conformity in "indifferent" matters was not only morally wrong but accomplished little but fraudulent uniformity. Force could not compel a man to be any more or less devoted to his beliefs. The object of worship, God, Locke would maintain, was too important to be the subject of insincerity. Men must find their own way according to their own lights. He would extend this line of reasoning to secular or civil matters. At the time, though, it would not be inaccurate to say that early in his career, Locke was as much a skeptic as was Thomas Hobbes, whose major work, *Leviathan*, he

undoubtably read and must have agreed that "sovereign power is not so hurtful as the want of it."

Like many other lukewarm Calvinists then, Locke conformed to the Anglican Church at the Restoration. It was an expedient action and cost him nothing of his convictions; the ceremonies were "indifferent." But in the second year of his fellowship, he wrote a friend that "Phansye" ruled the world, and he wondered "where is that great Diana... Reason?" He would find it, at first, at Oxford.

Contributing to the development of his later views were Locke's friendships with Robert Boyle (of Boyle's Law fame) and other prominent British empiricists of the time, many of whom would become charter members of the Royal Society of London for the Improving of Natural Knowledge. Boyle, a noted chemist, physicist, and essayist on theological issues, had declined many lucrative clerical appointments to devote himself to scientific investigation and experimentation. This unconventional but respected thinker helped to influence Locke's unconventional decision not to follow the path of most other Christ Church Fellows and take orders for the Church of England, but instead to pursue the study of medicine. Although he never took a medical course and pursued his studies independently, he attained a bachelor's degree in medicine in 1674. His knowledge of the subject, together with the apparent efficacy of his advice to others on their health, were to garner him a reputation as a physician second only to his reputation as a political theorist.

In 1663, Locke wrote a series of *Essays on the Law of Nature*, which discuss the reality-based ethics he claimed ought to govern the actions of rational men. These *Essays* were a kind of overture to the *Two Treatises* and the *Essay concerning Human Understanding*, as they reveal the development and direction of his thinking. At the same time, he practiced medicine with a Dr. David Thomas of London, a close friend, until 1666.

As a respite from his lecturing duties at Oxford, Locke went abroad in 1664 as secretary to Sir Walter Vane, Charles II's envoy to Frederick William, the Great

Elector of Brandenburg. In a letter to John Strachy, a boyhood friend, Locke described Christmas visits to several churches near Cleve, including Catholic ones, and expressed pleasant surprise that so many religious sects could reside peacefully in one town. "I have not met with any so good-natured people, or so civil, as the Catholic priests," he wrote. These were not the ogres he had expected to encounter. His observations abroad would lead him to compose and publish anonymously in 1689 *A Letter concerning Toleration*, perhaps the most important and effective argument for the separation of church and state ever written.

Locke returned from the diplomatic mission in May 1666 and resumed his duties and studies at Christ Church. In July he received a letter from Dr. Thomas, asking him to give medical advice to Anthony Ashley Cooper—later the first earl of Shaftesbury—who was in Oxford to drink the supposedly healthy waters of nearby Astrop. Lord Ashley had fought with the Royalists in the Civil War, then in 1643 went over to the Roundheads and had been a member of Cromwell's Council of State. He was known to his contemporaries, writes Lockean scholar Richard Ashcraft, to be "opposed to religious persecution in general and to popery in particular, and as an advocate of the rights of Dissenters and of Parliament"—that is, he argued in the House of Lords and among friends and idealogues against state-enforced Catholicism, absolute monarchy, and the theory of the divine right of kings. Locke said Shaftesbury was "a vigorous and indefatigable champion of civil and ecclesiastical liberty."

THE TWO MEN formed such a warm friendship that Locke moved into Shaftesbury's London household the next year and acted as his personal physician and confidential advisor. In 1668 he performed a successful operation on his patron's abscessed liver, saving Shaftesbury's life and earning his constant gratitude.

Shaftesbury was the most important member of the Lords Proprietors of Carolina and appointed Locke secretary of that organization. When it drafted a new constitution for the colony, the two men coauthored a document that provided for an elective assembly and religious freedom. Shaftesbury was named Lord High Chancellor in November 1672, and he subsequently made Locke secretary for the Presentation of Benefices and a year later secretary to the Council of Trade and Plantations.

This last office introduced Locke to the realm of finance and economics; and what he learned during his year-and-a-half tenure enabled him to offer intelligent advice to Parliament, as it debated the Coinage Act of 1696. In his pamphlet *Some Considerations of the Consequences of the Lowering of Interest and Raising the Value of Money*, Locke argued that laws which lowered interest rates on private loans in favor of debtors amounted to theft. And although he was an original subscriber to the Bank of England (for £500, in 1694), Locke wrote that "I cannot but think a monopoly of money by the bank, as well as a monopoly of merchandising by the Act of Navigation, must prove a great prejudice to the trade of the nation."

While Locke was beginning to take and develop copious notes for his *Essay concerning Human Understanding*—in 1671, after a meeting with a small group of friends who could not agree on why they knew what they knew—the match was struck that would lead to a major political conflagration. Shaftesbury, an implacable advocate of toleration, had been influential in moving Charles II to proclaim, in March 1672, the Declaration of Indulgence, whose purpose was to free Nonconformists and Catholics from political and religious restrictions. Parliament responded by forcing the king to withdraw it, on the rationale that such an edict did not lay within proper royal power. The next year brought the revelation that James, the duke of York and the king's brother, had already converted to Catholicism. Little more than a year before, Charles had signed a secret "first" Treaty of Dover with France; among its provisions was an agreement that should Charles II convert to Catholicism, Louis XIV would give him £200,000 a year for his wars with Spain and Holland and 6,000 troops in the event of an English

insurrection against Charles's conversion.

Shaftesbury, who had helped negotiate the "second" Treaty of Dover, a mere pact of alliance with France, now saw the ulterior motive behind the Declaration and began balking at the king's policies. He was dismissed as chancellor in November 1673 and a few months later imprisoned in the Tower of London for a year for having opposed the king and his court party. When he was released, he became the leader of the opposition to the king.

When his term as secretary to the Council of Trade expired (or was terminated), Locke departed for France on a four-year sojourn, ostensibly for his health, which had always been precarious. Or, as some maintain, he was deeply involved in anti-court intrigues in this period—1675–79—and had decided to get out of harm's way. Locke's journals are a record of his travels, medical and scientific observations, and meetings with many of France's intellectual lights. It is plausible that he had a hand in the composition of the anonymously published *A Letter from a Person of Quality to His Friend in the Country*, a pamphlet attributed to Shaftesbury, which suggested a conspiracy by the king, the church, and certain government ministers to extend royal powers and reduce Parliament and the church to money-raising devices for the king. Locke may have left for France if he believed he was suspected of having authored the pamphlet, condemned and burned in November 1675; Locke left in December.

He returned from France in April 1679 in time to witness the unfolding of the Exclusion Crisis—and undoubtedly contribute to it. After a brief stop at Oxford, he moved back into Shaftesbury's household in London, again as the peer's physician and advisor. In May the Scottish Covenanters rebelled against the crown and the repressive measures of John Maitland, the duke of Lauderdale and Charles's secretary of state for Scottish affairs. The revolt was eventually put down by James Scott, the duke of Monmouth and Charles's natural son.

Shaftesbury, now a member of the king's new Privy Council, not only pushed through Parliament the landmark

Habeas Corpus Act but sponsored a succession of exclusion bills, whose aim was to prevent Charles's Catholic brother from inheriting the throne. Charles dissolved two Parliaments for their attempts to get the bills passed. In this period the opposition "country" party and the pro-monarchy "court" party began to coalesce into what would become known as the "Whig" and "Tory" parties—Scottish and Irish terms of derision respectively for "horse drover" and "outlaw."

In March 1681, Charles opened the third and last Exclusion Parliament; he dissolved it after eight days, when it would not do his bidding. His opponents now grasped that the king wished to rule without a legislature. In July a Shaftesbury supporter, Stephen College, was arrested for having entertained exclusion bill supporters with a "cartoon" depicting Charles's tyranny and his removal by Parliament. When a London jury rejected the charges of treason against him, the crown moved his trial to Oxford, where he was convicted and executed. Shaftesbury was arrested for high treason and again put into the Tower. The crown, reading his seized papers, saw that he was at the center of an "association" or confederacy. Not only did it oppose Charles and his brother, but it advocated the subordination of the throne to Parliament and the resort to a force of arms to accomplish it.

This was a separate conspiracy from the Rye House Plot, and the duke of Monmouth, Lords Russell, Grey, and Essex, and Algernon Sidney were arrested in connection with it. Shaftesbury was acquitted and released from the Tower at the end of the year but knew that he could be rearrested at any time. Subsequently, Charles revoked the charters of the City of London and other corporations and had them rewritten to purge the courts and elective offices of Whig juries and the Whig sheriffs who empaneled them; he replaced them with Catholics, Tories, and other pro-monarchy men. The trials and executions continued with a vengeance. Essex committed suicide, the duke of Monmouth was pardoned and fled to Holland, and Lord William Russell was beheaded. Algernon Sidney, who knew Shaftesbury but not Locke, long ago had refused to leave his seat in Parliament when Cromwell dissolved the Rump in 1653. Now he was tried for treason with a known liar as the sole witness to his crime; the prosecution needed two witness for a conviction. The court turned to Sidney's *Discourses on Government*, finished in prison, and argued that the anti-monarchy pro-liberty tract was proof of a conspiracy. Like Stephen College, Sidney was convicted on what he had written, not what he had done. On the scaffold, he refused to recant his claim that resistance to tyranny was a right, and he was beheaded in November 1683.

Locke, busy fighting the battle of ideas, composed in this period the *Two Treatises of Government*. For a long time scholars believed they were written as an apologia for the Glorious Revolution of 1688. A Lockean scholar, Peter Laslett, in 1960 proved that Locke wrote the essay chiefly in response to the events of 1679–83. Shaftesbury's "association" manifesto was a watered-down version of the *Two Treatises* and not nearly as radical as Locke's work. The *Second Treatise* especially was part answer to the growing despotism of Charles and part answer to a pro-monarchy tract written in 1631, Sir Robert Filmer's *Patriacha*, trotted out in 1680 by Tory idealogues to counter numerous Whig publications. Filmer's fundamental premise was that "men are not naturally free" but that the sovereign was. Locke's fundamental premise was that "every man has a property in his own person. This nobody has any right to but himself." *Nobody* included sovereigns and other men, and a man whose life or property was threatened by force had a right to resist, even as far as armed rebellion— a "treasonous" notion.

Shaftesbury had fled England; he died in Holland in January 1683. Locke probably had already finished the *Two Treatises* before Sidney was executed. He knew most of the men implicated in the Rye House Plot. At Oxford University, all books asserting the right of resistance to tyranny were burned. Watching the course of events, Locke must have concluded that his days as a free man were numbered. After hastily arranging his private affairs, he sailed for Holland and settled in Amsterdam in September

1683. He would not see England again until he accompanied Princess Mary, wife of William of Orange, to Greenwich in February 1689. William and Mary were proclaimed king and queen the day after his return.

During his five and a half years of exile, Locke lived in Amsterdam, Rotterdam, and Utrecht. The Dutch province contained such a large number of English expatriates that Amsterdam was often called "little London." There were enough of them so that not only did Locke feel at home, but his friends could establish a network of "safe" houses for him to move between to elude the prying eyes of Charles II's spies and later James II's. Kidnapping and murder by the two kings' agents were distinct possibilities. Charles had Locke expelled from Oxford, which itself summoned Locke to return to answer charges of libel, and James II included his name in a list of 85 men to be extradited from Holland to stand trial. Charles died in February 1685, converting to Catholicism on his deathbed. The duke of Monmouth's subsequent rebellion against the accession of James II to the throne was crushed, and Monmouth was beheaded. Judge George Jeffreys embarked upon the Bloody Assizes, sentencing 200 men to death and 800 to slavery in the West Indies.

In his exile, Locke completed the *Essay, A Letter concerning Toleration*, and *Some Thoughts concerning Education*. In addition to these and other minor works, he must have been in correspondence with those who would orchestrate the Glorious Revolution. His ideas influenced the content and purpose of the Declaration of Rights, issued by the Convention Parliament of 1689–90. The Declaration, in effect, set the terms of rule accepted by William and Mary that severely curtailed a sovereign's power over the national purse, the courts, and legislation. The Act of Settlement of 1701 underscored the Declaration in addition to mandating a protestant succession.

ON HIS RETURN to England, Locke set about the publication of his works. His *Essay* and *Education* were published under his own name. The *Two Treatises* and *Toleration*, including two later es-

says on toleration, however, were published anonymously. Whether this was from modesty or from fear of reprisal by the still powerful Tories has been a subject of speculation; Locke would admit his authorship only in his will, in which he directed that his name appear under the titles of future editions of these works.

While he was in exile, Locke, with grave panache, declined offers from friends to plead on his behalf to the king for a pardon, saying that he did not think he had committed any action for which he needed to be pardoned. With equal verve, he declined King William's offer in 1689 of the ambassadorship to the Elector of Brandenburg on the grounds of his health and his inexperience in diplomatic affairs, adding that he would be at a disadvantage for being "the soberest man in the Kingdom"; he had abstained from liquor most of his life. He did accept the post of commissioner of appeals in excise and later served as a commissioner on the Board of Trade until 1700. These positions allowed him to stay home and oversee the publication of his works. His powers of persuasion influenced the government's coinage policies, and his connections in Parliament and the book trade convinced Parliament to let the ancient Licensing Act lapse without renewal in 1695, thus ending press censorship and the Stationers Guild's monopoly on bookprinting.

His last major conflict was over *The Reasonableness of Christianity*, published in 1695. It was furiously assailed by theological authorities, and Locke was embroiled in the controversy until his death. "Locke's version of Christianity," writes Lockean scholar David Wootton, "appeared to leave no place for the doctrines of original sin or the Trinity. Its stress upon reason seemed to make revealed truth subject to human judgement."

Locke, friends with many of the prominent men of his age, corresponded with such figures as William Penn, James Blair, and Isaac Newton. But there was only one woman in his life. He spent his last years as a permanent guest of Sir Francis and Lady Masham, in Oates, Essex. Lady Masham, whom he had met in 1681 when she was Damaris Cudworth, seemed to be his intellectual equal—and an early, unrequited romantic interest. She was the daughter of Ralph Cudworth, a noted Cambridge philosopher. Locke had converted her from her father's Platonism to his own Aristotelianism. Perhaps she was the only person whose agreement he treasured.

He was sitting in a chair at Oates, listening to her read from the Psalms, when he died quietly in October 1704.

WITHOUT LOCKE, there likely would have been no American Revolution; or, if there had been one, it would have suffered the fate of the English republic of the mid-17th century and collapsed into a heap of grand but unconnected and unsupportable ideas. But even though Locke sits at his age's pinnacle of political thinkers who championed life, liberty, and happiness, neither he nor his predecessors and contemporaries, nor even many who followed him, could imagine a politics without a monarch. The Founders were descendants of colonists who had carved a civilization out of a wilderness without the guidance of kings, bishops, or parliaments; in fact, had accomplished that feat despite their hindrances and obstructions. Thus, the Founders could imagine a politics without a monarch, without royal prerogatives, without parliamentary privileges, and insist, among many other things, upon a separation of church and state. To their credit, they built upon Locke's thought, and more than once they acknowledged their debt to him.

Ed Cline, *novelist and essayist, has probed Jefferson the bibliosavant for this journal, as well as Patrick Henry, Anthony Wayne, Edmund Pendleton, and (in the Autumn 1997 issue) Samuel Johnson.*

UNIT 2

Rationalism, Enlightenment, and Revolution

Unit Selections

6. **Descartes the Dreamer**, Anthony Grafton
7. **Benjamin Franklin: An American in London**, Esmond Wright
8. **A New Light on Alchemy**, Zbigniew Szydlo and Richard Brzezinski
9. **Matrix of Modernity**, Roy Porter
10. **Witchcraft: The Spell That Didn't Break**, Owen Davies
11. **The Passion of Antoine Lavoisier**, Stephen Jay Gould
12. **The First Feminist**, Shirley Tomkievicz
13. **Catherine the Great: A Personal View**, Isabel de Madariaga
14. **Napoleon the Kingmaker**, Philip Mansel

Key Points to Consider

- What did Descartes contribute to modernity?

- Why was Benjamin Franklin so friendly to England? What did he hope for?

- Why were the alchemists called the forerunners of modern chemistry?

- Why was Erasmus Darwin to become famous?

- Although the Age of Reason was to eliminate all superstition, why were there still many accusations of witchcraft?

- Describe how and why France's greatest scientist was victimized by the French Revolution.

- Does Mary Wollstonecraft's feminism compare to today's version? Why or why not?

- Does Catherine the Great deserve a better reputation? Why or why not?

- Why was Napoleon feared rather than applauded by his fellow monarchs?

 **Links: www.dushkin.com/online/**
These sites are annotated in the World Wide Web pages.

Adam Smith
http://cepa.newschool.edu/het/profiles/smith.htm
Eighteenth-Century Resources/JackLynch
http://andromeda.rutgers.edu/~jlynch/18th/
Napoleon Bonaparte
http://www.napoleonbonaparte.nl
Western European Specialists Section/Association of College and Research Libraries
http://www.lib.virginia.edu/wess/
Women and Philosophy Website
http://www.nd.edu/~colldev/subjects/wss.html

T his unit explores facets of the Age of Reason (seventeenth century) and the Enlightenment (the eighteenth century). These two phases of Western tradition had much in common. Both placed their faith in science and reason, both believed in progress, and both were skeptical about much of the cultural baggage inherited from earlier periods. Yet each century marked a distinctive stage in the spread of rationalism. In the seventeenth century, a few advanced thinkers, such as John Locke and René Descartes, attempted to resolve the major philosophical problems of knowledge—that is, to develop a theoretical basis for the new rationalism. The eighteenth century saw in the work of Immanuel Kant and David Hume continuation of that theoretical enterprise. But there was a new development as well: Voltaire, Denis Diderot, and others campaigned to popularize science, reason, the principles of criticisms, and the spirit of toleration. Increasingly, the critical attitudes engendered by rationalism and empiricism in the seventeenth century were brought to bear upon familiar beliefs and practices in the eighteenth century.

Several articles in this unit show the advance of critical reason. "Descartes the Dreamer" profiles the seventeenth-century thinker who epitomized the new rationalism, as does the "Matrix of Modernity" in depicting Erasmus Darwin's praise of enlightened values. "The First Feminist" reviews Mary Wollstonecraft's life and her arguments for "enlightened" treatment of women.

The new attitudes were often troublesome, even revolutionary. During the seventeenth and eighteenth centuries no tradition seemed safe from criticism. Even the Bible was searched for contradictions and faulty logic. Universities and salons became intellectual battlegrounds where the classicists confronted the modernists. The struggle went beyond a mere battle of books. Powerful religious and political institutions were subjected to the test of reason an often were found wanting. The goal was to reorganize society on a rational or enlightened basis and to develop a new morality based on reason, not religious authority.

Of course, rationalism was not confined to these centuries, as anyone familiar with the works of Aristotle or St. Thomas Aquinas knows. Nor did the influence of the irrational disappear during the Age of Reason. The period witnessed a great European witch craze and a millennarian movement in England. And those who doubt that irrational attitudes could surface among the rationalists need only read about the craze for phrenology or Sir Isaac Newton's interest in alchemy and Blaise Pascal's mysticism. Two articles, "A New Light on Alchemy" and "Witchcraft: The Spell That Didn't Break," highlight the irrational during this period.

As for the Enlightenment, many have questioned how deeply its ideals and reforms penetrated society. On occasion, radical ideas and social change produced unanticipated consequences. Sometimes the peasants stubbornly resisted the enlightened legislation passed on their behalf. And we are hardly surprised to learn that the enlightened despots on the Continent stopped short of instituting reforms that might have lessened their authority. Or else they manipulated education and the arts in order to enhance their own power. (For a contrary view, see Isabel de Madariaga's "Catherine the Great: A Personal View"). Nor did modern rationalism cause the great powers to rein in their ambitions, as international wars often broke out.

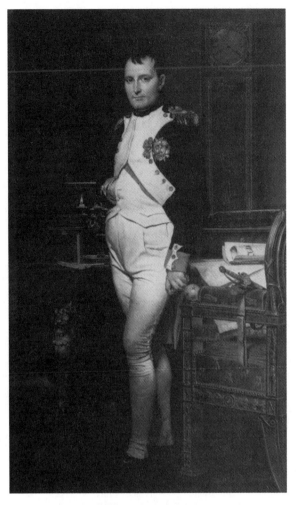

And while the doctrines of the Enlightenment may be enshrined in the noblest expressions of the French Revolution, it also witnessed mass executions and systematic efforts to suppress freedom of speech. The excesses of the Revolution are exemplified by the senseless execution of the most brilliant French scientist, Antoine Lavoisier, (see Stephen Jay Gould's article "The Passion of Antoine Lavoisier"). In "Napoleon the Kingmaker" Philip Mansel shows how Napoleon rearranged the monarchies of Europe while reverting to some of the ideas of the Old Regime.

In the last century, with its mass atrocities, world wars, and nuclear weapons, it is difficult to sustain the Enlightenment's faith in reason. But even before our recent disillusionments, rationalism provoked a powerful reaction—Romanticism. In contrast to the rationalists, romantics trusted emotions and distrusted intellect; they were not interested in discovering the natural laws of the universe, but they loved nature as a source of inspiration and beauty. They were preoccupied with self discovery, not social reform; and they often drew upon medieval experience for their images and models. Indeed, Rationalism has survived and lives on in our modern programs of education and social uplift under the concept called liberalism.

Descartes the Dreamer

No single thinker has had a more decisive influence on the course of modern philosophy—and general intellectual inquiry—than René Descartes (1596–1650). On the 400th anniversary of Descartes's birth, Anthony Grafton considers the forces that shaped the man and his thought.

by Anthony Grafton

All philosophers have theories. Good philosophers have students and critics. But great philosophers have primal scenes. They play the starring roles in striking stories, which their disciples and later writers tell and retell, over the decades and even the centuries. Thales, whom the Greeks remembered as their first philosopher, tumbled into a well while looking up at the night sky, to the accompanying mockery of a serving maid. His example showed, more clearly than any argument could, that philosophy served no practical purpose. Those who take a different view of philosophy can cite a contrasting anecdote, also ancient, in their support: after drawing on his knowledge of nature to predict an abundant harvest, Thales rented out all the olive presses in Miletus and Chios. He made a fortune charging high rates for them; better still, he showed that scholar rhymes with dollar after all.

At the other end of Western history, in the 20th century, Ludwig Wittgenstein held that propositions are, in some way, pictures of the world: that they must have the same "logical form" as what they describe. He did so, at least, until he took a train ride one day with Piero Sraffa, an Italian economist at Cambridge. Making a characteristic Italian gesture, drawing his hand across his throat, Sraffa asked, "What is the logical form of that?" He thus set his friend off on what became the vastly influential *Philosophical Investigations*, that fascinating, endlessly puzzling text which the American philosophers of my youth took as their bible, and to the exegesis of which they brought a ferocious cleverness that would do credit to any seminarian. If Helen's face launched a thousand ships, Sraffa's gesture launched at least a hundred careers.

In each case—and in dozens of others—the story has passed from books to lectures to articles and back, becoming as smooth and shiny in the process as a pebble carried along by a swift-flowing stream. In fact, these stories have become talismans of sorts: evidence that the most profound ideas, the most rigorous analyses, have their origins in curious, human circumstances and strange, all-too-human people. Such anecdotes accessibly dramatize the heroic originality and rigor of philosophers—qualities that one cannot always appreciate only by studying their texts, slowly and carefully.

It seems appropriate, then, that no philosopher in the Western tradition has left a more fascinating—or more puzzling—trail of anecdote behind him than the Frenchman René Descartes. Like Wittgenstein's philosophy, Descartes's began from curious experiences; but in his case the provocation was—or was remembered as—nothing so banal as a train ride.

Early in his life, Descartes became a soldier, serving two years in the Dutch army, before joining the Bavarian service. He writes that in the late fall of 1619, while stationed in the German city of Ulm, he "was detained by the onset of winter in quarters where, having neither conversation to divert me nor, fortunately, cares or passions to trouble me, I was completely free to consider my own thoughts." He refused all company, went on solitary walks, and dedicated himself to an exhausting search for... he did not quite know what. Suddenly he stumbled on what he called "the foundations of a marvellous science." After an almost mystical experience of deep joy, Descartes fell asleep, in his close, stove-heated room. He then dreamed, three times.

In the first dream, terrible phantoms surrounded him. His efforts to fight them off were hindered by a weakness in his right side, which made him stagger in a way that struck him as terribly humiliating. Trying to reach a chapel that belonged to a college, he found himself pinned to the wall by the wind—only to be addressed by someone who called him by name, promising that one "M.N." would give him something (which Descartes took to be a melon from another country). The wind died, and he awoke with a pain in is left side. Turning over, he reflected for some time, slept again, and dreamed of a clap of thunder. Waking, he saw that his room was full of sparks. In the third dream, finally, he found two books, which he discussed with a stranger. The second book, a collection of poems, included one about the choice of a form of life—as well as some copperplate portraits, which seemed familiar.

Waking again and reflecting, Descartes decided that these dreams had been divinely sent. He connected them, both at the time and later, with the discovery of the new method that would ultimately enable him to rebuild philosophy from its foundations. Paradoxically, Descartes, the pre-eminent modern rationalist, took dreams as the basis for his confidence in his new philosophy—a philosophy that supposedly did more than any other to deanimize the world, to convince intellectuals that they lived in a world uninhabited by occult forces, among animals and plants unequipped with souls, where the only ground of certainty lay in the thinking self.

Like Wittgenstein, Descartes enjoys a tribute that modern philosophers rarely offer their predecessors. He is still taken seriously enough to be attacked. Courses in the history of philosophy regularly skip hundreds of years. They ignore whole periods—such as the Renaissance—and genres—such as moral philosophy, since these lack the qualities of rigor, austerity, and explanatory power that win a text or thinker a starring position in the modern philosophical heavens. But Descartes continues to play a major role. In histories of philosophy, he marks the beginning of modernity and seriousness; he is, in fact, the earliest philosopher after ancient times to enjoy canonical status. Students of Descartes can rejoice in the existence of an excellent *Cambridge Companion to Descartes*, edited by John Cottingham, two helpful Descartes dictionaries, and even a brief and breezy *Descartes in Ninety Minutes*—as well as in a jungle of monographs and articles on Descartes's epistemology and ethics, physics and metaphysics, through which only the specialist can find a path. (One standard anthology of modern responses to Descartes's work extends to four thick volumes.) Descartes still provokes.

In a sense, moreover, he provokes more now than he did 20 years ago. In the last generation, developments in a wide range of disciplines—computer and software design, primate research, neurology, psychology—have made the question of how to define human consciousness more urgent, perhaps, than it has ever been. What would show that the computer or an ape thinks as humans do? Can one prove that the measurable physiological phenomena that accompany mental states should be identified with them? How can physical events cause mental ones, and vice versa? And who should settle such questions; philosophers, or scientists, or both in collaboration?

New interdisciplinary programs for the study of consciousness or artificial intelligence provide forums for the debate—which remains fierce—on these and other issues. And the debates are, if anything, becoming fiercer. Successes in solving particular problems—such as the creation of a machine genuinely able to play chess, rather than the man disguised as a machine unmasked by Poe—excite some of the specialists responsible for them to declare victory: if a computer has a mind, then the mind is a computer. Stalwart opponents swat these optimists with rolled-up newspapers, insisting that vast areas of mental and emotional experience—like the pain caused by the rolled-up newspaper—undeniably exist and matter even though they have no counterpart in computer models. From whatever side they come, a great many of the contributions to these debates start with a reference to, or amount to, a sustained attack on Descartes.

It is not hard to explain why this Frenchman, who has been dead for three and a half centuries, still seems modern enough to interest and irritate philosophers who otherwise feel contempt for most of their predecessors. He felt and wrote exactly the same way about his own predecessors.

Descartes, as is well known, began his career as a philosopher in a state of radical discontent with the resources of the intellectual disciplines. He described this state with unforgettable clarity, moreover, in the autobiography with which he began his most famous text, his *Discourse on the Method* (1637). Born in 1596, Descartes lost his mother as a baby and saw little of his father, a councilor in the *parlement* of Brittany at Rennes. For almost a decade, beginning around the age of 10, he attended the Jesuit college of La Flèche at Anjou. Here, he recalled, he made a comprehensive study of classical literature and science. He read—and wrote—much fine Latin, debated in public, learned how to produce an *explication du texte*. He knew all the clichés that humanists used to defend the classical curriculum, and he recited them with palpable irony: "I knew… that the charm of fables awakens the mind, while memorable deeds told in histories uplift it and help to shape one's judgment if they are read with discretion; that reading good books is like having a conversation with the most distinguished men of past ages."

But all this contact with traditional high culture left Descartes unconvinced. Knowledge of literary traditions and past events might give a young man a certain cosmopolitan gloss, but it could not yield profound and practical knowledge: "For conversing with those of past centuries is much the same as travelling. It is good to know something of the customs of various peoples, so that we may judge our own more soundly and not think that everything contrary to our own ways is ridiculous and irrational, as those who have seen nothing of the world ordinarily do. But one who spends too much time travelling eventually becomes a stranger in his own country; and one who is too curious about the practices of past ages usually remains quite ignorant about those of the present."

The humanists of the Renaissance had praised the Greeks and Romans, who did not waste time trying to define the good but made their readers wish to pursue it with their powerful rhetorical appeal. Descartes recognized fluff when he heard it: "I compared the moral writings of the ancient pagans to very proud and magnificent palaces built only on mud and sand. They extol the virtues, and made them appear more estimable than anything else in the world; but they do not adequately explain how to recognize virtue, and often what they call by this fine name is nothing but a case of callousness, or vanity, or desperation, or parricide." So much for the soft, irrelevant humanities—still a popular view in American and English philosophy departments. Descartes, in other words, was the first, though hardly the last, philosopher to treat his discipline as if it should have the austere rigor of a natural science.

Even the study of mathematics and systematic philosophy, however—at least as Descartes encountered them in his college—had proved unrewarding. The mathematicians had missed "the real use" of their own subject, failing to see that it could be of service outside "the mechanical arts." And the philosophers had created only arguments without end: "[philosophy] has been cultivated for many centuries by the most excellent minds, and yet there is still no point in it which is not disputed and hence doubtful." All previous thinkers, all earlier systems, seemed to Descartes merely confused.

He thought he knew the reason, too. All earlier thinkers had set out to carry on a tradition. They had taken over from their predecessors ideas, terms, and theories, which they tried to fit together, along with some new thoughts of their own, into new structures. Predictably, their results were incoherent: not lucid Renaissance palaces, in which all surface forms manifested the regular and logical structures underneath them, but messy Gothic pastiches of strange shapes and colors randomly assembled over the centuries. Such theories, "made up and put together bit by bit from the opinions of many different people," could never match the coherence of "the simple reasoning which a man of good sense naturally makes concerning whatever he comes across."

> *Descartes insisted that most of philosophy's traditional tools had no function.*

Descartes's "marvellous science" would be, by contrast, all his own work, and it would have the "perfection," as well as the explanatory power, that more traditional philosophies lacked. To revolutionize philosophy, accordingly, Descartes "entirely abandoned the study of letters." He ceased to read the work of others, turned his attention inward, and created an entire philosophical system—and indeed an entire universe—of his own. He hoped that this would make up in clarity and coherence for what it might lack in richness of content. And the first publication of his theories, in the form of the *Discourse* and a group of related texts, made him a controversial celebrity in the world of European thought.

As Wittgenstein, 300 years later, cleared the decks of philosophy by insisting that most of its traditional problems had no meaning, so Descartes insisted that most of philosophy's traditional tools had no function. Like Wittgenstein, he became the idol of dozens of young philosophers, who practiced the opposite of what he preached by taking over bits of his system and combining them with ideas of their own. Unlike Wittgenstein, however, he also became the object of bitter, sometimes vicious criticism, from both Protestant and Catholic thinkers who resented the threat he posed to theological orthodoxy or simply to the established curriculum. No wonder that he, unlike his opponents, remains a hero in the age that has none. What characterizes modernity—so more than one philosopher has argued—is its state of perpetual revolution, its continual effort to produce radically new ideas and institutions. Modern heroes—from Reformation theologians such as Martin Luther to political radicals such as Karl Marx—established their position by insisting that traditional social and intellectual structures that looked as solid and heavy as the Albert Memorial would dissolve and float away when seen from a new and critical point of view. The Descartes who wrote the *Discourse* belongs to this same line of intellectual rebels, and in this sense he is deservedly regarded as the first modern philosopher.

Again like Wittgenstein, Descartes refused to take part in normal or in academic high society. Though he devoted a period at the University of Poitiers to study of the law, he made little effort to follow a career as a lawyer—a path chosen by many intellectuals at the time. Though admired by patrons and intellectuals in France and elsewhere, he took little interest in court or city. He did not spend much time in Paris, where in his lifetime the classic French literary canon was being defined on stage and in the Academy and where the fashionable gossiped brilliantly about literature, history, and sex.

Descartes, who contributed so much to the development of that classic French virtue, clarity, kept aloof from his colleagues in the creation of the modern French language. He lived most contentedly in Holland, sometimes in towns such as Leiden and Deventer but often in the deep country, where he had at most one or two partners in conversation—one was a cobbler with a gift for mathematics—and led an existence undisturbed by great excitements. He only once showed great sorrow, when his illegitimate daughter Francine, who was borne by a serving maid named Hélène in 1635, died as a young child. And he only once departed from his accustomed ways: when he moved to the court of that eager, imperious student of ideas, texts, and religions, Queen Christina of Sweden. There he became mortally ill when she made him rise at four in the frozen northern dawn to give her philosophy lessons. He died at the age of 53, a martyr to intellectual curiosity, in February 1650.

Descartes's "marvellous science" portrayed a whole new universe: one that consisted not, like that of traditional philosophy, of bodies animated by a number of souls intimately connected to them, and related to one another by occult influence, but of hard matter in predictable motion. He cast his ideas not in the traditional form of commentary on ancient texts and ideas, but

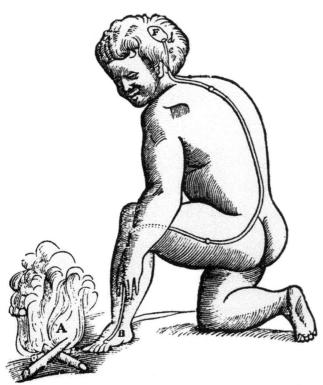

The drawing from Treatise of Man (1662) illustrates Descartes's theory of how nerves transmit sensations to "animal spirits" in the brain.

gebra and the inventor of analytical geometry. Like a mathematician, he tried to begin from absolutely hard premises: ideas so "clear and distinct" that he could not even begin to deny them. In these, and only in these, he found a place to stand. Descartes could imagine away the physical world, the value of the classics, and much else. But he could not deny, while thinking, the existence of his thinking self. Cogito, ergo sum.

From this narrow foothold he began to climb. He proved the existence of God in a way that he himself found deeply satisfactory though many others did not: the idea of God includes every perfection, and it is more perfect to exist than not to exist. Hence God must exist—and be the source of the innate faculties and ideas that all humans possess. He worked out the sort of universe that God would have to create. And he devised, over the course of time, a system that embraced everything from the nature of the planets to that of the human mind, from the solution of technical problems in mathematics to the circulation of the blood.

Wherever possible, precise quantitative models showed how Cartesian nature would work in detail: he not only devised laws for the refraction and reflection of light, for example, but also designed a lens-grinding machine that would apply them (and prove their validity). Parts of his system clanked and sputtered. His elaborate cosmology—which interpreted planetary systems as whirlpools, or vortices, of matter in motion—was technically outdated before it appeared. It could not account for the mathematical details of planetary motion established by Tycho Brahe and Johannes Kepler. Nonetheless, the rigor and coherence of his system inspired natural philosophers on the Continent for a century and more after his death.

The reception of Descartes's philosophy was anything but easy or straightforward. At the outset of his career as a published writer, in the *Discourse on the Method*, he invited those who had objections to his work to communicate them to him for reply. He circulated his *Meditations* for comment before he published them in 1641, and printed them along with systematic objections and his own replies. Thomas Hobbes, Marin Mersenne, Pierre Gassendi, and others now known only to specialists pushed him to define his terms and defend his arguments. At the same time, his thought became controversial in wider circles. Descartes long feared this outcome. Both a good Copernican and a good Catholic, he was appalled by the condemnation of Galileo in 1633. This led him both to delay publication of his treatise *The World* and to try to devise a metaphysics that would prove his natural philosophy legitimate.

But once his work reached print, Descartes could not avoid controversy. In 1639, his supporters in the faculty of the University of Utrecht began to praise his new philosophy, holding public debates about his theories. The influential theologian Gisbert Voetius defended traditional theology, not only against Cartesianism but against Descartes, whose beliefs and morality Voetius attacked. Descartes found himself forced to defend himself a series of pamphlets. He lost some sympathizers—such as the scholar Anna Maria van Schurmann, one of a

in the radically antitraditionalist one of systematic treatises that did not cite authorities—other than that of Descartes's own ability to reason. He said that he saw no point in weaving together chains of syllogisms, as the Scholastics of the Middle Ages had, in the vain hope that major and minor premises of unclear validity, drawn at random from old texts and swarming with unexamined assumptions, could somehow yield new and important conclusions. He did not try to protect his weaker arguments from attack by covering them with a thick, brittle armor plating of quotations from ancient and modern sources in the manner of the Renaissance humanists, who saw philology as the mainstay of philosophy.

Descartes, instead, claimed that he could build entirely on his own something new, coherent, and symmetrical. He liked to compare his work to that of the great town planners of his time, who saw the ideal city as a lucid walled polyhedron surrounding a central square, rather than an irregular, picturesque embodiment of centuries of time and change. The "crooked and irregular" streets and varied heights of the buildings in old cities suggested that "it is chance, rather than the will of men using reason, that placed them so," he said. Coherence, uniformity, symmetry attracted him: the Paris of the Place des Vosges rather then the palaces and alleys of the older parts of the city.

Descartes saw mathematics as the model for the new form of intellectual architecture he hoped to create. For he himself, as he discovered later than stereotypes would lead one to expect, was a very gifted mathematician, one of the creators of modern al-

number of women with whom he discussed theological or philosophical issues.

In the 1640s, Descartes's political and legal situation became extremely serious, and his life in the Netherlands increasingly exhausting and disturbing. Nor did he always agree with those who considered themselves his followers. Ironically, if inevitably, Descartes's philosophy mutated into Cartesianism—one more of the philosophical schools whose competing claims had driven the young Descartes to try something completely different. Some academic Cartesians—as Theo Verbeek and others have shown—even used his philosophy along with others in a deliberately eclectic way their master would have condemned.

Nonetheless, until recent years philosophers generally thought they had a clear idea both of what Descartes meant to do and about why he framed his enterprise as he did. The question of consciousness, of the nature of the mind and its relation to the body, provides a good example of how Descartes has generally been read. Earlier philosophers, drawing on and adding to a tradition that went back to Aristotle, explained life and consciousness in a way that varied endlessly in detail but not in substance. A whole series of souls, hierarchically ordered, each of them equipped with particular faculties, accounted for organic life in plants, movement in animals, and consciousness in humans. The number and quality of faculties possessed by each being corresponded to its position in the hierarchical chain of being, which determined the number and kinds of souls that being possessed. And the well-established nature and location of these faculties in the body could be used to show how body and soul were intimately and intricately connected. It made perfectly good sense to assume—as the astrologers, then almost as fashionable as now, regularly did—that celestial influences, acting on the four humors in the body, could affect the mind. No one could establish an easy, clear division between mind and body, man and nature.

Descartes, by contrast, drew a sharp line, here as elsewhere, both between his views and traditional ones and between physical and mental processes. He proved, as he insisted he could, that mind and body were in fact separate. Descartes could imagine that he had no body at all, but he could not imagine that he, the one imagining, did not exist. The mind, in other words, was fundamentally different from the body. Bodies had as their defining properties hardness and extension. Their other attributes—such as color and texture—were merely superficial, as one could see, for example, by melting a lump of wax. The material world, accordingly, could be measured, divided, cut. The mind, by contrast, was clearly indivisible; when conscious, one always had access to all of it. Descartes divided human beings, accordingly, into two components: a material, extended body, mobile and mortal, and an immaterial, thinking soul, located somewhere within the body but at least potentially immortal. He redefined the struggles between different souls which Saint Augustine had so influentially described in his *Confessions* and of which others regularly spoke as struggles between the body and the soul. These took place, Descartes argued, in a particular organ: the pineal gland, within the brain, the one point where soul and body interacted. He held that animals could not have minds, at least in the sense that human beings do. And the firm distinction he made between the physical plane that humans share with other beings and the mental operations that attest to their existence on more than a physical plane continues to irritate philosophers—just as his sharp distinction between the real world of solid matter in motion and the qualitative, unreal world of perception and passion once enraged T. S. Eliot and Basil Willey, who held him guilty of causing the 17th century's "dissociation of sensibility."

Descartes's position in the history of thought has seemed, in recent years, as easily defined as his innovative contributions to it. By the time he was born, in 1596, intellectual norms that had existed for centuries, even millennia, were being called into question. The discovery of the New World had challenged traditional respect for the cosmology and philosophy of the ancients. The Protestant Reformation had destroyed the unity of Christendom, offering radically new ways of reading the Bible. The Scholastic philosophers who dominated the faculties of theology in the traditional universities, though all of them worked within a common, basically Aristotelian idiom, had come into conflict with one another on many fundamental points, and some humanists claimed that their vast Gothic structures of argument rested on misunderstandings of the Bible and Aristotle.

Some thinkers looked desperately for moorings in this intellectual storm. Justus Lipsius, for example, a very influential scholar and philosopher who taught at both Calvinist Leiden and Catholic Louvain, tried to show that ancient Stoicism, with its firm code of duties, could provide an adequate philosophy for the modern aristocrat and military officer. Others began to think that there were no moorings to be found—and even to accept that fact as welcome, since it undermined the dogmatic pretensions that led to religious revolutions and persecutions. The philosophy of the ancient Skeptics, in particular, offered tools to anyone who wished to deny that philosophers could attain the truth about man, the natural world, or anything else.

Skepticism, as Richard Poplin and Charles Schmitt have shown, interested a few intellectuals in the 15th century, such as Lorenzo Valla. But it first attracted widespread interest during the Reformation. Erasmus, for example, drew on skeptical arguments to show that Luther was wrongly splitting the Catholic Church on issues about which humans could never attain certainty. The major ancient skeptical texts, the works of Sextus Empiricus, appeared in Latin translation late in the 16th century—just as the Wars of Religion between French Calvinists and Catholics were reaching their hottest point. Michel de Montaigne, the great essayist whom Descartes eagerly read and tacitly cited, drew heavily on Greek Skepticism when he mounted his attacks on intellectual intolerance. To some—especially the so-called Politiques, such as Montaigne, who was not only a writer but one of the statesmen who negotiated religious peace in France at the end of the 16th century—Skepticism came as a deeply desirable solution to religious crisis. To others, however—especially to Catholic and Protestant philosophers who still felt the need to show that their religious doctrines not only rested on biblical authority but also corresponded to the best possible human reasoning—Skepticism came as a threat to all intellectual certainties, including the necessary ones.

Descartes tried on principle to doubt everything he knew. (He called his method, eloquently, one of "hyperbolic doubt".) But he found, as we have seen, that there were some things even he could not doubt, and many others found his arguments convincing. Accordingly, Descartes appears in many histories of philosophy above all as one of those who resolved a skeptical crisis by providing a new basis for physics, metaphysics, and morality. Similarly, he appears in many histories of science, alongside Francis Bacon, as one of those who created a whole new method for studying the natural world.

For the last 20 years or so, however, this view of Descartes's place in the history of thought has begun to undergo scrutiny and criticism. Not only students of consciousness but historians of philosophy and science have begun to raise questions about Descartes's isolation in his own intellectual world. For all his insistence on the novelty of his views and the necessity for a serious thinker to work alone, he always looked for partners in discussion.

And this was only natural. "Even the most radical innovator," write the historians of philosophy Roger Ariew and Marjorie Grene, "has roots; even the most outrageous new beginner belongs to an intellectual community in which opponents have to be refuted and friends won over." Descartes, moreover, not only belonged to a community, as he himself acknowledged; he also drew, as he usually did not like to admit, from a variety of intellectual traditions.

For example, Stephen Gaukroger, whose intricately detailed new intellectual biography of Descartes elegantly balances close analysis of texts with a rich recreation of context, finds an ancient source for Descartes's apparently novel notion that certain "clear and distinct" ideas compel assent. The core of the Jesuit curriculum Descartes mastered so well was formed by rhetoric, the ancient art of persuasive speech. Quintilian, the Roman author of the most systematic ancient manual of the subject, analyzed extensively the ways in which an orator could "engage the emotions of the audience." To do so, he argued, the orator must *exhibit* rather than *display* his proofs." He must produce a mental image so vivid and palpable that his hearers cannot deny it: a clear and distinct idea.

Gaukroger admits that Roman orators saw themselves first and foremost as producing such conviction in others, while Descartes saw his first duty as convincing himself. But Gaukroger elegantly points out that classical rhetoric, for all its concern with public utterance, also embodied something like Descartes's concern with the private, with "self-conviction." The orator, as Quintilian clearly said, had to convince himself in order to convince others: "The first essential is that those feel-

ings should prevail with us that we wish to prevail with the judge."

Descartes's doctrine of clear and distinct ideas is usually described as radically new. It turns out, on inspection, to be a diabolically clever adaptation to new ends of the rhetorical five-finger exercises the philosopher had first mastered as a schoolboy. Gaukroger's negative findings are equally intriguing: he interprets Descartes's famous dreams as evidence not of a breakthrough but of a breakdown, and he argues forcefully that Skepticism played virtually no role in Descartes's original formulation of his method and its consequences.

Several other studies have revealed similarly creative uses of tradition in many pockets of Descartes's philosophy. As John Cottingham has shown, Descartes more than once found himself compelled to use traditional philosophical terminology—with all the problematic assumptions it embodied. Despite his dislike of tradition, he also disliked being suspected of radicalism, and claimed at times not to offer a new theory but to revive a long-forgotten ancient one—for example, the *"vera mathesis"* ("true mathematical science") of the ancient mathematicians Pappus and Diophantus. No one denies the substantial novelty of Descartes's intellectual program; but students of his work, like recent students of Wittgenstein, show themselves ever more concerned to trace the complex relations between radicalism and tradition, text and context.

Descartes's dreams—and his autobiographical use of them—play a special role in this revisionist enterprise. His earliest substantial work, composed in the late 1620s but left unfinished, takes the form of *Rules for the Direction of the Mind;* his great philosophical text of 1641 bears the title *Meditations.* In structure as well as substance, both works unmistakably point backward to his formation in a Jesuit college. There he had not only to study the classics and some modern science but to "make" the *Spiritual Exercises* laid down for Jesuits and their pupils by the founder of the Jesuit order, Ignatius Loyola. These consisted of a set of systematic, graded exercises in contemplation, visualization, and meditation. Students—and candidates for membership in the order—had to reconstruct as vividly as they could in their minds the Crucifixion, Hell, and other scenes that could produce profound emotional and spiritual effects in them. These exercises were intended to enable those who did them to discipline their minds and spirits, to identify and rid themselves of their besetting weaknesses, and finally to choose the vocation for which God intended them. Visions—and even mystical experiences—regularly formed a controlled part of the process, as they had for Ignatius himself. The similarity between these exercises in spiritual self-discipline and Descartes's philosophical self-discipline is no coincidence. Here too Descartes transposed part of the education he thought he had rejected into the fabric of his philosophy.

In seeing visions as a form of divine communication—evidence of a special providence that singled recipients out as the possessors of a Mission—Descartes remained firmly within the Jesuit intellectual tradition. He was, in fact, far from the only product of a good Jesuit education to trace his own development in minute interpretative detail. Consider the case of his near contemporary Athanasius Kircher—another mathematically gifted young man, who studied in Jesuit schools in south Germany before becoming the central intellectual figure in baroque Rome. Kircher's interests were as varied as Descartes's were sharply defined: he spelunked in volcanoes, experimented with magnets, reconstructed the travel of Noah's Ark, and studied languages ranging from Coptic to Chinese, with varying degree of success. But he defined the core of his enterprise with Cartesian precision, if in totally un-Cartesian terms, as an effort to decipher the ancient philosophy encoded in the hieroglyphic inscriptions on Egyptian obelisks. This effort attracted much criticism but also received generous papal support. Ultimately it inspired some of Bernini's most spectacular Roman works of sculpture and architecture, in the Piazza Navona and before the church of Santa Maria sopra Minerva.

Descartes would have found most of Kircher's project risible. Yet they had something vital in common. Kircher, like Descartes, tried to prove the rigor and providential inspiration of his work by writing an autobiography. Kircher's dreams and visions played as large a role in this work as his colorful and sometimes terrifying experiences. Like Descartes, he saw his unconscious experiences as evidence that God had set him on earth to carry out a particular plan. His accidental encounter with a book in which Egyptian hieroglyphs were reproduced and discussed exemplified—he thought in retrospect—the sort of special providences by which God had led him in the right direction. Evidently, then, Cartesian autobiography was actually Jesuit autobiography. Brilliant style, concision, and lucidity set off the beginning of the *Discourse on the Method* from Kircher's Latin treatise. But the enterprises were basically as similar as the larger enterprises they were meant to serve were different. And Descartes's dreams not only make a nice story to adorn the beginning of a lecture but actually shed light on the origins of his central intellectual enterprise.

In effect, then, Descartes has come back to new life in recent years—in two radically different ways. The Descartes who appears in so many studies of the philosophy and physiology of mind—the radical innovator, owing nothing to his predecessors, who devised the brutally simple theory about "the ghost in the machine"—seems hard to reconcile with the Descartes now being reconstructed by historians: the complex, reflective figure, whose relation to tradition took many different forms, and whose system embodied foreign elements even he did not recognize as such. Gaukroger's book marks a first and very rewarding effort to bring the two Descartes together. But the task will be a long one. It may prove impossible to fit Descartes the dreamer into traditional genealogies of modern thought—or to establish a simple relation between his theories of intelligence and current ones. Descartes lives, a troubling ghost in the machine of modern philosophy.

ANTHONY GRAFTON *is the Dodge Professor of History at Princeton University. He is the author of* Joseph Scaliger: A Study in the History of Classical Scholarship *(1983–1993)*, Forgers and Critics: Creativity and Duplicity in Western Scholarship *(1990), and* Defenders of the Text: The Traditions of Scholarship in an Age of Science, 1450–1800 *(1991). His study*, The Tragic Origins of the German Footnote, *appeared in 1997.*

From *The Wilson Quarterly*, Autumn 1996, pp. 36-46. © 1996 by Anthony Grafton. Reprinted by permission.

Benjamin Franklin:
An American in London

*Esmond Wright recalls the life of the American philosopher, scientist
and man of letters in his years in a street near Charing Cross.*

BENJAMIN FRANKLIN, a poorly-educated Boston boy who ran away from home to find his fortune in Philadelphia as journalist, editor, printer and publisher, founder of its University and of the American Philosophical Society, was the nearest to a genius of all the Founding Fathers of the United States. He was a practical man as well as a theorist. He was fascinated by natural phenomena, and constantly asked the question 'Why?'. When a steady succession of appalling winters and dry summers hit Europe in the 1780s, he traced the cause to a volcanic eruption in Iceland. These climatic conditions produced famines across Western Europe and were among the causes of the French Revolution. From his frequent journeys across the Atlantic, Franklin discovered and mapped the Gulf Stream. From his observations of climate he concluded that lightning was electricity. He devised and played the harmonica, his 'musical glasses'. He realised—though he never fully explored the reasons for—the contagious character of the common cold. He was, in the Italian phrase, *l'uomo universale*, a renaissance man, or, as the Scots put it, 'a man o' pairts'.

For seventeen years (1757–75) he lived in London, in 'four rooms and very genteel', as he put it. In these years, though he was proud to be an American, he was, also, in his own phrase, 'an Old England man' and proud of that too. He sought to avert the political separation that he saw coming. When it came to war, he went to Paris to secure the support of France that ensured American success. He was present in 1787 in Philadelphia at the Convention that drew up the Constitution.

When Mary Munn of Philadelphia married the 10th Earl of Bessborough in 1948, perhaps she did not realise that in London she would renew acquaintance with the most famous Philadelphian of all, Benjamin Franklin. Or maybe she did: The 2nd Earl of Bessborough in the eighteenth century as Postmaster General had been in charge of Franklin's activities as a colonial post officer-in-chief. For the last thirty years Lady Bessborough and a group of trustees have campaigned to raise money in the US and in the UK to restore the house in which Franklin lived during his London years as the agent for Pennsylvania (and eventually for Massachusetts, New Jersey and Georgia) from 1757 to his return home on the outbreak of the War for American Independence in 1775.

He made 36, Craven Street in the Strand a home from home. Franklin was as much at ease in London as he was in Philadelphia in the hurly-burly of business. Goods were landed from the river at the foot of the street and transported to the Hungerford Market at the top, where it meets the Strand. As the wits put it, there was craft on the river, and craft on the street; and Franklin, a strong swimmer, was at ease with both, the lawyers and journalists at one end, the tradesmen—and the tides—at the other. Opposite 36, Craven Street then stood the large and daunting Northumberland House, the town-house of the Dukes of Northumberland, and a thriving social centre—on the site of what is now Charing Cross Station.

His domestic circle included not only his landlady, Mrs Stevenson, and Polly, her daughter, but Franklin's grandson, Temple, and Sarah Franklin, daughter of one of his Northamptonshire cousins. The latter lived in Craven Street, and was as a second daughter to him.

The *Craven Street Gazette*, a newspaper which he produced for fun, testifies to his contentment. It is clear that he ruled over his 'Court'—at least in 'Queen Margaret's' infrequent absences—as 'Big Man', 'Great Person' and 'Dr Fatsides'. He hoped that Polly might marry his son, but they both had other ideas. Polly married a surgeon, William Hewson, but became in fact the 'intellectual daughter' that his own daughter Sarah

'The Charing Cross Evening Frolick' by L.P. Boitard, 1756, shows a party of drunken revellers passing a coffee stand by the statue of Charles I, late one night.

(back in Philadelphia) never was. William had jettisoned his fiancée in Philadelphia, became a devotee of the Northumberland House connection—he visited it more often than the Inns of Court, where he was nominally a student—and in 1762 was appointed royal Governor of New Jersey; and stayed a Loyalist to the end. Polly would be persuaded to spend a winter with Benjamin in France when he was there, and finally moved to Philadelphia with her own family—her husband having died in 1774—and was with him there when he died in 1790.

Franklin was a man who attracted friends very easily, wherever he happened to be. He was so happy on the British 'side of the Water' that he had decided in 1762

> to settle all my Affairs [in America] in such a Manner, as that I may then conveniently remove to England, provided we can persuade the good Woman [his wife Deborah] to cross the Seas.

Speaking of London, Franklin said there were opportunities of displaying one's talents among the 'Virtuosi of various kingdoms and nations'. The conversation, he said, was not only agreeable but 'improving'. As he told his son William in 1772, he found in Britain,

> a general respect paid me by the learned, a number of friends and acquaintances among them with whom I have a pleasing intercourse; a character of so much

weight that it has protected me when some in power would have done me injury... my company so much desired that I seldom dine at home in winter, and could spend the whole summer in the country houses of inviting friends if I chose it. Learned and ingenious foreigners, that come to England, almost all make a point of visiting me, for my reputation is still higher abroad than here; several of the foreign ambassadors have assiduously cultivated my acquaintance, treating me as one of their corps, partly I believe... that they may have an opportunity of introducing me to the gentlemen of their country who desire it.

This happiness was reinforced by another factor, the political respect in which (we now forget) not only the government of Britain, but the monarchy itself, was held in what became the United States. Franklin came in 1757 to persuade the British government to abrogate the proprietary charter of Pennsylvania. He wanted royal government, not the domination of the Penns. The Penn family had ceased to live in Philadelphia, and had become Anglicans. He saw opportunities for America in royal government rather than in government by a proprietor, or by anything more democratic. He hoped that the loyalty that he felt for Britain could be translated into a general loyalty, in the concept of a royal colony.

The almost universal 'respect for the mother country, and admiration of everything that is British' on the part of the colo-

HT ARCHIVES

Savaged by a dead sheep? A trade card for Robert Crow's warehouse for men's clothes, near Hungerford Market and a stone's-throw from Craven street.

nists, Franklin wrote in *The London Chronicle* in 1759, was 'a natural effect' not only of their constant intercourse with England, by ships arriving almost every week from the capital' but also, and more importantly, of an ingrained loyalty to a country that, for all free whites, permitted far more liberty than was enjoyed by the colonists of any European power. 'Delegates of British power' in the colonies might indeed lose the respect of and 'give Jealousy to' the colonists, either by their corrupt behaviour, or 'by continually abusing and calumniating the People'. But such actions did not diminish colonial faith in imperial institutions. 'Confidence in the Crown' remained 'as great as ever', and Parliament was held in the highest esteem as the ultimate protector of British liberty—in the colonies as well as in Britain.

This was linked to Franklin's awareness of the importance of the West. He told Lord Kames, one of his closest friends, with whom he stayed in Scotland, that the expulsion of the French from Canada in 1763 would mean that,

> all the Country, from the St Lawrence to the Mississippi will in another Century be fill'd with British People; Britain itself will become vastly more populous by the immense Increase of its Commerce; the Atlantic Sea will be cover'd with your Trading Ships; and your naval Power then continually increasing, will extend your Influence round the whole Globe, and awe the World.

There is no republican here, nor an American either. This is British imperialism as Joseph Chamberlain would have understood it, or American imperialism as Teddy Roosevelt would

have understood it: a sense that the future rested with the empire 'on that side'. Franklin was ridiculed by Josiah Tucker in one of his pamphlets, who said that Franklin's constant plan had actually been to remove the seat of government of the British empire to America. Although he never quite said that, Franklin did have his plan for a colony in the West. Called variously the Ohio Scheme or Vandalia, Franklin's expectation was that there would be a post or posts for him or his friends, the Washington family, and the Morgans of Philadelphia. This grand Ohio plan failed, primarily because of the opposition of Lord Hillsborough, afraid of the emigration of his Irish tenants to the New World. In 1768 Hillsborough became Secretary of State for American Affairs, a newly created department. There were other reasons for hesitation about a western colony; a British colony without seaports would mean a colony beyond naval control; its products would be sold primarily inside North America, and it would not therefore fit into the colonial system. So there were many reasons why, seen from a rather narrow-focused London point of view, this was a dangerous step; but Franklin saw his British Empire as much on the Ohio as on the Thames: it was a great misfortune for him that nothing came of Vandalia.

Tucker ridiculed Franklin, claiming his intention was to remove the seat of government of the British empire to America.

There was, of course, another good reason why Franklin was an 'Old England man', devoted to the throne. His son William was not only a royal governor throughout these years, but a very good one, as his father heard John Pownall, the permanent secretary of the new American Department, testify to Lord Hillsborough. Sadly, from an American point of view, William stayed a Loyalist when war broke out in 1776, and was imprisoned; his wife was not allowed to see him again, and she died without doing so. William's Loyalism destroyed the relationship between father and son. There was never any forgiveness. Benjamin Franklin, full of blarney and craft, was ruthless about Loyalists, even his own son.

In 1768 a new department was set up. There is no direct evidence, but my own reading suggests that Benjamin Franklin hoped he would become a permanent secretary at that new American desk, the department for North American Affairs (the post that went to John Pownall). Of course it would fold up again in 1782 after the war was over, but it was a post that might have made a profound difference. It might even have averted the War for American Independence.

As late as 1769 Franklin still believed that,

> nothing that has happened or may happen will diminish in the least our Loyalty to our Sovereign, or Affection for this Nation in general. I can scarcely conceive

HT ARCHIVES

The 'Colonies Reduced', a card designed by Franklin in late 1765, with which he lobbied London's 'Men of Power' about the injustice of the Stamp Act.

a King of better Dispositions, or more exemplary Virtues, or more truly desirous of promoting the Welfare of all his Subjects. The experience we have had of… the two preceding mild Reigns, and the good Temper of our young Princes so far as can yet be discovered, promise us a Continuance of this Felicity. The Body of this People too is of a noble and generous Nature, loving and honoring the Spirit of Liberty, and hating arbitrary Power of all Sorts.

---

*'While I have been thought here
too much of an American,
I have in America been deemed
too much of an Englishman.'*

To this one has to add—and here the pattern begins to change and is less orthodox—Franklin's pride in being a member of an empire was rooted in his faith in American population growth, whatever his criticisms of some British political and mercantile policies. His great optimism about the connection between England and America stemmed from the knowledge that the rate of population increase was so much greater in the New World than in the Old. He had written in 1751 his famous *Observations concerning the Increase of Mankind*, in which he calculated that in due course the daughter colony would become very much more populous, successful and prosperous than the mother country.

Franklin lived a long life. He moved on to other places, notably Paris, and did other things. Indeed it is said that he would have been asked to write the Declaration of Independence but for the risk that he would have put a joke in it. For all his affection for Britain, he was a man who was at times unable to read the portents, and who was unaware in 1764 of the coming conflict over stamp duty that was going to erupt within eighteen months in Boston and most of the coastal ports, and who was keen to appoint his friends to jobs as stamp distributors. Maybe the very affluence which he enjoyed in London hid such matters from him. His best friends in London—'Straney' (his name for William Strachan, the publisher and editor), Sir John Pringle, Caleb Whitefoord—were Scots, or, like Price and Priestley, Dissenters; outsiders looking in. In London, as in Philadelphia, Franklin was an addict of newspapers and gazettes, replying to criticisms of America and Americans, regularly contributing, both openly and under pen-names, often printing tall tales and spoofs as he had done in his own *Pennsylvania Gazette*. It went down well among coffee-house gossips; but it was not the way to acceptance by the decision-making aristocratic Establishment. Again, perhaps his appointment to the agency for Massachusetts in 1770, as well as that for Pennsylvania, pushed him in more radical directions than he would naturally have gone.

In London in January 1760, Franklin heard of Wolfe's seizure of Canada from the French, and wrote to Lord Kames,

No one can rejoice more sincerely than do I on the Reduction of Canada: and this, not merely as I am a Colonist, but as I am a Briton. I have long been of Opinion that the Foundations of the future Grandeaur and Stability of the British Empire, lie in America; and tho', like other Foundations, they are low and little seen, they are nevertheless broad and Strong enough to support the greatest Political Structure Human Wisdom ever yet erected.

It might have been so. If so, it is likely that a *pax Anglo-Americana* would have been obtained. But in the eighteenth-century the Atlantic was not an easy ocean to bridge; and in 1768, as again in 1774, Franklin was not given the chance to try to do so. As it was, he paid the price of every man who tries too long to sail down the middle of the stream. 'Hence it has often happened to me, that while I have been thought here [in England] too much of an American, I have in America been deemed too much of an Englishman', as he ruefully complained.

Franklin wrote to his former good friend, Lord Howe, who in 1776 was in charge of the British forces sent to put down the American rebellion,

Long did I endeavour, with unfeigned and unwearied zeal, to preserve from breaking that fine and noble china vase, the British Empire, for I knew that, being once broken, the separate parts could not retain even their shares of the strength or value that existed in the whole, and that a perfect reunion of those parts could scarce ever be hoped for.

By this time, Franklin charged, the Empire had become devoted to war, conquest, dominion, and commercial monopoly rather than the true interest of the mutual advantage of colonies and mother country.

Her Fondness for Conquest, as a warlike Nation, her lust of Dominion, as an ambitious one, and her wish for a gainful Monopoly, as a commercial One, (none of them legitimate Causes of War), will all join to hide from her Eyes every view of her true Interests, and continually goad her on in those ruinous distant Expeditions, so destructive both of Lives and Treasure, that must prove as pernicious to her in the End, as the Crusades formerly were to most of Nations in Europe.

Equally stimulated by absence and by that distance that lends enchantment, Franklin came more and more to express often his love for his 'dear Country'. A new note was now emerging: of pride in America as a distinct entity.

Upon the whole, I have lived so great a part of my life in Britain, and have formed so many friendships in it, that I love it, and sincerely wish it prosperity; and therefore wish to see that Union, on which alone I think it can be secured and established. As to America, the advantages of such a Union to her are not so apparent. She may suffer at present under the arbitrary power of this country; she may suffer for a while in a separation from it; but these are temporary evils that she will outgrow. Scotland and Ireland are differently circumstanced. Confined by the sea, they can scarcely increase in numbers, wealth and strength, so as to over-balance England. But America, an immense territory, favoured by Nature with all advantages of climate, soil, great navigable rivers, and lakes, must become a great country, populous and mighty; and will, in a less time than is generally conceived, be able to shake off any shackles that may be imposed on her, and perhaps place them on the imposers. In the meantime every act of oppression will sour their tempers, lessen greatly, if not annihilate the profits of your commerce with them, and hasten their final revolt; for the seeds of liberty are universally found there, and nothing can eradicate them. And yet, there remains among that people, so much respect, veneration and affection for Britain, that, if cultivated prudently, with kind usage, and tenderness for their privileges, they might be easily governed still for ages, without force, or any considerable expense. But I do not see here a sufficient quantity of the wisdom, that is necessary to produce such a conduct, and I lament the want of it.

Next door to number 36 Craven Street lived the Scotsman, David Whitefoord, with whom Franklin had many a drink in the coffee-houses on the Strand. Ironically, Whitefoord in 1783 was a member of the British negotiating team which drew up the terms of the Treaty of Paris, which ended the War of American Independence, and which recognised the independence of the United States. The friendship of Franklin, the chief American negotiator, and Whitefoord, made the peace-making much easier. At the signing ceremony, and looking at the French team, Whitefoord said prophetically, 'And remember that the colonists, now independent, and their descendants will all speak English'.

FOR FURTHER READING:

Esmond Wright, *Franklin of Philadelphia* (Harvard UP, 1986); Edmund Morgan (ed.), *Prologue to Revolution* (Chapel Hill, University of North Carolina, 1959); A.O. Aldridge, *Benjamin Franklin and Nature's God* (Duke UP, 1967); Bernard Bailyn, *The Ideological Origins of the American Revolution* (Harvard UP, 1967); Jonathan Dull, *Franklin the Diplomat* (American Philosophical Society, 1982); Claude Lopez, *Mon Cher Papa: Franklin and the Ladies of Paris*, (Yale UP, 1966). William Randall, *A Little Revenge: Benjamin Franklin and his son.* (Little, Brown, Boston, 1984); Sheila L. Skemp, *William Franklin, son of a Patriot, servant of a King*, (OUP, 1990).

Esmond Wright, Emeritus Professor of US History in the University of London, is former Director of the Institute of US Studies in London. He is the historical adviser to the Benjamin Franklin House project.

This article first appeared in *History Today*, March 2000, pp. 18-25. © 2000 by History Today, Ltd. Reprinted by permission.

A New Light On Alchemy

Fools' gold, Dr. Faustus—traditional images of a Renaissance black art. But was there more to it than that? **Zbigniew Szydlo** and **Richard Brzezinski** offer an intriguing rehabilitation.

In June 1897 the French journal *La Nature* reported that the United States Assay office had, on April 16th, purchased the first ever gold ingot manufactured from silver. Six months later, an article in a popular newspaper related that the inventor, Dr. Stephen H. Emmens, was 'producing enough gold to bring him at the Assay Office a profit of $150 a week'. Emmens, an American of British descent, bragged that he had finally mastered the alchemists' art and could produce gold commercially. He let slip that his Argentaurum' process worked by the action of high pressure and intense cold on silver, but was eventually exposed as a fraud when he claimed that his process was endorsed by a leading physicist, Sir William Crookes. By 1901 Emmens was nowhere to be traced.

Three centuries earlier, in 1590s Prague, an unknown alchemist of Arabic origin made a flamboyant appearance in a city with a reputation as the alchemical capital of Europe. After courting merchants and bankers, he invited twenty-four of the wealthiest to a banquet, during which he promised to multiply gold. He obtained 100 gold marks from each guest, and placed the coins in a large crucible with a mixture of acids, mercury, lead, salt, eggshells and horse dung. But, as he prepared to operate the bellows of his furnace, there was a tremendous explosion which left the guests spluttering in a fog of fumes. By the time the smoke had cleared, the alchemist had vanished, along with the 2,400 gold marks.

Such stories of fraudsters form the modern stereotype of the alchemist, and alchemy is widely seen as little more than the art of changing base metals into gold. With hindsight we know the alchemists were wasting their time: it is impossible to transmute' elements by chemical means, and nothing short of bombardment by neutrons in a nuclear reactor will produce gold from lead, and then only in microscopic amounts.

Although modern chemists are prepared to admit that the alchemists invented many of the chemical processes in use today, alchemy is still often condemned as mumbo-jumbo, and at worst, bundled in with astrology and necromancy as an occult pseudo-science. No wonder then that alchemy was dismissed in 1831 by Thomas Thomson as the 'rude and disgraceful' beginnings of chemistry.

But is this view of alchemy justified? When we hear that some of the greats of science, Sir Isaac Newton (1642–1727) and Robert Boyle (1627–91—of Boyle's law fame) had a keen interest in alchemy, perhaps it is time to think again. When we examine more closely the obscure texts of alchemy and venture behind the baffling terminology and mystical allusion, we see revealed a long and ancient line of philosophers and experimenters searching for secrets far more precious than gold.

The origins of alchemy go back at least four millennia to ancient Mesopotamia, India, China and Egypt and the first reasoned attempts to make sense of the diversity of nature. Aristotle, the tutor of Alexander the Great, brought many of these ideas together when he proposed that all worldly substances were made up of four elements: air, earth, fire and water. A fifth element, the ether or quintessence (from Latin *quinta essentia*, fifth essence) was the stuff of the heavens.

A refinement to this picture was made by Arab alchemists in the eighth century AD, in particular by Jabir ibn Hayyan, known in Europe as Geber. He proposed that all metals were formed of mercury and sulphur mixed in various proportions. White metals had very little sulphur, and yellow metals like gold, had more. It seemed like common sense, and was an open invitation for attempts at gold-making.

Increasingly alchemy gained a mystical side—perhaps from frustration at failed experiments. Into it came a strange concoction of Christian, Gnostic and neo-Platonic ideas. Adepts began to believe that experiments would only work when they were in a state of spiritual elevation achieved through prayer.

Central to the mysteries of alchemy was the belief that ancient texts contained forgotten secrets of nature. The most definitive of these texts was the *Tabula Smaragdina* or Emerald Tablet, which, according to legend, had been discovered by Alexander the Great in the Egyptian tomb of Hermes Trismegistos ('thrice-great'), the Greek counterpart of the Egyptian god of

The elixir of life—or a charlatan's potion? A late 16th-century illustration of an alchemist's workshop.

wisdom and magic, Thoth. The Emerald Tablet was inscribed with thirteen axioms. Unfortunately, they were rather difficult to understand. The riddle-like language of the fourth is typical: 'Its father is the sun, its mother the moon; the wind carries it in its belly, its nurse is the earth'. This cryptic style was emulated by the alchemists, who christened themselves sons of Hermes' or Hermetic philosophers.

It is impossible here to go into the full world picture the alchemists had developed by the sixteenth century; but the key to it was *panvitalism*—the idea that the universe and everything in it was alive: animals, plants and minerals. Animals had the shortest lives but most complicated structures; minerals, the longest lives and simplest forms—that they were alive seemed logical after observations of volcanoes erupting, and crystals growing.

Minerals were believed to grow from seeds—the equivalent of plant seeds and human semen. These grew deep in the earth and rose to the surface, maturing as they moved. Depending on the path taken, they developed into different types of rocks. If a young mineral rose quickly along a poor route it emerged in a 'corrupt' form, such as lava; if it rose slowly along a pure and perfect vein it matured into gold. Even until the early twentieth century, English farmers were convinced that stones were growing in the ground and rising up like weeds that periodically needed be removed.

When a true alchemist, as opposed to a quack, was attempting to make gold he was not merely lusting for wealth: gold, because of its rarity, lack of reactivity, and glowing lustre was the mineral world in its ultimate state of perfection. By dis-

covering how to make gold, the alchemist would, it was thought, also have the means of perfecting the plant and animal worlds. In order to produce gold in the laboratory, alchemists attempted to replicate and speed up the natural processes thought to take place deep in the earth. Their main goal was to discover the mysterious substance through which gold travelled on its way to the surface—this material they knew as the Philosopher's Stone. When found, the Stone would be the means of bringing perfection to the human world, giving health and eternal salvation to the fortunate alchemist. In effect, the search for the Philosopher's Stone was much like the quest for the Holy Grail.

The Philosopher's Stone was a major goal of alchemy, but to claim it was the only one is like saying the Grand Unified Theory is the sole aim of physics, or Fermat's Last Theorem was the same to mathematics. Alchemy had the general aim of making sense of nature in all its complexity. To be sure, there were other concrete goals: the *alkabest* or universal solvent which could dissolve all substances, and the universal medicine or Elixir of Life, which would cure all diseases and was related to the Philosopher's Stone. More bizarre, and verging on the occult was *palingenesis*—the reincarnation of plants and animals from their ashes; and attempts to generate miniature human beings (*homunculi*) from semen incubated in rotting horse dung.

Alchemy had already been given a sizeable kick in the direction of a practical science by the extraordinary Swiss physician Paracelsus—or to give his full name, Philippus Theophrastus Aureolus Bombastus von Hohenheim (1493–1541). After travels to the east, and work as a military surgeon, Paracelsus

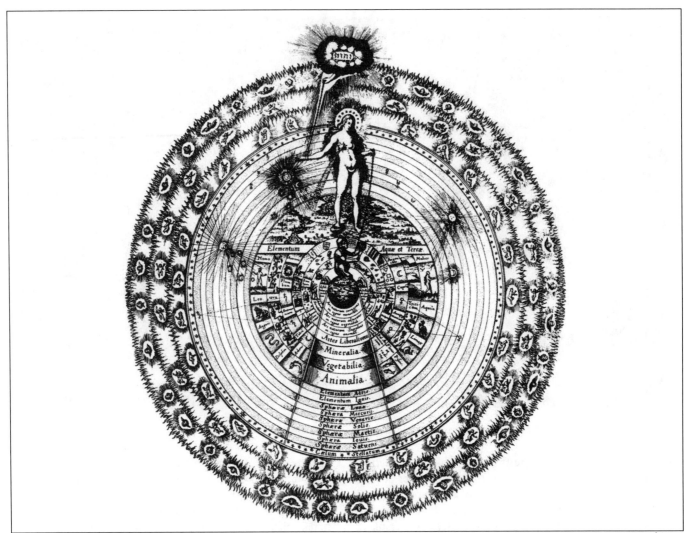

Holding up the mirror to nature: the frontispiece to *Utriusque Cosmi...* (1617) by Robert Fludd, one of the disseminators of Sendivogius' theories in the West.

declared that most traditional medicines were useless, so he devised his own, with spectacular results. When appointed physician to the city of Basel in 1527, he celebrated by publicly burning the works of Galen and Avicenna, the established authorities on medicine.

The only way to learn anything about nature, said Paracelsus, was to go out and observe it at first hand. Only the Bible was infallible, everything else was open to question. Paracelsus disputed Aristotle's four elements theory because fire was nowhere mentioned in Genesis. Borrowing from Geber's theory of metals, he decided that there were three fundamental substances: sulphur, mercury and salt—though he defined them in a broader sense than the modern materials of these names.

Paracelsus' revolutionary ideas spawned a new school of medical alchemists. Many of them were attracted to Prague and the liberal court of the German emperor, Rudolf II, who sponsored a bustling community of proto-scientists and artists. Among Rudolf's alchemical protégés, and shining out above them was a Polish doctor, Michal Sçdziwój (latinised as Sendivogius). Recognised by his contemporaries as one of the greats

of early European natural philosophy, he has now slipped back into obscurity. Sendivogius was to signal the next remarkable transformation of alchemy.

Michael Sendivogius (1556–1636) has suffered more than most from the poor reputation of alchemy. Until recently, his life was known only in legendary accounts, replete with tales of spectacular transmutations, imprisonment by jealous rulers and improbable escapes from dungeons and burning towers. In the contemporary record Sendivogius emerges as a very different man. Born in Sacz, Poland, his name appears on the registers of Altdorf and Leipzig universities and in 1591 he matriculated from Vienna University. After serving as a courtier and doctor of medicine at Rudolf's court in Prague, he returned to Poland where he was taken into the confidence of King Zygmunt III. He became involved in the Polish metallurgical industry, and helped set up several factories in the Czestochowa and Silesia regions. He travelled regularly to the German empire on secret diplomatic missions, taking the opportunity to maintain contact with leading academics such as Johann Hartmann, Europe's first professor of chemistry (appointed in 1609).

Sendivogius' most influential book was published in Prague in 1604 as *De lapide pbilosopborum* (On the Philosophers' Stone), but was soon retitled *Novum lumen cbymicum* (A New Light of Alchemy). Over the next two centuries it was to go through at least fifty-six editions in Latin, German, French, English, Russian and Dutch. Sir Isaac Newton owned a copy, now in the British Library, which has marginal notes in his handwriting, and corners turned down to mark passages. The great French chemist, Antoine Laurent Lavoisier, also had a copy—now at Cornell University and marked with his bookplate. What was it about this work that gave it such a distinguished following?

As was common with alchemical tracts, the author of *A New Light of Alchemy* concealed his name in an anagram: *Divi Leschi Genus Amo*—I love the divine race of the Lechites' (i.e. Poles). Yet the book is surprisingly easy to read and is largely devoid of mystical terminology, quite unlike the opaque writings of Paracelsus. The book is a remarkable exposé of the world-view of Renaissance alchemy, which Sendivogius states had developed greatly beyond the wisdom of the ancients.

In his preface to the first English edition (1650), the translator, John French, a successful doctor of medicine, could hardly have praised Sendivogius' book more highly:

> In that treatise of his thou shalt see the mystery of Deity, and Nature unfolded .... So that if anyone should ask me, What one book did most conduce to the knowledge of God and the Creature, and the mysteries thereof; I should speake contrary to my judgement, if I should not, next to the Sacred Writ, say Sandivogius.

Alongside his explanation of the workings of nature, much of which went back to traditional alchemical ideas, Sendivogius had put something quite new:

> Man was created of the Earth, and lives by virtue of the Aire; for there is in the Aire a secret food of life…whose invisible congealed spirit is better than the whole earth.

For the first time Sendivogius revealed that air is a mixture, not a single fundamental substance as proposed by Aristotle. This was a great step. The implications to alchemy were momentous.

By the mid-sixteenth century, the alchemists were convinced there was a 'universal spirit'—a vapour or soul—pervading all matter. It was in this that the life-substance of all entities (including minerals) was believed to be located. Before Sendivogius nobody had managed to identify this universal spirit with a real substance. Sendivogius' 'aerial food of life' seemed to be the true Elixir of Life—sought after by alchemists for centuries.

Sendivogius saw the 'aerial food' percolating through all life, by way of an innocent-looking, colourless, crystalline solid: saltpetre (nitre or potassium nitrate). By observing over time the main source of saltpetre—farmyard soils—Sendivogius became convinced that the 'food of life' was condensing out of the air and growing into living saltpetre crystals. Salt-

petre's life-giving power was visible in fertilizers and dynamically demonstrated in gunpowder, of which it was the key ingredient. Saltpetre also seemed to have other miraculous properties: it was used in medicines and freezing mixtures and in the manufacture of the acid, *aqua regia* (the 'queen of waters') which could dissolve gold.

'Aerial nitre'—what modern chemists would call oxygen—seemed to be the key to nature; in its gaseous form, it made all animal life possible; condensed into solid form, as saltpetre (or nitre), it gave life to plants and minerals. It was, in Sendivogius' words: 'Our water that wets not our hands, without which no mortal can live, and without which nothing grows or is generated in the world'. To the great satisfaction of the Hermetic philosophers, Sendivogius' aerial nitre also seemed to be the solution to the fourth riddle of the Emerald Tablet—'the wind carries it in its belly, its nurse is the earth'. Sendivogius' aerial nitre theory was a landmark breakthrough in the understanding of nature. Alchemy was never to be the same again.

The study of the nature of air quickly became a major topic of scientific enquiry. Research was, however, soon interrupted by the horrors of the Thirty Years' War of 1618–48, and Sendivogius himself was brought to the verge of bankruptcy. But a number of central European scientists fled to the relative safety of England, and through contacts like Robert Fludd (1574–1637) and Sir Kenelm Digby (1603–65), the Sendivogian theory received a wide audience in England. Thanks to the so-called 'Invisible College' interest in air survived the English Civil Wars and Cromwell's Commonwealth. By the 1660s air and its properties had grown into a key field of research at Oxford University. The chief experimenters included Robert Hooke (1635–1703), John Mayow (1641–79), and, of course, Robert Boyle. Although they made no mention of the anonymous man who had inspired their research, the influence of Sendivogius is clear in their writings, and it would be appropriate to call them the 'Oxford Sendivogians'.

Even with these great minds at work, the composition of air was to defy the investigators for nearly two centuries. Air contains one-fifth oxygen and four-fifths nitrogen, but the smaller quantities of carbon dioxide and water vapour make its chemical behaviour highly complex and difficult to understand. The subject was confused for many decades by the German 'Phlogiston' theory of about 1700, which was a radical departure from Sendivogian views. But Sendivogius' influence was still in evidence in 1732, when one of the earliest (and greatest) teachers of chemistry, the Flemish author, Herman Boerhaave, restated the importance of Sendivogius' discovery:

> Air possesses a certain occult virtue which cannot be explained by any of those properties previously investigated. That in this virtue the secret food of life lies hidden, as Sendivogius clearly said, some chemists have asserted. But what it really is, how it acts, and what exactly brings it about is still obscure. Happy the man who will discover it!

And happy he was. When Joseph Priestley isolated 'dephlogistigated air' in 1774, he tried breathing some of it. He found that his 'breast felt peculiarly light and easy for some time afterwards'. He went on:

> Who can tell, but that, in time, this air may become a fashionable article in luxury. Hitherto only two mice and myself have had the privilege of breathing it .... Nothing I ever did has surprised me more, or is more satisfactory.

In fact, Priestley was probably not the first person to breathe pure oxygen.

In 1621 an unusual event took place in London. A vessel rowed by twelve oarsmen sailed from Westminster to Greenwich *under water*. The voyage was witnessed by James I and thousands of Londoners. This, the first recorded submarine, was constructed by the Dutch inventor and alchemist Cornelis Drebbel (1572–1633), one of the great lost figures of Renaissance science. Drebbel had become internationally famous after building a perpetual motion machine (which, in fact, was solar-powered); and from about 1604, he worked for James I, building a variety of automata, refrigerators, barometric devices, and probably the first microscope seen in England (1621).

Much of the interest in Drebbel's submarine lay not in its construction and military potential—but in an air-freshening technique that Drebbel had devised, and kept a close secret. The great Robert Boyle described Drebbel's vessel in his *New Experiments Physico-Mechanicall, Touching the spring of the Air, and its effects* (Oxford, 1660). Boyle was especially curious about a 'Chymicall liquor, which he [Drebbel] accounted the chiefe Secret of his submarine Navigation'. Boyle interviewed Drebbel's son-in-law, and discovered that when the air in the submarine became stuffy, Drebbel 'would by unstopping a vessel full of this liquor, speedily restore it to the troubled Air such a proportion of Vitall parts, as would make it againe, for a good while, fit for respiration'. Although Boyle describes Drebbel's secret substance as a 'liquor', several other writers of the period insist it was a gas. But could it have been oxygen?

In his *Treatise on the Elements of Nature* (1608), Drebbel gives a clue to how he might have manufactured oxygen. In a passage on the origin of thunder, he writes: 'Thus is the body of the saltpetre broken up and decomposed by the power of the fire and so changed in the nature of the air'. This suggests he was aware that heating saltpetre causes it to give off a gas—and realised that this gas was the same substance that allows humans to breathe.

Modern scientists have not been comfortable with the idea that Drebbel isolated oxygen over 150 years before Lavoisier. The idea of a gas did not yet exist (the term was coined by van Helmont in the 1640s); and formal techniques for experimenting with gases were only developed around 1700 by the Englishman, Stephen Hales. Even so, behind the complex medieval terminology of spirits, vapours and exhalations, it is clear that the alchemists understood more about gases than we give them credit for. It had been known for centuries that breathing or burning things in an enclosed space reduces the quality of air, and glass apparatus had made big advances by about AD 1150

when pure alcohol was first obtained in Italy by distilling wine. In practice, there is no reason why Drebbel could not have used oxygen in his submarine, even if he did not understand the full chemical significance of what he had done.

It is likely that Drebbel learnt how to produce oxygen from Sendivogius. Drebbel belonged to a scientific and artistic elite that was already by the sixteenth century, cosmopolitan. Such men travelled Europe seeking wealthy patrons and most of them knew each other. Drebbel visited Rudolf's court at Prague in 1594 and again in 1610–11, and it was here that he may have met Sendivogius, and found out how to manufacture the 'secret food of life' by heating saltpetre.

But if Sendivogius discovered how to make oxygen in around 1600 and Drebbel used it in a practical way in 1620 why is it that nobody knows about it today? How is it that Priestley, Scheele and Lavoisier got all the credit in the 1770s? In part the answer is that the alchemists were highly secretive and believed only the worthy should be enlightened. They wrote in an obscure style so that only the 'sons of Hermes', who were prepared to spend years in study, would be able to understand their texts. Making such knowledge public, they said, was 'casting pearls before swine'. There was also the danger that the knowledge would fall into the wrong hands and be used for evil ends.

Despite its essentially honest objectives, alchemy was, even in its own time, viewed with contempt and regarded as little removed from magic and astrology. It was banned by universities, popes and kings, and Ben Jonson lampooned it furiously in *The Alchemist* (1610). The respected figures of medicine generally ignored the subject. The Imperial Count Palatine Michael Maier (1569–1622) was different.

Maier had known Sendivogius since they had studied together at Altdorf University in 1594, and got to know him better when he was employed as doctor at the Imperial court from 1609 until 1611. Maier had initially been highly sceptical about alchemy, but through Sendivogius he became a committed alchemist and one of its most ardent champions. Along with Sendivogius, Maier seems to have played a key role in the formation of secret philosophical societies, the details of which are only now beginning to emerge. In his 1617 book *Atalanta Fugiens*, Maier wrote that alchemy was the 'noblest of the scholarly disciplines, directly after theology, for its subject matter is the investigation of the greatest secrets of God's creation'.

Alchemy was also accorded respect by Robert Boyle, the archetypal enemy of Aristotelian beliefs, and often described as the world's first true scientist. Boyle believed in the possibility of transmuting base metals into gold, and was influential in obtaining Parliamentary repeal of the Act against gold multipliers in 1689. Sir Isaac Newton was another closet alchemist. In spite of his pioneering work in the 'respectable' sciences—mechanics, optics and calculus—it has recently emerged that Newton spent the bulk of his career secretly attempting to decipher the mysterious texts of alchemy.

There was another problem that prevented Sendivogius' theories from becoming common knowledge: the church. Hermetic philosophy was knowledge about nature in addition to that in the Bible. To have openly identified a 'spirit of life' that corresponded to a real substance was risking censure. Copernicus had dared publish his theory only on his death bed; Galileo published and got into serious trouble with the Inquisition; Darwin dreaded the church's reaction, and refused to discuss his ideas in public. Sendivogius got over the problem by publishing anonymously, but then took little credit for his discovery.

Today, the identification of a 'food of life' in air by a now obscure Polish alchemist may appear to be of only trivial interest, yet the repercussions on the progress of science were profound. Sendivogius shone a bright new light on alchemy, away from attempts at gold-making towards the investigation of air. By doing so, he set in motion an explosion of protoscientific enquiry which was to end when Lavoisier identified and named oxygen in 1779. With that event, chemistry in its modern form was born.

Sendivogius still does not hold the historical status and respect he deserves; neither does alchemy. In an unscientific age, the alchemy of the hermetic philosophers was the closest there was to a science. But alchemy was more than just a predecessor to chemistry—it was a 'living chemistry'—the study of which encompassed the entirety of nature. Lavoisier has been called the father of chemistry. It is perhaps time that alchemy was acknowledged as the mother of chemistry, rather than just a wayward cousin.

FOR FURTHER READING

John Read, *Prelude to Chemistry* (London, 1936); E.J. Holmyard, *Alchemy* (London, 1957, reprinted Dover Publications, 1990); Betty Joe Dobbs, *The Foundations of Newton's Alchemy or the "Hunting of the Greene Lyon"* (Cambridge University Press, 1975); Z.R.W.M. von Martels, *Alchemy Revisited* (E.J. Brill, 1990); P. Rattansi & A. Clericuzio (Editors), *Alchemy and Chemistry in the 16th and 17th Centuries* (Kluwer Academic Publishers, 1994).

Zbigniew Szydlo*, is a chemistry teacher at Highgate School, London, and author of* Water which does not wet Hands: The Alchemy of Michael Sendivogius. *(Polish Academy of Sciences, Warsaw, 1994). Available from Chthobios Books, Hastings, tel: 01424-433302. Price £22.50.*

Richard Brzezinski *is a science and history writer and editor. He is author of* The Army of Gustavus Adolphus *(2 vols, Osprey 1991, 1993).*

This article first appeared in *History Today*, January 1997, pp. 17-23. © 1997 by History Today, Ltd. Reprinted by permission.

Matrix of Modernity

In his recent Royal Historical Society Gresham Lecture, Roy Porter discusses how the British Enlightenment paved the way for the creation of the modern world.

THIS MILLENNIUM YEAR LED HISTORIans to address moments in the past which represent epochs in human affairs. The Enlightenment comprised such a turning-point, since it secularised the worldview and trained eyes and attention towards the future. British thinkers played an influential part in this intellectual revolution—though that is a contribution often ignored or played down, by contrast to that of France.

In the eighteenth century, attention became focused, perhaps for the first time ever, on the future rather than the past, and the drive to create a better future generated a belief in progress. The achievements of scientists like Isaac Newton (1642–1727) and philosophers like John Locke (1632–1704) bred new faith in man's right and power to achieve knowledge of himself and the natural world, and encouraged practical action in such fields as overseas exploration, technology, manufactures, social science and legal reform. Philosophers became committed to the ending of religious strife, bigotry, ignorance, prejudice and poverty, and the creation of polite new social environments and lifestyles.

History is progressive, proclaimed the enlightened activists. 'Rousseau exerts himself to prove that all was right originally', commented Mary Wollstonecraft (1759–97), 'a crowd of authors, that all is now right: and I, that all will be right'. Sights became trained on the future—not the Apocalypse of orthodox Christian es-

chatology but one continuous with the here-and-now. Indeed, the Enlightenment brought the birth of science fiction—Samuel Madden's futurological *Memoirs of the Twentieth Century* (1733), for instance, or the anonymous and not too chronologically inaccurate *The Reign of George VI, 1900–1925* (1763).

The scent of progress was in the air. The Anglican Edmund Law (1703–87) professed his faith in the 'continual Improvement of the World in general', while the Glasgow Professor John Millar taught that 'one of the most remarkable differences between man and other animals consists in that wonderful capacity for the improvement of his faculties'. Improvement seemed so visible and tangible. 'Who even at the beginning of this century', asked the Unitarian minister Richard Price (1723–91), fired by rational Dissent:

> … would have thought, that, in a few years, mankind would acquire the power of subjecting to their wills the dreadful force of lightning, and of flying in aerostatic machines? … Many similar discoveries may remain to be made… and it may not be too extravagant to expect that… the progress of improvement will not cease till it has excluded from the earth most of its worst evils, and restored that Paradisiacal state which, accord-

ing to the Mosaic History, preceded the present state.

Late-Enlightenment belief in progress was, to be sure, a secular theodicy but Mary Wollstonecraft's 'all will be right' was not complacent. The world, as she explained, was not perfect yet: rather it was mankind's duty to perfect it, through criticism, reform, education, knowledge, science, industry and sheer energy. The dynamo of advancement, proclaimed the psychologist David Hartley, was 'the diffusion of knowledge to all ranks and orders of men, to all nations, kindred, tongues, and peoples', a progress which 'cannot now be stopped, but proceeds ever with an accelerated velocity'. And all this optimism about the future was buoyed up by the conviction, in the thinking of the likes of Hartley, Price and Joseph Priestley, that Divine Providence guaranteed such developments or that social progress was underwritten by the surge of biological evolution at large.

Traditional historical pessimism was addressed and allayed by Edward Gibbon (1737–94). Would not, as many believed, the calamities which had destroyed Imperial Rome recur in 'this enlightened age'? No: the great 'source of comfort and hope', explained the *Decline and Fall*, was the permanency of improvement. From savagery, mankind had 'gradually arisen to command the animals, to fertilise the earth, to traverse the ocean, and to measure the heavens'.

The 'experience of four thousand years should enlarge our hopes', soothed Gibbon, and since technical skills could never be lost, no people 'will relapse into their original barbarism'. Mankind could, therefore,

> acquiesce in the pleasing conclusion that every age of the world has increased, and still increases, the real wealth, the happiness, the knowledge, and perhaps the virtue, of the human race.

Crucial to the birth of the modern was a rethinking of economics. Greek philosophy and Christian theology had each condemned the love of money. The Churches had deemed lucre filthy, greed evil, profit without labour usurious. The Christian duty to conduct personal economic dealings in a just manner had been mirrored in Tudor commonwealth thinking at large. 'Mercantilism'—the economic outlook which dominated the Stuart century and beyond—took good housekeeping as its model. It measured economic well-being principally in terms of a favourable balance of trade generated by export surpluses: being in pocket. Associating wealth with money or gold and silver, mercantilism's advocates approved the hoarding of reserves, the promotion of exports, the limitation of imports, and the management of vital national monopolies.

Enlightened thinking attacked such policies for being unscientific and hence futile. David Hume's essay 'Of the Balance of Trade' (1741) argued that a nation never need be apprehensive of losing its money so long as it preserved its people and its industry, because an automatic self-adjusting mechanism operated which 'must for ever, in all neighbouring countries, preserve money nearly all proportionable to the art and industry of each nation'. In place of regulation, labour and consumption were to be set at the heart of the new thinking.

Mercantilism's faith in interference, critics argued, was superficial, opportunistic, and often poisonous. Regulation had made bad worse. What was needed instead was an informed grasp of the macro-economics of cash transfers, the relations between wealth and bullion,

money and commodities, the short and the long term.

A profound revaluation of economic activity itself was under way. The old 'moral economy' was coming under fire from a new 'political economy' which laid claim to a scientific grasp of wealth-creation and consumer satisfaction. Enlightened analysts insisted that economic activity was governed by fundamental laws of its own. Ideals such as the just price, the proper reward for labour and other aspects of the moral economy, might be admirable, but they did not reflect human nature. Man was, if not nakedly rapacious, at least an accumulating creature, and to ignore such omnipresent motives was pie-in-the-sky.

The new political economy prided itself upon being grounded on a proper grasp of motives, ends and means—natural science, in particular Newtonian physics, often being invoked to prove how economic forces 'gravitated' to an equilibrium: prices were 'continually gravitating…', wrote Adam Smith, 'towards the natural price'. Like water, economic activity would find its own level, and regulation was thus counter-productive. Since profit-seeking was only human nature, it was best to leave trade free and let the economic players get on with it. As the economist Dudley North (1641–91) opined,

> The main spur to Trade, or rather to Industry and Ingenuity, is the exorbitant Appetites of Men, which they will take pains to gratifie, and so be disposed to work, when nothing else will incline them to it; for did Men content themselves with bare Necessaries, we should have a poor World.

The pioneering figure among the liberal theorists of this school was John Locke. Not only private property but exchange and money were, in his scheme, pre-established in the state of Nature, subject to the laws of Nature and human rationality. Value itself was determined by labour. Hence economic regulation formed no part of the state's day-to-day remit. The new political economy thus repudiated moral or statesmanly policing of wealth.

Adam Smith (1723–90) systematised the new political economy, grounding it in a science of human appetite, 'the desire of bettering our condition'. Selfishness made the world go round:

> It is not from the benevolence of the butcher, the brewer, or the baker, that we expect our dinner, but from their regard to their own interest.

His formula—let demand decide—expresses the enlightened inclination to trust in Nature. In so doing, Smith was forced to confront the old civic humanist worries about private wealth and greed. Could *enrichissez-vous* prove compatible with socio-political stability? Would not the pursuit of affluence compromise virtue, and 'luxury' subvert liberty, set class against class, and corrupt the commonwealth?

Smith's *Inquiry into the Wealth of Nations* (1776) must be assessed in terms of its wider contribution to enlightened discussions about freedom, justice, subject/state relations, and the quality of life in commercial society. Smith proposed 'opulence and freedom' as 'the two greatest blessings men can possess'. The pairing packed some punch. Two contrasting concepts of liberty had been in circulation since Antiquity. In the Stoic view, freedom was a state of tranquillity in which the cravings of the flesh were curbed by the rational will. There was also the 'civic' view, proposed by Cicero and Livy, for whom liberty lay in political activity and public service. Smith though held that the true key to freedom was commerce, and that it achieved its full expression only in a nation of shopkeepers.

Like Hume, Smith held that the proper stage for human energies was not honour and glory in the Senate, but private, self-regarding pursuits. For Graeco-Roman thinkers, time spent meeting household needs was beneath the dignity of the true male citizen; for Smith, by contrast, it was the natural business of humanity. Indeed, it was a public benefit, for economic exchange forged supportive social networks.

For Smith, dependency was corrupting—a view central to the civic humanist

The secrets of the brewhouse, from the *Complete Dictionary of Arts and Sciences,* 1764-66, by Temple Henry Crocar.

equation of freedom with independence. Yet he insisted that 'commerce is one great preventive' of its occurrence. Economic activity was thus not pathological but prophylactic, preservative of a sound constitution.

'Industry and the machine have been the parent of happy change.'

Science too was a mighty generator of optimism. In the wake of the great age of Newton, the culture of science spread. While the Royal Society remained the nation's senior scientific society, further bodies were added in the capital, notably the Linnean Society of London (1788) and the Royal Institution (1799). The Royal Society of Edinburgh was set up in 1783, and its counterpart, the Royal Irish Academy, in 1785, while science, Dissent and political reformism joined forces from the 1760s in literary and philosophical societies in Manchester, Newcastle and other industrial centres. Science was acclaimed as vital not just to utility but to the civilising process, the leading light in Manchester, Thomas

Henry, pronouncing the pursuit of natural philosophy preferable to 'the tavern, the gaming table, or the brothel'.

The most energetic of such gatherings embodying enlightened faith in science was the Lunar Society in Birmingham, formed by Matthew Boulton whose machine-tool-producing Soho factory was internationally famous. From about 1765 a group of friends—leading industrialists, scientists, educators, dissenting ministers and physicians—began to meet at Boulton's home to discuss innovations in science and technology and the new industrial order they were helping to create. They met once a month at full moon, to help light them home. William Hutton found there an ethos he had not encountered elsewhere:

I had been among dreamers, but now I saw men awake.

Through such associations, Paul Langford tells us, 'a nation of Newtons and Lockes became a nation of Boultons and Watts'.

Scientific improvement was a label often applied to the land, serving as a code-word for capitalist farming, notably enclosure. The improving spirit in agriculture was increasingly associated

with the application of science. In the 'Introduction' to his *Phytologia* (1800), Erasmus Darwin, for instance, expressed his view that agriculture had to be made businesslike, through the teachings of political economy:

…for the invention of arts, and production of tools necessary to agriculture, some must think, and others labour; and as the efforts of some will be crowned with greater success than that of others, an inequality of the ranks of society must succeed.

Farming became regarded as a form of manufacturing, with Robert Bakewell's fat sheep serving, rather like Newton's prism, as icons of Enlightenment. That Leicestershire stockrearer bred sheep, cattle, and pigs as meat-producing engines, selected so as to maximise expensive cuts and minimise bones and waste: animals were thus turned into machines.

But it was another field of progress which now received the warmest accolades: manufacturing. Progressives had long expressed their fascination with industry in the traditional meaning of skilled work, praising *homo faber.* Manufacturing's appeal to enlightened

Spreading the word: enlightened practice in the farmyard did much to boost productivity, and one technique for recycling organic nitrates was presented in this illustration of 1756.

minds was potent and many-sided. Technology was the cutting-edge of novelty. Water-wheel design became a model of experimental efficiency, and the engineer John Smeaton (1724–92) perfected the lighthouse. In 1758 the 'Improved Birmingham Coach' had blazoned on its side, a touch over-optimistically, 'FRICTION ANNIHILATED', and by 1801 Richard Trevithick (1771–1833) had put a steam carriage on the road. Textiles technology was transformed and the steam engine revolutionised power. Industry was also a prime instance of disciplined rationality. Josiah Wedgwood (1730–95), the potter, aimed to 'make such machines of Men as cannot err', introducing clocking-on to ensure punctuality among his workforce. Surveying the progress so visible across the West Midlands, he declared,

Industry and the machine have been the parent of this happy change. A well directed and long continued series of industrious exertions, has so changed, for the better, the face of our country, its buildings, lands, roads and the manners and deportment of its inhabitants, too.

Business promoted not just wealth but well-being.

Manufacturing, moreover, seemed to be producing a new breed of heroes, principally the self-made 'captain of industry'. One of the children's tales in Anna Barbauld's primly improving *Evenings at Home: Or the Juvenile Budget Opened* (1794) celebrated Sir Richard Arkwright's rise to fame and fortune. 'This is what manufacturers can do', explained Papa to his children: 'here man is a kind of creator, and like the great Creator, he may please himself with his work and say it is good'. Showing his youngsters round a factory, the fictional father insisted what fun it all was: there was 'more entertainment to a cultivated mind in seeing a pin made, than in many a fashionable diversion'.

The entrepreneur was applauded as the exemplar of modern energy. 'I shall never forget Mr Boulton's expression to me', recalled James Boswell of a visit to the Soho works: '"I sell here, Sir, what all the world desires to have,—power". He had about seven hundred people at work... he seemed to be a father to this tribe'.

Like Boulton, his friend Josiah Wedgwood was one of a remarkable new breed of men conspicuous for applying enlightened thinking to business. Though of meagre formal education, he displayed a consummate faith in reason, and a passion for measuring, weighing, observing, re-

cording and experimenting: all problems would 'yield to experiment'. His rational outlook extended beyond business to Unitarianism in religion and radicalism in politics—he was hostile to slavery, and a warm supporter of the American colonists and later the French Revolution. He thought big: 'I shall ASTONISH THE WORLD ALL AT ONCE', he declared to his partner, Thomas Bentley, 'for I hate piddling you know'. Becoming 'vase-maker general to the universe', he died worth half a million.

It is Robert Owen (1771–1858), however, who offers the perfect illustration of the application of enlightened ideas to the empire of industry. Born in mid-Wales, Owen got his first employment as an errand-boy; then he moved into drapery, rising to a partnership in a Manchester firm, before, at the turn of the century, becoming partner and manager of the New Lanark Mills on Clydeside. For the next two decades he combined entrepreneurship with social reform. In his *A New View of Society* (1813) Owen urged rational social rebuilding on the basis of universal education. Manufacturing would provide the foundation for happiness, but only once divested of the arbitrariness of the dog-eats-dog market and reorganised according to social utility. Character could be moulded by correct environmental influence. If the labouring classes were ignorant, brutalised and criminal, they were victims and it was society that must shoulder the blame.

But Owen was no Smithian. *Laissez-faire* was useless for ensuring long-term prosperity and welfare—market forces would 'produce the most lamentable and permanent evils', unless there were 'legislative interference and direction'. Though industrialisation held out the promise of untold human benefit, under the competitive system some grew fabulously rich while others were pauperised. Co-operation was needed to effect industry's potential social advantages. Since people were products of circumstances, education would make all the difference according to Owen's plan. In his New Lanark factory village, the provision of schooling, along with such amenities as a museum, would programme workers for happiness. Here was a veritable social experiment in action, 'one which cannot fail to prove the certain means of renovating the moral and religious principles of the world, by showing whence arise the various opinions, manners, vices and virtues of mankind.' An unbeliever, Owen secularised Christian aspirations in envisaging

> …the foretold millennium… when the slave and the prisoner, the bondman and the bond-woman, and the child and the servant, shall be set free for ever, and oppression of body and mind shall be known no more.

Owen was thus a logical terminus *ad quem* of certain strands of Enlightenment thought, envisaging comprehensive benevolent control within a scheme of industrialisation, and showing both a concern with education and discipline over his 'human machines'.

Many penned anthems to improvement, uniting science and imagination, poetry and social theory. The most notable poetic prophet of progress, however, was Erasmus Darwin. A physician first and foremost, Darwin practised for some forty years, and his magnum opus, *Zoonomia* (1794–96), was essentially a work of medical theory. Despite his busy medical practice, he poured his boundless energies into many channels. In 1771 he was dabbling with a mechanical voicebox; in the next year he had long discussions with Wedgwood and the engineer James Brindley about extending the Grand Trunk Canal; with his friend Brooke Boothby, he founded the Lichfield Botanic Society, which in time brought out translations of Linnaeus' classification system. His gardening interests also blossomed on a site west of Lichfield, where in 1778 he established a botanic garden, the inspiration of his later poem of the same name.

Progress proved to be the ultimate Enlightenment gospel.

Uniting arts and sciences, medicine, physics and technology, Darwin was the embodiment of enlightened values. 'All those who knew him will allow that Sympathy and benevolence were the most striking features', wrote Keir:

> He despised the monkish abstinences and the hypocritical pretensions which so often impose on the world. The communication of happiness and the relief of misery were by him held as the only standard of moral merit.

Darwin embraced a humanitarian benevolence hostile to Christian values and judgements. From early on, he rejected Christianity in favour of Deism. Indeed, he found the Christian Almighty quite repellent: how could a truly loving Father visit terrible diseases upon innocent children?

Politically, Darwin was a dyed-in-the-wool-liberal. His books and letters echo with condemnations of despotism, slavery and bloodshed: 'I hate war'. 'I have just heard', he raged on one occasion to Josiah Wedgwood, 'that there are muzzles or gags made at Birmingham for the slaves in our island. If this be true, and such an instrument could be exhibited by a speaker in the House of Commons, it might have a great effect'. He supported the French Revolution, and after the 1791 Birmingham riots he wrote to Joseph Priestley deploring his victimisation by fanatics—while also politely advising him to quit his theological maunderings and get on with something more useful, namely scientific experiments. Darwin's politics were, however, never revolutionary. Law, order and property were essential ingredients for the social progress which would be achieved within the framework of free-market capitalism and industrialisation.

As the summation of his myriad ideas, Darwin developed the first comprehensive theory of biological evolution: 'would it be too bold to imagine, that all warm-blooded animals have arisen from one living filament, which THE GREAT FIRST CAUSE endued with animality?' The endless mutual competition of burgeoning organic forms within the terraqueous globe also resulted in death, destruction and even extinction.

Nevertheless, rather as for Adam Smith, the law of competition brought about net improvement, and the aggregate rise of population spelt not Malthusian misery but an augmentation of happiness. Darwin's evolutionism provided the British Enlightenment's clinching theory of boundless improvement.

The epic of progress, implicit or explicit in most late-enlightenment opinion and given a scientific grounding by Darwin, stands in stark contrast to such earlier visions of the human condition as *Paradise Lost* (1663) and Pope's *Essay on Man* (1733–34). For Milton, what was fundamental was the relationship between God and man: Adam's offence lay in violation of God's command; man's destiny was couched in a transcendental revelation. Darwin, by contrast, painted a wholly optimistic, naturalistic and this-worldly picture, grounded on evolution, biological and social. Human capacities were the products of biological and physiological development which extended to 'the progress of the Mind'. Not only was there no Miltonic Lucifer and Fall, but to Darwin, man alone had consciousness of the natural order. Whereas Pope had scorned pride as hubristic, for Darwin pride and its triumphs had their legitimate basis in Nature.

Progress proved the ultimate Enlightenment gospel. Darwin and his peers presented a man-centred view of man making himself—a Promethean vision of infinite possibilities. God had become a distant cause of causes; what counted was man acting in Nature.

Erasmus Darwin's evolutionary theories were not accepted in his own day. Evolutionary thinking long lay under a cloud, being condemned as materialistic and atheistic and associated with that great abomination, the French Revolution. Therein lay one of the reasons why his grandson, Charles, was so hesitant about publishing his own evolutionary theory, and why, when *The Origin of Species* finally saw the light of day in 1859, it still created such a storm.

Something similar happened with many of the other key ideas of the Enlightenment. Original and challenging, they had never met with universal acceptance, and there always remained powerful groupings of High-Flying churchmen, Jacobites, Tories, traditionalists, Methodists and so forth for whom the enlightened accent on critical reason was an absurdity or an obscenity.

Undergoing socio-political growing pains and tensions, and in particular when confronted by the French Revolution, the Revolutionary and Napoleonic Wars, and their backlashes, liberal ideologies began to shiver into fragments. For some, libertarian rhetoric led to Jacobin radicalism—witness Tom Paine's very titles: *Common Sense, The Age of Reason*, and *The Rights of Man*. Bourgeois liberalism put a different face upon enlightened ideology: individualism was to obey the iron laws of political economy; social progress demanded time-and-work discipline, penology and scientific poor laws; while humanitarian impulses bled into proto-Victorian sentimentality. Meanwhile, establishment apologists began to draw conclusions of their own from enlightened premises. Malthus put a new gloss on desire, recruiting science to prove how legislative action could not, after all, relieve suffering and starvation. More dramatically, French Revolutionary turmoil led many to change sides: Wordsworth, Southey and Coleridge, for instance.

Yet, in the long run, enlightened ideologies were not discarded. They continued to inform Victorian self-help liberalism and free-market ideology. By touting rational self-help, they promised a meliorist, moralised future which immunised native radicals against Marxist creeds of class war or communitarian socialism. Phrenology, secularism and Fabianism were all, in their own ways, Enlightenment legacies.

None of these developments was without the most profound tensions. If I have argued that the Enlightenment generated the idea of progress, mine has been no simple tale of 'progress', but of the on-going war of ideas against ideas.

FOR FURTHER READING

Roy Porter, *Enlightenment: Britain and the Creation of the Modern World* (Allen Lane, 2000); David Spadafora, *The Idea of Progress in 18th Century Britain* (Yale Univ. Press, 1990); Jan Golinski, *Science as Public Culture: Chemistry and Enlightenment in Britain*, 1760–1820 (Cambridge University Press, 1992); Larry Stewart, *The Rise of Public Science: Rhetoric, Technology, and Natural Philosophy in Newtonian Britain, 1660–1750* (CUP); W.L. Letwin, *The Origins of Scientific Economics* (Methuen, 1963); Donald Winch, *Riches and Poverty: An Intellectual History of Political Economy in Britain, 1750–1834* (CUP, 1996).

This article is the revised text of the Gresham Lecture delivered by Roy Porter in November 2000. Roy Porter is Professor of the Social History of Medicine at the Wellcome Trust Centre, University College, London.

HT ARCHIVES

Witchcraft:
The Spell That Didn't Break

Owen Davies argues that a widespread belief in witchcraft persisted in eighteenth- and nineteenth-century rural Britain despite the influence of the Enlightenment.

THE ADVENT OF industrialisation and the rise of the so-called 'Enlightenment' during the eighteenth century has often been portrayed as a watershed in British cultural life. Advances in the field of science and medicine are presumed to have rapidly dispelled 'superstitious' beliefs, as the spread of rational knowledge gradually trickled down to the masses. The dark days of the witch-trials were left behind and the people were freed from the everyday fear of the witch. However, historians are starting to realise that the history of witchcraft does not end with the execution of the last witch or the legal denial of their existence.

ABOVE: 'The ride through the murky air'—a 19th-century illustration to Harrison Ainsworth's 'The Lancashire Witches' shows a literary image of witchcraft.

The Witchcraft Act of 1736 repealed the English Statutes against witchcraft of 1563 and 1604, and also the Scottish Statute of 1563 (the Irish statute of 1587 remained fossilized in legislation until its belated repeal in 1821). From thenceforth the law dictated that

> no Prosecution, Suit, or Proceeding, shall be commenced or carried on against any Person or Persons for Witchcraft, Sorcery, Inchantment, or Conjuration, or for charging another with any such offence, in any Court whatsoever in Great Britain.

The Act further made it an offence to 'pretend' to exercise or use any kind of witchcraft or sorcery. For the legislature at least, the concept of witchcraft, which had brought hundreds of innocent people to the gallows over the previous two centuries, was now a mere pretence, a false belief consigned to the dustbin of history. But the passing of the Act did not signify the mass rejection of witchcraft. Many educated and eminent people like Dr Samuel Johnson and William Blackstone, one of the foremost legal minds of the eighteenth century, continued to believe that there was such a thing as witchcraft. Not only did the irrefutable word of the Bible plainly speak of witches, but some of the most respected men of the previous century had expressed their belief in witchcraft. However, although Methodists and Scottish Presbyterians continued to fear the threat of Satan and his earthly vassals, and condemned the Act of 1736, by the mid-eighteenth century the intellectual classes had comfortably convinced themselves that witches no longer existed. Yet little thought was actually given to explaining why they had disappeared. As Dr Samuel Johnson observed, nicely dodging the issue, 'Why it ceased, we cannot tell, as we cannot tell the reason of many things'. In newly 'enlightened' Britain it was thought best not to dwell too much on the dubious events of the recent past.

Educated people like Dr. Johnson continued to believe that there was such a thing as witchcraft.

Although witchcraft became a matter of private debate among the middle and upper classes, it remained a reality for a large portion of the population. While for the ruling elites of early modern England and Scotland witchcraft had been seen as a satanic threat to their moral and spiritual authority, for much of the labouring population, both before and after 1736, witchcraft was essentially an economic crime. Up until the second half of the nineteenth century, the way of life for many in rural areas had not changed fundamentally for two hundred years. The majority of people were still part of an agrarian economy, and a large portion of the population was involved in some form of husbandry to supplement their income or diet. Other than the very meagre relief provided by the Poor Law, there was no safety-net to fall back on when serious misfortune struck. Thus the illness of a family member or of a pig or cow could cause considerable hardship and lead to suspicions of witchcraft. Most staple foodstuffs such as butter, cheese and bread continued to be produced within the home or farmstead, and when these failed witchcraft might also be blamed. When people suspected witchcraft, they often looked no further than their neighbours to find the culprit. Relations between neighbours were close-knit and intense, but far from harmonious. Borrowing, begging and trespass were continual sources of friction. There was little privacy and gossip was rife. In such an environment personal conflicts were bound to occur frequently.

From the 1680s onwards, the number of witch-trials heard in English and Welsh courts diminished to a trickle, and the last execution for witchcraft was in 1684. In Scotland, too, the number of trials began to decline around the same time, though the courts remained more willing to accept evidence against

witches, and exercised little restraint in their sentencing. Thus a serious outbreak of accusations occurred in 1697, resulting in the execution of seven supposed witches, and the very last witch to be burnt was in 1722. The decline in indictments some thirty years before the repeal of the witchcraft laws was not, as has sometimes been assumed, an expression of declining belief. There is no evidence to suggest that there was a decrease in the number of complaints made to justices. Instead, as the trials became a legal embarrassment, justices increasingly dismissed complaints outright or dealt with them informally.

For the majority of the population who continued to consider witchcraft a serious threat, there must have been a good deal of frustration at the withdrawal of the justices and the courts from the arena. Yet the evidence would suggest that people were very slow to realise that there was no longer a general consensus concerning the need to suppress witches. Right up until the late nineteenth century magistrates up and down the country continued to receive requests for the arrest of suspected witches. In May 1870, for example, Mr Lushington, a magistrate at the Thames police court, was asked by a poor woman to arrest a neighbour named Biddy Coghlan for being a witch. The plaintiff had a hen that had died after laying a few abnormally small eggs, and Coghlan was held responsible. Not surprisingly, Lushington had little time for such complaints, and told the complainant to go about her business.

In the absence of a legal means of trying witches, people continued to resort to the trial by water, otherwise known as witch-swimming. This had been employed throughout the seventeenth century under quasi-official sanction. It was not, in fact, a legally recognised form of proof, but it was often accepted as such by judges and juries. The suspected witches had their thumbs tied to their toes, and a rope bound round their waists. They were then thrown into a pond or river to see whether they would sink or float. If the water rejected them and they floated, this was deemed a divine sign that they were guilty. If, however, they sank, then God had embraced them, thereby proving their innocence. Swimming must have been a terrifying ordeal for those subjected to it. Both before and after the actual immersion the victims were often subjected to much violent abuse, and many of those who 'proved' their innocence by sinking nearly drowned anyway. These witch-swimmings continued to occur fairly frequently up until the early nineteenth century and could attract hundreds of people. In 1737, for instance, a woman was swum in the River Ouse, at Oakley in Bedfordshire. A large crowd gathered, including the vicar of Oakley, and there were cries of 'A witch! Drown her! Hang her!'. Quite often magistrates, or some other passing 'gentleman', would intercede and stop the proceedings, but legal action was rarely taken against those who organised such brutal events, unless someone died. One of the few prosecutions occurred in Hertfordshire in 1751 when Thomas Colley stood trial for the murder of Ruth Osborne who was swum in a pond near Tring. A crowd, which one witness estimated as being some five thousand strong, gathered to see the swimming, and a collection was even held to recompense the organisers. Tragically, Osborne died from her repeated immersions, and Colley was subsequently hanged for his role in the affair.

HT ARCHIVES

'Credulity, superstition and fanaticism—a medley.' An engraving by William Hogarth mocks the continuing resistance to rationalism in the Age of Reason.

The Tring case was widely reported in the press at the time, and became something of a national sensation. It provided ample proof of the strong hold that witchcraft still held over the minds of the people. Yet there was an undoubted reluctance on the part of the authorities to get involved in any way in what they considered 'vulgar' affairs. As a result there was no campaign against the continued persecution of supposed witches. This led to the wholly unsatisfactory situation whereby some of those accused of witchcraft actually volunteered to undergo the ordeal by water because local justices were deaf to their pleas for succour. This is exactly what happened to an old woman of

Stanningfield, Suffolk, in 1792. She pleaded with Sir Charles Davers and the Rev. John Ord to protect her against charges of witchcraft that had 'very much disordered her head'. They said they could no nothing, however, and so she decided to let herself be swum before the community in order to clear her name. Her husband and brother complied with her request as they feared she would otherwise kill herself, and they held the rope at her swimming to ensure that she was not mistreated. Fortunately she sank, though she was dragged out 'almost lifeless'.

It is important to realise that throughout the early modern period recourse to the law was just one of several options that vic-

HT ARCHIVES

The fatal 'swimming' of suspected witch Ruth Osborne in Hertfordshire in 1751 led to the hanging of Thomas Colley for her murder. But 5,000 had seen her die.

tims of witchcraft could choose. People did not go running to the courts every time they considered themselves bewitched. So after 1736 the pattern of response to witchcraft was not that different. Some went to those intriguing magical practitioners known as cunning-folk to be cured. A counter-spell such as a witch-bottle might be employed. Numerous examples of these have been found dating from the seventeenth to the twentieth century. In its simplest form a witch-bottle consisted of a bottle filled with the bewitched person's urine. Into this was put some sharp objects such as thorns, pins or nails. The bottle was then sealed, and either buried in the ground, placed under the hearthstone, or heated in a fire. The bottle represented the witch's bladder, and the thorns and pins were meant to cause him or her such excruciating pain that they would be forced to remove their spell. However, the most potent method of breaking witches' power was to scratch them in order to draw blood. Since this constituted a physical assault, some who employed it found themselves in court for their violent actions. It is these cases, arising from the act of scratching, which form the bulk of what are effectively witch-trials in reverse. These were court cases in which accused witches were no longer appearing as defendants charged with a capital crime, but as prosecutors seeking legal retribution against those who assaulted them. Most of these prosecutions were heard before the summary court of petty sessions, although some were deemed serious enough to be brought before the quarter sessions or assizes.

In the mid-nineteenth century among rural folk 'belief in witchcraft is all but universal'

A general trawl of secondary sources and a brief random sampling of newspapers from England and Wales has revealed over seventy reverse witch-trials from the mid-eighteenth century to

the early twentieth century, as well as numerous prosecutions involving cunning-folk. The majority of these date from the nineteenth rather than the eighteenth century, partly because there was greater concern over the continued belief in witchcraft then, and also because the introduction of a professional police force facilitated the lodging of official complaints. Indeed, a systematic survey of nineteenth-century Somerset newspapers has uncovered twenty-six reverse witch-trials from that county alone, and no doubt several more went unrecorded. Based on these samples I would suggest that the number of such cases from England, Wales and Scotland probably number well over two hundred. If we further consider that these represent only those assaults which came to court, then we get some idea of the continued level of violence against suspected witches in an age when agents of the British Empire were complaining of the 'heathen' behaviour of many of its colonial subjects. The comparison was not lost on everyone. In the mid-nineteenth century the educationalist, James Augustus St John, bemoaned how

> here in England, in the midst of our civilization, with the light of Christianity, ready to pour into the meanest and darkest hovels [violence against witches was] still prevailing in our rural districts, while the belief in witches is all but universal.

There were numerous women with the scars to prove it. In 1935 a doctor from Poole, Dorset, wrote about an old woman of his acquaintance whose back and chest were covered with scars from being scratched. At the time of the assault she had twenty-two wounds that required stitching up.

The source of the majority of these assaults lay in the prolonged and inexplicable illness of family members. For all the advances in the understanding of human biology, the medical profession's ability to cure remained rudimentary. Until the development of aspirin and antibiotics during the twentieth century, doctors and vets could provide little comfort for a wide range of human and animal medical conditions. Some serious illnesses, such as internal cancers, remained undiagnosable, and so appeared mysterious to both doctor and patient. When people fell ill, witchcraft was not usually suspected straight away, and general practitioners were called in to apply their medicines. It was only if their treatment failed to provide any significant relief that suspicions sometimes grew that there might be some supernatural cause. A cunning-man or -woman might then be consulted to identify the witch responsible and to instruct on the best course of action. One example amongst many that could be given to illustrate this process occurred in 1854. A man from Heavitree near Exeter fell ill, and went to be treated by the local Poor Law Union surgeon. Finding little relief in the medicine given to him he discontinued his attendance and went to consult a 'wizard doctor'. This gentleman told him that the 'Union doctor was a consummate fool, and did not know what was the matter with him, for he was "bewitched"', and for the large sum of thirty shillings he provided him with a charm that would break the witch's spell.

Most of the rest of the reverse witch-trials resulted from the death or illness of horses, cattle and pigs, from the failure of do-

A Devonshire village 'wise man' of the late 19th century: such 'cunning folk' were consulted about counter-charms when witchcraft was suspected.

across the country. The local production of foodstuffs declined. Bread, butter, milk and cheese were now being brought in and sold by burgeoning retail outlets. People became increasingly divorced from the traditional agricultural rhythm of life. Once largely self-sufficient communities became wholly dependent on goods produced outside the community. As a result, the everyday toing and froing among neighbours buying, borrowing and begging from each other, which helped foster intimate neighbourhood relations, became less frequent. While communities were losing their cohesion and becoming less introspective, life in general was also becoming more financially secure. The spread of trade unionism, the beginnings of the welfare state—particularly the advent of old age pensions in 1909—the rise of personal insurance, and the eventual setting up of wage boards, meant that the impact of those misfortunes which had often led to accusations of witchcraft was lessened. Witchcraft gradually ceased to serve a function for those who believed in it, and although stories of witches continued to be told and believed in, fewer and fewer people attracted the reputation of being witches as the social circumstances which produced accusations dwindled. However, while the long-held popular tradition of witchcraft was becoming obsolete, a new phase in the modern history of witchcraft was beginning.

The last straw was a bewitched pudding that swelled so much in the pot it was impossible to remove.

During the late nineteenth century there occurred what has been described as the 'Occult Revival'. This was a renewed learned interest in ceremonial magic that grew out of the Masonic movement, and which was encouraged by the popularity and influence of spiritualism. There had been a small number of erudite, experimental magicians throughout the eighteenth and nineteenth centuries, but what defined the Occult Revival was the shift from solitary to collective magical practice, coupled with the formulation of a new magical tradition bringing together ancient pagan beliefs and the Christian occult philosophies of early modern Europe. To legitimise the credentials of this new brand of occultism, some occultists claimed that they were the inheritors of a secret pagan movement. Powerful support for this nascent tradition was provided by the work on witchcraft by the respected Egyptologist Margaret Murray. In 1921 her book, The Witch-Cult in Western Europe, was published. In it she argued that those persecuted as witches in the past were not Devil worshippers but members of a pre-Christian religion who gathered together at 'sabbaths' to venerate and supplicate a horned god. This notion of a pagan witch-cult was further developed by the founder of the modern witchcraft movement, Gerald Gardner. This freemason and spiritualist was a great admirer of Murray's work, and in a series of books published after the Second World War, he set out to trace the history of this ancient religion that came to be called 'Wicca', and to formulate a ritual structure for new members.

mestic food processing, or from poor fishing catches. Admittedly, only one case involving fishing has been found, but further newspaper research in counties with large fishing communities would probably reveal more. The case was heard by a court in Peterhead, Scotland, in September 1872, and concerned a man who drew blood from his wife to ensure that he would have a good catch of herring. In several instances people experienced a series of inexplicable misfortunes. Thus in 1895 a poor, elderly woman of Long Sutton, Lincolnshire, was assaulted by a farming couple for having supposedly bewitched their cows, pigs, hens, and butter. The last straw was a bewitched pudding that swelled so much in the pot that it was impossible to remove. Although people continued to interpret misfortune in terms of witchcraft, and individuals continued to be subjected to violent attack for being witches right up until the early decades of the present century, from the late nineteenth century onwards the cultural environment in which witchcraft functioned was undergoing a profound transformation. The mechanisation of agriculture, the opening up of a global market for meat and wheat, severe agricultural depression, emigration, and urbanisation led to the fracturing of communal relations

A coven of witches: a familiar image of a cult that was all too real for many rural people. From 'The Lancashire Witches'.

However, the concept of witchcraft propounded by the neo-magicians of late nineteenth- and early twentieth-century Britain was very different from the popular experience of witch-craft. There is absolutely no evidence in the modern historical record that those accused of witchcraft were pagan worshippers. In the opinion of those who accused and assaulted them, witches were guilty of malice and spite, not of subversive religious practices. A growing number of Wiccans are accepting this historical fact, and are distancing themselves from the Gardnerian claims for an inherited witchcraft tradition. Those who continue to claim for their religion people labelled as witches in the past, should remember that those who carried the scars of popular persecution were often God-fearing, church-going folk who would probably have been as horrified to be embraced as a pagan as scratched for a witch.

FOR FURTHER READING

Bob Bushaway, *Tacit, Unsuspected, but still Implicit Faith: Alternative Belief in Nineteenth-Century Rural England, in* Tim Harris (ed.), *Popular Culture in England, c. 1500-1850* (Macmillan, 1995); Ronald Hutton, *The Triumph of the Moon: A History of Modern Pagan Witchcraft* (Oxford University Press, forthcoming); Ralph Merrifield, *The Archaeology of Ritual and Magic* (Guild Publishing, 1987); James Sharpe, *Instruments of Darkness: Witchcraft in England 1550-1750* (Hamish Hamilton, 1996).

Dr. Owen Davies is the author of Witchcraft, Magic and Culture, 1736–1951 (Manchester University Press, 1999).

The Passion of Antoine Lavoisier

With its revolution, France founded a rational republic and lost a great scientist

Stephen Jay Gould

Galileo and Lavoisier have more in common than their brilliance. Both men are focal points in a cardinal legend about the life of intellectuals—the conflict of lonely and revolutionary genius with state power. Both stories are apocryphal, however inspiring. Yet they only exaggerate, or encapsulate in the epitome of a bon mot, an essential theme in the history of thinking and its impact upon society.

Galileo, on his knees before the Inquisition, abjures his heretical belief that the earth revolves around a central sun. Yet, as he rises, brave Galileo, faithful to the highest truth of factuality, addresses a stage whisper to the world: *eppur se muove*—nevertheless, it does move. Lavoisier, before the revolutionary tribunal during the Reign of Terror in 1794, accepts the inevitable verdict of death, but asks for a week or two to finish some experiments. Coffinhal, the young judge who has sealed his doom, denies his request, stating, "La république n'a pas besoin de savants" (the Republic does not need scientists).

Coffinhal said no such thing, although the sentiments are not inconsistent with emotions unleashed in those frightening and all too frequent political episodes so well characterized by Marc Antony in his lamentation over Caesar: "O judgment! thou are fled to brutish beasts, And men have lost their reason." Lavoisier, who had been under arrest for

months, was engaged in no experiments at the time. Moreover, as we shall see, the charges leading to his execution bore no relationship to his scientific work.

But if Coffinhal's chilling remark is apocryphal, the second most famous quotation surrounding the death of Lavoisier is accurate and well attested. The great mathematician Joseph Louis Lagrange, upon hearing the news about his friend Lavoisier, remarked bitterly: "It took them only an instant to cut off that head, but France may not produce another like it in a century."

I feel some need to participate in the worldwide outpouring of essays to commemorate the 200th anniversary of the French Revolution. Next month, on July 14, unparalleled displays of fireworks will mark the bicentenary of the fall of the Bastille. Nonetheless, and with no desire to put a damper on such pyrotechnics, I must write about the flip side of this initial liberation, the most troubling scientific story of the Revolution—the execution of Antoine Lavoisier in 1794.

The revolution had been born in hope and expansiveness. At the height of enthusiasm for new beginnings, the revolutionary government suppressed the old calendar, and started time all over again, with year I beginning on September 22, 1792, at the founding of the French republic. The months would no longer bear names of Roman gods or emperors, but would record the natural passage of sea-

sons—as in *brumaire* (foggy), *ventose* (windy), *germinal* (budding), and to replace parts of July and August, originally named for two despotic Caesars, *thermidor*. Measures would be rationalized, decimalized, and based on earthly physics, with the meter defined as one tenmillionth of a quarter meridian from pole to equator. The metric system is our enduring legacy of this revolutionary spirit, and Lavoisier himself was the guiding force in devising the new weights and measures.

But initial optimism soon unraveled under the realities of internal dissension and external pressure (the powerful monarchists of Europe were, to say the least, concerned lest republican ideas spread by export or example). Governments tumbled one after the other, and Dr. Guillotin's machine, invented to make execution more humane, became a symbol of terror by sheer frequency of public use. Louis XVI was beheaded in January, 1793 (year one of the republic). Power shifted from the Girondins to the Montagnards, as the Terror reached its height and the war with Austria and Prussia continued. Finally, as so often happens, the architect of the terror, Robespierre himself, paid his visit to Dr. Guillotin's device, and the cycle played itself out. A few years later, in 1804, Napoleon was crowned as emperor, and the First Republic ended. Poor Lavoisier had been caught in the midst of the cycle, dying for his former role as tax collector on May 8, 1794, less than three months before the fall of Robespierre on July 27 (9 Thermidor, year II).

Old ideas often persist in vestigial forms of address and writing, long after their disappearance in practice. I was reminded of this phenomenon when I acquired, a few months ago, a copy of the opening and closing addresses for the course in zoology at the Muséum d'Histoire naturelle of Paris for 1801–2. The democratic fervor of the revolution had faded, and Napoleon had already staged his *coup d'etat* of 18 Brumaire (November 9, 1799), emerging as emperor de facto, although not crowned until 1804. Nonetheless, the author of these addresses, who would soon resume his full name Bernard-Germain-Etienne de la Ville-sur-Illon, comte de Lacépède, is identified on the title page only as C^{en} Lacépède (for *citoyen*, or "citizen"—the democratic form adopted by the revolution to abolish all distinctions of address). The long list of honors and memberships, printed in small type below Lacépède's name, is almost a parody on the ancient forms; for instead of the old affiliations that always included "member of the royal academy of this or that" and "counsellor to the king or count of here or there," Lacépède's titles are rigorously egalitarian—including "one of the professors at the museum of natural history," and member of the society of pharmacists of Paris, and of agriculture of Agen. As for the year of publication, we have to know the history detailed above—for the publisher's date is given, at the bottom, only as "l'an IX de la Rèpublique."

Lacépède was one of the great natural historians in the golden age of French zoology during the late eighteenth and early nineteenth century. His name may be overshadowed in retrospect by the illustrious quartet of Buffon, Lamarck, Saint-Hilaire and Cuvier, but Lacépède—who was chosen by Buffon to complete his life's work, the multivolumed *Histoire naturelle*—deserves a place with these men, for all were *citoyens* of comparable merit. Although Lacépède supported the revolution in its moderate first phases, his noble title bred suspicion and he went into internal exile

during the Terror. But the fall of Robespierre prompted his return to Paris, where his former colleagues persuaded the government to establish a special chair for him at the Muséum, as zoologist for reptiles and fishes.

By tradition, his opening and closing addresses for the zoology course at the Muséum were published in pamphlet form each year. The opening address for year IX, "Sur l'histoire des races ou principales variétés de l'espèce humaine" (On the history of races and principal varieties of the human species), is a typical statement of the liberality and optimism of Enlightenment thought. The races, we learn, may differ in current accomplishments, but all are capable of greater and equal achievement, and all can progress.

But the bloom of hope had been withered by the Terror. Progress, Lacépède asserts, is not guaranteed, but is possible only if untrammeled by the dark side of human venality. Memories of dire consequences for unpopular thoughts must have been fresh, for Lacépède cloaked his criticisms of revolutionary excesses in careful speech and foreign attribution. Ostensibly, he was only describing the evils of the Indian caste system in a passage that must be read as a lament about the Reign of Terror:

> Hypocritical ambition,… abusing the credibility of the multitude, has conserved the ferocity of the savage state in the midst of the virtues of civilization…. After having reigned by terror *[regné par la terreur]*, submitting even monarchs to their authority, they reserved the domain of science and art to themselves [a reference, no doubt, to the suppression of the independent academies by the revolutionary government in 1793, when Lacépède lost his first post at the Muséum], and surrounded themselves with a veil of mystery that only they could lift.

At the end of his address, Lacépède returns to the familiar theme of political excesses and makes a point, by no means original of course, that I regard as the central structural tragedy of the nature of any complex system, including organisms and social institutions—the crushing asymmetry between the need for slow and painstaking construction and the potential for almost instantaneous destruction:

> Thus, the passage from the semisavage state to civilization occurs through a great number of insensible stages, and requires an immense amount of time. In moving slowly through these successive stages, man fights painfully against his habits; he also battles with nature as he climbs, with great effort, up the long and perilous path. But it is not the same with the loss of the civilized state; that is almost sudden. In this morbid fall, man is thrown down by all his ancient tendencies; he struggles no longer, he gives up, he does not battle obstacles, he abandons himself to the burdens that surround him. Centuries are needed to nurture the tree of science and make it grow, but one blow from the hatchet of destruction cuts it down.

The chilling final line, a gloss on Lagrange's famous statement about the death of Lavoisier, inspired me to write about the founder of modern chemistry, and to think a bit more about the tragic asymmetry of creation and destruction.

Antoine-Laurent Lavoisier, born in 1743, belonged to the nobility through a title purchased by his father (standard practice for boosting the royal treasury during the *ancien régime*). As a leading liberal and rationalist of the Enlightenment (a movement that attracted much of the nobility, including many wealthy intellectuals who had purchased their titles to rise from the bourgeoisie), Lavoisier fitted an astounding array of social and scientific services into a life cut short by the headsman at age fifty-one.

We know him best today as the chief founder of modern chemistry. The textbook one-liners describe him as the discoverer (or at least the namer) of oxygen, the man who (though anticipated by Henry Cavendish in England) recognized water as a compound of the gases hydrogen and oxygen, and who correctly described combustion, not as the liberation of a hypothetical substance called phlogiston, but as the combination of burning material with oxygen. But we can surely epitomize his contribution more accurately by stating that Lavoisier set the basis for modern chemistry by recognizing the nature of elements and compounds—by finally dethroning the ancient taxonomy of air, water, earth, and fire as indivisible elements; by identifying gas, liquid, and solid as states of aggregation for a single substance subjected to different degrees of heat; and by developing quantitative methods of defining and identifying true elements. Such a brief statement can only rank as a caricature of Lavoisier's scientific achievements, but this essay treats his other life in social service, and I must move on.

Lavoisier, no shrinking violet in the game of self-promotion, openly spoke of his new chemistry as "a revolution." He even published his major manifesto, *Traité élémentaire de chimie*, in 1789, starting date of the other revolution that would seal his fate.

Lavoisier, liberal child of the Enlightenment, was no opponent of the political revolution, at least in its early days. He supported the idea of a constitutional monarchy, and joined the most moderate of the revolutionary societies, the Club of '89. He served as an alternate delegate in the States General, took his turn as a *citoyen* at guard duty, and led several studies and commissions vital to the success of the revolution—including a long stint as *régisseur des poudres* (director of gunpowder, where his brilliant successes produced the best stock in Europe, thus providing substantial help in France's war against Austria and Prussia), work on financing the revolution by *assignats* (paper money backed largely by confiscated church lands), and service on the commission of weights and measures that formulated the metric system. Lavoisier rendered these services to all governments, including the most radical, right to his death, even hoping at the end that his crucial work on weights and measures might save his life. Why, then, did Lavoisier end up in two pieces on the *place de la Révolution* (long ago re-

named, in pleasant newspeak, *place de la Concorde*)?

The fateful move had been made in 1768, when Lavoisier joined the infamous Ferme Générale, or Tax Farm. If you regard the IRS as a less than benevolent institution, just consider taxation under the *ancien régime* and count your blessings. Taxation was regressive with a vengeance, as the nobility and clergy were entirely exempt, and poor people supplied the bulk of the royal treasury through tariffs on the movement of goods across provincial boundaries, fees for entering the city of Paris, and taxes on such goods as tobacco and salt. (The hated *gabelle*, or "salt tax," was applied at iniquitously differing rates from region to region, and was levied not on actual consumption but on presumed usage—thus, in effect, forcing each family to buy a certain quantity of taxed salt each year.)

Moreover, the government did not collect taxes directly. They set the rates and then leased (for six-year periods) the privilege of collecting taxes to a private finance company, the Ferme Générale. The Tax Farm operated for profit like any other private business. If they managed to collect more than the government levy, they kept the balance; if they failed to reach the quota, they took the loss. The system was not only oppressive in principle; it was also corrupt. Several shares in the Tax Farm were paid for no work as favors or bribes; many courtiers, even the King himself, were direct beneficiaries. Nonetheless, Lavoisier chose this enterprise for the primary investment of his family fortune, and he became, as members of the firm were called, a *fermier-général*, or "farmer-general."

(Incidentally, since I first read the sad story of Lavoisier some twenty-five years ago, I have been amused by the term farmer-general, for it conjures up a pleasantly rustic image of a country yokel, dressed in his Osh Kosh b'Gosh overalls, and chewing on a stalk of hay while trying to collect the *gabelle*. But I have just learned from the *Oxford English Dictionary* that my image is not only wrong, but entirely backward. A farm, defined as a piece of agricultural land, is a derivative term. In usage dat-

ing to Chaucer, a farm, from the medieval Latin *firma*, "fixed payment," is "a fixed yearly sum accepted from a person as a composition for taxes or other moneys which he is empowered to collect." By extension, to farm is to lease anything for a fixed rent. Since most leases applied to land, agricultural plots become "farms," with the first use in this sense traced only to the sixteenth century; the leasers of such land then became "farmers." Thus, our modern phrase "farming out" records the original use, and has no agricultural connotation. And Lavoisier was a farmer-general in the true sense, with no mitigating image of bucolic innocence.)

I do not understand why Lavoisier chose the Ferme Générale for his investment, and then worked so assiduously in his role as tax farmer. He was surely among the most scrupulous and fair-minded of the farmers, and might be justifiably called a reformer. (He opposed the overwatering of tobacco, a monopoly product of the Ferme, and he did, at least in later years, advocate taxation upon all, including the radical idea that nobles might pay as well.) But he took his profits, and he provoked no extensive campaign for reform as the money rolled in. The standard biographies, all too hagiographical, tend to argue that he regarded the Ferme as an investment that would combine greatest safety and return with minimal expenditure of effort—all done to secure a maximum of time for his beloved scientific work. But I do not see how this explanation can hold. Lavoisier, with his characteristic energy, plunged into the work of the Ferme, traveling all over the country, for example, to inspect the tobacco industry. I rather suspect that Lavoisier, like most modern businessmen, simply jumped at a good and legal investment without asking too many ethical questions.

But the golden calf of one season becomes the shattered idol of another. The farmers-general were roundly hated, in part for genuine corruption and iniquity, in part because tax collectors are always scapegoated, especially when the national treasury is bankrupt and the people are starving. Lavoisier's position was particularly precarious. As a scheme to prevent the loss of taxes from widespread smuggling of goods into Paris, Lavoisier advocated the building of a wall around the city. Much to Lavoisier's distress, the project, financed largely (and involuntarily) through taxes levied upon the people of Paris, became something of a boondoggle, as millions were spent on fancy ornamental gates. Parisians blamed the wall for keeping in fetid air and spreading disease. The militant republican Jean-Paul Marat began a campaign of vilification against Lavoisier that only ended when Charlotte Corday stabbed him to death in his bath. Marat had written several works in science and had hoped for election to the Royal Academy, then run by Lavoisier. But Lavoisier had exposed the emptiness of Marat's work. Marat fumed, bided his time, and waited for the season when patriotism would become a good refuge for scoundrels. In January 1791, he launched his attack in *l'Ami du Peuple* (the Friend of the People):

> I denounce you, Coryphaeus of charlatans, Sieur Lavoisier [coryphaeus, meaning highest, is the leader of the chorus in a classical Greek drama] Farmer-general, Commissioner of Gunpowders.... Just to think that this contemptible little man who enjoys an income of forty thousand livres has no other claim to fame than that of having put Paris in prison with a wall costing the poor thirty millions.... Would to heaven he had been strung up to the nearest lamppost.

The breaching of the wall by the citizens of Paris on July 12, 1789, was the prelude to the fall of the Bastille two days later.

Lavoisier began to worry very early in the cycle. Less than seven months after the fall of the Bastille, he wrote to his old friend Benjamin Franklin:

> After telling you about what is happening in chemistry, it would be well to give you news of our Revolution.... Moderate-minded people, who have kept cool heads during the general excitement, think that events have carried us too far... we greatly regret your

absence from France at this time; you would have been our guide and you would have marked out for us the limits beyond which we ought not to go.

But these limits were breached, just as Lavoisier's wall had fallen, and he could read the handwriting on the remnants. The Ferme Générale was suppressed in 1791, and Lavoisier played no further role in the complex sorting out of the farmers' accounts. He tried to keep his nose clean with socially useful work on weights and measures and public education. But time was running out for the farmers-general. The treasury was bankrupt, and many thought (quite incorrectly) that the iniquitously hoarded wealth of the farmers-general could replenish the nation. The farmers were too good a scapegoat to resist; they were arrested en masse in November 1793, commanded to put their accounts in order and to reimburse the nation for any ill-gotten gains.

The presumed offenses of the farmers-general were not capital under revolutionary law, and they hoped initially to win their personal freedom, even though their wealth and possessions might be confiscated. But they had the misfortune to be in the wrong place (jail) at the worst time (as the Terror intensified). Eventually, capital charges of counter-revolutionary activities were drummed up, and in a mock trial lasting only part of a day, the farmers-general were condemned to the guillotine.

Lavoisier's influential friends might have saved him, but none dared (or cared) to speak. The Terror was not so inexorable and efficient as tradition holds. Fourteen of the farmers-general managed to evade arrest, and one was saved as a result of the intervention of Robespierre. Madame Lavoisier, who lived to a ripe old age, marrying and divorcing Count Rumford, and reestablishing one of the liveliest salons in Paris, never allowed any of these men over her doorstep again. One courageous (but uninfluential) group offered brave support in Lavoisier's last hours. A deputation from the Lycée des Arts came to the prison to honor Lavoisier and crown him with a wreath. We read in the minutes of that organiza-

tion: "Brought to Lavoisier in irons, the consolation of friendship... to crown the head about to go under the ax."

It is a peculiar attribute of human courage that when no option remains but death, criteria of judgment shift to the manner of dying. Chronicles of the revolution are filled with stories about who died with dignity—and who went screaming to the knife. Antoine Lavoisier died well. He wrote a last letter to his cousin, in apparent calm, not without humor, and with an intellectual's faith in the supreme importance of mind.

> I have had a fairly long life, above all a very happy one, and I think that I shall be remembered with some regrets and perhaps leave some reputation behind me. What more could I ask? The events in which I am involved will probably save me from the troubles of old age. I shall die in full possession of my faculties.

Lavoisier's rehabilitation came almost as quickly as his death. In 1795, the Lycée des Arts held a first public memorial service, with Lagrange himself offering the eulogy and unveiling a bust of Lavoisier inscribed with the words: "Victim of tyranny, respected friend of the arts, he continues to live; through genius he still serves humanity." Lavoisier's spirit continued to inspire, but his head, once filled with great thoughts as numerous as the unwritten symphonies of Mozart, lay severed in a common grave.

Many people try to put a happy interpretation upon Lagrange's observation about the asymmetry of painstaking creation and instantaneous destruction. The collapse of systems, they argue, may be a prerequisite to any future episode of creativity—and the antidote, therefore, to stagnation. Taking the longest view, for example, mass extinctions do break up stable ecosystems and provoke episodes of novelty further down the evolutionary road. We would not be here today if the death of dinosaurs had not cleared some space for the burgeoning of mammals.

I have no objection to this argument in its proper temporal perspective. If you choose a telescope and wish to peer into an evolutionary future millions of years away, then a current episode of destruction may be read as an ultimate spur. But if you care for the here and now, which is (after all) the only time we feel and have, then massive extinction is only a sadness and an opportunity lost forever. I have heard people argue that our current wave of extinctions should not inspire concern because the earth will eventually recover, as so oft before, and perhaps with pleasant novelty. But what can a conjecture about ten million years from now possibly mean to our lives—especially since we have the power to blow our planet up long before then, and rather little prospect, in any case, of surviving so long ourselves (since few vertebrate species live for ten million years).

The argument of the "long view" may be correct in some meaninglessly abstract sense, but it represents a fundamental mistake in categories and time scales. Our only legitimate long view extends to our children and our children's children's children—hundreds or a few thousands of years down the road. If we let the slaughter continue, they will share a bleak world with rats, dogs, cockroaches, pigeons, and mosquitoes. A potential recovery millions of years later has no meaning at our appropriate scale. Similarly, others could do the unfinished work of Lavoisier, if not so elegantly; and political revolution did spur science into some interesting channels. But how can this mitigate the tragedy of Lavoisier? He was one of the most brilliant men ever to grace our history, and he died at the height of his powers and health. He had work to do, and he was not guilty.

My title, "The Passion of Antoine Lavoisier," is a double-entendre. The modern meaning of *passion*, "over-mastering zeal or enthusiasm," is a latecomer. The word entered our language from the Latin verb for suffering, particularly for suffering physical pain. The Saint Matthew and Saint John Passions of J. S. Bach are musical dramas about the suffering of Jesus on the cross. This essay, therefore, focuses upon the final and literal passion of Lavoisier. (Anyone who has ever been disappointed in love—that is, all of us—will understand the intimate connection between the two meanings of passion.)

But I also wanted to emphasize Lavoisier's passion in the modern meaning. For this supremely organized man—farmer-general; commissioner of gunpowder; wall builder; reformer of prisons, hospitals, and schools; legislative representative for the nobility of Blois; father of the metric system; servant on a hundred government committees—really had but one passion amidst this burden of activities for a thousand lifetimes. Lavoisier loved science more than anything else. He awoke at six in the morning and worked on science until eight, then again at night from seven until ten. He devoted one full day a week to scientific experiments and called it his *jour de bonheur* (day of happiness). The letters and reports of his last year are painful to read, for Lavoisier never abandoned his passion—his conviction that reason and science must guide any just and effective social order. But those who received his pleas, and held power over him, had heard the different drummer of despotism.

Lavoisier was right in the deepest, almost holy, way. His passion harnessed feeling to the service of reason; another kind of passion was the price. Reason cannot save us and can even persecute us in the wrong hands; but we have no hope of salvation without reason. The world is too complex, too intransigent; we cannot bend it to our simple will. Bernard Lacépède was probably thinking of Lavoisier when he wrote a closing flourish following his passage on the great asymmetry of slow creation and sudden destruction:

Ah! Never forget that we can only stave off that fatal degradation if we unite the liberal arts, which embody the sacred fire of sensibility, with the sciences and the useful arts, without which the celestial light of reason will disappear.

The Republic needs scientists.

Stephen Jay Gould taught biology, geology, and the history of science at Harvard University.

The First Feminist

In 1792 Mary Wollstonecraft wrote a book to prove that her sex was as intelligent as the other: thus did feminism come into the world. Right on, Ms. Mary!

Shirley Tomkievicz

The first person—male or female—to speak at any length and to any effect about woman's rights was Mary Wollstonecraft. In 1792, when her *Vindication of the Rights of Woman* appeared, Mary was a beautiful spinster of thirty-three who had made a successful career for herself in the publishing world of London. This accomplishment was rare enough for a woman in that day. Her manifesto, at once impassioned and learned, was an achievement of real originality. The book electrified the reading public and made Mary famous. The core of its argument is simple: "I wish to see women neither heroines nor brutes; but reasonable creatures," Mary wrote. This ancestress of the Women's Liberation Movement did not demand day-care centers or an end to women's traditional role as wife and mother, nor did she call anyone a chauvinist pig. The happiest period of Mary's own life was when she was married and awaiting the birth of her second child. And the greatest delight she ever knew was in her first child, an illegitimate daughter. Mary's feminism may not appear today to be the hard-core revolutionary variety, but she did live, for a time, a scandalous and unconventional life—"emancipated," it is called by those who have never tried it. The essence of her thought, however, is simply that a woman's mind is as good as a man's.

Not many intelligent men could be found to dispute this proposition today, at least not in mixed company. In Mary's time, to speak of *anybody's* rights, let alone woman's rights, was a radical act. In England, as in other nations, "rights" were an entity belonging to the government. The common run of mankind had little access to what we now call "human rights." As an example of British justice in the late eighteenth century, the law cited two hundred different capital crimes, among them shoplifting. An accused man was not entitled to counsel. A child could be tried and hanged as soon as an adult. The right to vote existed, certainly, but because of unjust apportionment, it had come to mean little. In the United States some of these abuses had been corrected—but that the rights of man did not extend past the color bar and the masculine gender was intentional. In the land of Washington and Jefferson, as in the land of George III, human rights were a new idea and woman's rights were not even an issue.

In France, in 1792, a Revolution in the name of equality was in full course, and woman's rights had at least been alluded to. The Revolutionary government drew up plans for female education—to the age of eight. "The education of the women should always be relative to the men," Rousseau had written in *Emile*. "To please, to be useful to us, to make us love and esteem them, to educate us when young, and take care of us when grown up, to advise, to console us, to render our lives easy and agreeable; these are the duties of women at all times, and what they should be taught in their infancy." And, less prettily, "Women have, or ought to have, but little liberty."

Rousseau would have found little cause for complaint in eighteenth-century England. An Englishwoman had almost the same civil status as an American slave. Thomas Hardy, a hundred years hence, was to base a novel on the idea of a man casually selling his wife and daughter at public auction. Obviously this was not a common occurrence, but neither is it wholly implausible. In 1792, and later, a woman could not own property, nor keep any earned wages. All that she possessed belonged to her husband. She could not divorce him, but he could divorce her and take her children. There was no law to say she could not grow up illiterate or be beaten every day.

Such was the legal and moral climate in which Mary Wollstonecraft lived. She was born in London in the spring of 1759, the second child and first daughter of Edward Wollstonecraft, a prosperous weaver. Two more daughters and two more sons were eventually born into the family, making six children in all. Before they had all arrived, Mr. Wollstonecraft came into an inheritance and decided to move his family to the country and become a gentleman farmer. But this plan failed. His money dwindled, and he began drinking heavily. His wife turned into a terrified wraith whose only interest was her eldest son, Edward. Only he escaped the beatings and abuse that his father dealt out regularly to every other household member, from Mrs. Wollstonecraft to the family dog. As often happens in large and disordered families, the eldest sister had to assume the role of mother and scullery maid. Mary was a bright, strong child, determined not to be broken, and she undertook her task energetically, defying her father when he was violent and keeping her younger brothers and sisters in hand. Clearly, Mary held the household together, and in so doing forfeited her own childhood. This experience left her with an everlasting gloomy streak, and was a strong factor in making her a reformer.

At some point in Mary's childhood, another injustice was visited upon her, though so commonplace for the time that she can hardly have felt the sting. Her elder brother was sent away to be educated, and the younger children were left to learn their letters as best they could. The family now frequently changed lodgings, but from her ninth to her fifteenth year Mary went to a day school, where she had the only formal training of her life. Fortunately, this included French and composition, and somewhere Mary learned to read critically and widely. These skills, together with her curiosity and determination, were really all she needed. The *Vindication* is in some parts long-winded, ill-punctuated, and simply full of hot air, but it is the work of a well-informed mind.

Feminists—and Mary would gladly have claimed the title—inevitably, even deservedly, get bad notices. The term calls up an image of relentless battle-axes: "thin college ladies with eye-glasses, no-nonsense features, mouths thin as bologna slicers, a babe in one arm, a hatchet in the other, grey eyes bright with balefire," as Norman Mailer feelingly envisions his antagonists in the Women's Liberation Movement. He has conjured up all the horrid elements: the lips with a cutting edge, the baby immaculately conceived (one is forced to conclude), the lethal weapon tightly clutched, the desiccating college degree, the joylessness. Hanging miasmally over

the tableau is the suspicion of a deformed sexuality. Are these girls man-haters, or worse? Mary Wollstonecraft, as the first of her line, has had each of these scarlet letters (except the B.A.) stitched upon her bosom. Yet she conformed very little to the hateful stereotype. In at least one respect, however, she would have chilled Mailer's bones. Having spent her childhood as an adult, Mary reached the age of nineteen in a state of complete joylessness. She was later to quit the role, but for now she wore the garb of a martyr.

Her early twenties were spent in this elderly frame of mind. First she went out as companion to an old lady living at Bath, and was released from this servitude only by a call to nurse the dying Mrs. Wollstonecraft. Then the family broke up entirely, though the younger sisters continued off and on to be dependent on Mary. The family of Mary's dearest friend, Fanny Blood, invited her to come and stay with them; the two girls made a small living doing sewing and handicrafts, and Mary dreamed of starting a primary school. Eventually, in a pleasant village called Newington Green, this plan materialized and prospered. But Fanny Blood in the meantime had married and moved to Lisbon. She wanted Mary to come and nurse her through the birth of her first child. Mary reached Lisbon just in time to see her friend die of childbed fever, and returned home just in time to find that her sisters, in whose care the flourishing little school had been left, had lost all but two pupils.

Mary made up her mind to die. "My constitution is impaired, I hope I shan't live long," she wrote to a friend in February, 1786. Under this almost habitual grief, however, Mary was gaining some new sense of herself. Newington Green, apart from offering her a brief success as a schoolmistress, had brought her some acquaintance in the world of letters, most important among them, Joseph Johnson, an intelligent and successful London publisher in search of new writers. Debt-ridden and penniless, Mary set aside her impaired constitution and wrote her first book, probably in the space of a week. Johnson bought it for ten guineas and published it. Called *Thoughts on the Education of Daughters*, it went unnoticed, and the ten guineas was soon spent.

Mary had to find work. She accepted a position as governess in the house of Lord and Lady Kingsborough in the north of Ireland.

Mary's letters from Ireland to her sisters and to Joseph Johnson are so filled with Gothic gloom, so stained with tears, that one cannot keep from laughing at them. "I entered the great gates with the same kind of feeling I should have if I was going to the Bastille," she wrote upon entering Kingsborough Castle in the fall of 1786. Mary was now twenty-seven. Her most recent biographer, Margaret George, believes that Mary was not really suffering so much as she was having literary fantasies. In private she was furiously at work on a novel entitled, not very artfully, *Mary, A Fiction*. This is the story of a young lady of immense sensibilities who closely resembles Mary except that she has wealthy parents, a neglectful bridegroom, and an attractive lover. The title and fantasizing contents are precisely what a scribbler of thirteen might secretly concoct. Somehow Mary was embarking on her adolescence—with all its daydreams—fifteen years after the usual date. Mary's experience in Kingsborough Castle was a fruitful one, for all her complaints. In the summer of 1787 she lost her post as governess and set off for London with her novel. Not only did Johnson accept it for publication, he offered her a regular job as editor and translator and helped her find a place to live.

Thus, aged twenty-eight, Mary put aside her doleful persona as the martyred, set-upon elder sister. How different she is now, jauntily writing from London to her sisters: "Mr. Johnson... assures me that if I exert my talents in writing I may support myself in a comfortable way. I am then going to be the first of a new genus...." Now Mary discovered the sweetness of financial independence earned by interesting work. She had her own apartment. She was often invited to Mr. Johnson's dinner parties, usually as the only female guest among all the most interesting men in London: Joseph Priestley, Thomas Paine, Henry Fuseli, William Blake, Thomas Christie, William Godwin—all of them up-and-coming scientists or poets or painters or philosophers, bound together by left-wing political views. Moreover, Mary was successful in her own writing as well as in editorial work. Her *Original Stories for Children* went into three editions and was illustrated by Blake. Johnson and his friend Thomas Christie had started a magazine called the *Analytical Review*, to which Mary became a regular contributor.

But—lest anyone imagine an elegantly dressed Mary presiding flirtatiously at Johnson's dinner table—her social accomplishments were rather behind her professional ones. Johnson's circle looked upon her as one of the boys. "Wollstonecraft" is what William Godwin calls her in his diary. One of her later detractors reported that she was at this time a "philosophic sloven," in a dreadful old dress and beaver hat, "with her hair hanging lank about her shoulders." Mary had yet to arrive at her final incarnation, but the new identity was imminent, if achieved by an odd route. Edmund Burke had recently published his *Reflections on the Revolution in France*, and the book had enraged Mary. The statesman who so readily supported the quest for liberty in the American colonies had his doubts about events in France.

Mary's reply to Burke, *A Vindication of the Rights of Men*, astounded London, partly because she was hitherto unknown, partly because it was good. Mary proved to be an excellent polemicist, and she had written in anger. She accused Burke, the erstwhile champion of liberty, of being "the champion of property." "Man preys on man," said she, "and you mourn for the idle tapestry that decorated a gothic pile and the dronish bell that summoned the fat priest to prayer." The book sold well. Mary moved into a better apartment and bought some pretty dresses—no farthingales, of course, but some of the revolutionary new "classical" gowns. She put her auburn hair up in a loose knot. Her days as a philosophic sloven were over.

Vindication of the Rights of Woman was her next work. In its current edition it runs to 250-odd pages; Mary wrote it

in six weeks. *Vindication* is no prose masterpiece, but it has never failed to arouse its audience, in one way or another. Horace Walpole unintentionally set the style for the book's foes. Writing to his friend Hannah More in August, 1792, he referred to Thomas Paine and to Mary as "philosophizing serpents" and was "glad to hear you have not read the tract of the last mentioned writer. I would not look at it." Neither would many another of Mary's assailants, the most virulent of whom, Ferdinand Lundberg, surfaced at the late date of 1947 with a tract of his own, *Modern Woman, the Lost Sex*. Savagely misogynistic as it is, this book was hailed in its time as "the best book yet to be written about women." Lundberg calls Mary the Karl Marx of the feminist movement, and the *Vindication* a "fateful book," to which "the tenets of feminism, which have undergone no change to our day, may be traced." Very well, but then, recounting Mary's life with the maximum possible number of errors per line, he warns us that she was "an extreme neurotic of a compulsive type" who "wanted to turn on men and injure them." In one respect, at least, Mr. Lundberg hits the mark: he blames Mary for starting women in the pernicious habit of wanting an education. In the nineteenth century, he relates, English and American feminists were hard at work. "Following Mary Wollstonecraft's prescription, they made a considerable point about acquiring a higher education." This is precisely Mary's prescription, and the most dangerous idea in her fateful book.

"Men complain and with reason, of the follies and caprices of our Sex," she writes in Chapter 1. "Behold, I should answer, the natural effect of ignorance." Women, she thinks, are usually so mindless as to be scarcely fit for their roles as wives and mothers. Nevertheless, she believes this state not to be part of the feminine nature, but the result of an equally mindless oppression, as demoralizing for men as for women. If a woman's basic mission is as a wife and mother, need she be an illiterate slave for this?

The heart of the work is Mary's attack on Rousseau. In *Emile* Rousseau had set forth some refreshing new ideas for the

education of little boys. But women, he decreed, are tools for pleasure, creatures too base for moral or political or educational privilege. Mary recognized that this view was destined to shut half the human race out of all hope for political freedom. *Vindication* is a plea that the "rights of men" ought to mean the "rights of humanity." The human right that she held highest was the right to have a mind and think with it. Virginia Woolf, who lived through a time of feminist activity, thought that the *Vindication* was a work so true "as to seem to contain nothing new." Its originality, she wrote, rather too optimistically, had become a commonplace.

Vindication went quickly into a second edition. Mary's name was soon known all over Europe. But as she savored her fame—and she did savor it—she found that the edge was wearing off and that she was rather lonely. So far as anyone knows, Mary had reached this point in her life without ever having had a love affair. Johnson was the only man she was close to, and he was, as she wrote him, "A father, or a brother—you have been both to me." Mary was often now in the company of the Swiss painter Henry Fuseli, and suddenly she developed what she thought was a Platonic passion in his direction. He rebuffed her, and in the winter of 1792 she went to Paris, partly to escape her embarrassment but also because she wanted to observe the workings of the Revolution firsthand.

Soon after her arrival, as she collected notes for the history of the Revolution she hoped to write, Mary saw Louis XVI, "sitting in a hackney coach… going to meet death." Back in her room that evening, she wrote to Mr. Johnson of seeing "eyes glare through a glass door opposite my chair and bloody hands shook at me…. I am going to bed and for the first time in my life, I cannot put out the candle." As the weeks went on, Edmund Burke's implacable critic began to lose her faith in the brave new world. "The aristocracy of birth is levelled to the ground, only to make room for that of riches," she wrote. By February France and England were at war, and British subjects classified as enemy aliens.

Though many Englishmen were arrested, Mary and a large English colony stayed on. One day in spring, some friends presented her to an attractive American, newly arrived in Paris, Gilbert Imlay. Probably about four years Mary's senior, Imlay, a former officer in the Continental Army, was an explorer and adventurer. He came to France seeking to finance a scheme for seizing Spanish lands in the Mississippi valley. This "natural and unaffected creature," as Mary was later to describe him, was probably the social lion of the moment, for he was also the author of a best-selling novel called *The Emigrants*, a farfetched account of life and love in the American wilderness. He and Mary soon became lovers. They were a seemingly perfect pair. Imlay must have been pleased with his famous catch, and—dear, liberated girl that she was—Mary did not insist upon marriage. Rather the contrary. But fearing that she was in danger as an Englishwoman, he registered her at the American embassy as his wife.

Blood was literally running in the Paris streets now, so Mary settled down by herself in a cottage at Neuilly. Imlay spent his days in town, working out various plans. The Mississippi expedition came to nothing, and he decided to stay in France and go into the import-export business, part of his imports being gunpowder and other war goods run from Scandinavia through the English blockade. In the evenings he would ride out to the cottage. By now it was summer, and Mary, who spent the days writing, would often stroll up the road to meet him, carrying a basket of freshly gathered grapes.

A note she wrote Imlay that summer shows exactly what her feelings for him were: "You can scarcely imagine with what pleasure I anticipate the day when we are to begin almost to live together; and you would smile to hear how many plans of employment I have in my head, now that I am confident that my heart has found peace...." Soon she was pregnant. She and Imlay moved into Paris. He promised to take her to America, where they would settle down on a farm and raise six children. But business called

Imlay to Le Havre, and his stay lengthened ominously into weeks.

Imlay's letters to Mary have not survived, and without them it is hard to gauge what sort of man he was and what he really thought of his adoring mistress. Her biographers like to make him out a cad, a philistine, not half good enough for Mary. Perhaps; yet the two must have had something in common. His novel, unreadable though it is now, shows that he shared her political views, including her feminist ones. He may never have been serious about the farm in America, but he was a miserably long time deciding to leave Mary alone. Though they were separated during the early months of her pregnancy, he finally did bring her to Le Havre, and continued to live with her there until the child was born and for some six months afterward. The baby arrived in May, 1794, a healthy little girl, whom Mary named Fanny after her old friend. Mary was proud that her delivery had been easy and as for Fanny, Mary loved her instantly. "My little Girl," she wrote to a friend, "begins to suck so manfully that her father reckons saucily on her writing the second part of the Rights of Woman." Mary's joy in this child illuminates almost every letter she wrote henceforth.

Fanny's father was the chief recipient of these letters with all the details of the baby's life. To Mary's despair, she and Imlay hardly ever lived together again. A year went by; Imlay was now in London and Mary in France. She offered to break it off, but mysteriously, he could not let go. In the last bitter phase of their involvement, after she had joined him in London at his behest, he even sent her—as "Mrs. Imlay"—on a complicated business errand to the Scandinavian countries. Returning to London, Mary discovered that he was living with another woman. By now half crazy with humiliation, Mary chose a dark night and threw herself in the Thames. She was nearly dead when two rivermen pulled her from the water.

Though this desperate incident was almost the end of Mary, at least it was the end of the Imlay episode. He sent a doctor to care for her, but they rarely met

again. Since Mary had no money, she set about providing for herself and Fanny in the way she knew. The faithful Johnson had already brought out Volume I of her history of the French Revolution. Now she set to work editing and revising her *Letters Written during a Short Residence in Sweden, Norway, and Denmark*, a kind of thoughtful travelogue. The book was well received and widely translated.

And it also revived the memory of Mary Wollstonecraft in the mind of an old acquaintance, William Godwin. As the author of the treatise *Political Justice*, he was now as famous a philosophizing serpent as Mary and was widely admired and hated as a "freethinker." He came to call on Mary. They became friends and then lovers. Early in 1797 Mary was again pregnant. William Godwin was an avowed atheist who had publicly denounced the very institution of marriage. On March 29, 1797, he nevertheless went peaceably to church with Mary and made her his wife.

The Godwins were happy together, however William's theories may have been outraged. He adored his small stepdaughter and took pride in his brilliant wife. Awaiting the birth of her child throughout the summer, Mary worked on a new novel and made plans for a book on "the management of infants"—it would have been the first "Dr. Spock." She expected to have another easy delivery and promised to come downstairs to dinner the day following. But when labor began, on August 30, it proved to be long and agonizing. A daughter, named Mary Wollstonecraft, was born; ten days later, the mother died.

Occasionally, when a gifted writer dies young, one can feel, as in the example of Shelley, that perhaps he had at any rate accomplished his best work. But so recently had Mary come into her full intellectual and emotional growth that her death at the age of thirty-eight is bleak indeed. There is no knowing what Mary might have accomplished now that she enjoyed domestic stability. Perhaps she might have achieved little or nothing further as a writer. But she might have been able to protect her daughters from some part of the sadness that overtook them; for as things turned out, both Fanny and Mary were to sacrifice themselves.

Fanny grew up to be a shy young girl, required to feel grateful for the roof over her head, overshadowed by her prettier half sister, Mary. Godwin in due course married a formidable widow named Mrs. Clairmont, who brought her own daughter into the house—the Claire Clairmont who grew up to become Byron's mistress and the mother of his daughter Allegra. Over the years Godwin turned into a hypocrite and a miser who nevertheless continued to pose as the great liberal of the day. Percy Bysshe Shelley, born the same year that the *Vindication of the Rights of Woman* was published, came to be a devoted admirer of Mary Wollstonecraft's writing. As a young man he therefore came with his wife to call upon Godwin. What he really sought, however, were Mary's daughters—because they were her daughters. First he approached Fanny, but later changed his mind. Mary Godwin was then sixteen, the perfect potential soul mate for a man whose needs for soul mates knew no bounds. They conducted their courtship in the most up-to-the-minute romantic style: beneath a tree near her mother's grave they read aloud to each other from the Vindication. Soon they eloped, having pledged their "troth" in the cemetery. Godwin, the celebrated freethinker, was enraged. To make matters worse, Claire Clairmont had run off to Switzerland with them.

Not long afterward Fanny, too, ran away. She went to an inn in a distant town and drank a fatal dose of laudanum. It has traditionally been said that unrequited love for Shelley drove her to this pass, but there is no evidence one way or the other. One suicide that can more justly be laid at Shelley's door is that of his first wife, which occurred a month after Fanny's and which at any rate left him free to wed his mistress, Mary Godwin. Wife or mistress, she had to endure poverty, ostracism, and Percy's constant infidelities. But now at last her father could, and did, boast to his relations that he was father-in-law to a baronet's son. "Oh, philosophy!" as Mary Godwin Shelley remarked.

If in practice Shelley was merely a womanizer, on paper he was a convinced feminist. He had learned this creed from Mary Wollstonecraft. Through his verse Mary's ideas began to be disseminated. They were one part of that vast tidal wave of political, social, and artistic revolution that arose in the late eighteenth century, the romantic movement. But because of Mary's unconventional way of life, her name fell into disrepute during the nineteenth century, and her book failed to exert its rightful influence on the development of feminism. Emma Willard and other pioneers of the early Victorian period indignantly refused to claim Mary as their forebear. Elizabeth Cady Stanton and Lucretia Mott were mercifully less strait-laced on the subject. In 1889, when Mrs. Stanton and Susan B. Anthony published their *History of Woman Suffrage*, they dedicated the book to Mary. Though Mary Wollstonecraft can in no sense be said to have founded the woman's rights movement, she was, by the late nineteenth century, recognized as its inspiration, and the *Vindication* was vindicated for the highly original work it was, a landmark in the history of society.

From *Horizon, Spring 1972.* © *1972 by Forbes, Inc. Reprinted by permission of American Heritage* magazine, a division of Forbes, Inc.

Catherine the Great
A Personal View

Isabel de Madariaga looks at the personality and achievement
of the controversial Empress of Russia.

Since I first took Catherine seriously as a ruler, some forty years ago, I have grown to like her very much. This is not therefore going to be an exercise in debunking, it is a personal portrait of someone who has become a close friend.

For nearly two hundred years the Empress Catherine II of Russia (1762–96), or Catherine the Great, as she is known, has had a very bad press as a German usurper from a minor ducal family, without any claim to the Russian throne. Women on the throne were an anomaly and it was expected that they would rule through favourites or husbands. But Catherine had blotted her copy book in a more serious way: she had mounted the throne as the result of a military *coup d'etat* in June 1762, over the body of her murdered husband, Peter III, the grandson of Peter the Great. From Catherine's point of view at the time it was a question of 'who whom', as Lenin later put it. Peter was supposed to have been about to repudiate her, disinherit her son and marry his mistress. Catherine's many friends in the army joined in a plot to dethrone Peter and seized power with her full approval and participation. She circumvented the men who helped her to seize the throne in 1762 and was wise enough never to enter into a publicly recognised marriage. She shocked opinion even further by having many publicly acknowledged lovers at a time when virtue

was still demanded of a woman. By modern standards, Catherine was not really promiscuous. She had only twelve well-documented lovers in some forty-four years. But neither Victorian England nor Victorian Russia approved. Alexander Herzen (1812–70), the great Russian revolutionary, who later sought asylum in England, exclaimed in the mid-nineteenth century that 'the history of Catherine the Great cannot be read aloud in the presence of ladies'.

The prejudice was so great that for a long time it prevented an objective study of the events of Catherine's reign, and fostered the assumption that she had achieved nothing. Nineteenth-century historians, often populists or Marxists, viewed her proclamation of the tenets of the French enlightenment as hypocrisy—as did the poet Alexander Pushkin in his young days—because she did nothing to free the serfs. With the coming of the Bolsheviks, the publication of Catherine's official papers ceased almost entirely and study of the class war superseded study of the action of individuals. It is only since the fall of Communism that Russian historians have been freed to undertake fresh documentary research, and to approach their past in an objective spirit. Historians have thus rescued their most impressive and intellectually distinguished ruler from the undeserved neglect she has suffered in

the country she ruled over so successfully for thirty-four years.

Sophia of Anhalt-Zerbst, the name of the girl baptised Catherine on her conversion from Lutheranism to the Orthodox religion, arrived in Russia in 1744, aged fourteen, and was married at sixteen to a seventeen-year-old who failed to consummate the marriage for some years. The reigning Empress Elizabeth, Peter the Great's daughter, was so perturbed at the lack of an heir to the throne that she conveyed a message to Catherine urging her to produce one, if not by her husband, then by someone else, which Catherine duly did, and her son Paul, probably fathered by a courtier known as 'handsome Serge' Saltykov, was born in 1754.

The Empress Elizabeth died in 1762, and Catherine's husband became emperor. He soon showed himself as unsatisfactory as a ruler as he had proved as a husband. It was not so much what he did, but the way in which he did it. His gracelessness and his lack of judgement alienated all the powerful social groups, including his wife for whom he had ceased to have any regard: 'she will squeeze you like a lemon', he had said 'and then she will throw you away'. But Catherine through her lover, the guards officer Grigory Orlov and his four dashing brothers, won over the army to her cause, and by sheer force of personality, many of the high officials as well, even those close to Peter III. Her supporters proclaimed her not as regent for her son Paul, as some had hoped, but as ruler in her own right, as Empress regnant.

What sort of woman was she? By the time she came to power, she had spent eighteen years steering her way through the many pitfalls of the Russian court. During this time she had given birth to one son by a lover, to a daughter, who died, by another lover, Stanislas Poniatowski, and to a second son by her lover Grigory Orlov, born in secret only four months before her *coup*, who was not recognised by Peter III. She had had to manoeuvre between the many factions in the Russian court, her friends had been removed, some disgraced and sent into exile, leaving her at times in considerable solitude. And yet always she had had to share a bed with a totally uncongenial man, who for instance court martialled a rat caught in her bedchamber and executed it. She took refuge from boredom in reading, mainly history, politics, and philosophy, a great deal of French literature and a life of Henri IV of France, who became her model of a king. In this way Catherine accumulated a considerable fund of knowledge of the theory of government, and of comparative politics. She was greatly influenced by Montesquieu's *Esprit des Lois* which became for a while her bedside book and profoundly affected her legislation; she read Voltaire, of course, with whom she began a regular correspondence. When Diderot met with obstacles over the publication of the *Great Encyclopedia* in France, Catherine offered to publish it in Russia. A translation fund she established published works by Voltaire, Rousseau, Mably, *Gulliver's Travels*, Robertson's *History of America*, and in 1778 a translation of Sir William Blackstone's *Commentaries on the Laws of England* (from the French) which exercised a great influence on her political and legal thinking until her death.

Brought up a Lutheran, religion sat very lightly on her. She fulfilled all her Orthodox religious duties punctiliously, was courteous to the Russian hierarchy but gave the Church no access to political institutions, and confiscated its lands. She turned a blind eye to the presence and ac-

tivities of the Old Believers, wound down Orthodox missionary activity among Muslims and pagans and allowed 'reputable' religions to build churches, run their own schools and practise their religion freely though under state inspection of their organisation and finances. In theory, religion was no obstacle to participating in elective local government posts—even for Jews whose number within the borders of Russia increased considerably after the first partition of Poland in 1772. Who knows what she believed in? She would attend all-night services in church but sat at a little table out of sight where she could pass the time with a pack of cards, playing patience.

Catherine was also extremely hardworking. She rose early, read or wrote, copied out her drafts, and discussed them with her advisers. Thousands of sheets of paper covered in her handwriting have survived, and her writings, both political and *belles lettres*, occupy twelve substantial volumes. The most outstanding of them was her *Great Instruction*, published in 1767 in order to lay before an assembly of elected representatives of the nobles, the townspeople, cossacks, tribesmen and state peasants (not the serfs) the general principles on which laws should be codified by this assembly. The *Instruction*, comprising some 650 articles in all, defined the functions of social estates and laid down the means of establishing the rule of law and the welfare of the citizens. Catherine drew on a number of important German and French thinkers of the time, and there is even a suggestion that she may have known about the work of Adam Smith. She was very proud of her compilation, which was published in over twenty-five languages, including English. It was so radical that it was condemned by the Sorbonne in Paris.

From the Italian jurist Cesare Beccaria, Catherine drew her condemnation of torture in judicial proceedings in her *Great Instruction*:

The innocent ought not to be tortured; and in the eye of the law every person is innocent whose crime is not yet proved.

This axiom, which sounds so familiar to an English ear, was completely novel

in eighteenth-century Russia. One cannot say that the Empress succeeded in eliminating torture entirely from Russian legal procedure, but she did succeed in reducing its sphere of operation. It is not unfair to Catherine's predecessors to state that she was the first ruler of Russia to have any sense of legality, of what the rule of law meant. Indeed, there was no university in Russia until 1755, no teaching of jurisprudence except by Germans who taught in Latin. The first professor of Russian law (trained in Glasgow) teaching in Russian was appointed by Catherine II in 1773. As a result Russian officials were prone to override the decisions of judges in favour of what they might regard to be common sense, convenient, or politically desirable.

In a document intended to teach her subjects how to draft laws, Catherine spent some time in defining how laws should be written: in the vernacular, in simple, concise language, bearing in mind that they were written for people of moderate capacities; they should be published as a small book which could be bought as cheaply as the catechism, and which should be used in schools to teach children to read. Napoleon had the same idea.

What is striking about Catherine's *Instruction* is that it formed part of a plan to shake up the political culture of Russia in a dramatic way. It was a pedagogical instrument designed to instruct public opinion in the assembly which was to draft her new code. It was read through in public every month from cover to cover from August 1767 until the Assembly was disbanded in autumn 1768 on the outbreak of war with Turkey. The deputies were thus subjected to a flood of unheard of ideas in what amounted to a speech from the throne.

It is worth pausing for a moment to consider this aspect of Catherine as a ruler. She had a profound understanding of the nature and importance of public opinion, and of the need to mould it. Her correspondence with Voltaire, Diderot, Falconet, Grimm and others, served to promote her interests and to portray her personality and ideas in the most attractive light. Thus the proceedings of the Assembly were public, and accounts of its activities were published in the Moscow and St Petersburg gazettes. No such gathering had been held in Russia since the seventeenth century, nor was one to meet again until after the revolution of 1905. It is a tribute to Catherine's political courage, that a mere five years after seizing the throne, she did not fear that such a gathering might provide a focus for opposition to her rule. Indeed, the sluices were opened for a freedom of speech unheard of in Russia and rendered possible by the fact that the deputies needed only to start their contributions with the words: 'As the Empress says in para xyz of her *Instruction*'.

Much of Catherine's future programme of legislation is to be found in embryo in her *Great Instruction*, and in the documents collected by the Assembly, which provided her with a vast amount of information about the state of her realm. What of the serfs who were not represented? There was of course much information about them available in the form of the murder of landowners and local risings on private estates which had to be put down by troops. Catherine herself was opposed to serfdom and she took some steps to introduce non-servile tenures on imperial estates which proved highly unpopular with the serfs. Chapter XI of her *Instruction* dealt with serfdom and slavery. She showed it to some of her advisers who cut out vast portions. The leading Russian dramatist of the period, A.P. Sumarokov, complained that the nobles would have neither coachman nor cook nor lackey, for they would all run away to better paid jobs, whereas at present the nobles all lived quietly on their estates. Catherine did not agree; she noted in the margin of Sumarokov's comments: 'and have their throats cut from time to time'.

It was only in 1907 that the suppressed portions of Chapter XI were brought to light, so that the Empress's real views were simply unknown to the general public for more than a century. She had, for instance, suggested that serfs should be entitled to purchase their freedom, or that servitude should be limited to a period of six years. Subsequently she stopped up many holes which enabled people to be enserfed, but she did not pursue total emancipation.

Historians have also criticised her for giving away thousands of 'free' peasants to her favourites and public servants, thus enserfing them. Stated bluntly like that of course it sounds terrible, and what actually happened is probably not much better. For, in fact, three-quarters of the peasants she gave away were already serfs on estates acquired in the partitions of Poland. This has been known by historians since 1878, but... shall we say forgotten?

What marks Catherine's approach is the careful planning of a programme of interrelated measures, steadily pursued over a number of years. Local government and the judiciary were remodelled in 1775, with elected participation by nobles, townspeople and state peasants and separation of the new network of courts based on social rank from the administration. Local responsibility for certain welfare functions such as schools, hospitals and almshouses was also established, and a national network of primary and secondary schools, free and co-educational, which even serf children could attend with the permission of their owners. The civil rights of nobles and townspeople were set out in terms which reflect English legal thought in charters issued in 1785. Some of Catherine's work survived until 1864, some until the Bolsheviks in 1917.

Thus far the ruler. What of the woman? After Sergey Saltykov, Catherine found another lover, Count Stanislas Poniatowski, a Polish noble, who came to St Petersburg in the suite of the English ambassador, Sir Charles Hanbury Williams, and may well have introduced Catherine to the pleasures of collecting. Poniatowski was handsome, well bred, cultured, and fell genuinely in love with Catherine, who in turn found a soul mate and an intellectual companion for the first time in her life. In dangerous and sometimes farcical circumstances Catherine conducted her affair and gave birth to their daughter. But a political crisis in 1758 cut short their relationship, and Poniatowski returned to Poland. Love for a handsome guards officer, Grigory Orlov, as well as concern for her own safety led Catherine into a new affair, in which she proved remarkably faithful since it lasted twelve years.

In 1772, kind friends warned Catherine about her lover's infidelities and she dismissed him. Emotionally vulnerable and at a loss, Catherine was also faced with a political crisis: by the winter of 1773, the Pugachev revolt was in full swing, the war against the Ottoman Porte marked time, and her son Paul attained his majority, which might threaten her hold on the throne. At this point her whole emotional life changed gear for good. She summoned to her side Grigory Potemkin, ten years her junior, a man who had reached the rank of Lt General on the battlefields, whom she knew since he had played a minor part in her *coup d'etat*, and who had the authority to impose himself on the armed forces, the imagination and the political acumen to make his way to the top of the political tree, and the energy to sweep all rivals aside. He also offered her total devotion, both as a woman and as his liege lady. (I use this archaic phrase deliberately because it represents how he thought of her to his dying day.) He was a handsome man (though he had lost an eye), imposing, witty and well-educated. Their meeting was explosive, and led to a stormy, passionate and well-documented love affair. Potemkin was conscious that his position was insecure and was very jealous of Catherine's past lovers. He sulked and made scenes, but so great was Catherine's trust in him that it is generally accepted now that she went through a religious ceremony of marriage with him, thus giving him, as her husband, the security he needed. For after barely two years, the passion between them wore out, though the love remained. Catherine needed him as her partner in government, particularly in military affairs, and he loved her and served her unconditionally. They found a way out of their dilemma by separating sex from love: Catherine chose a series of lovers, one after the other, and he chose his mistresses, starting with three of his nieces who became protégées of the Empress and much loved by her. To the surprise of Catherine's public servants and courtiers, Potemkin continued in greater favour than ever, and remained by the Empress as unacknowledged prince consort until his death fifteen years later in 1791.

But there were occasional difficulties with Catherine's lovers. She seems to have been easily bored, and broke with several of them, sending them away to travel abroad or to live in Moscow, well endowed. Some of them deserted her. We cannot tell how important the sexual aspect of this relationship was to her, but what is clear from her letters to others is that there was a strong dose of maternal feeling for them. She valued them as participants in her intellectual and artistic occupations.

As a woman, Catherine was generous, considerate and humane and not at all vindictive. There are endless examples of her servants' love for her. An early riser, she would make up her fire herself in order not to rouse her stoker. My favourite example of her thought for others occurred one day when she entered a room in the Winter Palace where a young soldier, supposedly on guard, was sitting reading at a table. Horrified at being caught off guard, he sprang to his feet. The empress asked him what he was reading and talked for a while with him. A few days later she gave orders to set aside a room and to establish a library for the palace staff. Her easy manners and lack of social pretensions were commented on by all who attended court. When she travelled to the Crimea in 1787, she stopped in many towns on her way to attend receptions and emerged from the crush with her cheeks covered with rouge from kissing the highly made-up bourgeois ladies. Her simplicity of manner is what made working for her pleasurable. She chose her senior advisers—her ministers—well and kept them on for years. Prince A. A. Vyazemsky, to all intents and purposes her Home Secretary and Finance Minister, worked for her from 1764 to 1792, and when he became too ill to continue, her minister of commerce from 1772 to 1792. When she received the news of the death of Potemkin in 1791 she had to be bled, wept for days, and was never the same again. None of her senior public servants was ever exiled or sent to Siberia, so that high office became a safe occupation. She spoke freely to her advisers and welcomed frank speaking to her; she did not dismiss her staff for making mistakes, not even for losing battles, she merely encouraged them to do better next time. This contributed greatly to the stability of the regime and the sense of security and continuity in government.

Catherine loved the theatre and wrote for it herself. 'I cannot see a sheet of blank paper without wanting to write on it.' She wrote short pieces for a satirical journal, and quite a number of plays, 'because I enjoy it'. She was among the first to take an interest in Shakespeare, whose plays she read in German translation. She commented:

> imitations of Shakespeare are very convenient, for since they are neither comedies nor tragedies and have no other rules but tact, but a feeling for what the spectator can bear, I think we can do anything with them.

She tried to imitate Shakespeare in a play called *How to have both the linen and the basket*, based on the *Merry Wives of Windsor*, and also wrote historical plays like 'From the life of Ryurik, an imitation of Shakespeare without the dramatic unities' in which there are many echoes of *Henry IV* parts I and II. She wrote fairy tales for her grandchildren, treatises on conduct, education and bringing up children (I should perhaps mention that children in the Foundling Homes she established were given muesli for breakfast). She issued an *ukaz* recommending the cultivation of potatoes with instructions on how to cook them and potatoes were even served in the palace. She even devised a special garment for babies which could be easily pulled off with one tug of a tape, and sent the pattern to the King of Sweden for his wife.

So far I have shown the side of Catherine that won her many admirers. I must now try to find a few faults. First of all she was vain, vain of her achievements, but also of her role as a woman on the throne who outshone many men as a successful modern and reforming ruler, as a correspondent of leading minds in Paris and Germany, as an art collector. She was proud of the victories of her armies, and determined to assert the equality of Russia—a newcomer—with the other great powers in Europe. She was delighted at the successful dispatch of several Russian Baltic fleets to the Mediterranean in 1769–74. It did indeed astound most European countries, and could not have been achieved without the help of Britain. But her letter to her ambassador in London notifying him of her intention reads almost like that of a gleeful little girl:

> We have aroused the sleeping cat, and the cat is going to attack the mice and you will see what you will see, and people will talk about us and nobody expected us to make such a rumpus ...

The Rules

1. All ranks shall be left outside the doors, similarly hats, and particularly swords.
2. Orders of precedence and haughtiness, and anything of such like which might result from them, shall be left at the doors.
3. Be merry, but neither spoil nor break anything, nor indeed gnaw at anything [a reference to Potemkin who bit his nails.]
4. Be seated, stand or walk as it best pleases you, regardless of others.
5. Speak with moderation and not too loudly, so that others present have not an ear-ache or headache.
6. Argue without anger or passion.
7. Do not sigh or yawn, neither bore nor fatigue others.
8. Agree to partake of any innocent entertainment suggested by others.
9. Eat well of good things, but drink with moderation so that each should be able always to find his legs on leaving these doors.
10. All disputes must stay behind closed doors; and what goes in at one ear should go out of the other before departing through the doors.

If any shall infringe the above, on the evidence of two witnesses, for any crime each guilty party shall drink a glass of cold water, ladies not excepted, and read a page from the 'Telemakhida' out loud.

As she grew older her vanity took on a Russian nationalist flavour with an unpleasant tendency to browbeat her enemies. Her strong nerves enabled her to overcome the anxieties of indecisive campaigns, but during the Ochakov crisis in 1791 she had to be bullied into climbing down by the pressure of Potemkin, more aware than she of the military danger of a Prussian attack on land and of a possible British naval attack in the Baltic, but she was saved from total surrender by the collapse of Pitt's policy in England. There is one aspect of her increasingly brash attitude to other powers which I personally find unforgiveable and that is her treatment of her ex-lover Stanislas Poniatowski as a man, and of Poland as a nation. The destruction of Poland was carried out with a ruthlessness and an undercurrent of raillery which is extremely unpleasant and Catherine's bullying of Stanislas himself was downright cruel. For she could be ruthless in defence of her own position, and the existing political and social structure.

Yet she had an original and creative political mind, and the disciplined temperament of a statesman. To the end of her life she continued to ponder over possible ways of associating elected representatives of the Russian nobility, townspeople and peasantry with a decision-making body in the government of Russia, drawing often on English models. Her attitude to government can be summed up in a remark attributed to her by Potemkin's one-time secretary, V.S. Popov. When he expressed his surprise to her at the blind obedience with which her every order was treated:

She condescended to reply: It is not as easy as you think. In the first place my orders would not be carried out unless they were the kind of orders which could be carried out. You know with what prudence... I act in the promulgation of my laws. I examine the circumstances, I take advice, I consult the enlightened part of the people and this way I find out what sort of effect my law will have. And then when I am already convinced in advance of general approval, then I issue my orders, and have the pleasure of observing what you call blind obedience. And that is the foundation of unlimited power.

FOR FURTHER READING:

Catherine II, *The Correspondence with Voltaire and the Instruction of 1767 in the English Text of 1768*. Edited under the title *Documents of Catherine the Great* by W.F. Reddaway (Cambridge University Press, 1931); Carol S. Leonard, *Reform and Regicide: the Reign of Peter III of Russia* (Indiana University Press, 1992); Isabel de Madariaga, *Russia in the Age of Catherine the Great* (reprint forthcoming, Phoenix Press, January 2002); Isabel de Madariaga, *Catherine the Great: A Short History* (Yale University Press, 1991); Isabel de Madariaga, *Politics and Culture in Eighteenth Century Russia* (Longmans, 1998); T. Alexander, *Catherine the Great—Life and Legend* (Oxford University Press, 1989); Simon Sebag Montefiore, *Prince of Princes, The Life of Potemkin* (Weidenfeld and Nicolson, 2001).

Isabel de Madariaga, FBA, FRHistSoc is Professor Emerita of Russian Studies, at the School of Slavonic and East European Studies, UCL.

Napoleon the Kingmaker

With his own elaborate imperial court, with his family ensconced on thrones across the continent, and with his overthrow of several historic republics, Napoleon brought Europe to a pinnacle of monarchism, argues **Philip Mansel.**

Thomas Rowlandson had presented a forthright contrast between liberty in Hanoverian Britain and Jacobin France in the early 1790s. Though Napoleon hid some of the anarchy beneath the restored trappings of monarchy, few argued that the ills Rowlandson had pointed to were alleviated under the Empire.

The period after 1789 has been so often labelled an age of revolution that its character as an apogee of monarchy has been ignored. Yet, unlike those of 1830 and 1848, the revolution of 1789 inspired more revulsion than imitation abroad. From Naples to St Petersburg rulers previously interested in reforms reverted to conservatism. The Habsburg monarchy, under Joseph II in the vanguard of Enlightenment, became a citadel of censorship and repression: in 1798 a Viennese crowd attacked the house of the first ambassador from the French Republic simply for flying the Tricolour. England was swept by Loyalist movements convinced of the truth of Thomas Rowlandson's famous cartoon of 1792, *The Contrast*, which depicted 'British Liberty' above the caption 'National Prosperity and Happiness', in con-

trast to the figure of 'French Liberty' representing 'National and Private Ruin' and 'Misery'.

Russia provides the clearest example of the increase in authoritarian monarchy. An emphasis on discipline and order replaced Catherine's efforts to promote local initiative and participation. In 1796–97, in the first year of Paul I's reign, according to one of his secretaries, he issued 48,000 orders, rules and laws. The new Tsar also initiated the return to grandeur which was a feature of nineteenth century courts, after the fashion for such royal retreats as the Hermitage, the Trianon, and Joseph II's pavilion in the Augarten. On May 4th, 1797, the imperial ambassador Count Cobenzl wrote that Paul I had multiplied:

… so far as it has been possible the occasions for grand etiquette and representation on the throne. It is unbelievable to what degree Paul I loves great ceremonies, the importance which he attaches to them and the time which he employs for them.

No mere brushing of the lips, but full formal kissing of the imperial hand, was demanded from his officials. The central moment of his day, whatever the temperature, was the guard parade. It was at once an endurance test, the chief ceremony of state and a means by which Paul I exerted direct control over his officers and his empire. During his reign three regiments and his own 2,400 'Gatchina troops' were added to the Imperial Guard. According to his biographer Roderick McGrew, Paul 'pointed society, with the state in the vanguard, towards a severely hierarchical and essentially militarised mode of organisation'.

Thus when Bonaparte seized power in 1799, while much of Europe had been conquered by the armies of the French Republic, the powers united against it in the Second Coalition were more monarchical and conservative than before. Earlier than is generally thought, the First Consul Bonaparte aligned himself with this monarchical trend, acquiring in succession a guard (1799), a palace (1800), court receptions and costumes (1800–02), a household (1802–04), a dynasty (1804), finally a nobility (1808).

By January 3rd, 1800, the Garde des Consuls, created in November 1799, numbered 2,089—more than Louis XVI's Garde Constitutionelle of 1792. From the beginning it was an elitist unit with taller men, more splendid uniforms, and privileges of pay and rank over line units. On February 10th, 1800, escorted by his guard, Bonaparte moved into the Tuileries palace. He soon established what his architect Pierre Fontaine called 'the magnificence due to his rank'. The weekly, later monthly, reviews which Bonaparte held in the Tuileries courtyard, riding a white horse which had once belonged to Louis XVI, inspired widespread admiration, not least from Paul I. According to one English visitor 'their presence alone maintains public tranquility and causes a sensation'. An Austrian later called such a review 'the finest military spectacle it is possible to see'. In the autumn of 1800, as he withdrew from the Second Coalition, Paul I suggested that Bonaparte make the throne of France hereditary in his family.

The Hofburg, rather than Versailles, was the model for the regular receptions which Bonaparte began to hold in the Tuileries, and after the autumn of 1802 at St Cloud. Rank at the French court was now based on service to the state rather than noble birth, and was revealed by space not time; by which room an officer or official could enter in the state apartments, rather than what time a courtier could enter the king's bedroom. Officers down to the rank of captain were admitted into the fourth room before the Salle des Consuls, field officers into the third, generals into the second, ambassadors into the first. The English traveller, J.G. Lemaistre, who attended one of these receptions, wrote on March 7th, 1802: 'persons used to courts all agree that the audience of the First Consul is one of the most splendid things of the kind in Europe'. Bonaparte both employed 'all the requisites of show, parade, form and etiquette', and received 'flattery and cringing attention'.

Bonaparte's costume, as well as his guard and his receptions, revealed his monarchical ambitions. Heavily embroidered official uniforms were created in December 1799 for the consuls and ministers, and in May 1800 for prefects and senators. At a reception in the Tuileries after Bonaparte's review of the guard in March 1802, J.G. Lemaistre admired his 'grand costume of scarlet velvet richly embroidered with gold' and 'the handsome uniforms and commanding figures of the soldiery… the consular guards are the handsomest men I ever saw, scarcely any are less than six feet high'. He also wrote of foreign visitors, 'everyone not in uniform is in the full dress of the old court'.

For Bonaparte's court was already in some ways more old-fashioned than other courts. 'The full dress of the old court', which was imposed at the receptions for foreigners and Frenchmen without official positions, was more common in 1802 than it would be after 1814 under the Restoration. Foreigners bought their court dress in Paris, since elsewhere on the Continent it had, with a few exceptions, been abandoned. In 1800, in a gesture revealing desire at once for trade, splendour and peace, the city of Lyon had presented the First Consul with a cherry velvet *habit à la française*, embroidered with olive branches in gold and silver thread. Bonaparte wore this costume in preference to his official First Consul's uniform at the Te Deum for the signature of the Concordat with the pope at Nôtre Dame on April 18th, 1802, and subsequently on other state occasions. He later devised a special lace and velvet court costume for himself, *the petit costume de l'Empereur*, such as no other monarch possessed. Costume was an instrument of power. When a group of men dared visit the Second Consul Cambacérès, future Archichancelier de l'Empire, in black tail coats, he asked: 'Are you in mourning? I would like to express my sympathy for the loss you have suffered'.

The proclamation of the empire in May 1804, the establishment of the households of the Emperor, the Empress and the Imperial Family in July, the coronation by the pope in December of that year, were confirmations of an existing monarchical reality. From the start members of the old nobility—Segur, Talleyrand, Rohan, La Rochefoucauld—were among the court officials, as they had been among the first government officials nominated in 1800.

Napoleon never wavered on such gains of the Revolution as equality before the law, religious toleration, the confiscation and sale of ecclesiastical property, and careers open to talents (although between 1805 and 1814 the proportion of non-nobles in court office fell by half). However, at the same time as he extended French territory by force of arms, Napoleon extended the principle of monarchy by imperial decree. He personally organised the destruction of the last city states in Europe. Already in 1797, after a thousand years, Venetian independence had been abolished on his orders; Genoa also lost its independence forever in 1805, when the Ligurian Republic was annexed to the French Empire. In 1805, when Napoleon crowned himself king in Milan cathedral, the Italian Republic became the Kingdom of Italy with its own viceroy, Eugène de Beauharnais, its own court and nobility. One of the best surviving examples of a Na-

The Treaty of Tilsit, signed on July 7th, 1807, confirmed Napoleon's mastery of Europe, following the diplomatic wooing of Tsar Alexander I (centre) and humiliation of Queen Louise and King Frederick William III of Prussia.

poleonic palace interior can be seen in Venice, in what is now the Museo Correr on the Piazza San Marco: from 1807 to 1814 it served as one of Napoleon's palaces as King of Italy. In 1805 another ancient urban republic, Dubrovnik, which had recently experienced a commercial renaissance, was also abolished and annexed to the Kingdom of Italy.

The same year the Republic of Lucca—a free city since the twelfth century—became a principality under Napoleon's brother-in-law Felix Baciocchi, who was crowned in pomp in Lucca cathedral on July 14th, 1805. In 1806, acting as self-appointed overlord of Europe, Napoleon transformed the Batavian Republic, one of the bastions of European bourgeois life, into the Kingdom of Holland, under his brother Louis-Napoleon. Despite murmurs from the citizens, the great symbol of seventeenth-century urban prosperity and independence, the Town Hall of Amsterdam, became a Royal Palace, as it still is; one of the building's attractions was that the square in front could contain 5,000 soldiers to subdue any potential popular disturbance. Meanwhile, King Louis-Napoleon introduced court costumes for the first time into the Netherlands: 'the intention seems to be to compensate them for never having worn embroidery in this country' wrote Stanislas de Girardin, a chamberlain of Napoleon.

In 1806, Napoleon transformed another great commercial city, Frankfurt, self-governing since the twelfth century, into the capital of a Grand Duchy under the last Archbishop Elector of Mainz, whom Napoleon had appointed Prince Primate of the Confederation of the Rhine. His heir was Eugene de Beauharnais, so that the expected second son of Napoleon I could become King of Italy. The same year, again acting as self-appointed overlord of Europe, the Emperor of the French elevated his allies, the rulers

of Bavaria, Württemberg and Saxony, to the rank of King, and the rulers of Baden and Hesse-Darmstadt to that of Grand Duke. Absorbing free cities, and independent ecclesiastical and noble territories, these monarchs enjoyed more power during and after the Napoleonic era than they had under the Holy Roman Empire. Further extensions of monarchy occurred when the Septinsular republic of the Ionian islands, established by the Second Coalition in 1799, was annexed to the French Empire in 1807, as were the free cities of Hamburg, Lubeck and Bremen in 1810.

Foreign conquests not only helped Napoleon extend monarchy in Europe but also helped him strengthen monarchy within his empire. Both the territorial titles of the *noblesse d'empire* created in 1808, and the domains and revenues assigned with them, were based on locations outside France. Hugues Maret, the Emperor's trusted Ministre secrétaire d'Etat, for example, became Duke of Bassano in northern Italy, while Joseph Fouché, Minister of Police, became Duke of Otranto in the Kingdom of Naples. In 1810, Napoleon married the Archduchess Marie Louise, the last of the nine marriages—to the Houses of Bavaria (twice), Baden, Württemberg, Hohenzollern-Sigmaringen, Salm-Salm, von der Leyen and Arenberg— by which he connected members of his family, his marshals or their relations, with dynastic Europe.

The imperial household, rather than the Senate, the Corps Legislatif and the Conseil d'Etat, became the power-centre of the state, the *Etiquette du Palais Impérial* a clearer guide to the power structure than the written constitution. The Emperor's *lever* and *coucher* became critical moments, as Louis XVI's had not been, used by ambitious courtiers, such as the chamberlain Stanislas de Girardin (who was ultimately successful), to restate their candidacy for a prefecture. In 1810 dukes obtained the *entrée* to the throneroom, while presidents of sections in the Council of State lost it. Count Regnault de Saint Jean d'Angély, Secretary of State of the Imperial Family, wrote to Cardinal Fesch on October 4th, 1810:

> … the ministers and grand officers of the Empire are also part of the Household of the emperor… This practice is consistent with the practice of the former French monarchy and the current practice of the other courts of Europe.

By September 1813 so many chamberlains were serving as officers in the army or prefects in the *departements* that not enough were available for duty at court. In addition the Emperor used his ADCs to check and control the power and patronage of the Minister of War. Ultra-monarchical etiquette was used to assert the Emperor's superiority over the Senate, the Corps Legislatif and the city of Paris—even, to the Representatives' fury, during the Hundred Days. Echoing many Parisians, Madame de Boigne wrote of Napoleon that she had never seen a monarch treat the public so cavalierly—by his failure to salute or bow to his subjects. Stendhal, who often attended court between 1810 and 1814 as 'inspector of the furniture and buildings of the crown', wrote in 1818 of

> … this court devoured with ambition [whose] pestilential air… totally corrupted Napoleon and exalted his armour propre to the state of a disease… he was on the point of making Europe one vast monarchy.

Indeed by 1812, Napoleon owned forty-four palaces, from Rome to Amsterdam, more than any other monarch; when the restoration begun in 1808 had been completed, he was also planning to use Versailles, which he inspected several times. As one of his secretaries Baron Meneval wrote, he saw himself as 'the pillar of royalty in Europe'. On January 18th, 1813, he wrote to his brother Jerome that his enemies, by appealing to popular feeling, represented 'upheavals and revolutions… pernicious doctrines.'

In Napoleon's opinion his fellow monarchs were traitors to 'their own cause' when in 1813 they began to desert the French Empire, or in 1814 refused to accept his territorial terms for peace. However, like the Kaiser in 1914, he over-estimated their commitment to authoritarian monarchy. Most monarchs admired Napoleon's genius, his skill at taming the Revolution, the excellence of his guard and army, the splendour of his court and palaces. They were ready to imitate Napoleonic models in those domains and to travel long distances to pay him court at Erfurt in 1808, Paris in 1809 and Dresden in 1812. In 1811 Metternich, a particular admirer of Napoleonic autocracy, thought of using French troops to suppress the Hungarian constitution. In 1813 both the King of Prussia and the Emperor of Austria dreaded war and hesitated to appeal to popular nationalism.

However, most monarchs feared Napoleonic expansion more than they admired Napoleonic autocracy. Moreover, there was a monarchical alternative to Napoleon I. In Vienna, Saint

Petersburg and London there flourished what Count S. Uvarov, future minister of education in Russia, but long resident in Vienna, called 'that sort of open conspiracy… that great war machine… the secret alliance of European opinion against the France of the time'. He was referring to networks of dedicated opponents of French expansion, united by feelings of European solidarity. They included the great writer Madame de Stael; Baron von Stein the Prussian reformer; Baron von Armfelt, a confidante of Alexander I; Count Pozzo di Borgo, one of his ADCs and the oldest and most implacable enemy of Napoleon since their youth on the island of Corsica; General Moreau, Napoleon's rival of 1800–04; and in Austrian service the great publicist, later called 'the Secretary of Europe', Friedrich von Gentz. They helped push Austria to attack the Napoleonic Empire in 1809, the Tsar to maintain resistance in 1812, and Bernadotte to join, that year, what Madame de Stael called 'the European cause.'

Some of these enemies of Napoleon had personal connections with the Bourbon emigre government which, from 1798 if not before, both the British and Russian governments had kept as a reserve card in their plans for redrawing the map of Europe. As Pitt had told the House of Commons in 1800, the British government considered: 'the Restoration of the French monarchy… as a most desirable object because I think it would afford the strongest and best security to this country and to Europe'—although it was never a *sine qua non* of peace.

The reappearance of the Bourbon dynasty on the European stage owed less to respect for its dynastic rights than to its commitment to France's traditional frontiers. This renunciation of territorial expansion, first evident at the Treaty of Aix-la-Chapelle in 1748, was maintained throughout the reign of Louis XVI (Vergennes wrote to Louis XVI in 1777, 'France as it is now constituted should far more fear than desire additional territory') and was repeatedly asserted in Louis XVIII's proclamations and letters. Even Napoleon, who continued to insist on retaining Antwerp and the 'natural frontiers', called a return to the 'old frontiers' 'inseparable from the reestablishment of the Bourbons'. This was the principal reason why Britain supported the Bourbons with money, asylum for Louis XVIII after 1807, assistance in distributing his proclamations in France and active encouragement for his nephew the Duc d'Angouleme behind British lines in south-west France in March 1814.

Like both Catherine II and Paul I, Tsar Alexander I remained more sympathetic to the Bourbon cause than is generally believed. His court, like the Swedish, went into mourning for the Bourbon prince, the Duc d'Enghien, executed on Napoleon's orders in 1804, and refused to recognise Napoleon's imperial title until 1807. Although opposed to fighting a war for the sole object of the restoration of the King of France, in 1805 he considered the restoration of a Bourbon with a constitution 'highly desirable'. Throughout the years of peace with Napoleon after the Treaty of Tilsit in 1807, the Russian government continued diplomatic contacts with, and paid a subsidy to, Louis XVIII.

In a private audience in May 1813, Alexander I told the Comte de La Ferronays, a representative of Louis XVIII, that he was prepared to consider supporting a Restoration, once allied armies had crossed the Rhine: 'Let us let circumstances do the work. I know better than anyone, believe me, that the re-establishment of legitimacy is the only base on which one can establish the peace and tranquility of Europe'. To Louis XVIII he wrote 'we need patience, circumspection and the greatest secrecy'.

Pozzo di Borgo was one of several royalist ADCs of the Tsar at allied headquarters from January to June 1814. In April, assisted by the growth of anti-Napoleonic feeling in France, and the Tsar's secret inclination, Pozzo insisted on the restoration of the Bourbons and Napoleon's abdication. It may have been Pozzo who suggested Elba, an island he knew well, as Napoleon's compensation.

As the Bourbons had found during their emigration, so Napoleon learnt in 1814: territorial interests mattered more than blood connections to what Marshal Bernadotte called 'the family of kings'. To Napoleon's surprise, after 1814 Francis I of Austria showed no more support for the dynastic interests of his grandson the King of Rome than the Bourbons of Spain, Naples or Parma had done, after 1793, for those of their French cousins. Francis I wrote to Metternich of Napoleon's exile to Elba (formerly subject to his brother the Grand Duke Ferdinand III of Tuscany);

> The island of Elba does not please me, for it is a loss to Tuscany; they give to others what belongs to my family, which cannot be allowed in future, and Napoleon remains too near to France and Europe.

The Empress Marie Louise was more loyal, but concerned above all to gain Parma as an independent sovereignty for herself: *'Parme ou rien est ma devise'*. Hence her switch of loyalties from husband to father in autumn 1814.

Napoleon I had hoped to link the sense of solidarity of the monarchs of Europe to the French Empire. Instead it had been turned against the Empire in the European coalition of 1813–15. From Moscow to London, consciously rivalling the monuments of the Napoleonic Empire, monarchs built triumphal arches, temples of victory and war memorials celebrating their victory over Napoleon. The picture by Peter Krafft of 'The Commander-in-Chief Prince Schwarzenberg presenting to Emperor Franz I, Emperor Alexander I and King Frederick William III captured French troops and standards after the Battle of Leipzig, October 18th, 1813', the Battle of the Nations which, more than Waterloo, marked the end of the Napoleonic Empire, is the finest memorial to 'Coalition Europe'. It was painted in 1817 for the Military Invalids Hospital of Vienna as a dynastic, artistic, humanitarian and European riposte to the similar picture by Baron Gerard, once on the ceiling of the hall of the Council of State in the Tuileries: 'Count Rapp presenting the banners of the defeated Russian Imperial Guard to Napoleon I on the battlefield of Austerlitz, December 2nd, 1805'. Fewer dead and wounded are depicted; three monarchs instead of one are shown; and they are humbly dismounted rather than, like Napoleon, portrayed on horseback.

After 1815 the monarchies of Europe owed relatively little, apart from a reinforced sense of Francophobia, to the Napoleonic Empire and epoch. The Napoleonic legend was a legend, not a political reality. None of Napoleon's innumerable changes to the map of Europe lasted, except for certain frontiers created for some of his German allies. All Napoleonic constitutions were abolished. Rather than continuing the military autocratic style and regime of Napoleon, many monarchs adopted liberal constitutions, based on the 1814 charter of Louis XVIII. By 1821 such constitutions had spread across half of the German Confederation; by 1848 to Spain, Piedmont and Prussia. Napoleon's most immediately important legacy was neither his guard, nor his court, nor his nobility, the majority of whom rallied to his successors, nor even perhaps the Code Napoleon, but his dynasty.

After 1815, the Bonapartes continued to function as a dynasty. Indeed, because of the plebiscites of 1804 and 1815 endorsing Napoleon I, they considered themselves, as Joseph Bonaparte wrote to La Fayette in 1830, more legitimate than the Bourbons. The son of Napoleon's admirer Lady Holland found in Rome in 1828 that Jerome-Napoleon, former King of Westphalia, kept 'the best mounted and most princely looking establishment' in the city, and 'will not go out where he is not received as a king'. As they had done at the Tuileries, in Rome the Bonapartes quarrelled over who had the right to a royal armchair at Madame Mére's family dinners; in the end she stopped giving them.

In addition to its internal French political programme of plebiscites and strong government, the dynasty was committed, in Europe, to reversing the two main legacies of the European coalition: the territorial settlement of 1814–15 and the Congress system. This was one reason for Louis-Napoleon's popularity and rise to power in 1848. It would be Napoleon III who, by the wars into which he led the French Empire against Russia in 1854, Austria in 1859 and Prussia in 1870, destroyed the alliance between the monarchs of Europe which had overthrown his uncle.

FOR FURTHER READING:

Louis Bergeron, *L'Episode Napoléonien* (Editions du Seuil, 1972); Charles J. Esdaile, *The Wars of Napoleon* (Longman, 1995); Pierre-Francois-Léonard Fontaine, *Journal*, 2 vols, Ecole Nationale Superieure des eaux-Arts, 1987; Paul W. Schroeder, *The Transformation of European Politics* 1763–1848 (Oxford University Press, 1994).

Philip Mansel's *latest book is* Constantinople: City of the World's Desire 1453–1924 *(Penguin 1997). He is currently working on a history of Paris between 1814 and 1848. He is editor of* The Court Historian, *newsletter of the Society for Court Studies.*

This article first appeared in *History Today*, March 1998, pp. 39-46. © 1998 by History Today, Ltd. Reprinted by permission.

UNIT 3

Industry, Ideology, Nationalism, and Imperialism: The Nineteenth Century

Unit Selections

15. **Arkwright: Cotton King or Spin Doctor?** Karen Fisk
16. **The Origins of Prussian Militarism**, Peter H. Wilson
17. **Slavery and the British**, James Walvin
18. **Scrooge and Albert: Christmas in the 1840s**, Christine Lalumia
19. **Nation-Building in 19th-Century Italy: The Case of Francesco Crispi**, Christopher Duggan
20. **Not So Saintly?** David van Biema
21. **Sweep Them Off the Streets**, John Marriott
22. **The Hunt for Jack the Ripper**, William D. Rubinstein
23. **Destroyers and Preservers: Big Game in the Victorian Empire**, Harriet Ritvo

Key Points to Consider

- What were Richard Arkwright's principal contributions to the industrialization of England?

- What were the first reasons given for the military victories of Prussia? What may be the real reasons?

- What were the economic and social reasons for the slave trade?

- Why did Christmas become so important in nineteenth century Britain? Why was Charles Dickens important for Christmas celebrations?

- Why is Francesco Crispi important for Italy? How did his ideas influence later ideas?

- Why is the canonization of Pope Pius IX so controversial?

- How did views change over the centuries in regard to the poor?

- Why did Jack the Ripper draw so much attention in London?

- How did Victorian views change in regard to animals?

 **Links: www.dushkin.com/online/**
These sites are annotated in the World Wide Web pages.

The Victorian Web
   http://www.victorianweb.org/victorian/victov.html
Historical U.S. Census Data Browser
   http://fisher.lib.virginia.edu/census/
Society for Economic Anthropology Homepage
   http://nautarch.tamu.edu/anth/sea/

The early years of the nineteenth century were marked by two powerful opposite forces. The French Revolution and industrialization proved the impetus for political, economic, and social change in Western civilization. The ideals of the French Revolution remained alive in France and inspired nationalistic movements in other parts of Europe. Industrialization brought material progress for millions, particularly the burgeoning middle class, but often at the expense of the unskilled workers who were victims of low wages and an impersonal factory system. Shifting demographic patterns created additional pressures for change. It had taken all of European history to reach a population of 180 million in 1800. In the nineteenth century, the European population doubled, causing major migrations on the continent from the countryside to the city, and sending waves of emigrants to America, Australia, and elsewhere. By 1919 about 200 million Europeans had migrated.

But forces of continuity also lingered on. Notwithstanding the impact of industrialism, much of Europe remained agrarian, dependent upon peasant labor. Christianity remained the dominant religion and the institution of monarchy reattained the loyalty of those who wanted to preserve an orderly society. In addition, millions of Europeans, having lived through the crises of the French Revolution and Napoleonic eras, were willing to embrace even the most repressive, reactionary regimes if they could guarantee peace and stability.

The interaction of tradition and change raised vital new issues and generated conflicts in politics and thought. By necessity the terms of political dialogue were redefined. The century was an age of ideologies: conservatism, with is distrust of untested innovations and its deep commitment to order and traditions; liberalism, with its faith in reason, technique, and progress; various forms of socialism, from revolutionary to utopian, each with its promise of equality and economic justice for the working class; and nationalism, with its stirring demand, at the same time unifying and divisive, that the nationalities of the world should be autonomous. Even Darwinism was misappropriated for political purposes. Transformed into Social Darwinism, it was used to justify the domination of Western nations over their colonies. Popular misconceptions of evolution reinforced prevailing notions of male supremacy.

In sum, the nineteenth century, for those who enjoyed economic and political status, was the "Golden Age" of human progress. For the rest, many of whom shared the materialist outlook of their "betters," it was a time of struggle to attain their fair share.

Several articles in this unit explore the dynamics of change in the nineteenth century. Economic forces and related political ideologies are covered in "Arkwright: Cotton King or Spin Doctor?" "Slavery and the British," "Nation-Building in 19th-Century Italy: The Case of Francesco Crispi," and "The Origins of Prussian Militarism." Middle-class values, which reached their heights in this century, are treated from diverse perspectives in "Scrooge and Albert: Christmas in the 1840s," "Sweep Them Off the Streets," and "The Hunt for Jack the Ripper." Finally, making imperialism compatible with conservation is surveyed in "Destroyers and Preservers: Big Game in the Victorian Empire."

Arkwright: Cotton King or Spin Doctor?

Was Richard Arkwright really the mechanical genius of the Industrial Revolution?
Karen Fisk *questions his record as Britain's first cotton tycoon.*

Sir Richard Arkwright (1723–92) is usually credited with revolutionising the technical basis of cotton production between 1768 and 1792, transforming it from a cottage industry to one of worldwide proportions. Apart from developing machinery to do the work, he is credited with creating the factory system, earning him such titles as a 'founding father' of the Industrial Revolution and the 'father of the factory system'. Undoubtedly an inspirational figure of the eighteenth century, he emerged from a working-class background and achieved immense wealth. However, closer scrutiny of the evidence raises uncertainties about the traditionally accepted view of Arkwright, the mechanical genius, and his technical achievements.

Indeed, it appears that Arkwright's first patent was obtained by simply improving existing spinning frames. Having trained as a barber, Arkwright was unlikely to have possessed the technical skills required to produce these machines himself. It therefore seems curious that Arkwright achieved such recognition for the invention, which proved a catalyst to all the events that followed. So how and why has Arkwright been made the Cotton King?

Until the early eighteenth century, most of Britain's cloth was made from wool in areas where there were both sheep and ample water for the various processes, such as the West Country, Yorkshire and Lancashire; with most of the manufacture being carried out in the workers' homes. The system had lasted for centuries, but in 1702 a major turning point occurred when Thomas Cotchett, an elderly barrister, together with the engineer George Sorocold, built a silk mill powered by a waterwheel on the Derwent at Derby. This mill has good claim to the title of being the first factory, in the sense that it was a single establishment with complex machinery, a source of power, and accommodation for a number of workers. Sir Thomas Lombe, a wealthy silk merchant of Norwich and London, made consider-

able additions to Cotchett's mill in 1717, which established the pattern of textile factories. The transformation within and around Derbyshire that this heralded was unique, not only for its radical repercussions for textile production and business, but in a wider sense that was to alter the course of modern society.

Later inventions, such as the 'Flying Shuttle' by John Kaye of Bury in 1733, further promoted the textile industry to new heights. The demand for yarn became so greatly increased that it became impossible to meet it merely by hand labour. A machine for carding cotton had been introduced into Lancashire in 1760, and, in 1761, the Society for the Encouragement of Arts and Manufactures offered a price of £50 for a successful spinning machine. Until 1767, spinning continued to be wholly by the old-fashioned jersey wheel. It was later in this year that James Hargreaves completed and patented the 'Spinning Jenny'. The jenny was, however, applicable only to the spinning of cotton for weft, being unable to give the yarn the degree of strength required in the longitudinal threads, or warp.

At his uncle's insistence, the highly-motivated Arkwright received more education than was customary for someone of his class. Eager to improve his lot of life, Arkwright made the most of his opportunities and soon realised that there was a fortune to be made, quite apart from a prize to be won, from designing an efficient spinning machine.

In 1768 Arkwright employed John Kaye, a clockmaker from Warrington, to assist in the construction of wooden models in an attempt to produce a workable machine. Arkwright was not alone in taking up the challenge. Lewis Paul and John Wyatt conducted many experiments between 1736 and 1745 and probably came closest in their attempts to invent a spinning machine, while Thomas Highs, a reedmaker at Leigh, was another who unsuccessfully attempted to design such a machine. Highs had also employed John Kaye to help him and it seems possible

COURTESY OF THE MUSEUM OF THE LANCASHIRE TEXTILE INDUSTRY.

A full-size water frame worked by Cromford Mill. The site was chosen, stated Arkwright in 1780, as `a place affording a remarkable fine Stream of Water... in a Country very full of inhabitants vast numbers of whom & small Children are constantly Employed in the Works'.

that Kaye copied some of Highs' ideas which he conveyed to Arkwright. Most of these early designs were similar and it was simply a matter of time before one person made a breakthrough in achieving the correct specifications. Arkwright may simply have modified certain components of Highs' basic attempt in achieving this goal.

Besides requiring considerable technical assistance, Arkwright could not have continued his spinning venture without adequate financial support. His business sense told him that his invention had more than just local potential, as it could be used in power-driven factories. However, a factory required much more capital than Arkwright possessed. His frame still needed perfecting and considerable investment would be necessary to make his venture a commercial success. Furthermore, to protect his ideas from being stolen and to ensure profit, he needed to take out a patent. Where a patent was granted, the holder alone had full entitlement to it for fourteen years. The machines could either be sold, or the holder could sell licences allowing other manufactures to use his invention. Anybody using the design without a licence or agreement was liable to prosecution. But patents themselves were costly to take out as legal fees had to be met and, again, Arkwright could not afford to patent his invention without further financial backing which he set about raising.

John Smalley, a publican and paint merchant of Preston, and David Thornley, a merchant of Liverpool, became Arkwright's first backers. Soon after the expansion of the partnership Thornley died, which is the reason his name rarely appears in

history books. John Smalley's name appears as a witness to Arkwright's first patent declaration. Shortly afterwards, however, the three associates must have run into difficulties as the partnership was enlarged to include Samuel Need and Jedediah Strutt. Both Need and Strutt had extensive connections with the textile industry. Need was probably the wealthiest hosier in Nottingham, while Strutt had established a flourishing hosiery trade centred in Derby. Together they masterminded the spinning project, ensuring that it became a profitable enterprise.

What is clear from this summary of Arkwright's quest to invent a successful spinning machine is that, in contrast to the traditional view of a struggling lone inventor and genius, the highly ambitious young man sought and received considerable assistance in achieving his goal. The new associates began their venture in a Nottingham Mill, which was driven by horses as had been envisaged in the patent. However, this method soon became too expensive, as well as unfeasible for production on a large scale. Arkwright resolved to use waterpower, an initiative he is often credited with pioneering but which had in fact already proved successful, notably in the Cotchett and Sorocold mill of 1702 and Thomas Lombe's Derby silk mill of 1717. The trials of the new spinning frame showed sufficient promise for the partners to take the momentous decision to erect a mill powered by a waterwheel and in 1771 a site at Cromford, near Matlock, was leased.

Arkwright took out a second patent for a series of adaptions and inventions to augment his existing machinery in 1775. The whole process of yarn manufacture, including carding, drawing,

COURTESY OF THE HISTORY TODAY ARCHIVES.

Women's work, factory style: carding, drawing and roving—an engraving from *Cotton Manufacture in Great Britain* **by Edward Baines.**

rolling and spinning, was now performed by a beautifully arranged succession of operations on one machine. The grant of this further patent removed every obstacle to providing an efficient supply of yarn to meet demand. Whatever the future held for Arkwright, the prosperity of cotton manufacture was guaranteed.

As the rapid increase of power-driven machines produced yarn more cheaply, English merchants were able to capture a large proportion of the world market for cotton cloth. More mills were established in England and Scotland to meet the demand, in turn creating greater demands for wood, iron, leather, bricks, timber and so on needed to make the machines and mills and the fuel to run them. Of course, other developments in iron manufacture and steam engine design contributed, but the expanding cotton industry stimulated technological advances in most areas. For example, expanding coal production enabled mines to meet the demands of the new coke furnaces used for smelting. The introduction in 1776 of the steam pumping-engines of James Watt enabled colliery owners to mine deeper coal seams. Iron was the master material of the early Industrial Revolution. Developments in Shropshire in 1709 by Abraham Darby introduced pig- and cast-iron, while Henry Colt established the manufacture of wrought iron. Between 1740 and 1850, iron produced in Britain alone rose from 17,000 to 1.4 million tons annually.

The meteoric development of the textile industry is still, however, the most dramatic story of the Industrial Revolution. In a few decades, the textile mills became the biggest employer of labour in Britain. All this, happening within a period of about fifty years, created great changes within the lifetime of a single individual. In Derbyshire, people who had been self-employed, or who had been out-workers in their own home, found themselves living in new villages such as Cromford, and working in large mills owned by a single employer. A new industrial community was developed, which was to change the face of society for ever.

Unexpected difficulties soon arose for Arkwright, for in the late 1770s he found he was running short of water to power his mill. When he first moved to Cromford, probably only the water frames (the spinning frame driven by water), and some of the winding frames were power-driven. As one after another of the preparatory stages was mechanised, hand processes were replaced by systems needing power. The site of the mill was also enlarged and this, too, meant more energy would have been required. Attempts were made to combat the water problem. The level of the pond supplying the mill was raised, generating a higher fall of water. In the meantime, Arkwright investigated the possibility of using steam power which had already proved successful in other industries at that time.

Evidence indicates that a steam engine was used to drive spinning machines at Papplewick near Nottingham in 1788. The majority of written accounts state that Papplewick was the first textile factory to use steam power for spinning cotton. The introduction in 1712 of the steam pump invented by Thomas Newcomen, later to be refined by James Watt in 1776, was first used in collieries to put out water. Water power, meanwhile, was in use at Derby's silk mill long before Arkwright was even born. Again we must ask why Arkwright has been granted such individual recognition for his role in the textile revolution.

Without a business-like approach and certain leadership qualities, Arkwright could not have made his immense fortune. He did not, however, have an easy relationship with his partners and made many enemies. He began expanding his empire by building several additional cotton mills. He licensed his patents to cotton spinners in the North and Midlands. His achievements inspired others to attempt similar projects. Little is known about the licences which the partners sold to allow rivals to construct their machines. Gordon and Pares, the partnership which built the mill at Calver in 1780, paid £2,000 for using the first patent, £5,000 for the second, and an annual payment of £1,000 thereafter. However, other manufacturers felt that Arkwright charged excessively for the privilege and this encouraged them to use his designs without seeking permission.

Arkwright decided to take steps to protect himself, and began approaching spinners who had infringed his carding patent. Three submitted and paid up. However, deciding to take nine more to trial, he discovered that the Lancashire manufacturers had organised resistance. Already in 1772 they had attempted to set the first patent aside on the grounds that Arkwright was not the original inventor. This was unsupported by evidence and the case ended with a verdict which confirmed the validity of the patent.

In 1781, Arkwright's second patent, obtained in 1775, was again attacked by the Lancashire manufacturers. A legal decision was obtained against him, not on the grounds of prior invention, but because he had not given an accurate description of the machinery in the specification. Descriptions and pictures of ten machines were given in the patent. The opening and cleaning machines depicted in the patent were never used, and no satisfactory machine for doing this was made until Snodgrass adapted the threshing machine to produce the 'scutcher' in 1808, while about the same time, William Strutt, son of Jedediah, invented the 'devil' at Belper. The devil began the process of opening and loosening the cotton which had been tightly compressed into a bale for trans-shipment. The scutcher also cleaned out the seeds and dirt. At Cromford this must have been done by women beating the cotton with sticks and picking out dirt by hand until it was ready for carding (disentangling the cotton fibres in their natural state and beginning to lay them parallel).

Arkwright succeeded in having the 1781 verdict reversed four years later. In June of the same year, several other cotton spinners, particularly those in Lancashire, went to court again. A formidable array of witnesses was brought against Arkwright. Amongst them emerged Thomas Highs, who for the first time claimed the credit for the roller-spinning invention. John Kaye, the clockmaker from Warrington, whom Highs had employed before 1768, was summoned to prove that he had communicated Highs' ideas to Arkwright. At the same trial, James Hargreaves' widow claimed that he had invented the 'crank and comb' (the answer to successful carding) thirteen or fourteen years earlier, and others claimed they had used it before 1775. Robert Pilkington gave evidence that he and Richard Livesay had made a carding engine in 1770 with the carding arranged in strips, thus preceding Arkwright by five years. Consequently, in June 1785, Arkwright lost the case and the rights to his patent. He tried to have the case re-opened the following November: he failed and finally the patents were freely available to all.

So why is it that Arkwright is acknowledged above all his peers? One deserving reason is that he cared about the welfare of his workers. Shift work was practised in most of these early mills and Cromford was no exception, with machinery running day and night. To contemporaries, this seemed wonderful, as did the fact that children could also earn a livelihood.

Mindful of the well-being of his employees, Arkwright built rows of cottages for his workers. The best example of this housing is North Street in Cromford, situated less than one mile from his mills. A school was founded for the children of his staff, churches and chapels were built with Sundays left free from work for church attendance, and the Greyhound Inn was also constructed for the local community. Farms were established for the provision of fresh vegetables, and loans were advanced to those wishing to buy a cow. In 1790, the right to hold a Saturday market was secured, and fairs were held twice yearly.

Arkwright was strict about the employment of children. He did not employ parish apprentices, nor any child under the age of ten, and no children were admitted into the mills until they could read. However, the pressure of parents to get their children mill work resulted in a lowering of standards. Consequently, children were taken on if they could read any small words at all.

Arkwright deserves credit for these early enlightened efforts which have been overshadowed by the malpractices of some later cotton masters of Lancashire. Many employed children at the age of five or six. The youngest began picking up waste cotton from the floor and going under machines in order to clean dust and dirt from the machinery. Bad health and stunted growth were often the price for those working in such cramped conditions.

Not everyone approved of the rapid changes, and mills were frequently under attack from rioters, or Luddites as they became known, who were opposed to the mechanised system which brought unemployment to those involved in hand-spinning. Lancashire mills, particularly, incurred trouble and many were destroyed by fire. However, the location of Arkwright's mills was generally remote from towns, with the risk of industrial unrest kept to a minimum. It was also said that within an hour, loyal supporters from his villages could gather together over 6,000 men, 1,000 guns and several cannons. Considered an understanding and fair employer, Arkwright was held in high esteem amongst the population at Cromford, which no doubt contributed to the expansion of his cotton empire.

On April 14th, 1781, Samuel Need died, ending the cotton partnership. John Smalley was paid over £3,000 by the remaining partners, and may also have been given a licence to build waterframes. He subsequently constructed a three-storey mill at Holywell. Jedediah Strutt bought land at Belper where he built three mills, and this was to become one of the largest cotton spinning sites in the country. Strutt also purchased land at Milford, and the famous warehouse was begun in which the Strutts experimented with a fireproof structure. His son William was the first man to design and build multi-storey fireproof buildings, the iron-framed construction and machinery being more ambitious than anything undertaken by Arkwright.

Establishing more mills in Derbyshire, Yorkshire, Worcestershire and Manchester, Arkwright began to expand throughout the country. He also opened a mill in Scotland after a visit took him to Lanark to see the Falls of Clyde. Here he realised their great potential as a source of water power. Further inventions, such as Samuel Crompton's Spinning Mule of 1779, helped the cotton trade continue to develop more rapidly than any other industry of its time in spite of the general economic depression and the American War of Independence. In 1751, Britain's export of cotton goods was valued at £46,000. By 1800 this had risen to £5,400,000 and by 1861 to £46,800,000— more than a thousandfold increase in value. Judged by the numbers employed, the Arkwright empire was the largest in the country. By 1782, he estimated his workforce at over 5,000.

In 1786 Arkwright was knighted by George III. In the following year, he reached the pinnacle of his social ambition when he was made High Sheriff of Derbyshire. To match his new rank, in 1789, Sir Richard bought a large estate around Cromford on which he built Willersley Castle. Arkwright had become socially acceptable where it mattered and this is no doubt another factor contributing towards his recognition as a great pioneer industrialist.

But, throughout his life, he had suffered from violent asthma and on August 3rd, 1792, aged sixty, a complication of disorders brought about his death. He was buried a week later at Matlock Church; the funeral procession was watched by a crowd of 2,000. Sir Richard's final resting place lies beneath the altar of a small chapel he had begun to build at Smelting Green Mill, close to Cromford Bridge. Arkwright's only son, thirty-seven-year-old Richard, inherited the greater part of his fortune. Included in this was the entire cotton-spinning empire. The younger Arkwright had been involved in cotton production for the whole of his working life, and was well qualified to inherit his father's legacy. However, within a year of his father's death, he had relinquished control of much of it, selling the mills at Nottingham and Wirksworth, retaining only the Cromford and Masson Mills.

Arkwright can perhaps be regarded as the first industrial tycoon in Britain. He was able to adapt other people's techniques and was an effective raiser of funds from other investors. Despite numerous setbacks, his sheer determination and commitment were a key factor in what was accomplished. He was not afraid to take risks. His perseverance, business sense and leadership must be seen as the driving force behind his success. James Hargreaves did not possess the vision required to create a lucrative business, while Samuel Crompton lacked Arkwright's commercial ability.

The debates surrounding Arkwright continue. However, the remarkable expansion which occurred in the eighteenth-century textile revolution is unquestionable. Without his contributions, the textile revolution might never have developed in Derbyshire from the domestic into the mill-based industry that played such a central role in the Industrial Revolution.

For Further Reading:

Brian Bailey, *Britains Industrial Past*, Whittet Books, London, 1985; R.S. Fitton, *The Arkwrights—Spinners of Fortune*, Manchester University Press, 1989; R.S. Fitton & A.P. Wadsworth, *The Strutts and the Arkwrights*, Manchester University Press, 1973; Richard L. Hills, *Richard Arkwright and Cotton Spinning*, Priory Press, London, 1973; Frank Nixon, *The Industrial Archaeology of Derbyshire*, David and Charles, Newton Abbot, Devon, 1969.

Karen Fisk is a freelance textile designer

This article first appeared in *History Today*, March 1998, pp. 25-30. © 1998 by History Today, Ltd. Reprinted by permission.

The Origins of Prussian Militarism

Peter H. Wilson *suggests that the aggressiveness of Wilhelmine Germany was not necessarily a direct consequence of the Prussian social system of the eighteenth century.*

THE STORY OF PRUSSIA'S transformation from potential victim of hostile international forces into a dominant and aggressive state often seems miraculous. To those who viewed it in the eighteenth century, it inspired a mixture of admiration and apprehension. These feelings gave way in the nineteenth century to a rather less critical glorification fostered by the authorities and German nationalist historians like Heinrich von Treitschke (1834–96), who saw Prussia's rise as the foundation of a united and dynamic imperial Germany. This vision disintegrated in the horrors of the first half of the twentieth century, after which Prussia's earlier rise appeared a historical 'wrong turn' (*Sonderweg*) on the path to modernity. It remains nonetheless a compelling tale that requires explanation.

Known as the 'sandbox of the Holy Roman Empire' on account of its poor soil and limited natural resources, the lands of the Prussian Hohenzollern dynasty were scattered across northern Europe from what is now modern Poland along the southern Baltic shore through to isolated enclaves on the Dutch border. When Frederick William (1620–88) became Elector or ruler of Brandenburg in 1640, he inherited a collection of different provinces lacking in common bonds or a uniform administration. Even the army, numbering a few thousand unreliable mercenaries, was split into regi-

ments funded separately by the different provincial administrations. By his death in 1688, Frederick William had faced off his Polish and Swedish enemies, ruthlessly suppressed domestic opposition, imposed new taxes, forged common institutions and established a permanent army of no fewer than 29,154 men. He would go down in history as the 'Great Elector'. His son and successor, Frederick I (1657–1713), would receive a less prominent place in Prussian history, but nonetheless acquired a royal title for Prussia itself in 1701 and added another 10,000 men to the army. This force was effectively doubled during the reign of King Frederick William I (r.1713–40), known to posterity as the 'soldier king' for his obsession with all things military and his passion for his 'giant grenadiers', a special regiment of exceptionally tall men stationed at his palace in Potsdam who, when the King was feeling unwell, would march through his bedroom to cheer him up. However, it was only under his son, Frederick II 'the Great' (r. 1740–86), that this well-drilled army was really tested in battle. Whereas only 15,000 sq km of new territory had been added to the Hohenzollern domains between 1648 and Frederick's accession in 1740, over 75,000 sq km were acquired by the time of his death in 1786 through the conquest of new lands, particularly at the expense of Poland and the Austrian Habsburg monarchy. A fur-

ther 113,500 sq km were seized in 1793–95 during the final carve-up that removed Poland from Europe's map until 1918. These gains increased the overall size of the Hohenzollern monarchy from around 1.6 million inhabitants in 1713 to at least 8.5 million by 1795. Impressive as these figures were, they failed to explain the phenomenal growth of the Prussian army, which already ranked fourth in size in Europe by 1740, while the country was only in thirteenth place in terms of population.

Contemporaries felt that this transformation was due to something more than the gritty determination and tactical skill of the Prussian monarchs and pointed to a deeper, underlying militarisation of Prussian state and society as the reason for the country's emergence as a great power. Among the most perceptive was the Austrian chief minister, Wenzel Anton von Kaunitz (1711–94), who identified the 'canton system' introduced between 1713 and 1733 by Frederick William I as the cause of a new militarism. This system was a form of conscription which divided the entire Prussian monarchy into cantons, or recruiting districts assigned to each regiment. In a practice known as enrolling lists were kept of all males from the age of religious confirmation. The regiment drew men from the list as required to keep it up to strength, training them for about a year before giving them furlough; in other words discharging them on unpaid leave. Industrial zones and those individuals who were wealthy or deemed of value to the state were exempt from service. The regiments remained in being thanks to a cadre of paid professionals serving throughout the year, many of whom were recruited from outside the Prussian monarchy, while the conscripts were recalled annually for a period of intensive training. This system enabled Prussia to maximise its military potential without destabilising its labour-intensive agrarian economy since the discharged conscripts were free to work their landlords' fields for most of the year, thus sustaining productivity and with it state taxes, while also mollifying the Junkers, the feudal aristocracy on whom the crown depended for its officers and administrators.

While recognising that it had certain technical military advantages, Kaunitz felt the canton system was 'repulsive' as it led to the total subordination of all civil life to military requirements, creating 'unending oppression and extortion', a slavish mentality on the part of the population and suffocating the freedom and patriotism he believed flourished in more progressive countries like Britain and the Dutch Republic. Moreover, the 'Prussian military state' was inherently unstable with an in-built propensity to war as it could only sustain itself through external aggression to acquire ever more territory and resources. This had led to a new kind of total war in 'that the king does not just exploit his own population, money and military potential, but also all the inhabitants, money, food and other materials of innocent and neutral neighbours as far as force enables him'.

Emperor Joseph II (r.1765–90) rejected Kaunitz's advice and introduced Prussian-style conscription into the Habsburg lands after 1771 in an effort to match the threat posed by Frederick the Great. However, subsequent historians have tended to agree with the minister's assessment of the fateful consequences of the canton system. In an influential thesis, the German post-war historian Otto Büsch argued that it consolidated the compromise between the Hohenzollern dynasty and the feudal Junker aristocracy that underpinned Prussian

absolutism since the reign of the Great Elector in the later seventeenth century. In return for voting taxes for the army and surrendering their say in determining foreign policy in the 1650s, the Junkers received confirmation and extension of their powers over their peasant tenants, tying them to perpetual servitude and forced labour. The subsequent expansion of the army under Frederick William after 1713 consolidated this by offering the Junkers socially prestigious and financially rewarding positions in the officer corps. The canton system completed the process by tightening the Junkers' grip on their serfs, especially since their monopoly of officer posts ensured that many aristocrats were simultaneously both captain and landlord over the same group of serf-conscripts. Since the army now regarded every man as a potential recruit, attempts to leave the country were equated with desertion so that military discipline reinforced feudal jurisdiction, creating what some have called a 'military-agrarian complex' or community of interest between monarchy, army and feudal aristocracy.

Though this system enabled Prussia to wage war successfully in the mid-eighteenth century, it became increasingly inflexible—as change to any part of this structure threatened the web of vested interests. This appears to account for the rigidity that contemporaries noted in the Prussian army after the Seven Years' War (1756–63) as it became a force drilled to perfection but unable to cope with any serious reverse. These weaknesses were exposed by the crushing defeat at the twin battles of Jena-Auerstadt in 1806 at the hands of the forces of dynamic Napoleonic France. The catastrophe led to a brief period of liberal reforms which partially modernised the army without seriously disturbing the social order. The canton system was replaced by what was heralded as patriotic universal military service in 1814, but the aristocracy reasserted its hold on the officer corps and the militarisation of society continued unabated once Napoleon had been defeated.

Büsch's views proved highly controversial and were rejected by the still largely conservative German historical establishment in the 1950s, delaying the

publication of his thesis by a decade. However, when it first appeared in 1962 it coincided with a wider trend in historical revisionism which sought not to explain the Nazi era as an aberration in an otherwise blameless German past, but as the direct culmination of earlier militarism. Rather than only briefly departing from the European norm in 1933–45, Germany now seemed to have been heading in the wrong direction since the early eighteenth century.

Büsch's explanation of what he termed 'the origins of German social militarisation' fitted so well with the wider assumptions of the 'wrong turn' theory that no one has seriously questioned it until comparatively recently. Improved access to the archives of the former GDR after German reunification in 1991 has been instrumental in this reappraisal since these contain material relating to the feudal heartlands of Brandenburg and Pomerania. New research has incorporated different methodologies, including historical anthropology and detailed 'micro-historical studies' of individual Junker estates. A greater readiness to compare Prussia to other German territories has also been important. Even by 1800 the Hohenzollern monarchy still only contained a fifth of the inhabitants of the Holy Roman Empire: clearly German history cannot be written simply by generalising from the Prussian experience.

Taken together, these findings reveal a very different picture of the relationship of army and society in old regime Prussia than presented by Büsch. In purely technical military terms, Prussia now appears less innovative than once thought. Key elements of the canton system like the practice of enrolling, furlough and assigning recruitment districts to individual regiments were all in use in other German territories, in some cases decades before their introduction in Prussia. Moreover, Prussia was not uniquely militarised as many smaller territories including Hessen-Kassel, Munster and even tiny Schaumburg-Lippe maintained more troops in proportion to their populations. Perhaps more significantly, the core assumptions behind the social militarisation thesis have been undermined and there is little evidence that serfdom and canton recruitment were necessarily mutually-reinforcing systems. Conscription was implemented throughout the Prussian monarchy, including in towns and areas like the Westphalian enclaves where serfdom and Junker manorial agriculture were not practised. More crucially, Junkers were rarely captains of their own serfs. Even in East Prussia, bastion of feudal Junkerdom, locally-born noblemen made up only half of the captains of regiments stationed in that province, while elsewhere the proportion could be as low as ten per cent. Being a native of that province did not mean one necessarily held land there. Many aristocratic officers were landless while those who still had estates generally had them outside the canton of their own regiment. Indeed, this was a necessity since tying officer appointments to only particular groups of estate owners would have rendered any kind of promotions and personnel policy impossible.

Some Junkers connived at draft dodging to prevent the loss of valuable workers.

Far from militarising society, the practice of discharging conscripts for most of each year partly civilianised the army which assumed many of the characteristics of a militia, despite the fact that Frederick William abolished the Prussian militia structure and even banned the use of the word *Miliz* in 1713. By regulating conscription, the canton system also made recruitment more predictable and easier to bear by the population. The internal administration of the canton was largely determined by the civilian settlement pattern of individual 'hearths' and communities which were permitted some role in the selection of recruits. Though obliged to serve for life if drafted, many conscripts were discharged early if others of a more suitable stature became available. All were permitted to return home for most of the year, enabling something approaching a

'normal' life despite military service. Soldiers retained their own homes and a relatively large proportion were allowed to marry, factors which gave the system considerable stability and discouraged desertion. The rules for surveillance and supervision by the military and civil authorities, though strict on paper, were not completely enforceable in practice and were open to manipulation from below as well as abuse from above. Some Junkers even connived at draft dodging to prevent the loss of valuable workers while the army's interest in preserving a pool of healthy recruits acted as a break on the excesses of tyrannical landlords. It is also telling that a significant minority of cantonists actually volunteered for service, joining the army as full-time paid professionals where they received a guaranteed minimum wage and were free to earn more money as hawkers, servants and building workers in their long off-duty hours. Those who were successful in finding such work could quadruple their basic pay, while those who were not could still supplement their wage by standing extra watch duty while their more entrepreneurial comrades engaged in more profitable civil employment.

These findings should not be taken as an attempt to return to the Hohenzollern legend propagated by nineteenth-century historians like Treitschke. The Prussian monarchy was far from being an impartial, strict yet benevolent guardian of common German interests. Canton conscription represented a heavy burden with at least five per cent of potential recruits serving in peacetime and double that number in war. Though service could be accommodated by those it took, it hardly offered a comfortable life: neither conscripts nor professional Prussian soldiers received a pay rise between 1713 and 1799! Frederick the Great's brilliant strategy may have ensured his country's survival during the Seven Years' War against impossible odds, but his battle tactics demanded a heavy price. Over 180,000 Prussian servicemen died in the conflict in addition to perhaps as much as ten per cent of the civil population. The army served the crown whose policies the bulk of the population had no say in determining and with which many, particularly the new Polish

subjects acquired after 1772, could not identify.

Nevertheless, the recent research does raise questions about the degree of continuity between eighteenth-century conditions and subsequent German militarism. The aggressive militarism after 1871 has been regarded as a product of the marriage brokered by Bismarck of the old Prussian tradition represented by the Hohenzollern dynasty and Junker aristocracy with liberal capitalists and the big industrialists like the arms manufacturer Friedrich Alfred Krupp (1854–1902). Continuity with the eighteenth century was sustained by the resilience of the old regime which rode out the storms of Napoleonic defeat in 1806 and the Reform Era of 1807–14 and survived the violent socio-economic change unleashed by rapid industrialisation by introducing sham democracy after 1871 and pursuing increasingly reckless diversionary strategies such as Kaiser Wilhelm's *Weltpolitik* bid for colonial empire and, ultimately, launching world war in 1914.

Like all teleological arguments, this is seductively persuasive but flawed in the light of the recent research into eighteenth-century Prussia. The lines of continuity, though surely still present, now seem less clear or straightforward and Frederick the Great no longer appears the direct antecedent of Kaiser Wilhelm, let alone Hitler. The eighteenth century nonetheless left a fateful legacy, but it was not the fabled canton system. The army did enjoy unusually high social prestige in Prussia—something that was deliberately fostered by the crown as part of its efforts to reconcile the Junkers to service in the officer corps. Prussia also witnessed a new kind of militarised patriotism which first flowered in the Seven Years' War and intensified with the experience of the 'War of Liberation' against Napoleonic France 1813–14. This re-evaluated the soldier's tragic death on the field of slaughter as the hero's glorious sacrifice for the fatherland. Significantly, this fatherland was no longer defined in terms of the decentralised, pacific, non-aligned and cosmopolitan Holy Roman Empire, but increasingly by reference to blood, soil, language and Protestantism.

However, this was not yet the exclusively reactionary, xenophobic nationalism associated with the Wilhelmine and Nazi eras which, in retrospect now appears more the product of the mid-nineteenth century experience. It was only the experience of revolution, especially that of 1848 when Prussian troops fired on crowds in Berlin and other cities, that heightened consciousness of the army as pillar of an increasingly obsolete social and political order. Additionally, the short and spectacularly successful wars of German unification in 1866 and 1871 left a very different memory of martial conflict than the prolonged bloodletting and near disaster of the Seven Years' War or Frederick the Great's last military engagement, the inglorious 'Potato War' of 1778–79 against Austria when deserters exceeded battle casualties by a factor of ten to one. It was these factors, rather than the experience of the eighteenth century, that conditioned the militarism that was to have such fateful consequences for Europe after 1914.

FOR FURTHER READING

Otto Büsch, *Military System and Social life in Old Regime Prussia 1713–1807: The Beginnings of the Social Militarisation of Prusso-German Society* (Humanities Press, 1997); Christopher Duffy, *The Army of Frederick the Great* (2nd ed., The Emperor's Press, 1996); Dennis Showalter, *The Wars of Frederick the Great* (Longman, 1996); Peter H. Wilson, *German Armies: War and German Politics 1648–1806* (UCL Press, 1998); Peter H. Wilson, 'Social militarisation in eighteenth-century Germany'. *German History*, 18 (2000), pp.1–39.

Peter H. Wilson is Reader in Early Modern European History at the University of Sunderland and the author of Absolutism in Central Europe *(Routledge, 2000).*

Slavery and the British

James Walvin *reviews current ideas about the vast network of slavery that shaped British and world history for more than two centuries.*

THE ENFORCED MOVEMENT OF MORE THAN ELEVEN MILLION Africans onto the Atlantic slave ships, and the scattering of over ten million survivors across the colonies of the Americas between the late sixteenth and early nineteenth centuries, transformed the face of the Americas. It also enhanced the material well-being both of European settlers and their homelands. The cost was paid, of course, by Africa: a haemorrhage of humanity from vast reaches of the continent, the exact consequences, even now, unknown. Though they were not its pioneers, by the mid-eighteenth century the British had come to dominate Atlantic slavery, a fact which in turn helped to shape much of Britain's status and power.

Historians have become increasingly interested in the concept of an Atlantic world: a world that embraced the maritime and littoral societies of Europe, Africa and the Americas, and one in which slavery played a crucial role. The Atlantic system developed a gravitational pull that drew to it many more societies than those formally committed to African slavery. Even the economies of Asia were ultimately linked to African slavery. European ships, bound for the slave coast of Africa, brimmed not simply with produce from their home towns, their hinterland and from Europe, but also with goods transhipped from Asia. Firearms from Birmingham, French wines, Indian textiles, cowrie shells from the Maldives, food from Ireland, all were packed into the holds of outbound ships, destined to be exchanged for Africans.

The bartering and trading systems on the coast fed a voracious demand for imported goods that stretched far deeper into the African interior than Europeans had seen or visited. In return, the traders who settled on the coast, and the transient captains, gradually filled the holds of their ships (suitably rearranged for human cargoes) with Africans.

European, American and Brazilian traders flitted nervously up and down the west African coast, always anxious to make a quick exchange and quit the dangers of the region for the welcoming currents that would speed their Atlantic crossing to the expectant markets of the Americas. We have details of some 26,000 voyages throughout the recorded history of the slave

A Boston advertisement for a cargo of slaves, probably from the early eighteenth century.

trade. Once described as a 'triangular trade', it was in fact a trading system of great geographical complexity, with routes cutting from Brazil to Africa, from North America to Africa and back, between Europe and the Caribbean—and of direct routes from the slave colonies back to the European heartlands. Ships crisscrossed the north and south Atlantic Caribbean, ferrying Africans and goods needed by all slave societies, finally hauling the vast cargoes of slave-grown produce back to European markets, to sate the appetite of the Western world for tropical and semi-tropical staples. This trading complexity was compounded by commercial transactions with native peoples on the frontiers of European settlement and advancement across the Americas.

This vast network, lubricated by slavery, drew together hugely different peoples from all over the world. Africans in the

Caribbean dressed in textiles produced in India, used tools made in Sheffield, and produced rum drunk by indigenous native peoples of the Americas. Tobacco cultivated by slaves in the Chesapeake was widely consumed, from Africa itself to the early penal colonies of Australia.

Though Africans were present in many of the early European settlements in the Americas, the drift towards African slavery was slow. Europeans tried a host of agricultural and social experiments in the Western Hemisphere before the mid- and late-sixteenth-century Brazilian development of sugar cane cultivation. Sugar had long been grown on plantations in the Mediterranean (it came later to the Atlantic islands), before being transplanted into the Americas in the late sixteenth century. But sugar plantations, even in their early form, were labour-intensive, and there was not enough labour available among local peoples, or migrating Europeans. Africa, though, could be made to yield people in abundance. From small-scale, haphazard origins (with Europeans tapping into local slave systems), the demand for labour in the New World spawned violent networks of slave-trading along the African coast and deep into the interior.

By the time the British forged their own early seventeenth-century settlements in the Caribbean and North America, black slavery had already taken root in Spanish, Portuguese and Dutch settlements. Informed by this earlier experience, and able to borrow the technologies of sugar cultivation, backed by Dutch money, and with domestic political support, the British found the commercial opportunities afforded by slavery irresistible. But they, too, tried other systems at first.

Sugar changed all. First in Barbados and the Leewards from the 1630s, then in late seventeenth-century Jamaica, British settlers converted ever more acreage into cane cultivation. In Barbados, sugar cultivation hastened the rise of larger plantations and the decline in the number of smallholdings—and, of course, a growing proportion of the population was black and enslaved. In 1650 there were perhaps 300 plantations on the island, by 1670, some 900. The black population in Barbados stood at about 20,000 in 1655 but less than thirty years later it had risen to over 46,000. In the same period, the white population had declined. The conversion of Barbados to a plantation society based on African slave labour was a pattern repeated across the Caribbean.

In the Chesapeake colonies of Virginia and Maryland, the drift to slavery followed local lines of tobacco cultivation (again on plantations), though they differed in size (and nature) from the sugar plantations of the West Indies. Later, in the early eighteenth century, rice cultivation (also on plantations) in the Carolinas was also driven forward by slavery. Though all depended on imported Africans, each region developed a distinctly different slave system. Plantations varied from crop to crop. Slave demography, social life and culture took different trajectories across the enslaved Americas. But one universal fact remained unflinching: the reduction of African humanity to the status and level (in law, economic and social usage) of property.

From the first, the slave's status clashed with a number of European legal and political practices and conventions. Europeans were turning their backs on bondage in their own continent at the very time they were creating and perfecting African slavery in the Atlantic economy. In turn, the expansion of slavery—British ships carried three million Africans between 1680 and 1807—spawned a confusion of justifications, many of which came to hinge on ideas of race; for what could be the justification for the relegation of humanity to the level of chattel, even when colonial (and imperial) law decreed it so? There consequently evolved a protracted social and political debate about colour and 'race' that entered the intellectual bloodstream of the Western world. By the time the slave systems reached their mature form in the English-speaking colonies in the mid-eighteenth century, to be black was to be enslaved: a piece of chattel. The obvious contradictions in such practices and beliefs were there for all to see. Nonetheless, the political (and legal) tensions generated by the property-status of slaves remained. Ultimately, this ideological core of the slave system was fatally fissured by the seismic impact of the French Revolution of 1789 and the *Declaration of the Rights of Man and the Citizen* passed by the Constituent Assembly in France the same year. And in Britain the assertion of equality encapsulated in the abolitionists' motto 'Am I not a Man and a Brother?', adopted in 1787, would ultimately prove corrosive of slavery.

But slavery and the Atlantic slave trade still continued. Even after 1789, the intellectual or political attachment to black freedom was often overridden by economic considerations. For much of its history, slavery had had its critics. But its basic commercial value served to marginalise whatever criticisms were raised by churchmen, philosophers and even political economists. For a long time the material well-being, visible on both sides of the Atlantic, that slavery brought to so many hushed all protest.

The benefits of slave labour could be seen, initially, in the colonies themselves. Africans and their local-born offspring converted swathes of the settled Americas to profitable agriculture. Though often little more than toe-holds on the American land mass and Caribbean islands, plantations became the means of bringing a luxuriant wilderness into commercial cultivation. Slaves re-ordered the confusions of the natural habitat into fields and fruitful land-holdings, the whole linked by man-made trails and pathways, to local river or coastal docks. Each plantation colony developed its own, often small-scale, urban centres. Towns, cities and ports were both centres of local political power and entrepôts forming a crossroads with the wider world, where goods (and peoples) flowed in from Europe and Africa, and whence produce and profits were dispatched back, across the Atlantic, to Europe.

From the sixteenth to the early nineteenth century, European conflicts were also played out in the Americas, as each emergent colonial power sought to gain advantage over its rival. In the islands, Europeans built massive fortifications to keep other marauding Europeans at bay, and to prevent their own settlements from being destroyed or usurped. The magnificent fortifications that survive along the Caribbean island chain testify to the military threat experienced by each colonising nation, and to the vast expense invested in securing their strongholds. In time, however, the greatest threats came not from other Europeans, but from the enslaved armies toiling reluctantly for their colonial masters. The slave colonies, and the planters in their rural retreats, were permanently embattled against an encircling slave population they vitally needed but never trusted.

Colonial slave societies were held in place not simply by naval and local armed defences, but by ad-hoc federations of militia and armed whites (and by the late eighteenth century even by black troops) marshalled to over-awe and stifle any outburst which might erupt from the slave quarters. Throughout the British slave colonies, violence and resistance among the slaves was endemic (as they were wherever slavery existed). But so too was savage and remorseless repression. Slaves resisted their bondage in a variety of ways. From enslavement in Africa, to life in the squalor of the slave ships, through to the more settled but often brutal life on the plantations, slaves found ways to resist. Most spectacularly in the form of open revolt or rebellion, resistance more commonly took the form of mundane acts of non-compliance: feigning stupidity, failing to do what was required, sabotaging owners' plans and instructions, or simply by presenting the sullen reluctance that whites reported across the slave colonies. There were great dangers here for the slaves: resist too much, too far, and retribution would result in all too predictable a fashion. This was true for healthy young men in the fields (generally the most 'troublesome' group) and for their mothers and sisters working as domestics in white households. How far to go—the boundary between the tolerable and the dangerous—was always an early lesson young slaves had to learn from their elders. Throughout, physical assault, a simple cuff or beating, was an ever-present reality.

Not surprisingly, slaves ran away in all slave societies, though physical circumstances often determined what was possible. Barbados for example—much the same size as the Isle of Wight—offered few obvious escape routes once the island had been fully conquered and put into sugar cultivation. But in other colonies where geography allowed, slaves formed 'maroon' societies: communities of runaways, living beyond the pale of plantation life. Maroons were deeply disliked by planters and military alike. Seen as an obvious goal for potential runaways, they were viewed as a threat in many senses. Yet efforts to destroy them generally failed in the teeth of fierce resistance and the physical difficulties of the local environment (mountains or jungle, ideal country for what were, effectively, guerrilla bands.) Where the British could not bring maroons to heel, they were ultimately forced to [work] with them, conceding their independence, most importantly in return for the handing back of further would-be runaways.

Newspapers throughout the slave colonies were filled with advertisements for slave runaways. Most common was the slave runaway heading for a loved-one. While many were clearly on the run from their plantation or owner most were simply seeking family and friends: a lover or spouse, a child or parent. Runaways might more easily escape notice in urban communities. Curiously, at times, slave owners seemed not to mind when slaves ran away (when food was short, for example, or when the demands of the agricultural year were slack), on condition that they returned—eventually. Always, of course, slaves had to prove their right to roam. Unless they had an obvious task to do, slaves on the move were inevitably suspect, and runaways generally moved furtively, needing the help of other slaves for food

or shelter. There were, however, many other slaves with a legitimate reason to be on the move—to and from their own markets, between plantations and the nearest river or port, transporting exports and imports, goods and beasts, along the lines of local (and even international) communication.

Open revolt bloodied the history of the slave colonies. The insurrection of the 1790s in the French colony of Haiti was the only example of slaves in the Americas succeeding in the complete destruction of the system that oppressed them, though not for want of trying elsewhere. African slaves (many with military experience in their African homelands) tended to be more resistant than those born in the New World, with numbers trying, but invariably failing, to escape their bondage by plots, revolt and physical defiance. Failure was measured out in bloody retribution by means of summary executions, dismemberments and exemplary tortures which colonial penal codes (to say nothing of plantocratic instinct) made possible. Nowhere was the 'bloody code' more bloody, and more widely used, than in the slave islands. And each failed slave revolt saw a tightening of plantocratic repression: a vicious cycle of resistance and repression which showed no prospect of change.

One element in the growing British disenchantment with slavery was with the brutality required simply to keep the slaves in their place. What might have gone unquestioned in 1700 had, by the 1820s, become unacceptable. By then there was a changing sensibility about slavery that was partly religious, partly secular but which, when placed in the context of growing economic doubts (was slavery really more efficient than free labour?) helped to undermine the metropolitan attachment to a system that had served Britain so well for two centuries. Moreover, as British missionaries began to win over increasing numbers of slaves to their chapels and churches, they reported back to their British congregations the full nature of slave experience and sufferings, to the growing concern of fellow British worshippers. What kind of system was it that persecuted black Christians, their preachers and their places of worship? By the 1820s few doubted that the British slave system was doomed.

From the late eighteenth century, the adoption of Christianity transformed slave life in the islands. From the first, slaves had evolved distinctive cultures from one colony to another, which blended Africa with local European and colonial life. Belief systems and languages, folk customs (from cooking to health care and dress) and family patterns imported from the slaves' varied African communities, were transformed by the process of enslavement, transportation and settlement in the Americas. Africans in the slave quarters may have sought out their 'own people' (whose language and habits they understood) but they were also forced into the company of other Africans, local-born slaves and Europeans, with whom they had to live and work. The creole cultures that grew from such blendings imposed a distinct style and tone on each and every slave society.

Despite the ubiquitous repression and violence of slavery, slave-owners learned that they secured the best returns on their human capital not by unrelenting pressure, but by allowing free time: breaks at weekends, at high days and holidays. The calendar of the local agricultural year or the Christian Year provided slaves with a breathing space. In those breaks from drudgery, slaves evolved their own particular social activities, investing their breaks with ritual and ceremonies: dressing up in elaborate fashion (in sharp contrast to the everyday dress of the workplace), enjoying particular customs with music, food, drink and elaborate carnival. Equally, the patterns of family and community life—notably birth, marriage and death—evolved their own distinctive patterns and rhythms. Outsiders were often amazed at the vigour and material bounty displayed by slaves in their social life. Where and how did they acquire such elaborate clothing and finery: jewellery and musical instruments, money for lavish food and drink? In fact, they bought such luxuries from the fruits of their own labours. Individual skills (such as music-making, nursing, sewing or craftsmanship) could generate earnings. Gardens and plots, tending animals, cultivating foodstuffs and so on, gave slaves the material wherewithal for barter and trade, for sale and purchase. Such efforts formed the basis of the slave markets which came to characterise the slave islands. All this took place after the normal working day: at evenings, weekends or in other free time. It meant that even in their rare moments of leisure slaves had to toil. Whatever advancement they made (and many clearly did make their lives more comfortable) came from their own sweat and application.

The greatest beneficiaries of slave efforts were of course their owners and their imperial backers. This brings us to the thorny issue of profit and loss. For more than fifty years, historians have squabbled about the economics of the British slave system. What role did slavery play in the transformation of Britain itself? More especially, what was its significance in enabling Britain to become an industrial power from the late eighteenth century onwards? Equally, were Britain's decisions to turn its back first on the slave trade (1807), and then on slavery itself (1834), economically inspired? At one level it is implausible to discount the importance of the Atlantic slave system, it was so massive, its ramifications so ubiquitous, its defenders so tenacious in their attachment to it. In the development of Liverpool, for instance, can we ignore the some 6,000 slave voyages that departed from that port? And can we adequately grasp the nature of Bristol's (or London's) earlier, seventeenth-century involvement in the slave trade and settlement of the slave colonies? Moreover, the accountancy of the system—the facts and figures so carefully researched and teased apart by historians in the past twenty-five years—do not always convey the full social impact of slavery on Britain itself. Whatever the level of profit (or loss) of particular voyages, of specific trading companies and plantations, here was a system that by the mid-eighteenth century had become part of the warp and weft of British life itself. To those at home, slavery was, in general, out of mind and out of sight. Yet its consequences, most obviously the fruits of slave labour (the sugar and rum, the tobacco, rice and coffee) served to transform the social life of Britain (and the West in general.) Africa was obliged to consume vast amounts of Western produce in return for bartered slaves. Plantation societies were kept alive by British imports, from the hats on the slaves' heads, to the hoes in their hands, from equipment in the fields, to the wines on the planters' tables. And a host of British ports, with their immediate economic hinterland, thrived on supplying the whole, filling the ships, plying African markets and the American plantations with vital goods and services: with their manpower (black and white), their finance, firepower and military defences. In the enslaved Atlantic, Britain may have ruled the waves. But even the victorious Royal Navy, hard at its massive task of protecting the British colonies and the sea-lanes from the predatory threats of other Europeans, kept its men at their unenviable tasks by lavish helpings of rum. And who made the rum?

The results of slave labours were inescapable, from the smoke-filled atmosphere (courtesy of Virginian tobacco) of London's myriad coffee houses, to the insatiable appetite of British common people for sugar to take with the tea. Yet the slaves were thousands of miles distant. What gave the slave system a local, British focus was that small band of blacks, living in London, mainly domestics, sometimes slaves, who flit in and out of view; in parish registers, fashionable portraits, as the subject of legal arguments, and often the victims of aggression by employer or owners. They serve as a reminder, however apparently removed from the centre of Atlantic slavery, of other Africans, measured in their millions, whose brutal enslavement and transportation was so fundamental a part of the rise to greatness of eighteenth-century Britain.

FOR FURTHER READING.

Robin Blackburn, *The Making of New World Slavery* (Verso, 1997); David Eltis, *The Rise of African Slavery in the Americas* (Cambridge University Press, 2000); *The Oxford History of the British Empire: The Eighteenth Century* P.J.Marshall, ed, (Oxford University Press, 1998); James Walvin, *Making the Black Atlantic* (Cassell, 2000).

James Walvin is Professor of History at the University of York.

This article first appeared in *History Today,* March 2002, pp. 48-54. © 2002 by History Today, Ltd. Reprinted by permission.

Scrooge and Albert

Christmas in the 1840s

Christine Lalumia

Today it is somewhat of a cliche to say that Christmas as we know it in Britain was either invented or largely created by the Victorians. In fact, historians never seem to tire of debating the role of the Victorians in forming our modern concept of the Christmas celebration. Was it invention or re-invention? Was it an act of myth-making or simply a case of repackaging older traditions in a form that suited their modern age and appealed to the general mood?

There is ample evidence, as well as many good scholarly arguments and critical studies, to convince us that the latter is probably closer to the truth. Christmas, as we know it today, is essentially a nineteenth-century mixture of all that was best and most popular from English Christmases past, continually tempered by new sensibilities, ideas and prevailing concerns. What is surprising is that much of this repackaging and revivification was vigorously undertaken early in Victoria's reign, during the 1840s—in the first full decade of her monarchy and her marriage. Why was this period historically significant in the story of Christmas? And what were the foundations upon which this 'new' Christmas was constructed?

The answer lies, in part, in the reaction to the social changes that threatened the middle classes. Increasing urbanisation in England had brought about high concentrations of poverty, overcrowding, insanitary conditions and disease. The middle classes were perhaps more vulnerable to the threats posed by urbanisation and the poor owing to proximity in the city and the insecurity arising from often similar social backgrounds, than the upper classes who were at some remove. To protect themselves, the early Victorian middle classes built a world of strict moral codes and strong religious beliefs, with an emphasis on hard work and achievement. This was underpinned by the idea of the family as the most acceptable social unit and so the type of Christmas the Victorians fashioned reinforced all their social and moral beliefs. The middle classes almost used it as an exercise in social engineering, to encourage others to be equally moral and upright, even though they might be less fortunate. Christmas also provided a cultural anchor, a life raft of familiarity in changing times.

Christmas as the celebration of the birth of Christ was integrated with an already established festival over which the Church itself had remarkably little influence. As a cultural festival, its influences were many and although in the 1840s the Christian faith was an important part of the season, Christmas, then as now, seems to have been a festival of family and kinship in which charity toward others was perhaps the strongest element.

There was undoubtedly a growing interest in the history and traditions of Christmas during this period. This can be seen as part of a larger trend of the late-eighteenth and early-nineteenth centuries to examine and understand English history in a new way. The nation's history became of interest not just to antiquarians but to a wider public. The preceding centuries were useful not only as a mirror in which those in the nineteenth century could see and understand themselves but also provided a fertile picking ground for historical role models. A 'magpie' approach was employed as selected elements of Christmas across the ages were considered suitable for adaptation. The Christmas-makers of the early-nineteenth century were attempting to create a festival—to reflect a society—that was better, morally and socially, than the immediate past. For this reason they were highly selective about which 'past' suited their purpose, and the result was an eclectic mix of the traditional and modern.

In this constructed idea of festivity, the immediate past seemed not to appeal. A common perception was that the Regency period had lacked substance, was cold-hearted and characterised by unbalanced excess and overspending. Christmas during this period was viewed as having become a soulless shadow of what it had once been. Something more robust, both morally and in terms of sheer celebration, was required. The medieval and, in particular, the Elizabethan periods provided the most suitable models. 'Olde Christmas' was perceived as a vigorous, heartfelt festival, which struck the right balance between hedonistic pleasures and an awareness of communal relationships and responsibilities. The celebrations of the sixteenth and early seventeenth centuries were considered to

The *Illustrated London News* commended 'the poor who are kind to the poor' in this engraving by Leech, 'Fetching home the Christmas Dinner', of 1848.

have been both morally sound and exceedingly jolly. As the Scottish poet and editor Thomas K. Hervey observed in *The Book of Christmas* in 1836:

> If the old festivals and commemorations in which our land was once so abundant—and which obtained for her, many a long day since, the name of 'merrie England'—had no other recommendation than their convivial character, the community of enjoyment which they imply, they would on that account be worthy of all promotion, as an antidote to the cold and selfish spirit which is tainting the life-blood and freezing the pulses of society.

'Merrie England' and 'Olde Christmas' provided most of the raw materials with which to revive and re-shape Christmas into something both spectacular and appropriate for this new age. Traditions like burning the yule log and the emphasis on bringing light to the darkest days of the year, feasting and decorating the home with evergreens were sixteenth-century cus-

toms embraced, and in some cases enhanced, by the Victorians. Most of these ancient customs were still familiar and popular across all bands of society and were therefore strong enough to stand some modernisation.

Carol-singing was a popular medieval custom that was thought to be in decline at the beginning of the nineteenth century. The middle classes in particular worried that the songs themselves would be forgotten and lost forever. To counter this, antiquarians in the 1820s and 1830s began to compile collections of traditional carols. At the same time, inexpensive printed carol sheets and books, such as *The Star of Bethlehem: a selection of excellent carols* (1825) and *The Evergreen: Carols for the Christmas Holidays* (1830) became widely available. Medieval songs and even some from the eighteenth century, such as 'O Come, all ye faithful' and 'Hark the Herald Angels Sing', were revived. New carols, such as 'Once in Royal David's City', written by Mrs Cecil Frances Alexander in 1845, were also added to the repertoire.

Concern that Christmas had become an anaemic version of its former self and that some of the more vibrant traditions of the past were on the verge of disappearing altogether was noted by several writers in the 1820s and 1830s. Thomas Hervey worried that society would suffer if 'right joyous festivals' such as Christmas were lost:

> The natural tendency of the time to obliterate ancient customs and silence ancient sports, is too much promoted by the utilitarian spirit of the day.... It is, alas! but too true that the spirit of hearty festivity in which our ancestors' met this season has been long on the decline; and much of the joyous pomp with which it was once received has long since passed away.

Hervey quoted Washington Irving who, in the 1820s, also worried about the diminution of the festival. William Hone expressed a similar view in *The Every Day Book* of 1826–27, where he noted that Christmas was no longer 'kept with anything like the vigour, perseverance and elegance of our ancestors'. All these writers expressed the fear that an interest in the 'merriest month of the year' might be lost.

Although the first three Hanoverian courts certainly celebrated Christmas at home, following the seasonal customs familiar to them from Germany, it seems to have been a fairly private affair, and not something about which the general populace were aware of or could copy. In addition, during the second half of the eighteenth century, London's social elite tended to view Christmas as a rather down-market festival and reduced their celebrations to nothing more than elegant dinner parties. So in general and particularly in London, Christmas may have gone through a rather lacklustre phase. However, the fears that the celebration of Christmas would disappear altogether seem somewhat exaggerated. Other contemporary accounts from the early nineteenth century suggest Christmas was far too strongly embedded within the national psyche and English culture to be seriously endangered. Instead, it is more likely that it was at a turning point, ripe for re-evaluation.

As the 1840s began, Christmas, like many other social customs which bonded society, needed new advocates. Two of the most powerful of these were the new monarch Queen Victoria and her husband, Prince Albert, whose influence on the celebration should not be underestimated. Although they created far less then they are often credited with, their simple support and embracing of Christmas was influential and gave the celebration a tremendous boost. Their personal delight and interest in Christmas became apparent soon after their marriage in 1840. That, combined with their emphasis on a happy domestic life and pleasure in the raising of their many children, seems to have inclined them to view Christmas as a particularly special annual event. It provided a respite from the daily grind of official life and they seem to have enjoyed hugely those times when domestic celebrations and rituals took centre stage. On December 26th, 1841, a member of Victoria's household observed that 'Christmas has brought the usual routine of festivity...'. Victoria herself described Christmases spent with Albert and her growing family as 'a most dear happy time'.

Details of the royal family's Christmases at Windsor Castle in the 1840s were spread widely by newspapers, periodicals and word of mouth. Victoria and Albert were popular and their activities set styles among much of the population, particularly among the growing middle classes. With a revised template and the royal stamp of approval, Christmas was once again fashionable. The royal couple's focus on their children at Christmas was a very important model, as Christmas until this time had largely been an adult festival. From the 1840s onwards, children gradually became more central to the celebrations. The popular view today that Christmas is 'really for children' would, however, have surprised the Victorians as it was still seen as a festival equally for adults.

It is a common misconception that Albert brought the Germanic custom of the Christmas tree to England. It was, in fact, an eighteenth-century, or earlier, introduction. Charlotte, wife of George III and herself German, was known in the 1780s and 1790s to have decorated and lit a fir tree in the house. Victoria herself described 'two large round tables on which were placed trees hung with lights and sugar ornaments' when she was fourteen years old in 1833. However, it was undoubtedly Victoria and Albert's joint enthusiasm for these trees and their presence every year at Windsor that popularised this custom. Each year from 1841 the royal family decorated trees under which they would place gifts for one another. In fact, in 1847 Albert decorated the trees for the children himself. But it was the tree of 1848 which was to have the greatest impact on the celebration of Christmas. In that year, the *Illustrated London News* printed a picture of the royal family, showing five children round the tree with their parents and grandmother. This image was widely published in periodicals at home and abroad. *The Times* of December 27th, 1848, described it thus:

> ...The tree employed... is a young fir, about eight feet high, and has six tiers of branches. On each branch are arranged a dozen wax tapers. Pendant from the branches are elegant trays, baskets, and bonbonniers, and other placements for sweetmeats of the most varied kind, and all forms, colours, and degrees of beauty.

The royal couple also gave trees to schools and army barracks, and the fashion spread. From the late 1840s, a German springelbaum became a must for homes throughout the land. Gradually, through various media, word spread from the royal household that Christmas was indeed a 'right joyous festival', suitable for the time.

The other important, well-known advocate of Christmas in the 1840s was, of course, Charles Dickens, although he was not, as some have said, the creator of the modern festival. Dickens' genius, rather, lay in being able vividly to express, through an examination of Christmas, contemporary social concerns. His vision immediately captured the hearts and minds of the nation. *A Christmas Carol*, and his other Christmas writings, show Dickens' genuine delight in the joys of the season. But this was tempered by a concern for the welfare of the less fortunate, a subject that had coloured debate about the health of society for several years.

In 1843, the year *A Christmas Carol* was first published, a piece in Punch asked,

This image of 1848 showing the royal family at Windsor Castle spread the fashion for Christmas trees and helped redefine the festival as a family affair.

What have you done, this 'merry Christmas', for the happiness of those about, below you? Nothing? Do you dare, with those sirloin cheeks and that port-wine nose, to answer—Nothing?

As early as 1836 Thomas Hervey said

Above all, we love those seasons… which call for the exercise of a general hospitality, and give the poor man his few and precious glimpses of a plenty which, as the world is managed, his toil cannot buy; which shelter the homeless wanderer, and feed the starving child, and clothe the naked mother, and spread a festival for all….

How easily this could be mistaken for a passage from Dickens! As Scrooge's nephew (perhaps the voice of Dickens himself?) says, Christmas was a 'good time; a kind, forgiving, charitable, pleasant time'. Clearly the idea of being a truly inclusive charitable society, even if only for twelve days of the year, seemed to appeal in equal measure in the 1840s both to those giving and receiving. *A Christmas Carol* vividly reflected a prevailing mood and marked a change in perception from Christmas as a celebration of general festivities and conviviality toward one more specifically preoccupied with family and goodwill toward others. The story was an immediate success, touching the conscience of the middle classes and must have influenced behaviour.

Humorous seasonal 'advertisements' from the *Illustrated London News*, 1848.

The highlight of Christmas Day for many, then as now, was a big meal, often shared with extended family and friends. Preparations were extensive and as much money and time as was available would be spent on making a memorable feast. In the early-nineteenth century the traditional Christmas dinner was similar to that found on tables throughout Britain today. The centre-piece of the main course was beef in the north of England and goose in the south. Turkey had been bred in England since the sixteenth century but had not yet become a widely popular dish, though it was a prize turkey that Scrooge sent to the Cratchits on Christmas Day, suggesting they were fairly easily available but expensive. The meat was accompanied by a variety of vegetables and sauces. Other courses included mince

pies and Christmas cake (a descendant of the ancient Twelfth-Night cakes traditionally served at Epiphany) and plum pudding. The latter, a peculiarly English creation, had been around for centuries and by the early Victorian period had become a symbol of seasonal hospitality. This 'speckled cannonball' was to be found in houses of all classes across the land. According to Hervey, writing in 1836:

> Plum pudding is a truly national dish, and refuses to flourish out of England. It can obtain no footing in France.

The food historian Maggie Black has called it a 'democratic dish', a 'unifying dish' that was economical with fuel and inexpensive in ingredients but created a wonderful and, to most, a delicious result. An image of Mrs Cratchit boiling the plum pudding over the family fire vividly comes to mind. All this would be washed down with wines and warming drinks.

Consumption and spending were already a well-established part of Christmas in the early nineteenth century. William Hone observed in 1827 that 'the charms of Christmas give temporary bustle to most classes of tradesmen'. David W. Bartlett, a visitor to London from the United States in 1847–48, was impressed by the array of foodstuffs available in London:

> Perhaps a week before Christmas, we noticed that all the markets began to increase in the quantity and quality of their stores, and in front of them all, green branches of holly were hung as emblems of the coming holiday. The game shops were full of pheasants, rabbits, and venison; the confectioners exhibited a richer than usual assortment of saccharine toys; at the bookshops, Christmas presents began to appear, consisting of every variety of beautiful books. As the day approached, all these shops, in fact all the shops of whatever kind, increased in the splendour and quantity of their wares; the very countenances of the people in the streets were brighter than usual....

When finally Christmas Day arrived, he was not disappointed:

> And when at last we all gathered around that groaning table... it indeed seemed that Christmas in England was a happy festival.

Shopping for food was as important in the 1840s as it is now, and although shopping for presents was slightly more restrained, it was also an important part of the season. The same American visitor observed that 'the streets on Christmas Eve were one continuous blaze of show and ornament', Victoria and Albert seem mainly to have given improving gifts such as books and paintings, although Victoria gave Albert a small pin for Christmas the year before their marriage, saying 'I hope you will sometimes wear it'. Picture frames, perfume bottles, small pieces of jewellery, binoculars for the theatre and albums were also widely popular. And gifts made and bought especially for children became more common.

Two enduring Christmas traditions were conceived in the 1840s, though both took some time to filter into the mainstream. The first was the commercial Christmas card which, unlike the Christmas tree, was an English idea. It was common practice in the early nineteenth century to write seasonal messages on calling cards or in personal letters. The Queen herself sent correspondence to Lord Melbourne in 1841 'upon paper adorned with many quaint and humorous Christmas devices'. In response, Melbourne 'begs to offer... most sincerely and most fervently, the good wishes of the Season'. However, it was Sir Henry Cole who took the idea of sending seasonal greetings a step further with his conception in 1843 of the first commercial Christmas card. Cole and his friend John Horsley devised and printed a small batch of cards, intended to save Cole from handwriting dozens of business and personal messages at Christmas. Within two decades the sending of printed seasonal messages had become an indispensable way of spreading yuletide cheer and maintaining social and familial contacts.

Tom Smith of London was responsible for the other important Christmas invention of the 1840s, the Christmas cracker. First conceived in 1847, this party item was loosely modelled in appearance on a French *bon-bon*, but with the essential added excitement of the 'pop' or 'crack'. It took Smith until 1860 to perfect the cracker with the addition of the salt-petre strip needed to make the distinctive bang, but once he had achieved this, his crackers became an instant success. By the 1906 one London shop alone could offer up to sixty-five types.

The *Illustrated London News* during the second half of the 1840s shows how closely our modern interests and preoccupations mirror those of the early Victorians. The edition for the week ending December 26th, 1846, gave pride of place on the front page to an article entitled 'Christmas in two centuries'. There were also short pieces on Christmas presents, Christmas in Germany, the legend of the Christmas tree and Christmas morning. For the week ending December 25th, 1847, there were short features on the traditional game of snap dragon, the Christmas party, the children's Christmas party and the carol. In the *Christmas Supplement* of 1849 there were a number of familiar topics: Christmas in town and country, plant profiles on choice evergreens such as mistletoe, holly and ivy, Christmas presents, old Christmas customs, Christmas charities, the Christmas pudding, and the meeting of families at Christmas.

By the end of the 1840s, the celebration had all the central ingredients of what we today consider to be a traditional Christmas: strong family feeling, sentimentality, charity and goodwill toward others, consumption and expenditure, fun and games, feasting and drinking. The Victorians certainly did not invent Christmas; they simply picked up a work in progress, begun by previous generations, and finished it with great flair. They mixed old traditions and new sensibilities to create a celebration that had broad appeal, was largely inclusive and was marked by an emphasis on goodwill. This suited a vision of

HT ARCHIVE

Scrooge and the Ghost of Christmas Present from *A Christmas Carol*, 1843. The book inspired a great outpouring of Christian charity.

themselves as good citizens in an ideal society. In a cultural sense, Christmas was the perfect festival on which to build cohesion and a sense of order and security in a rapidly changing society. The seeds for this notion of Christmas were sown before Victoria came to the throne, but they germinated and began to flourish during her first full decade as monarch, forming the core elements of the celebration as we know it today.

For Further Reading

Simon Carter, *Christmas Past Christmas Present: Four Hundred Years of English Seasonal Customs 1600–2000* (Geffrye Museum, 1997); Mark Connelly, *Christmas: A Social History* (Tauris Publishers, 1999); Christopher Hibbert, *The Illustrated London News: A Social History of Victorian Britain* (London, 1976); Delia Millar, 'The Dear, Dear Fashion', *Country Life*, December 3rd, 1992; J.A.R. Pimlott, *The Englishman's Christmas, A Social History* (The Harvester Press Ltd, 1978).

Christine Lalumia is the Deputy Director of the Geffrye Museum, London, which mounts an annual exhibition 'Christmas Past— Seasonal Traditions in English Homes' each December.

Nation-building in 19th-Century Italy

The case of Francesco Crispi

***Christopher Duggan** recalls the contribution of a forgotten Italian statesman.*

THE RE-EMERGENCE OF NATIONALISM as a powerful and virulent factor in international relations—in the Balkans, the former Soviet empire, and elsewhere—together with the increasing momentum in Europe towards ever-greater political integration, has focused minds in the last decade on problems of national identity. The question famously posed in a lecture of 1882 by the French philosopher and historian, Ernest Renan, 'What is a nation?' has acquired a new relevance. Following the pioneering work of Benedict Anderson, Eric Hobsbawm and Ernest Gellner in the 1980s, issues of how (and when) national identities are constructed, the degree to which they co-exist and interact with other more local or cosmopolitan identities (religious, linguistic, ethnic), and whether material (economic, social) or non-material factors (ideas, images) can better explain their formation and continuance, have produced a good deal of speculation and debate.

Nowhere was the problem of constructing the nation more acutely felt than in Italy in the half-century that followed the country's sudden and largely unexpected unification in 1860. This period of Italian history had not been well served. It has frequently been portrayed by Anglo-Saxon historians as a rather dull interlude between the Risorgimento and Fascism, between the heroics of Garibaldi and the buffooneries of Mussolini. It has been characterised as an era of colourless politicians, ill-judged initiatives in foreign policy, tentative reforms, parliamentary corruption, and economic weakness. Italian historians, too, have not always given the period its due—in part, perhaps, because of a widespread desire after 1945 to see Fascism as a 'parenthesis', a rupture with the liberal idealism of the era of Mazzini (1805–72) and Garibaldi (1807–82), and not as something whose roots may in fact have reached deep into the culture of the Risorgimento itself.

Up till now no academic biography has been written of the life of the man who dominated Italian politics in the last two decades of the nineteenth century, Francesco Crispi (1818–1901). The omission is all the more surprising in that Crispi was one of the towering figures of the Risorgimento: a revolutionary and a conspirator, a close friend of Mazzini, and a key player in the events of 1860. Without him Garibaldi would almost certainly not have set sail for Sicily, and probably not have reached Naples. When he was prime minister in the late 1880s and 1890s Crispi was internationally famous. He was the subject of hagiographies in many languages, and was often bracketed along with Bismarck, Gladstone and Salisbury in the pantheon of world statesmen. His death in 1901 resulted in lengthier obituaries in Europe's press than for any Italian politician since Cavour (1810–61).

Why then has he received so little attention from historians? In part because his career ended amid controversy and failure: he got caught up in a major banking scandal and fell from power in 1896 following a disastrous colonial defeat in Africa. But the main reason for his neglect is also, ironically, the reason why he deserves most to be studied today. During the 1920s and 1930s Crispi was celebrated extravagantly by the Fascist regime. He was feted as the 'precursor' of Mussolini, and as the only figure of the liberal era, apart from Cavour, who deserved to be honoured. He was the subject of a day of national commemoration in 1927. Streets and buildings were named after him, and monuments erected. However, with the collapse of Fascism Crispi's reputation was left fatally tarnished. A pall of embarrassed silence settled over his name. How could it be that this friend of Mazzini and Garibaldi had ended up being hailed as a fore-runner of the Duce?

Francesco Crispi was born in Sicily in 1818 into a middle-class family of Greek-Albanian extraction. He studied law at Palermo University, but like many of his background and generation he soon got sidetracked into the exciting world of political and literary romanticism. In the mid-1840s, with his legal career faltering (the Bourbons could quietly block the professional advancement of those they regarded as politically suspect—the hope was that even the most obdurate would eventually give way and sell their souls to them), he went to Naples, and became active in liberal conspiratorial circles. When revolution broke out in Sicily in January 1848, he hurried to Palermo, where he was elected a deputy and served in the civil service of the revolutionary government. He had particular responsibility for defence. When the revolution collapsed ignominiously in the spring of 1849, Crispi fled into exile, first to Marseille, then to Turin, Malta, London and Paris.

In these early years, Crispi's main focus of patriotism was Sicily. He probably did not believe, like many of his fellow islanders, that Sicily was a nation that deserved to be independent of rule from Naples; but he certainly referred to Sicily as his 'country' (*paese*) and his 'homeland' (*patria*). In the revolution of 1848–49 he supported the idea of linking the various Italian states into a federation; but the inability of the revolutionary governments throughout the peninsula to co-operate, and the ease with which they were crushed in the course of 1849, helped convince him that federalism was not viable. Centuries of war and rivalry had left Italy too divided for such an arrangement to be durable. In exile in the 1850s, and partly under the influence of Mazzini, who befriended him when he was in London, Crispi came to the view that the only way to safeguard freedom and independence for all parts of the peninsula was if Italy became a strong unitary state.

Like Mazzini, Crispi was acutely aware that the vast majority of the 22 million Italians in the peninsula had little sense of what 'Italy' was and no feelings of loyalty to it. Middle-class audiences may have cheered at references to 'L'Italia' in Verdi's operas in 1848–49, but their enthusiasm had not been converted into a willingness to take up arms on its behalf. This is why for Mazzini and his supporters the key issue was education: teaching Italians that it was their God-given duty to struggle and if need be to die for the cause of national unity. Mazzini's principal model was the early Christian church. Christ's disciples had won converts through preaching and acts of martyrdom: the apostles of Italian unity (and the words 'apostle' and 'apostolate' punctuated Mazzini's writings, together with terms such as 'martyr', 'faith' and 'cult') had to do likewise. The shedding of blood was important: one reason why Mazzini persisted in organising insurrections, even when they had little or no chance of succeeding, was so as to create 'martyrs'.

Crispi never fully shared Mazzini's more extreme religious views, but all his life he retained a conviction that politics was essentially a matter of faith. 'Patriotism'—the glue that bound the people to the political institutions and made nations morally great—was in essence a religious sentiment. In exile in Paris

and London he had been struck by the depth of national sentiment, even among ordinary people, and of the strength of collective historical memories (above all of great military and naval victories). He noted, too, how patriotism enabled governments to weather major reverses (such as the Indian Mutiny) and allowed the authorities to take a relaxed approach to freedom of speech and association. He recalled attending republican and atheist rallies in London at which there had been no policemen present, and which had ended with renditions of the national anthem.

The contrast with the situation in Italy was marked. Italy had no obviously 'national' historical memories to fall back on. Its past glories had been essentially regional: Piedmontese, Milanese, Venetian, Genoese, Florentine, Neapolitan, Sicilian, not Italian. Furthermore, the most authoritative moral force in the peninsula, the Catholic Church, was avowedly universal, not national, in its claims. In making Italy, what Crispi and his fellow democrats longed for was a great popular insurrection, culminating in victory over the Bourbons, the Austrians, and if need be, the French, with the new nation-state inaugurated magnificently in Rome, on the ruins of the papacy, with a constituent assembly. The genesis of the new nation, they hoped, would have the same kind of symbolic and emotional aura and power as the French Revolution had had for France, or the American War of Independence for the United States, or the Glorious Revolution for England.

As it turned out, the events of 1860—in which Crispi played a leading role, helping to foment the rising in Sicily and acting as Garibaldi's Secretary of State during the expedition of 'the Thousand'—were glorious, but not as glorious or as revolutionary as had been hoped. Rome was not captured (the dream of a revolutionary 'march on Rome' was bequeathed to subsequent generations); there was no constituent assembly; and far from being a wholly new entity, fashioned by the people, the Kingdom of Italy was largely an extension of the old Kingdom of Piedmont-Sardinia. Italy's constitution, administrative system, tariffs, and legal codes were adopted wholesale from Piedmont. And the capital of the new state was Turin. To add insult to injury, the King, Victor Emmanuel II of Piedmont-Sardinia, did not even bother to change his title. He remained Victor Emmanuel II of Italy.

To Crispi and many like him on the left (and on the right, too) this was deeply galling. Italy had been made, but not in such a fashion as to 'make Italians'. Most of those who had fought with Garibaldi were sent home unceremoniously by the new government under the premiership of Count Cavour (1860–61), and the promises of land and reforms that Crispi had been careful to make when Secretary of State, went unhonoured. The imposition of Piedmontese rule made many, especially in the south, feel that they had been conquered, not liberated. Furthermore, the fact that in the course of the 1860s the government resorted frequently to martial law to maintain order within the kingdom exacerbated the divisions between the masses and the state, between what was soon referred to as 'real Italy' and 'legal Italy'.

How under these circumstances could Italians be 'made'? Some of Crispi's friends on the left decided the only hope was to break with the new regime and agitate for a popular revolution and a republic. Crispi, however, remained loyal to the monarchy. He felt that in a country like Italy, with strong absolutist traditions, the king was a powerful unifying symbol—potentially at least. As he said in a speech in 1864: 'The monarchy unites us, and a republic would divide us.' Crispi was also, perhaps, under the illusion that the new liberal regime would seem to many Italians to be superior to the *ancien régime* states that had preceded it, even when run by an insensitive and conservative northern clique, and that they would be won over in due course. His own sufferings and years of exile had probably led him to over-estimate greatly the degree to which the old rulers in Italy had been disliked. They may not have been much loved, but they had not on the whole been detested. The new state, by contrast, with its compulsory military service and its high taxes was soon widely reviled.

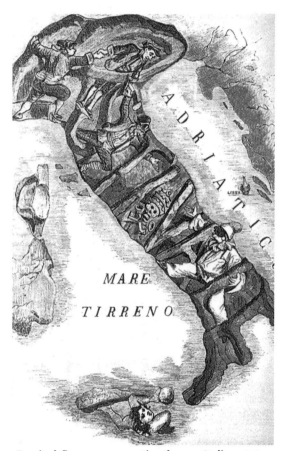

Carnival figures representing former Italian states, divided by a symbol of the Papacy, clamber through the letters of 'Lo Stivale' ('the boot'), trying to complete unification, in this caricature of 1866.

One way Crispi hoped to 'make Italians' was through reforms. If parliament was able to pass laws that would raise the standing of the political institutions, improve economic and social conditions, and gradually, through extensions of the vote, draw the masses inside the framework of the state, this might help to bridge the gap between 'legal' and 'real' Italy. In the years after 1860 Crispi pressed insistently for a broad raft of major reforms, including universal suffrage for literate males,

progressive taxation, and a clear separation between the powers of the executive and the administration. As prime minister between 1887 and 1891 he pushed through an extraordinary package of radical measures (together they constituted the most remarkable legislative achievement of any Italian prime minister) that laid the foundations for public health and welfare services in Italy, liberalised the penal code, and greatly extended local democracy.

But, as Crispi came increasingly to accept, reforms could have only a limited impact in 'making Italians'. The romantic faith that he had had as a young man in the intrinsic virtue of the people, and their capacity to shake off the legacies of centuries of despotism and Catholic rule and become dutiful, free citizens, began to evaporate in the course of the 1860s and 1870s. The old Italian vices (as he saw them) of clientelism, individualism, factionalism, intolerance, materialism and disdain for the state and the law were more tenacious than he had supposed. And far from curing such vices, the new parliamentary system risked exacerbating them: it simply mirrored the country's weaknesses. The scandals that began to rock parliament from the mid-1860s, the lack of party discipline, the failure of deputies to stick to programmes or principles, and the tendency of public officials to exploit their positions for private gain—all made Crispi feel that Italy needed more than just reforms if it was to become 'morally' a nation.

Hence his growing obsession from the 1870s with what he called Italy's 'political education' in order to 'make Italians'. Indeed until the process of 'political education' had been completed, Crispi argued, certain liberal reforms and safeguards might have to be put on hold. This was particularly the case given the growth of organised Catholicism from the 1870s, and the first stirrings of socialism. If the suffrage was enlarged, or freedom of speech and association extended, or government decentralised, there was a danger that this would simply give the enemies of the state more space and opportunity to mobilise against it. From the late 1870s Crispi increasingly came to see a centralised state not as an evil, as he had done before, but as a necessary instrument for controlling and educating Italians.

But how, exactly, were Italians to be educated? Like Mazzini, Crispi's main model was the Catholic Church. Catholicism afforded a brilliant example of successful mass mobilisation. Rituals, ceremonies, grandiose buildings, feast days, charismatic leaders, saints, martyrs and miracles—all these needed to be replicated on a secular level. In the 1880s and 1890s Crispi worked tirelessly to create a national myth out of the Risorgimento, and fostered 'cults' (a key word in his lexicon) of Garibaldi and Victor Emmanuel II. He strove to get Garibaldi's embalmed body interred in the Pantheon in Rome: he wanted the Pantheon to become a centre for national 'pilgrimages'. He promoted the erection of statues and monuments. He organised celebrations of key events, such as the 25th anniversary of the expedition of the Thousand, the 25th anniversary of the taking of Rome in 1870 and the 600th anniversary of the Sicilian Vespers. And he worked hard at his own image—the more parliament seemed prey to weakness and corruption, the more he felt Italians would look to a 'great man' for salvation.

But there was another crucial strand to 'political education' as Crispi envisaged it, and this was war. For all its humanitarian impulses, the Risorgimento had a pronouncedly bellicose and sanguinary side to it. Blood, sacrifice, revenge, martyrdom and slaughter of the tyrannous foreigner were all crucial themes in Italian patriotic writings in the mid-nineteenth century. Garibaldi may have cultivated the image of a reluctant warrior, but he was a soldier through and through, and was fond of quoting the Spanish proverb, '*la guerra es la verdadera vida del hombre*' ('war is the true life for a man'). Mazzini found it repugnant to keep birds in a cage, but he promoted terrorism and insurrections, and believed that Italians would only become conscious of their duty towards the nation when they had learned to kill and be killed for Italy.

Bloodshed had a powerful symbolic value: through it nations were fashioned. The French nation (or at least one version of it) had been forged in the crucible of revolution and war. Italy's genesis, in comparison, had been tame. The battles of 1859 in northern Italy against the Austrians had been fought mainly by the soldiers of Napoleon III; the expedition of the Thousand in 1860 had been deprived of its final consummation. For many, both conservatives and democrats, Italians needed the collective experience of a war to make the nation. The opportunity presented itself in 1866 with the outbreak of hostilities between Austria and Prussia. Crispi called in parliament, to thunderous applause, for a 'baptism of blood'. Italy joined in the war, but suffered two humiliating defeats the same year at the hands of the Austrians at Custoza and Lissa.

The defeats of 1866 were deeply galling, and accentuated insecurities on both the right and the left about the Italian nation. In the years that followed, Crispi called repeatedly for Italy to increase its armaments and to be ready for war. He also wanted Italians to be trained to fight. One historic defect of the Italian character, he argued, was a proneness to indiscipline, humanitarianism and meekness. He urged 'the nation in arms' and wanted all young men to be trained in weaponry (indeed as prime minister he was to consider making military education compulsory in schools). And he was far from being alone in all this. The idea of the 'nation in arms' was one of the central tenets of the democratic left in the Risorgimento. Garibaldi, the republican, Carlo Cattaneo (1801–69), and the famous revolutionary Nicola Fabrizi (1804–85), to name but a few, had been passionate advocates of compulsory military service and of regular drill and practice in target-shooting in the interests of creating their ideal of the 'soldier-citizen'.

By the mid-1880s there was a widespread feeling that Italy was hovering on the brink of moral collapse and physical disintegration. The social situation was worsening, above all in the countryside, and strikes and disorder were spreading. Socialism and republicanism were gaining support, and the Catholic Church, which was still implacably opposed to the liberal state, was becoming more militant. The gap between 'real' and 'legal' Italy was wider than ever. Parliament under the now ailing and lack-lustre prime minister, Agostino Depretis (during his second term in 1881–87), appeared weak, corrupt and incapable. To make matters worse, Italy had suffered a series of humbling reverses in foreign policy, beginning with the Congress of Berlin in 1878, which together had created a sense that the country was being surrounded by its principal rival in the Mediterranean, France, and risked being stifled. When, early in 1887, a force of 500 Italian soldiers was massacred in Africa, there was a national outcry and demands for strong government. Crispi's hour had come.

Crispi's first period as prime minister lasted from 1887 until 1891. For much of that time he enjoyed overwhelming support in both parliament and in the country, and acted almost dictatorially. Though he had a clear agenda on the domestic front, his main concern was with foreign policy. His hope was to involve Italy in a great and successful war. This, he believed, would prove the making of Italy (a view shared by many—in the military, at court, in the foreign ministry, and in government, as well as by some of the most influential writers and intellectuals of the period). Crispi hurriedly signed a secret military convention with Germany—a country that he admired enormously: had not Bismarck, Count Moltke and the Prussian king together 'made' Germany with three carefully orchestrated military campaigns?—and then embarked on a programme of massive rearmament. He justified this by claiming that a European war could break out at any moment, such was the level of international tension, and that Italy had to be ready to defend herself.

An Italian army of 17,000 was annihilated by Ethiopian forces at the Battle of Adowa.

In reality, Crispi's intentions were more aggressive than defensive. He knew that Bismarck had little stomach for another war, but he was aware that many in the German military were convinced that Germany needed to launch a pre-emptive strike against Russia and France before the combined forces of these two exceeded those of the Triple Alliance—as, it was believed, they soon would. By agreeing to send 200,000 Italian troops to the Rhine front, Crispi hoped to make the war option as appealing as possible to the likes of General von Waldersee (a key figure in the so-called 'war party' in Berlin), Moltke, and the young and impetuous Wilhelm II, who became Kaiser in 1888.

Crispi tried time and again in 1888–90 to provoke the French and trigger a war. The French needed to be made to seem the aggressor. British support for the Triple Alliance was crucial, and that could only be guaranteed if Italy seemed the victim of Gallic *hubris*. It was a difficult game, and one that Crispi played with unnerving skill. He counted in part on the strongly nationalist atmosphere that had been whipped up in France in recent years by the revanchist rabble-rouser General Boulanger. Crispi concocted numerous 'trumpery quarrels' (in the words of Lord Salisbury, who found Crispi a nightmare to deal with) and even began mobilising the Italian army in mid-July 1889 (just as the celebrations for the centenary of the French Revolution were reaching a peak), claiming that the French government had hatched a plot with the Pope to launch an imminent attack on Italy.

War, of course, did not break out in Europe on this occasion. Bismarck, Salisbury and the French government managed to keep their nerve and thwart Crispi—who by the second half of 1890 had grown despondent and contemplated doing a deal with the French and quitting the Triple Alliance. Crispi fell from power early in 1891. He returned at the end of 1893, when Italy was being rocked by a huge banking scandal and threats of a socialist insurrection. Again he looked to war for a solution to the country's problems. He hoped to convert the crisis over Constantinople in late 1895 into a European conflagration; but again he was frustrated. Instead he had to be content with Africa, where he became embroiled in a major conflict in Ethiopia. However, he had bitten off more than he could chew, and on March 1st, 1896, an Italian army of 17,000 was annihilated by Ethiopian forces at the Battle of Adowa. Crispi fell from power. He died five years later, convinced that a man of genius was needed to complete Italy's moral unity and finally 'make Italians'.

Crispi's extraordinary career sheds light on the problem of nation building in Italy. Like many of his contemporaries, Crispi was acutely aware that national sentiment was lacking in Italy in 1860. Morally, the nation did not exist. He hoped initially that the beneficial effects of freedom would win over Italians, bind them to the liberal regime, and generate patriotism. His disappointment, in this respect, led him increasingly to believe, from the 1870s onwards, that the state needed to engage in an active process of 'political education' in order to 'make Italians'. The ideas and practices Crispi espoused strongly foreshadowed many of those ideas that were to be taken up by the Fascists in the 1920s and 1930s: the sacralisation of politics, charismatic leadership, obligatory military training, mass mobilisation through war and the threat of war, the manufacture of foreign scares, the cult of energy and enthusiasm, and the creation of national myths. The roots of these ideas and practices, however, can be clearly discerned in the Risorgimento, where the problem of how to make the 'Italian nation' was first mooted.

FOR FURTHER READING

D.Mack Smith, *Modern Italy. A Political History*, (Yale University Press, 1997); F. Chabod, *Italian Foreign Policy—the Statecraft of the Founders*, (Princeton University Press, 1996); A. Russell Ascoli and K.von Henneberg (eds), *Making and Remaking Italy. The Cultivation of National Identity around the Risorgimento* (Berg, 2001); J.A. Davis (ed.), *Italy in the Nineteenth Century* (OUP, 2000); N.Doumanis, *Italy* (Arnold, 2001).

Christopher Duggan is Reader in Italian History at the University of Reading. His biography of Francesco Crispi will be published by Oxford UP in 2002.

Not So Saintly?

This week the Catholic Church beatifies Pius IX. The flawed 19th century Pontiff, who once referred to Jews as "dogs," is an odd candidate for canonization

By DAVID VAN BIEMA

OFFICIALLY THE RITE IS CALLED Recognition. On April 4, a delegation of bishops and monsignors in full regalia arrived at Rome's Basilica of St. Lawrence Outside the Walls. They descended to the 6th century cathedral's crypt and were led to a white stone tomb. A casket was opened for them. At this point, wrote Monsignor Carlo Liberati of the Vatican's Congregation for the Causes of Saints, "there was a moment of profound and intense commotion." The body within, that of 19th century Pope Pius IX, was "almost perfectly conserved." Pius, known universally in Rome as Pio Nono, died in 1878. Yet here he was "in the beauty of his humanity, just as he is seen in the photographic documentation" of his deathbed, back when the entire city came "and admired the beautiful face of the Pontiff smiling in the sleep of death." Although Pius' face is now masked, Liberati's observations suggest that the old Pope is smiling still.

If so, he is in a minority. The April exhumation cleared the way for Pio Nono's beatification, scheduled for this Sunday. Beatification will confirm Pius' "heroic virtue," affirm a miracle (a nun's broken kneecap healed) and encourage Catholics to venerate his remains, which will be transferred to a clear crystal casket. The next step will be canonization, or sainthood.

Although the Vatican will not admit it, Pio Nono is a last-minute substitution for a controversial successor, Pius XII.

The beatification of the later Pius was to have balanced that of Pope John XXIII, the liberal hero who called the Second Vatican Council. The past 40 years, however, have seen an unabating storm of complaint that Pius XII did not do enough to oppose the Holocaust. Postponing Pius XII's "cause" and replacing it with that of Pio Nono—also a conservative favorite—must have seemed a good idea at the time.

But in actuality the Vatican has exhumed far more than just a venerable body. "I am appalled that the Catholic Church wants to make a saint out of a Pope who perpetuated... an act of unacceptable intolerance," declared a professor named Elena Mortara in Rome. Pio Nono, it turns out, had a Jewish problem of his own. Mortara is the great-grandniece of Edgardo Mortara, who was taken from his Jewish parents at age six in 1858 by the papal police and raised—in part by Pius himself—as a Catholic. The incident typified Pius' ham-fisted treatment of the Jews, and many feel his beatification contradicts Pope John Paul II's embrace of that people and his apologies for their treatment by church members. Israel's Ambassador to the Holy See, Aharon Lopez, while stressing that beatification is a church "internal matter," told TIME that Pius' might have "implications" for Israeli-Vatican cooperation in "bridging difficult periods" of history.

Pius, in fact, is one of the modern church's problematic giants. His papacy as a whole was far more controversial than Pius XII's. He was the longest-serving Pope since St. Peter, reigning 32 years from 1846 to his death. He lost the Papal States, the Vatican's worldly kingdom. He promulgated two of Catholicism's most triumphal doctrines—the Immaculate Conception of the Virgin Mary and papal infallibility. He pioneered the papal personality movement that John Paul embodies so brilliantly. Many historians believe he created the modern papacy.

Yet some also think his narrowness crippled his church. Pius reigned just as the old order in the West was giving way to new notions of God, the state and the citizen. His response—a wholesale rejection of modernity—dominated Catholicism for almost a century after his death and continues to color its present. A true reactionary who saw the secular state, and indeed civil rights, as satanic manifestations, he made it difficult for generations of believers to claim intellectual independence or integrity. Says journalist-historian Garry Wills, who savages Pius in his best seller *Papal Sins*: "He was a disaster, and his influence has been bad ever since. If you beatify him now, there will be a whitewashing of him, which will involve the church in more dishonesty." Pius is the heavy in the well-reviewed *The Kidnapping of Edgardo Mortara*, by Brown University historian David Kertzer, which is being adapted for Broadway by playwright Alfred Uhry (*Driving Miss Daisy*). Even the author of the definitive, three-volume Pius biography, Jesuit historian Giacomo Martina, does not favor his subject for sainthood.

The Vatican has long been aware of Pius' explosiveness as a candidate for canonization. As Kenneth Woodward reports in his book *Making Saints*, the first time Pius' cause was formally addressed, every firsthand witness criticized his papacy's conduct. His beatification was repeatedly postponed, most recently in the 1980s, when churchmen apparently deemed it not to be "opportune." That seems to have changed. It will be interesting to see whether the upcoming ceremony will end the debate or spark an even more thorough public airing of this larger-than-life Pope's remarkable career.

GIOVANNI MASTAI-FERRETTI WAS born at a disadvantage. The ninth child of a minor count in the town of Senigallia, he applied early to join the Pope's Noble Guards. They rejected him: guards did not have epilepsy. A biographer quoted him complaining that because of his condition, he "could not concentrate on a subject for any length of time without having to worry about his ideas getting terribly confused." He was ordained in 1819 on condition that another priest always be present when he celebrated Mass. By 1827 he was Archbishop of Spoleto.

The position plunged him into a supremely complicated religious and political game. Throughout Europe the old order of divinely sanctioned kingdoms was battling models of popular sovereignty and citizenship inspired by the Enlightenment, the French Revolution and the adolescent U.S. The Italian peninsula was a crux of this struggle. The Pope himself was a monarch, ruler of the states girdling the boot approximately from Naples to Venice, playing survival politics amid what historian Kertzer describes as "a patchwork of duchies, grand duchy, Bourbon and Savoyard kingdoms [and] Austrian outposts." Would-be nation builders plotted Italy's unification from the south and the north. Revolutionaries, writes Kertzer, goggled across papal borders at those who regarded "the notions that people should be free to think what it pleased them to think [as] heretical."

For a few brief years, it seemed as though Mastai might bridge the gap. In Spoleto he had brokered a peaceful surrender of 4,000 Italian revolutionaries to the archconservative Austrian forces. This led to his 1846 election to the papacy as a moderate. Once installed, he gave amnesty to political prisoners in the Papal States, bestowed on Rome a constitution and a Prime Minister and talked about creating an Italian federation. He unlocked the Jewish ghetto and allowed its wealthier inhabitants to live among the Christian population. Austria's Prince Metternich, the genius of the ancien régime, quipped that he "had allowed for everything in Italy except a liberal Pope."

The détente didn't last long. In 1848, as revolutions blazed throughout Europe, Italian nationalists tried to enlist Pius in their plan to expel the Austrian forces and attain unification. He refused. Achieving an Italian Republic anyway, they slit his Prime Minister's throat. Pius fled Rome disguised as a priest and wearing tinted spectacles. When he returned three years later, supported by French troops, he was a different Pope.

"The knock came at nightfall." So begins *The Kidnapping of Edgardo Mortara*. Kertzer's echo of Holocaust literature is daring but eerily appropriate. The unwanted visitors to the Jewish Mortara family in June 1858 were papal police; they left with Edgardo. A family servant, thinking he was mortally ill, had secretly baptized him, and law required that he be removed from Jewish influence and brought up by the church. Pius may not have initiated the action, but he soon embraced it, and Edgardo, wholeheartedly. In a memoir, Edgardo later recalled that "like a good father, [Pius] had fun with me hiding under his great red cloak and said, jokingly, 'Where is the boy?' and opening up the cloak, he showed all those standing around, 'Here he is!'" Edgardo eventually became a priest, lecturing on the miracle of conversion to Catholicism.

To Pius' astonishment, the child's abduction became an international scandal, a focus for global ambivalence regarding the church. The New York *Times* ran 20 articles on it in a month; the New York *Herald* cited "colossal" interest in the matter. Pius' response set the tone for his next 20 years. "The newspapers can write all they want. I couldn't care less about what the world thinks," he told a Jewish delegation. And he added a threat: "Take care. I could have made you go back into your hole." In fact he had already confined the Jews to the ghetto again and rescinded their civil rights. In 1870 he declared them "dogs... there are too many of them in Rome, and we hear them howling in the streets."

PIUS WAS A DIVIDED PERSONALITY. A biographer wrote that "looking into [his] sparkling eyes and hearing the warm measure of his sentences, you felt how beautiful the world could be." He was famously accessible. He played billiards with the Swiss Guard and was the first modern Pontiff to grant audiences to commoners. He personally tended cholera victims, Gentile and Jewish, during an epidemic. He was truly pious. However, he was also excitable, oversensitive and bullying. Sometimes this expressed itself in wit. The benediction he bestowed upon a group of Protestant clergy was borrowed from the prayer over incense: "May you be blessed by Him in whose honor you shall be burnt." But often he employed the bludgeon: bishops who displeased him were ordered to kiss his foot. Later, members of the Vatican's saintmaking congregation seriously questioned whether he had lacked the essential Christian virtue of charity. (A related objection involved his sustaining of the death sentences of two anarchists. His successor reportedly remarked, "This fact alone would impede [his] canonization.") Biographer Martina describes a "siege complex": unable to understand liberals on political or psychological terms, he saw them as "unbelievers... [operating] a war machine against the church."

In 1864 this intemperance was writ very large indeed. The Vatican released the *Syllabus of Errors*, an index of don'ts that summed up Pius' response to modernity—by spitting in its face. The 80 delusions in question included separation of church and state, freedom of conscience, civil rights and rationalism. Error No. 80 was that "the Roman Pontiff can... reconcile himself to any compromise with progress, liberalism and modern civilization." Writes Wills: "The *Syllabus* dumbfounded the world." It still has its defenders. Theologian Don Gianni Baget Bozzo says Pius "simply refused to accept the tenets of liberalism in their entirety." It is true that the knee-jerk antireligious sentiment and materialism that irked Pius plague Western culture today. Still, the tract defined Catholicism in the negative—and placed good Catholics at odds with modern Western governance. Wills maintains that it "gave ammunition" to anti-Catholics "down to the time when John Kennedy was running for President and many felt no Catholic could be free—that the church was opposed to democracy in every way."

Many of the *Syllabus'* most egregious positions were repudiated 35 years ago at the Second Vatican Council. But Vatican II let stand what may be Pio Nono's most lasting achievement, the doctrine of papal infallibility. By 1869 most Catholics already believed that a Pope could, alone, define the word of God through church dogma. But no Pontiff had ever said so explicitly, and some bishops thought this might drive an even greater wedge between Catholicism and the rest of the world. Pius' war on the dissenters featured deception, obfuscation and railroading. When the Archbishop of Bologna complained that church tradition in Europe argued against infallibility, Pius roared, "I *am* tradition!" and reassigned the Archbishop to a monastery. (He came around.)

Said British Cardinal John Henry Newman: "It is not good for a Pope to live 20 years. He becomes a God [and] has no one to contradict him." No one but history. In 1870, Piedmont's King Victor Emmanuel arrived at Rome to complete the unification of Italy and end the church's 1,116-year history as a

worldly monarchy. The Pope, 79, long white hair flying, climbed the Scala Santa staircase on his knees and told his troops to show token resistance and then surrender honorably. Victor Emmanuel offered him some powers in return for recognition. Pius excommunicated him and vowed to become a "prisoner of the Vatican." He never again left the grounds. Many Catholics loved him for it. The Italians did not; after his death, a Roman rabble tried to toss his coffin into the Tiber.

BAPTISM BY FORCE Taken from his parents, Mortara grew up under Pius IX's wing in a home funded by levies on Jews. He became a priest.

T HE JUDGMENT OF THE MOB WAS TOO harsh," wrote ethicist Daniel Callahan in a 1966 essay. "Pius IX was no villain. But he was... a man who used the wrong weapons at the wrong time to fight for the wrong cause." Most historians concur. Yet someone clearly loves Pius, someone with the power to make saints. Vaticanologists have suggested that he is a "hero" of John Paul II's. The two Pontiffs do share a special reverence for the Virgin Mary, a generally conservative world view and an impatience with church dissenters. But John Paul's conservatism is tempered with an un-Pius-like humanism. Pius' comfort with executions runs counter to John Paul II's campaign against the death penalty. And then there are the Jews. Vittorio Messori, collaborator with John Paul on the best seller *Crossing the Threshold of Hope*, says, "I think Pius' cause is something of a problem. When John Paul II asked for forgiveness for the church's treatment of the Jews over the centuries, I think perhaps he was thinking of Pius IX."

If not John Paul, then who? Each year a group of aging, high-ranking clerics

convenes for a special Mass on Feb. 7, Pius' birthday. They share a belief that a Pope's administration of worldly states (and by extension Pius' treatment of the Jews) has little bearing on his sanctity. Saintmaking's fine print sets great store by a candidate's intent. And so, says Austrian Cardinal Alfons Stickler, presenter of Pius' case in 1985, "you can't condemn someone for something he believed was an act of virtue." Most important, the group feels, was that Pius successfully preserved the church's great truths during a period of unbelief.

But if the Feb. 7 Club alone could prevail, it would have done so in the 1980s. Some see this year's events as the work of parties less keen on Pius himself than on blunting the thrust of the Second Vatican Council. As John Paul becomes weaker, liberals hope someday to interpret Vatican II's watchwords of openness and dialogue to revive seemingly shut issues like women priests. Guido Verucci, a Roman historian, is among those who see conservatives using Pius' beatification to reaffirm his contrasting "vision of a strong, unerring Church."

There is one other possibility: the Vatican simply needed a beatifiable Pope in a hurry. Even liberals admit the wisdom of balancing John XXIII with a conservative. Says Kertzer: "There are not so many recent Popes who can represent the right wing. Pio Nono's cause went through the administrative hoops in the 1980s, so everything was ready. He was from so long ago—who knew him? They thought he'd just slide by."

And so he has, after a fashion. Somewhere in Rome, a crystal casket is being readied. Pius will be beatified, and all will get a clear look at him. They will quite likely still be arguing about what they've seen years later, when his canonization rolls around.

—With reporting by Martin Penner/
Rome

SWEEP THEM OFF THE STREETS

John Marriott *looks at attitudes to the London poor since the seventeenth century.*

RECENT PUBLICITY over the numbers of those sleeping rough on the streets of London has served to remind us that the poor are not only still with us but continue to be perceived as an urgent problem. According to *The Observer* of November 14th, 1999, for example, Louise Casey, head of the government's Rough Sleepers' Unit, claimed that the policies of charitable organisations just perpetuated the problem of the homeless, and called for radical new strategies to 'sweep them off the streets'.

There is something familiar about such pronouncements. As early as 1700, 'M.D.' worried that:

> The number of Beggars increases daily, our Streets swarm with this kind of People, and their boldness and impudence is such that they often beat at our Doors, stop Persons in the ways, and are ready to load us with Curses and Imprecations if their Desires be not speedily answered.

At particular moments, usually following demobilisation from the army and navy, the number of beggars increased dramatically. So too did the levels of anxiety expressed by observers. The early 1750s were distinctly troubled years. Not only did beggars proliferate, but they were linked to the more serious matter of crime. An anonymous pamphlet of 1751 argued:

> The first sources... of the many robberies committed in our streets... is the prodigious and scandalous encrease of publick beggars... [T]here are more publick beggars in London and Westminster alone than in all the great cities of Europe put together, tho' the revenue of collected for the use of the poor in these cities exceeds the revenue of some very respectable sovereign states.... At least 20,000 live by the publick trade of begging and pilfering, and other arts of that sly profession.

To Henry Fielding, then a Westminster magistrate, beggars on London streets were a lesser source of concern than was the criminal underclass taking refuge in London's infested courts,

rookeries and alleys. In *An inquiry into the recent encrease of robberies in the metropolis* (1751), he set out to think through the nature and extent of metropolitan crime. What comes over is a sense of bewilderment:

> Whoever indeed considers the Cities of London and Westminster, with their late vast addition of their Suburbs; the great irregularity of their Buildings, the immense Number of Lanes, Alleys, Courts and Byeplaces; must think, that, had they been intended for the very Purpose of Concealment, they could scarce have been better contrived. Upon such a View, the whole appears as a vast Wood or Forest, in which a Thief may harbour with as great Security, as wild Beasts do in the Desarts of Africa or Arabia.

For most of the eighteenth century the poor remained an object of fear, disgust and embarrassment to the elite: worse, they seemed increasingly unknowable. By the end of the century it was evident that ignorance prevailed. An inquiry into the state of mendicity initiated in 1796 by Lord Pelham, with the support of the Society for Bettering the Condition of the Labouring Classes, was abandoned six years later. The secretary, Matthew Martin, who had in the course of the inquiry interviewed more than 2,000 beggars, conceded defeat, pleading the 'complicated nature and extent of the misery'.

Others, though, were ready to take up the challenge. Patrick Colquhoun, like Fielding a London magistrate, established soup kitchens in Spitalfields, and advocated national schemes of education. More significant, however, were his writings on the plunder of riverside trade, which showed the poor as a threat to the empire itself. In his *A treatise on the police of the metropolis* (1795) and *A treatise on the commerce and police of the River Thames* (1800), Colquhoun remapped the moral, political and spatial boundaries of poverty and crime. The exotic and fanciful descriptions of street crime found in eighteenth-century writings were displaced by the idea of a criminal culture at the heart of commerce and empire. Most notable here was large-scale theft from riverside trades committed by 'nautical vagabonds' employed in the docks and on the river. He suggested the exist-

Outdoor relief, from James Grant *Sketches in London* (1838)

ence of an endemic, predatory and organised international underclass, located in an extensive network of receivers and dealers in stolen goods in the riverside areas of East London, far from the traditional sites of criminal activity in the City and Westminster. Colquhoun revealed the culture of London poverty through the radical methodology of rational inquiry, detailed statistics, reports and survey techniques. 'It may naturally be expected,' he wrote, 'that such an accumulation of delinquency, systematically detailed, and placed in so prominent a point of view, must excite a considerable degree of astonishment in the minds of those readers who have not been familiar with subjects of this nature.'

He was correct, for his writings found a ready audience. Politicians, social reformers and evangelicals found them a rich source of information and ideas. Colquhoun's role in the establishment of the Metropolitan Police is well remembered, but arguably of greater significance was his influence on the redefinition of poverty and crime; the concept of a casual residuum located in the East End was to frame much of nineteenth-century thought on poverty in the metropolis.

Much scholarly work has been devoted to poverty in nineteenth-century London, and we have a good understanding of the economic forces that shaped it. Less is known of the ways in which the poor came to occupy a symbolic centrality in the minds of the metropolitan bourgeoisie. A range of concerns about social order, citizenship, progress and the future of the imperial race were articulated around the poor. Accounts written by those who worked, lived and moved amongst the poor exerted a formative influence on Victorian perceptions of the problem. Men such as Henry Mayhew and Charles Booth

were part of an impressive body of work that attempted for the first time to grasp in totality the nature of poverty and the culture of those affected by it. Of particular significance were the tracts, articles and books that recorded the observations of evangelicals and urban explorers.

From the end of the eighteenth century London provided a focus for evangelical endeavour. Organisations such as the Society for Bettering the Condition of the Poor began to turn attention to the practical and ethical problems of poverty. Then in the 1830s evangelicals embarked on a campaign to bring the gospel to the poor, principally through the work of the London City Mission (LCM). Inspired by the work of people like Thomas Chalmers in Glasgow, the LCM was formed in 1835 aggressively to proselytise the poor through house to house visits. At the height of its activities in 1855 nearly one and a half million households were visited, and over two million tracts distributed.

This massive intervention transformed knowledge of the poor. Agents were required to keep daily logs of their visits, and wrote enthusiastically of their experiences. These accounts had historical antecedents in the spiritual autobiographies of sixteenth- and seventeenth-century preachers. In them, human existence was seen as a pilgrimage: after conversion to religious faith, the narrator abandoned material and social wealth to undertake an arduous spiritual journey in search of the promised land. His (and for the first thirty years or so only male agents were employed) example, it was hoped, would be followed by the poor themselves.

These accounts and the vast body of religious material distributed were used to articulate a wide range of concerns over the threat of the poor to the religious and social fabric of the nation. Thomas Beames, for example, wrote *The Rookeries of London* in 1848. How, he asked, was it possible that a poor remained among the ancient Anglo-Saxon people whose wise and civilising influence had been felt throughout the world? The question was urgent, for an unreformed poor might soon seek violent retribution, subjecting Britain to the same convulsions that had shaken the rest of Europe.

Similar sensibilities were voiced by Frederick Meyrick in his 1858 *The outcast and the poor of London*. This effectively constructed the poor as a race apart, and for the first time linked them with imperial subjects. Meyrick warned of the dangers of allowing the 'evil beast' within the poor to continue without the 'wholesome restraints of Christian precept and example'. Among a middle class readership reeling from the trauma of the Indian uprising, the warning would not have gone unheeded.

This 'racialisation' of the poor intensified as the metaphors of dirt and degeneration took hold. W.R. Cosens' *London dens and mission work among them* (1863) identified opium dens off the Ratcliffe Highway as symbolic sites of degeneration within the imperial race, and colonial subjects as a degenerate form of an idealised white, Anglo-Saxon race. This moral taxonomy was reinforced by accounts of overseas mission work. Joseph Mullens, for example, reflected in *London and Calcutta* (1869):

> There are slums in London, known only to city missionaries and the men who work with them, in which violence and vice abound to a degree which cannot be

told. But the slums of heathenism go a long way lower. They reach the very horrors of immorality.

No publication more powerfully captured unease over the gap between the poor and the 'decency and civilization' offered by evangelicals, than Andrew Mearns' *Bitter cry of outcast London* (1883). It lacked coherence and had none of the flair or originality of Mayhew, but it sold in vast numbers and was quoted in Parliament. Perceptions of the danger of revolution attendant upon this separation also informed the other great evangelical work of the time. William Booth's *In Darkest England* (1890) drew upon the same rhetoric of degeneration and moral contagion within the 'dark jungles' of the poor. In influentially promoting an interventionist response to poverty, however, it also closed the chapter on Victorian evangelicalism.

Colquhoun claimed there was a predatory underclass and an extensive network of dealers in stolen goods in East London, far from the traditional criminal areas of the City and Westminster.

Evangelicals inquiring into urban poverty were accompanied by social explorers, whose early nineteenth-century writings took the form of travelogues in which the innocent observer, usually on the visit from the countryside, encountered the criminal underworld in its various guises, emerging with new-found wisdom. Later, melodrama came to exert a powerful influence. Most of the important writers in this tradition—Henry Mayhew, Charles Dickens, Watts Phillips, John Hollingshead and Pierce Egan—had an abiding interest in the theatre. Melodramatic narratives of good versus evil, and of class and sexual exploitation, enabled them to explore the plurality of metropolitan life.

The work that defined this new genre was Pierce Egan's *Life in London*, first published after serialisation in 1821. It was an account of the exploits of the rustic Jerry Hawthorne, who is taken on a guided tour of the metropolis by Corinthian, Tom and Bob Logic. They encounter the highs and lows of London life, including the clientele of an East End gin house. But the book's extraordinary popularity was mainly due to its exploration of the darker sides of metropolitan life.

This desire to extend inquiry into the realm of the metropolitan poor found more rational forms in the writings of the journalist and devout Calvinist James Grant. In *The great metropolis* (1838), *Sketches in London* (1838) and *Lights and shadows of London life* (1841) he did as much as anyone to bring the plight of the poor to popular attention. Grant's guiding principle was to present to the reader 'such information respecting this modern Babylon, as may prove instructive as well as amusing', but at the same time entirely reliable.

In their attempts to capture the complex totality of the metropolis, Egan, Grant and their contemporaries widened the range of urban inquiry, and laid the foundations for the 'problem' novels of the 1840s and the first endeavours to listen to the poor themselves. Out of this milieu emerged Charles Dickens and Henry Mayhew. Both had direct links with Egan. In Dickens, there is the same celebration of metropolitan life, even though the poor remained minor and shadowy figures. Only in his journalistic peregrinations around London did he bring his acute powers of observation to reveal their plight. Mayhew, on the other hand, took Egan to heart and recorded patiently the minutiae of street life.

Many of the social explorers that followed Egan, Dickens and Mayhew demonstrated their influence, often transmitted through personal acquaintance. James Greenwood came to dominate the genre. During his forty-year career, Greenwood wrote thirty-nine books and numerous articles. Most of his investigations were based on personal observation by the then unusual device of disguising himself as one of the poor.

The poor were increasingly defined by the social explorers (as by the evangelicals) as a race apart. 'Racial' discourses were apparent in embryonic form in Mayhew, but Watts Phillips and Greenwood employed the language of dirt and degeneration to impart a menacing turn. Phillips recalled courts near Holborn which

> Swarm with dirty unwashed men, who bear, Cain-like, on every brow a brand that warns you to avoid them— with rude, coarse women, whose wild language, fierce eyes, and strange lascivious gestures strike terror to the spectator's heart…. Children… swarm about the road, half-naked, shaggy-headed little savages, who flock about you, and, with canting phrase and piteous whine, solicit charity for their dying father—that broad shouldered, burly-looking Milesian, who has just reeled from the tavern-door.

Towards the end of the century, the threat from the poor took on a new urgency. In the writings of George Sims and George Haw, even more extreme sentiments were expressed. Unsurprisingly given the new wave of immigration to the East End, the Jew now featured prominently—a theme consolidated by Arnold White in *The problems of a great city* (1886), which mapped the terrain for a new racialisation of the metropolis.

Race, degeneration and sexuality were now articulated in an imaginative framework within which the poor were presented as a crowd dwelling in the abyss. The 'crowd', a force of destructive mass irrationality, thus displaced the 'tribes' of the poor. The survey of Charles Booth, *Life and labour of the people of London* (1889), defined this transition, but this consciousness found its most imaginative expression in the writings of Charles Masterman and Ford Madox Ford. Masterman described the 'dense black masses' streaming across the bridges from the marshes and desolate places beyond the river:

> We have seen a ghost; we are striving to adjust our stable ideas. But within there is a cloud in men's minds,

and a half-stifled recognition of the presence of a new force hitherto unreckoned; the creeping into conscious existence of the quaint and innumerable populations bred in the abyss.

Bart Kennedy may be little known now, but at the time was one of very few writers who could claim to speak as a member of the early twentieth-century urban poor. In *The hunger line* (1908), a radical denouncement of corrupt and ineffective politicians, his final assessment was only too predictable:

London is being turned into the world's slum. The scum of the races of Europe is pouring in upon us. We are being invaded by hordes of wastrel aliens who are devouring the substance that belongs to our own people.

Herein were echoes of the eighteenth century and traditions of urban inquiry in the nineteenth, but their continued resonance is heard today.

John Marriott is Senior Lecturer in History at the University of East London.

This article first appeared in *History Today*, August 2000, pp. 26-28. © 2000 by History Today, Ltd. Reprinted by permission.

THE HUNT FOR
Jack the Ripper

William D. Rubinstein *reviews the achievements of the 'Ripperologists'
and lends weight to the argument surrounding the Ripper Diaries.*

The brutal murders of five prostitutes in London's East End in the autumn of 1888 by an unknown killer who came to be called 'Jack the Ripper' are probably the most famous unsolved crimes in history. During the past forty years a plethora of theories has been offered as to the identity of the Ripper. In recent years, the Ripper industry has mushroomed: it is likely that more has been written on this case than on any other staple of amateur historiography (the true identity of Shakespeare and the Kennedy assassination possibly excepted). The number of books about Jack the Ripper published internationally shows this dramatically: 1888-1909–nine; 1910-49–five; 1950-69– four; 1970-79–ten; 1980-89–twelve; 1990-99–thirty-nine. Most of these offer original 'solutions' to the question of the Ripper's identity. There has also been a stream of films, television programmes and novels. Two high quality British journals, *The Ripperologist* and *Ripperana*, are devoted to the subject, as are two others in America. The 'Cloak and Dagger Club', with a membership of over 220, is devoted almost exclusively to presenting talks and seminars on Jack, almost always with the aim of identifying the killer.

The five prostitutes were stabbed to death in Whitechapel between August 31st and November 9th, 1888, always late at night. Then, for unknown reasons, the killings stopped. Each of the women—Mary Ann (Polly) Nichols (August 31st, 1888), Annie Chapman (September 8th), Elizabeth Stride and Catharine Eddowes (both September 30th, about half-a-mile apart), and Mary Jane Kelly (November 9th)—was not merely murdered, but horribly mutilated, with organs removed and a strong possibility of cannibalism. The last victim was mutilated almost beyond recognition. Even today, the photographs of the bodies are still deeply shocking.

Jack the Ripper is often said to have been the first 'serial killer' (apparently random, sequential murders of the same type of victim) in the modern sense. Nothing like this had ever been known before in Britain. As the killings unfolded, fear gripped the East End, a near-riotous situation developed, and hundreds of extra police were drafted in to patrol the streets of Whitechapel. Although the Ripper was reportedly seen by several witnesses, he was never caught, and seemed time and again to slip through the dragnet like magic. While the police had many suspects, in the final analysis they remained baffled. Among those suspected were doctors, or slaughtermen (the, removal of the victims' organs implied anatomical knowledge), Jews or other foreigners from the large local community of recent immigrants, Fenians, lunatics and eccentrics of all shades, local workingmen, and associates of the murdered women. No one was ever charged. Since 1888 dozens, perhaps hundreds, of candidates have been proposed as the Ripper, ranging from dukes to dustmen, from Oxford scholars and millionaires to lunatics.

Whitechapel, adjacent to the City of London, and only a mile from the Bank of England, was synonymous with urban poverty and squalor. It was often known to middle-class Londoners as the 'Abyss.' Nevertheless, it is important not to exaggerate conditions there. According to Charles Booth's *Life and Labour of the People in London*, (1891–1903), the 90,000 inhabitants of Whitechapel (out of 900,000 in the East End) did indeed have the highest percentage in poverty of any London district (47 per cent), but nearly 53 per cent were living in what Booth described as 'comfort', that is, enjoying a normal working-class standard of living or higher. The district had a normal infrastructure of local government, shops, businesses, transport, and services. Many of the recent Eastern European Jewish and other immigrants were upwardly mobile in a determined way, working hard towards starting their own businesses. Each religious and ethnic group maintained its own network of charitable and educational institutions. Above all the East End was not seriously violent. In 1887 not a single murder was recorded in Whitechapel. (A total of eighty murders occurred in the whole of London in 1887, almost exactly the same, in *per capita* terms, as the number, 142, of murders in London in 1997.) It was the rarity of homicides in the East End, let alone grotesque multiple killings, which made the Ripper so infamous.

More is now known about the lives of the murdered women than any other group of working-class women in Victorian England.

What distinguished London's East End from most other large British cities was the absence of factory capitalism. Although there were large-scale employers of labour, such as the major breweries and railways, most firms were small-scale, with the largest form of employment, the docks, being notorious for hiring on a daily, casual basis. The East End was thus characterised by chronic under-employment which left tens of thousands constantly on the borderline of dire poverty. This was an even more drastic situation for women than men. In the north of England, most working-class girls were employed for a few years in a factory, enabling them to build up a small nest-egg before marriage. The East End was largely lacking in this possibility. There was a vast transitory population of sailors on shore leave, dock and building workers, recent unattached male immigrants, and slumming City men. As a result, prostitution was endemic, and even married women sold themselves to help make ends meet. In October 1888, at the height of the Ripper killings, the Metropolitan Police reported that there were believed to be 1,200 'low class' prostitutes in Whitechapel, in sixty-two brothels. (There may well have been thousands of other 'streetwalkers.') Most were in poor health, many suffering from venereal disease and alcoholism. They walked the streets, often late at night. It was from this class that the Ripper chose his victims.

The notoriety of the Whitechapel killer was augmented by other factors. The name 'Jack the Ripper' derives from a postcard sent to 'Dear Boss,' the head of the Central News Agency, on September 25th, 1888, signed 'Yours truly, Jack the Ripper.' Many believe that this postcard was actually written by a journalist, though there is no clear evidence for this. The only clue apparently left by the Ripper was the so-called 'Goulston Street Graffito [graffiti].' The words 'The Juwes are the men that Will not be Blamed for nothing', were chalked, seemingly by the murderer, on a doorway immediately above a portion of the bloodstained apron of victim Catharine Eddowes. What these words might mean—if, indeed, they were written by the Ripper—has been hotly debated. Some believe that 'Juwes' was a code-word for the Freemasons, who allegedly employ similar terminology in their ceremonies. If the commonsense meaning is the intended one, it is unclear whether the graffiti was supposed to blame the Jews or point to their innocence. Fearful of the message leading to antisemitic rioting, the London police quickly erased the graffiti.

It is probably the elusiveness of a true solution to the Ripper mystery that remains its central attraction to researchers. Most believe that some rearrangement of the evidence combined with a lucky new find will enable them to crack the secret. Perhaps it will. The association of the Ripper with the London of Sherlock Holmes, with fogs, riverside opium dens, the haunts of prostitutes and criminals, virtually adjacent to great wealth and the aristocracy, is enticing to many. Added to this, many amateur Ripper historians are Londoners, often with ancestral roots in the East End. For them, Jack the Ripper is a part of their heritage. Meanwhile, the prolific output of research on the Ripper has had many benefits for social historians. The five murdered women have been investigated in minute detail to see if any association can be found with any Ripper suspect or with each other (none has been discovered). As a result, probably more is known about the lives of these five than of any other group of working-class women in Victorian England. Detailed research on the Ripper crimes has also shed considerable light on a range of late Victorian institutions, from the police to the press.

There are about fifteen leading candidates for the true identity of the Ripper. None is wholly satisfactory, although one suspect in particular is highly convincing. Modern research on the Ripper is often dated from 1959, with the publication that year of the 'MacNaghten Memorandum', a document apparently written in the 1890s, naming three prominent Scotland Yard suspects. Sir Melville MacNaghten (1853–1921) had joined Scotland Yard in June 1889, eight months after the last Ripper murder, and served as Assistant Chief Constable and Chief Constable of Scotland Yard. The three chief suspects named in his document were Montague Druitt; 'Kosminski', a Polish Jew; and 'Michael Ostrog, a Russian doctor.' Druitt and Kosminski remain viable candidates who have been examined in detail by researchers. Ostrog, it appears, was a harmless conman and lunatic who was probably in Paris at the time of the killings.

For twenty years or more, Montague Druitt (1857–88) was probably the number one suspect. There appeared to be a good deal of evidence linking him with the Ripper. In 1913, MacNaghten told the *Daily Mail* that he had 'a very clear idea' who the Ripper was, but had 'destroyed all the documents and there is now no record of the secret information which came into my possession at one time or another.' A journalist with good police contacts, G.R. Sims, stated in 1903 that 'the body of the man suspected by the chiefs of Scotland Yard, and by his own friends, who were in communication with the Yard, was found in the Thames.' Druitt indeed committed suicide in the Thames around November 30th, 1888, shortly after being dismissed as a schoolteacher in Blackheath, and three weeks after the last Ripper murder. Druitt, who was also a barrister, had chambers at King's Bench Walk, within walking distance of the East End, and apparently had a cousin who was a doctor with offices in the Minories, on the border of the East End.

Given the general air of mystery surrounding his life, it is not surprising that Druitt was the preferred candidate of many Ripperologists. During the past two decades, however, his star has

I shant quit ripping them till I do get buckled. Grand work the last job was, I gave the lady no time to squeal. How can they catch me n I love my work and want to start again. You will soon hear of me

PUBLIC RECORD OFFICE

The letter of September 25th, 1888, signed 'Jack the Ripper', was believed to be genuine by the police at the time, but this is disputed by some modern researchers. Ripper victims Chapman and Stride and (right) Alice Mackenzie, murdered in July 1889 and once claimed as a Ripper victim, although the police did not think so at the time.

waned. Extensive research has failed to find evidence clearly linking him to the Ripper crimes. In 1959, for instance, the Ripper researcher Daniel Farson was told of a pamphlet entitled *The East End Murderer—I Knew Him*, allegedly written by a Dr Lionel Druitt, Montague's cousin, and published in Victoria, Australia in 1890. It is now apparent that tales of the work are no more than a garbled account of several other works published around the same time, none of which relate to Druitt. MacNaghten's information about Druitt was also highly inaccurate: in the Memorandum he described him as a doctor rather than a barrister and overstated his age by ten years. It is curious and regrettable that MacNaghten destroyed evidence which may have been crucial. The suspect's suicide seems to have been occasioned either by a scandal at his school or by severe depression, perhaps inherited (his mother was in an asylum). Recently it has been discovered that Druitt was playing cricket at Camford, Dorset, six hours after the Polly Nichols murder. Further attempts to link him with the Royal/ Freemason theory of the murders are often made, but are fanciful. Because of MacNaghten, Druitt will always remain a serious candidate, but one so far lacking in any direct supportive evidence.

The 'MacNaghten Memorandum' mentioned 'Kosminski, a Polish Jew' of Whitechapel, who 'indulg[ed] in solitary vices' and had 'a great hatred of women and strong homicidal tenden-

cies', as the second most likely suspect. According to Mac-Naghten, this young Eastern European Jewish immigrant was 'removed to a lunatic asylum about March 1889.' Mac-Naghten's suspicion was echoed by other senior Scotland Yard men: both Dr Robert Anderson and Donald Swanson believed that Aaron Kosminski's identity was known to other East End Jews, who refused to give evidence against him for fear of hanging a fellow Jew. The researcher Martin Fido believes that the Ripper might well have been not Aaron Kosminski but Aaron Davis Cohen, another East End Jew, who was sent to Colney Hatch lunatic asylum in December 1888, where he died less than a year later. Others believe that the East End Jew in question might have been Nathan Kaminsky, who was being treated for syphilis in a local infirmary.

There are, however, problems with these theories. Neither Kosminski nor Kaminsky was dangerous or violent: despite MacNaghten, there is no evidence that Kosminski was ever 'homicidal.' As to Cohen, it is difficult to believe that a senior Scotland Yard man, even one biased against Jewish immigrants, would confuse his name with 'Kosminski.' Although Cohen was violent when placed in the asylum, there is no evidence that he was ever violent before this. More importantly, there are considerable difficulties with the notion of an East End Jew being the Ripper. Whitechapel's MP at this time, Samuel Montagu

BRIDGEMAN ART LIBRARY/PRIVATE COLLECTION
25-year-old Irish-born Mary Kelly, the ripper's last victim, was killed in her room in Miller's Court.

The Royal and Masonic Ripper theory appears to be nonsense from beginning to end.

The alleged Royal/Ripper connection is probably the most popular of all the theories. This dates from a work published in French in 1962 by Dr Thomas Stowell, and given wide publicity before his death in 1970. Stowell was the son-in-law of the son-in-law of Sir William Gull, the Royal Physician frequently alleged to have had a direct hand in the Ripper murders. According to Stowell, the Ripper was Prince Albert Edward, Duke of Clarence, the eldest son of the Prince of Wales, later Edward VII. Clarence was only twenty-eight when he died in 1892; his younger brother, the Duke of York, married Clarence's fiancee, Princess Mary of Teck, and succeeded to the throne in 1910 as King George V. Clarence, a sexual sadist, was in the last stages of syphilis in 1889 and allegedly killed the five prostitutes, with the assistance of Gull. The Royal theory was taken a step further in 1973 in a television documentary in which a man named Joseph Sickert, claiming to be the illegitimate son of the artist Walter Sickert, alleged that Clarence had contracted an illegal marriage with his grandmother, Annie Crook, and that one of the witnesses was Mary Kelly, the last victim. In 1976, in *Jack the Ripper: The Final Solution*, the researcher Stephen Knight went further still, arguing that Gull and a conspiracy of Freemasons, acting on the orders of prime minister Lord Salisbury, killed Mary Kelly and the other prostitutes who were collectively trying to blackmail the British government through their knowledge of the secret Royal marriage. According to this view, much in the five murders was redolent of the language and customs of the Freemasons, and was, in fact, a Masonic 'ritual murder.' Most recently Sue and Andy Parlour have suggested that the instigator of the murders—carried out by Sir William Gull, possibly with the assistance of Montague Druitt and also James Kenneth Stephen (1859–92), Virginia Woolf's cousin, who was a Cambridge graduate who was committed to an asylum in 1891 and is frequently mentioned as a possible Ripper associate—was the Prince of Wales (later Edward VII), who was being blackmailed by Kelly. The Parlours have also discovered some curious features of Gull's burial in 1890.

The Royal/Masonic Ripper theory appears to be palpable nonsense from beginning to end, without a shred of evidence to support it. The whereabouts of senior royals is known with considerable precision: Clarence was in Scotland or Yorkshire at the time of all of the murders. There is no evidence that any member of the Royal family ever set eyes on any Ripper victim, or that Mary Kelly was blackmailing a Royal or anyone else. There is no evidence that Clarence entered into an illegal marriage with anyone. Sir William Gull was seventy-one in 1888 and had suffered two serious strokes the year before. The five Ripper victims were not associates: there is no evidence that they had even met. If Gull and his collaborators murdered Mary Kelly, they would surely have lured her into a carriage, chloro-

(later Lord Swaythling), was extremely close to the East End Jewish community. Although a millionaire City banker, he was one of the founders and patrons of the Federation of Synagogues, whose Orthodox religious practice was similar to that known in Eastern Europe and popular with the recent immigrants as a result—in contrast to the more acculturated, mainstream United Synagogue headed by the Chief Rabbi. Montagu was also a notable philanthropist to Jewish causes in the East End. If the Ripper had been a local Jewish lunatic, it is difficult to believe that Montagu and other Anglo-Jewish leaders would not have heard rumours about his identity, and moved to have him placed in an asylum as quickly as possible. Yet in September 1888 (after the second killing), Montagu offered a 100 [pounds sterling] reward for the Ripper's capture, and five weeks later (after the fourth killing) he sent Scotland Yard a local petition for police protection.

Equally plausible, at first glance, are the theories that the Ripper was an ordinary East End workingman, someone who knew the district well and could come and go without attracting undue attention. A number of such persons, including known associates of Mary Kelly, the last victim, have been proposed. However, the police did not believe that any such man was the Ripper. Had any evidence existed, it would have been relatively easy to secure the conviction of an impoverished workingman, but none did.

One whore no good,
decided Sir Jim strike another.
I showed no fright and indeed no light
damn it, the tin box was empty

BRIDGEMAN ART GALLERY/ROGER-VIOLLET/PRIVATE COLLECTION

The 'Ripper Diaries' apparently contain information that would have been virtually impossible for a forger to know: here he mentions an empty tin box found at the scene of Catherine Eddowes's murder, and he calls himself 'Sir Jim'.

formed her, hit her on the head, and thrown her into the Thames: the apparent drowning of a drunken East End prostitute would not have received five lines in any newspaper.

The discovery of a 'Diary of Jack the Ripper' 104 years after the crimes gave rise to deep suspicion.

As for the Freemason link, over the past 250 years tens of thousands of Englishmen have been Freemasons in hundreds of lodges, without any Masonic 'ritual murders' being reported. The 'Masonic link' is of like ilk to the 'Popish Plot' and *The Protocols of the Elders of Zion* and belongs in the same dustbin.

Most notable among the other serious candidates are the Polish-born barber George Chapman (ne Severin Klosowski), the American doctor Dr Francis Tumblety, and Robert Donston Stephenson, a freelance journalist, drug addict and student of the occult, who was taking a voluntary rest-cure in a Whitechapel hospital at the time of the killings. None of them can be totally overlooked. Dozens of others proposed as the true Ripper can be dismissed outright. Among those named as the Ripper are Lewis Carroll, Lord Randolph Churchill, Dr Barnardo, three insane medical students at London Hospital, and four Portuguese sailors on shore leave. The notion that 'Jack' was actually 'Jill' surfaced early during the spate of killings themselves, and had an advocate of sorts in Sir Arthur Conan Doyle, who argued that the male killer was able to pass through Whitechapel disguised as a bloodstained midwife. Several theorists have suggested that 'Jill' was actually an abortionist (who plainly botched the job!). None of the Ripper victims, however, appears to have been pregnant.

James Maybrick (1838-89) was a Liverpool cotton broker who in May 1889 died of apparent arsenic poisoning. His wife Florence Maybrick (1862-1941) was tried for his murder, convicted, sentenced to death. She was reprieved, spent fifteen years in prison, and passed the rest of her life in America (where

she was born), dying in dire poverty in a shack in rural Connecticut. Prior to 1992, there was nothing to connect James Maybrick with Jack the Ripper, and he was never named as a possible suspect, or indeed in connection with the case. Then, out of the blue, a handwritten. sixty-three page diary turned up in the possession of an ordinary couple in Liverpool, Michael and Anne Barrett (known, since her divorce as Anne Graham). Signed 'Jack the Ripper' and dated May 3rd, 1889, eight days before Maybrick's death, it gives apparently accurate information on Maybrick's life as a well-to-do cotton broker living in 'Battlecrease', a large house in Aigburth, Liverpool, and gruesome details of the Ripper killings, including Maybrick's penchant for cannibalism. According to the diary Maybrick embarked on his killing spree for motives of vicarious revenge at the behaviour of his wife, who was having an affair, probably with Alfred Brierley, another Liverpool merchant. Maybrick was a long-term arsenic addict. Arsenic, in small doses, produces a 'high' similar to other addictive substances, and Maybrick committed the Ripper crimes as, in effect, a drug addict. The diary suggest that Maybrick selected Whitechapel as a joke to parallel the Whitechapel district of Liverpool, and he rented a flat on Middlesex Street (Petticoat Lane), a very close to where four of the five killings occurred. Maybrick knew the East End of London well, and had business interests in the City. By the time of the diary's conclusion, Maybrick had repented the Ripper crimes, and he was actively contemplating suicide. Since its discovery in 1992 the 'Diary of Jack the Ripper' has become the most controversial and hotly-debated item in the world of Ripperology.

The discovery of an unknown 'Diary of Jack the Ripper', quickly marketed by mainstream publishers 104 years after the crimes, rightly gave rise to the deepest suspicions. It was denounced as a crude forgery, dating from a year or two before it was made public, Even to those inclined to view it as genuine, its provenance remains unclear. As a work it is in many respects highly unsatisfactory. It is not a diary in the normal sense, containing no dates prior to that given in the last line. It is incoherently written in a stream-of-consciousness style, but for the most part contains boasting, near-hysterical passages by Maybrick of anticipation at killing prostitutes, fooling the police, and avenging his wife's adultery. It also contains semi-coherent descriptions of the five Ripper murders. (Maybrick also claimed to have killed a prostitute in Manchester before beginning his spree in London.) The diary provides no information on many of the aspects of the Ripper killings which would most interest historians—why he chose the five victims; how, precisely, he killed them; the exact circumstances of the 'Jack the Ripper' letters; why he stopped—and, even assuming it is genuine, it adds little to our knowledge of the crimes beyond the identity of the killer and his motives. The diary is puzzling in other respects, too. Its handwriting appears to resemble some but not all of Maybrick's own writings, and it is written in an old scrapbook, not a real diary.

Numerous scientific test have concluded that the diary appears to date from the late-nineteenth century or soon after. The facts of its provenance are as follows: it was allegedly seen by Anne Graham's father, William Graham, in 1943 while he was on leave from the army, in a black tin box in his mother's house in Liverpool. It was allegedly seen by Anne Graham herself, in a trunk in a cupboard in her house in Liverpool in the late 1960s. Anne Graham took possession of it in the mid-1980s when her father moved house. In marital difficulties, she gave the diary to a friend of her husband Michael Barrett (who was unemployed) to give to her husband to keep him intellectually occupied. For reasons related to her marital breakdown, she did not admit its actual provenance, leading to the spread of (untrue) stories that it was dug up from the floor-boards of Battlecrease House. The diary became public knowledge in 1992, receiving widespread publicity thanks to the literary agent Robert Smith and the researcher Shirley Harrison. In 1993 Michael Barrett (apparently also for reasons related to his marriage breakdown) claimed to have forged the diary. This claim is not now accepted, even by those who are sceptical of its authenticity.

The key question is the diary's whereabouts between Maybrick's death in 1889 and William Graham's sighting in 1943. The most popular theory is that the diary was taken from Battlecrease in the confusion following Maybrick's sudden death by a servant, Alice Yapp (who certainly stole items from the household). It is believed that Yapp (who died in 1938) eventually passed the diary to William Graham's stepmother, Edith Formby, who was probably a family friend. (William Graham was a professional soldier in the 1930s who was overseas at this time.) Another theory is that William Graham was the son of the illegitimate son of Florence Maybrick and a shipowner named Henry Flinn. (Florence Maybrick used the pseudonym 'Mrs Graham' after her release from prison.) According to this view, Alice Yapp left the diary to the Graham family because she knew they were Florence's descendants. After leaving the army, Graham, who worked for many worker in a Dunlop tyre factory, had no interest in the diary. He later told Shirley Harrison, 'If I'd known what was it was worth, I'd have cashed it years ago. Blimey, I wouldn't have been slaving away in Dunlops....'

There are other reasons for believing that the diary is not a recent forgery. A 'Diary of Jack the Ripper' forged c.1990 might be expected to contain pornographic descriptions of Maybrick's sexual arousal during his encounters with the prostitutes (and with other women). However, while it does contain horrifying descriptions of mutilation and cannibalism, the diary has no explicit sexual content of any kind. This is consistent with the likelihood that the Ripper did not have sexual relations with the prostitutes he killed (although arsenic was frequently used in Victorian England as an aphrodisiac, and Maybrick, aged 50 in 1888, might well have experienced failing sexual powers).

More importantly, all attempts to show that the diary is a forgery and who its creator may be have failed. In the eight years since its appearance, no one has come forward to smirk at the gullibility of so many 'experts'. Moreover, if the diary were a modern forgery, its author was taking an enormous risk. There could well be evidence unknown to the forger that proves irrefutably that Maybrick could not have been in London at the time of a Ripper killing—a report in an obscure trade journal, say, that mentioned he was speaking at a meeting of cotton brokers in Liverpool at a certain time of day. No forger could ever be confident that he had studied every such possible source. But no evidence discounting the possibility that Maybrick could be the Ripper has ever come to light.

Furthermore, the diary appears to contain information that is virtually impossible for any recent forger to have known. In particular, Maybrick often refers to himself in the diary as 'Sir Jim' or 'Sir Jack.' In 1993, the researcher Paul Feldman, who has done more than anyone else to investigate the diary, found that in the summer of 1888 the Maybricks had as their guest an eight-year-old American girl, Florence Aunspaugh, the daughter of a business friend of James. In 1941–42, following Florence Maybrick's death, Trevor Christie, a New York journalist, conducted a correspondence with Aunspaugh, then aged sixty-two and living in Dallas, as background material for the book he was writing on the Florence Maybrick poisoning case. Neither Christie nor Aunspaugh had any idea that Maybrick might have been the Ripper. In 1970 Christie's widow deposited the Aunspaugh correspondence in the American Heritage Center in the University of Wyoming at Cheyenne. Feldman sent Keith Skinner, an eminent authority on the Ripper case, to photostat the whole Aunspaugh files. Buried in a long, hand-written, unpublished letter there, Florence Aunspaugh recalled that Alice Yapp had said 'she certainly would be glad when that damned little American left Battlecrease… she did not see why Sir James (Mr Maybrick) ever brought me there any way.' (Aunspaugh also recalled in 1941–42 that 'a current of mystery seemed to circulate all around' at Battlecrease, and that Maybrick, though charming, had a 'morose, gloomy disposition and extremely high temper' and was an 'arsenic addict [who] craved it like a narcotic fiend.') There is no evidence that anyone read these papers prior to Skinner and Feldman. There are three possible explanations: the forger made use of an unpublished source in an obscure archive; that by sheer chance the forger hit upon the unusual nickname actually used by Maybrick in his own household; or that the diary is authentic, or at least written by someone completely familiar with the secrets of the Maybrick family.

For all of these reasons, many of the Ripperologists who continue to doubt the authenticity of the diary now believe that it is an old forgery, probably contrived in the Edwardian period. An obvious candidate is James's brother Michael, a talented composer who used the pseudonym 'Stephen Adams.' Michael Maybrick, who died in 1913, almost certainly knew far more about the events of 1888–89 than he stated in public.

There are, however, objections to the proposition that the diary is an old forgery. The forger must have had precise knowledge of both the Maybrick household in Liverpool and the Whitechapel murders. In Edwardian times, most of the police involved in the hunt for the Ripper were still alive, as were dozens of people in Liverpool who knew Maybrick well. Had the diary become known at the time, the slightest mistake about either Liverpool or Whitechapel would have exposed the diary as a fraud. Even more important, it apparently contains information that could not have been known by an earlier forger. The diary refers to a 'tin box' which was 'empty' and which was found and left by Maybrick at the murder of Catharine Eddowes, the fourth victim. There was indeed '1 tin match box, empty' in a list of her effects drawn up by the police, but this list did not appear in print until 1987, and the existence of the empty tin box was unknown until then.

One theory favoured by some (although it has, apparently, never appeared in print) is that the diary was indeed written by James Maybrick, but as a Walter Mittyish fantasy, his attempt, perhaps, to gain 'revenge' at his wife's adultery by 'murdering' prostitutes on the written page. This ingenious theory has several flaws. As we have seen, the diary contains information that no one except the Ripper could have known in 1888–89. Also, if Maybrick was the author of the diary it must have been written before he died in May 1889. At the end of the diary the author has sincerely repented of his crimes and it is clear that there will be no more Ripper killings. But if Maybrick was not the Ripper, he could not have known that there would be no more killings: so far as he knew the Ripper was still at large and might strike again at any time. It thus seems almost impossible for the diary to be a recent forgery, an old forgery, or a fantasy created by Maybrick himself.

The case that Maybrick was the Ripper is strong even without the diary. Perhaps the most striking evidence for this is to be found in a number of unknown letters discovered by Paul Feldman from Liverpool sources. On October 9th, 1888, the *Liverpool Echo* printed a story (based on a letter it had received) that Jack the Ripper was about to strike in Dublin. The following day the same newspaper published the following, written on a postcard:

> I beg to state that the letters published in yours of yesterday are lies. It is somebody gulling the public. I am the Whitechapel purger. On 13th, at 3pm, will be on Stage, as am going to New York. But will have some business before I go.
> Yours Truly,
> Jack the Ripper DIEGO LAURENZ
> (Genuine)

Feldman asks 'What does Diego Laurenz mean? I have no idea. Is it a clue?' In my opinion, indeed it is—arguably the most im-

portant clue that we have. 'Diego' is Spanish for James, while 'Laurenz' is meant to rhyme with 'Florence.' If this is what it means, then this constitutes virtual proof that James Maybrick was Jack the Ripper. (Anyone familiar with the diary will know Maybrick's penchant for puns and word-games. And why was a letter written with such assurance sent to a Liverpool newspaper?) Another previously unpublished letter, sent by 'Jack the Ripper' to the Metropolitan Police from New York in October 1888, also said that the Ripper was temporarily there, but would be back. There was, indeed an inexplicable gap of five weeks between the two murders on September 30th, 1888, and the fifth killing on November 9th, which has always puzzled researchers. Maybrick himself was known to have made regular business trips to New York throughout his career.

The diarist states that he confessed to his wife that he was Jack the Ripper.

Why the Ripper stopped killing after November 9th, 1888, has always been one of the central mysteries of the Ripper question. With Maybrick there is a good explanation. On November 19th, Maybrick changed doctors, consulting Dr. J. Drysdale, who treated him with homeopathic remedies. Drysdale treated Maybrick five more times before his death, apparently with a gradual improvement. (Drysdale gave testimony under oath at Mrs. Maybrick's trial.) It is clear from the diary that Maybrick slowly but surely lost interest in further killings, feeling considerable remorse just before his death.

The diary also states that, just before he died, Maybrick confessed to his wife that he was Jack the Ripper. A letter written just before Maybrick's death from his wife to her lover Alfred Brierley figured prominently at her trial. In this Florence noted that her husband was 'delirious' and that 'he is perfectly ignorant of everything.' She later mysteriously remarks that 'The tale he told me was a pure fabrication and only intended to frighten the truth out of me.' This statement occurs abruptly and is not elaborated upon. It is possible a clever forger might have noted this sentence buried in a long letter in a published account of the trial and worked backwards from it. But it still does not answer the question of what the tale designed to frighten her might have been.

In another episode suggesting a link between Maybrick, Liverpool and the Ripper, William Graham told Feldman that as a boy (he was born in 1913) he lived near Battlecrease House and that he and his friends would run past it 'pretending we were Fred Archer, the jockey, smack our backsides and shout "Look out, look out, Jack the Ripper's about"….' Archer, the most famous jockey of the nineteenth century, committed suicide at the age of twenty-nine in 1886, only two years before the Ripper killings. If authentic, this story seems incomprehensible unless there was something to connect Battlecrease with the Ripper, presumably whisperings from the servants to their friends.

Furthermore, the name 'Jack the Ripper' may itself have had a Liverpool origin. Between 1884 and 1886 Liverpool's local newspapers made great play over the alleged existence of a murderous 'High Rip Gang' which, it was claimed, terrorised passers-by in the Scotland Road slums. There was considerable debate about whether such a gang actually existed, and mention of the 'High Rip' seems to have ceased in early 1887. However, the 'High Rip' and its association with street violence would have been well-known to any Liverpudlian in 1888.

On top of all this, in 1992 a watch (made in 1846) was found in Liverpool by a local man named Albert Johnson. Scratched on the inner case Johnson found the signature 'J. Maybrick', the words 'I am Jack', and the initials of the five Ripper Victims. Examination with a scanning electron microscope revealed that the scratchings are almost certainly not recently made, but are compatible with a date of 1888–89. Johnson contacted the *Liverpool Post* after the story of the diary came to light.

Beyond this there is a good deal of indirect evidence that points to Maybrick as opposed to other suspects. All five murders were committed on Friday, Saturday or Sunday. (This obviously noteworthy fact is, rather curiously, almost never mentioned in the Ripper literature.) The idea of weekend slaughter is itself strange: prostitutes walked the streets of Whitechapel every night, but there were more potential witnesses around on weekends. There could be any number of reasons for this, of course. One suggestion is that workingmen were traditionally paid on Thursdays. This would seem pertinent but for the fact that the Ripper did not pay the women he killed. (Indeed, he appears to have robbed them.) The weekend pattern also appears at variance with the Ripper being an upper- or middle-class Londoner. Well-to-do men might have spent the weekdays in town, staying at their club or a flat, but were more likely to be with their families in a suburban villa or the country at weekends. This pattern, however, is consistent with the lifestyle of a Liverpool cotton broker who spent the weekdays at the Liverpool Cotton Exchange but was free to travel on weekends (as Maybrick was).

All the murders took place late at night or early in the morning. Few men can be about at that hour without attracting attention from their family, neighbours, servants, landladies, or fellow tenants, let alone covered in blood and carrying a knife and the organs of their victims. Anyone out only on the nights when the Ripper crimes occurred would arouse suspicion. But Maybrick went to London alone and lived alone in the centre of the Ripper district, coming and going as he pleased.

I am personally more than 90 per cent convinced that James Maybrick was Jack the Ripper. Both evidence and inference appear overwhelmingly to point to him. However, if it can be proved that he was definitely not the Ripper—if, for instance, irrefutable proof were found that he was in Liverpool on the night a Ripper murder was committed—the identity of Jack the Ripper remains a mystery; none of the other suspects is remotely convincing.

FOR FURTHER READING

Paul Begg, Martin Fido, and Keith Skinner, *The Jack the Ripper A–Z* (London, 1996); Donald Rumbelow, *The Complete Jack the Ripper* (London, 1988) and Philip Sugden, *The Complete History of Jack the Ripper* (London, 1995); Maxim Jakubowski and Nathan Braund, eds., *The Mammoth Book of Jack the Ripper* (London, 1999); M.J. Trow, *The Many Faces of Jack the Ripper* (Chichester, 1997); Shirley Harrison, *The Diary of Jack the Ripper* (London, 1998); Paul H. Feldman, *Jack the Ripper: The Final Chapter* (London, 1998); Anne Graham and Carol Emmas, *The Last Victim* (London, 1999); William Beadle, *Jack the Ripper: Anatomy of a Myth* (Brighton, 1995); Andy and Sue Parlour, *The Jack the Ripper Whitechapel Murders* (London, 1997); Rob Sindall, *Street Violence in the Nineteenth Century: Media Panic or Real Danger?* (Leicester, 1990).

William D. Rubinstein is Professor of Modern History at the University of Wales.

This article first appeared in *History Today,* May 2000, pp. 10-19. © 2000 by History Today, Ltd. Reprinted by permission.

Destroyers and Preservers

Big Game in the Victorian Empire

*Continuing our History and the Environment series, **Harriet Ritvo** looks at the role of big-game hunting in spreading awareness of the need for conservation.*

Humans have, apparently, always hunted wild animals. At first for business, and subsequently, after the development of agriculture provided a more profuse and reliable source of calories, for pleasure, albeit pleasure with a purpose. Variously ritualised and institutionalised, the hunt has served the elites of many societies as recreation, status symbol, and para-military training. The killing of valuable animals has both enacted and represented social prestige and power. In Britain the exclusiveness of hunting had deep medieval roots. Access to game animals was limited both physically, through enclosure, and through laws that severely punished unauthorised slaughter. By the eighteenth century hunting was structured by a rhetoric of scarcity and privilege. Among sportsmen only fox hunters routinely claimed that their pastime served any useful purpose, and these claims were not especially persuasive.

The contributions of big game hunting to the imperial enterprise were multiple and complex. The vast territories of Asia, Africa, and North America were very different from the settings of domestic sport. Initially, there seemed to be little need for restraint or exclusivity. Game was plentiful, sometimes too plentiful. It could be large and ferocious, which made hunting both more dangerous and more useful. No longer purely recreational, the removal of wild animals could be appreciated as a service to humans, both colonists and indigenous inhabitants. Inevitably, imperial hunters adapted many of the sporting practices that they had learned at home, exchanging horses for elephants in some situations, guns for spears in others.

Despite such adjustments, however, the underlying meaning of the hunt did not change much. Killing large exotic animals emerged as both the quintessential activity and symbol of imperialism. Wild animals represented the obstacles that had hitherto prevented colonial territories from joining the march of progress, and that had to be eliminated before their native territories could enjoy the blessings of European civilisation. The hunt was thus a prized perquisite of colonial service in Africa and Asia, while the subsequent display of trophies and publication of stories excited and impressed expansionist sentiment at home. Rows of horns and hides, mounted heads and stuffed bodies, evoked the violent, heroic underbelly of imperialism. Such collections were readily available to the Victorian public. For example, the India Museum was founded in London in 1801 by the East India Company as a concrete representation of its commercial and political influence. The Museum soon boasted the largest collection of stuffed South Asian animals in Britain, and by the 1840s was attracting 10–20,000 visitors per year. The sporting prowess of native sons on imperial service adorned many local natural history museums, and the Great Exhibition of 1851 featured hunting trophies from around the globe.

The core appeal of such displays through their celebration of domination by naked force was further illustrated by the popular success of two mighty British hunters whose careers bracketed the most vigorous period of imperial expansion. Both Roualeyn Gordon Cumming (1820–66) and Frederick Courteney Selous (1851–1917) reaped the spoils of the chase a second time on the book, lecture and exhibition circuits. Cumming was drawn to imperial service at least partly by the promise of big game hunting. He entered the East India Company in 1838 but could not endure the climate. He returned to Scotland, but found the deer stalking too tame. He then enlisted in a Canadian regiment, but North America failed to provide the hunting opportunities he had anticipated. In 1843 he joined the Cape Mounted Rifles. When his military duties did not leave him enough time for sport, he resigned his commission in order to gratify 'the passion of my youth', the collection of hunting trophies. For the next five years he supported himself as an ivory hunter, then returned to England intending to capitalise on his African experiences. He co-ordinated his publicity cleverly, publishing a popular narrative of his adventures, *Five Years of a Hunter's Life in the Far Interior of South Africa*, in 1850, the same year that he opened his successful London exhibit of trophies and large canvases commissioned to illustrate his most dramatic escapades. Visitors could pay between one and three shillings to hear the lion-slayer describe his adventures to a musical accompaniment.

Frederick Selous presented a more austere figure. By the time he began to lecture in Britain in 1895, after more than twenty years as an ivory hunter and specimen collector in southern Africa, he had also participated in the military adventures that led to the British acquisition of Rhodesia. It was this colonial service that the Duke of Fife stressed in presenting Selous to a crowd that had packed the Great Hall of the Imperial Institute, London, in 1895. The Duke predicted that in the future Selous would be known as one of those who had advanced the cause of civilisation and helped to extend the British Empire. Despite the cheers that greeted this announcement, however, the audience had really come to hear about Selous' exploits. The lecturer obliged by recounting three perilous encounters in the bush, one with lions, one with elephants, and one with hostile natives, which commanded the rapt attention of his listeners for more than an hour and a half. Selous avoided the exaggeration associated with rough and ready figures like Gordon Cumming and the American Buffalo Bill Cody. But although he did not open his collection of hunting trophies to the public for a fee, he similarly used it to corroborate his prowess as a frontiersman. When he lectured, Selous arranged on the platform some of the most remarkable lions and other animals which had fallen to his gun, where they provided dramatic background and persuasive corroboration of his stories.

In Selous' rendition and through his example, the hunter emerged as both the ideal and the definitive type of empire builder. Even before his participation in the British annexation of Mashonaland, when he became renowned as a slayer of elephants, Selous was the hero of many boys preparing for colonial service at public schools. The arrival of big game hunters in regions previously untrodden by Europeans was seen as the harbinger of civilisation. One mid-century journalist attacked critics of hunting by presuming that 'it will hardly be maintained that… a huge portion of the globe [is to be] left unexplored, merely out of deference to… delicate feelings.'

When late Victorians began to worry about the waning of national purpose at home, they attributed this enfeeblement of spiritual and bodily vigour to the exhaustion of the new world of sport, which had lured at least two generations of doughty Britons into the hearts of Africa and Asia.

The pursuit of dangerous game rewarded generously both individual participants and the colonial order to which they belonged. Huntsmen enjoyed satisfying a lust for blood that was celebrated as a component of the national character. This basic pleasure was complemented by a sense of unrestrained freedom. The primary liberty of hunting, to wander and kill at will, was reflected in a range of releases from social convention, which were appreciated not only by men who had embraced bush life more or less permanently, but also by those on leave from the elaborately structured routine of colonial service. The enthusiasm with which officers and officials embraced this freedom suggests some of the psychological hazards of tropical service; and official concern about preserving stocks of game at the end of the nineteenth century corroborated the need to maintain this element of health in the lives of men stationed for long periods in debilitating climates. As a veteran sportsman put it:

When bile and nervousness become too intolerable; when you feel yourself too shaky and cross and yellow-faced for anything, get a leave of absence, and ride into the jungle.

Big game hunting also developed the qualities required in colonial officers and administrators in more positive ways. For young men posted to remote stations, who were at risk of falling into dissolute ways, hunting might prove their moral as well as their physical salvation; a day in the field would leave them (in the words of Parker Gillmore's *The Hunter's Arcadia*) 'too tired and too hungry to again go forth, yet invigorated and strengthened'. A civilian official who was also a sportsman could be expected to be a straight and honourable man, one likely to display feelings of humanity in appropriate circumstances. Even extended sporting expeditions were not considered wasted time. To the military hierarchy, the enthusiastic hunter was exercising many of the faculties needed by the good soldier in action.

As hunting success became an index of personal or professional worth, intense competition developed over the testimonials of prowess. Sometimes the object of contention was simply who took credit for a shared kill. But the real focus of competition was on that which could be measured, assessed and compared. The numbers could be enormous. A day's bag might include twenty-nine buffalo or nine bears, while a longer expedition might yield 150 hippopotami and 91 elephants. But such figures reflected an abundance that turned out to be evanescent. As improved rifles made shooting large animals easier, and diminishing game populations made massive bags seem vulgar, many hunters turned to accumulation based on connoisseurship rather than arithmetic.

During the final quarter of the nineteenth century, 'slaughter' and associated terms, which had previously been used as colourful synonyms for sport, were increasingly opposed to a moralised ideal of hunting. Distinctions were drawn between 'hunters' and 'butchers'. Elite sportsmen amassed their trophy collections with growing subtlety and restraint, although no less competitively. This was more widely echoed in the blend of physical force and judicious discrimination (rather than force alone) that was increasingly reflected in the magisterial functions exercised by the colonial ruling classes. Hunters whose goals were determined by aesthetic and qualitative considerations tried hard to ascertain in advance whether their intended prey was worth killing. They derived no satisfaction in killing an inferior head.

Big game hunting offered British officials respite from occupational stresses and made them better at their jobs. It also often came to constitute part of their imperial duties, for example when natives were threatened by man-eating predators. Business and pleasure overlapped for the colonials in the provision of such 'protective' services. The urgency with which beleaguered natives sought valiant sportsmen to rid them of such scourges reinforced the British sense of the fitness of the imperial structure and emphasised the physical and moral superiority of Europeans. On the other hand, in the absence of such native appeals for protection, it was less easy to justify big game hunting—symbol of imperial appropriation—as equally beneficial to the native populations.

As the nineteenth century wore on, native peoples ceased to express their gratitude to British sportsmen for delivering them from ferocious beasts, as these animals troubled them less frequently. Throughout the empire the dense accumulations of animals that had dazzled early adventurers were beginning to disappear. By the time the hunters noticed this diminution it had been in process for over a century in areas frequented by Europeans. At first, this phenomenon was not readily recognised or understood; the early casualties—mostly isolated populations like the dodo of Mauritius and the Steller's sea cow—were not perceived as straws in the wind. A creationist corollary made it difficult for many Christian believers to accept the possibility that the number of animal kinds represented in the Garden of Eden could be diminished by extinction any more than it could be enhanced by evolution.

As early as the 1790s, after his explorations of 1797 and 1798, John Barrow had complained that the Cape afforded but a narrow field for the inquiries of the zoologist because its wolves, hyenas, and antelopes had disappeared. Visitors to southern Africa routinely commented on the impoverishment of its originally rich and varied fauna. Before the end of the eighteenth century the southern tip of Africa had even lost one mammalian species, the blaubok, an antelope, to extinction. Elsewhere, in 1831 an Indian sporting journal expressed dismal forebodings that the Nilgiri elk would soon become extinct. A few years later a veteran hunter confirmed that in the past tigers had been more numerous.

At first, such observations were offered as matters of fact rather than of regret. The exigencies of imperial progress dictated that if new territories were to be appropriated by white settlers, who intended to exploit them more productively, their previous occupants, non-human as well as human, would inevitably have to give way. Thus, through most of the nineteenth century, the British government of India encouraged hunters to clear the game from large areas in order to make them available for cultivation. One civil servant celebrated the extermination of wild beasts in the great food-producing districts as one of the undoubted advantages which India had derived from British rule. In British Africa, where there was no centralised government to institute such a policy, observers noted that game tended to retreat before what was uniformly and appreciatively described as 'the advance of civilisation.'

Those who noticed that the game had vanished from a given locality assumed not that the animals had all been killed but that they had withdrawn to some wilder, less accessible place. And it was true that remoter territories were often more richly stocked. When Dr Livingstone saw a herd of buffalo parading slowly before his campfire, and numerous eland grazing fearlessly nearby, he confidently deduced that he was the first white visitor in the neighbourhood. By the 1880s, according to Selous, rhinoceros and Lichtenstein's hartebeest were only to be found in the 'fly country', the vast area within which horses and cattle quickly succumbed to sleeping sickness, and where, consequently, no Europeans could settle.

Well into the second half of the century optimistic sportsmen cherished the goal of discovering virgin hunting grounds, filled with animals that had not yet learned to fear men with firearms. But as exploration and conquest shrank the blank spaces on the map, it became more difficult to believe that the animals that no longer inhabited colonised districts had simply decamped to parts unknown. Reports from across the empire told the same tale of diminishing game populations. Not only were large areas at risk of losing some of their fauna, but in addition many whole species of animals were on the verge of vanishing permanently. The rapid disappearance of the vast bison herd that had roamed the Great Plains of North America shocked British sportsmen, even though bison hunting itself was considered no great loss. Although Yellowstone National Park was founded in 1872 to protect the few remaining animals, the success of this pioneering preservation effort was not assured for several decades. As late as 1875, an expedition to Matabeleland found more quagga, a striped relative of the zebra and the donkey that had once been numerous throughout southern Africa, and sable antelopes than any other game, but within little more than a decade the quagga had disappeared completely. The extinction of the quagga, wastefully hunted for the sake of its hide, was castigated as an example of human folly and greed and as a disgrace to latter-day civilisation.

Gradually, the idea that the elimination of wild animals from appropriated districts was an inevitable by-product of progress was replaced by one that viewed them as a valuable resource requiring protection. Still symbolic of uncivilised nature, game no longer represented a serious threat. Instead, it evoked a special kind of property, neither public nor private, that Britons felt they possessed in their Asian and African territories.

Little by little, late nineteenth-century colonial administrations throughout the empire placed legal restriction on human exploitation of big game animals. The most heavily settled jurisdictions were the first to adopt these codes. In Asia, British efforts such as the Nilgiris Game and Fish Preservation Act of 1879, which protected bison, sambars, ibex, jungle sheep, deer and hares, as well as a variety of birds and fish, and the Elephants Preservation Act of 1879, which prohibited the killing of wild elephants unless they threatened human life or property, supplemented the extensive game reserves maintained by the rajahs who ruled the Native States. In South Africa the hunting of buffalo, quaggas, zebras, hares and antelopes was limited by a Natal ordinance of 1866. The Cape Colony extended systematic protection to elephants, giraffes, hippopotami, buffalo, zebras, quaggas and antelopes in 1886. In the 1890s, the first game reserves were established in southern and eastern Africa.

If protection of threatened game now came to symbolise British stewardship of its colonies, then concern about the plight of creatures controlled by other powers may have been an oblique expression of Britain's claim to international preeminence. International co-operation was necessary for preservation measures to work, at least in Africa, where neither animals nor hunters were likely to acknowledge the arbitrary political boundaries that crisscrossed the continent. Thus in 1900 representatives of the European governments with colonies in sub-Saharan Africa met in London and eventually signed the Convention for the Preservation of Wild Animals, Birds and Fish in Africa, the substance of which had been proposed by the British delegation. The purpose of the Convention was 'saving from indiscriminate slaughter, and… insuring the preservation… of the various forms of animal life deemed either useful to man or are harmless'. Its provisions, reflecting the most self-consciously enlightened contemporary opinion, included absolute prohibitions on hunting those species considered to be threatened with extinction (this short list included the giraffe, gorilla, chimpanzee, mountain zebra, wild ass, white-tailed gnu, eland, and the pygmy hippopotamus); the protection of females and young of other species; the establishment of quotas for individual hunters; the establishment of game reserves within which no hunting would be allowed; the prohibition of hunting during the breeding season; the requirement that hunters purchase licences and that exporters of hides and horns pay duties; and the prohibition of such unsporting methods of killing as nets, pits, and dynamite.

Official correspondence over the next decade contained frequent references to lack of co-operation on the part of the Belgians, Germans and Portuguese suggesting that the other signatories of the Convention may not have been so interested in preservation as the British had come to be. The Colonial Office, however, implemented the spirit of the Convention to the extent that successive colonial secretaries urged colonial administrators to embody its recommendations in their laws and to report regularly on their success in enforcing them. Within a

few years ordinances and acts based on the model of the 1900 Convention had been promulgated throughout British Africa, and as far afield as Malaya.

Adopting regulations was one thing, enforcing them another. Generous with encouragement for preservation, the Colonial Office was stingy with funds to pay for policing vast unsettled areas. As a result, few violations were punished. The government of Uganda, for example, prosecuted only eleven people for shooting prohibited animals in 1906, and six of those were excused on grounds of self-defence. Moreover, not all colonial administrators were equally enthusiastic about protecting big game. Many sympathised strongly with sportsmen and enrolled in the Society for the Preservation of the Wild Fauna of the Empire (still active as the Fauna Preservation Society) when it was founded in 1903. The multiplicity of opinion on the big game issue was an index of how complicated imperial overlordship had become. It could no longer be represented by such straightforward dualities as European versus native, or civilised versus wild.

Far from uniting the inhabitants of a given colony, or even the European inhabitants, attempts to protect big game animals seemed to exacerbate their differences. Settlers often resented the superior privileges that game laws accorded civilian administrators, military officers, and sportsmen, licensing them to kill a few samples of most protected species, while restricting settlers to the most common antelopes. Wild animals competed directly with humans for land and other resources. Tracts set aside for game reserves could not be used for farming. Furthermore, as local planters in British Central Africa claimed in 1906 when they petitioned (ultimately with success) for the reduction of the Elephant Marsh Reserve, lions and other predators might emerge from the reserves to kill people and livestock; grazers and browsers from elephants to antelopes might raid and trample crops; and wild animals might infect domestic animals with disease.

Often complaints reflected the strength of the settlers' feelings more than the actual threat posed by the animals. For example, fears of contagion fo-

cused on sleeping sickness, to which many wild species were immune, and on rinderpest or cattle plague, which had demonstrably been introduced to both India and Africa by European cattle, subsequently decimating indigenous bovines, deer, and antelopes. Such representations were apt to be persuasive. In 1908 the game laws of British East Africa were restructured so as not to expose settlers to the depredations of wild animals, and the governor promised that future enforcement would respect the principle that 'the preservation of game cannot be allowed to interfere with the economic development of the country.'

Game laws also triggered expressions of white hostility toward native Africans. Although settlers sometimes cited black farmers as fellow sufferers from the raids of wild animals on field and fold, more often they joined ranks with sportsmen to protest against any special recognition of traditional hunting rights. Hunters faced with heavy licence fees and restrictions on their bags regarded local tribesmen as competitors with an unfair edge. One colonial complained that natives loved to show their zeal toward the government by reporting 'every elephant shot', while cases of a native reporting on another for breaking the game regulations were 'extremely few'. Despite the incontrovertible association between the advent of white hunters and the depletion of wild animal populations, it was often alleged that natives with modern weapons, and not white sportsmen, were responsible for the rapid disappearance of game. According to one sportsman in 1905, it was not the British gunner who was shooting the game, but 'the African himself, who, armed with a cheap gun, is dealing destruction daily and hourly, for ever creeping about the bush, and with endless patience, manoeuvring until he can gain a certain shot.'

Thus the kind of domination represented by big game hunting had altered significantly. No longer was it the emblem of armed European conquest of territories that seemed threatening and alien. Despite continual skirmishing, the main task of the late Victorian empire was administration, and the significance of hunting evolved to reflect this more sophisticated and less overtly brutal assignment. Killing large wild animals was redefined as a privilege for which the demand outstripped the supply. Hunting policy and rhetoric had to balance the competing interests of many groups, rather than prosecute a single appropriative purpose. The sporting code, which had been rough and ready for most of the nineteenth century, especially in Africa, began to impose more self-restraint on hunters. Furthermore, it compromised the easy camaraderie of the field by re-introducing the class distinctions of the old country.

Nevertheless big game hunting still represented dominion, even though its primary mode was protection rather than unrestrained slaughter. Predators that competed with people or were inclined to attack them were specifically excluded from protection under the convention of 1900 and under the many colonial ordinances based on its provi-

sions. In the first decade of the twentieth century the Indian government still offered rewards for killing tigers, while the Transvaal government rewarded lion slayers. Sir Harry Johnston, the High Commissioner for Uganda and an active preservationist, never attempted to check the slaughter of the hippopotami in the Shire River, which he characterised as very vicious and fond of pursuing and upsetting canoes. But these instances were exceptional; in general fewer and fewer threats were encountered. Big game hunting, the most atavistic and antagonistic connection between humans and animals, became the fitting emblem of the new style in which the British empire attempted to govern both the human and the natural worlds. The need to conquer through force had almost disappeared, giving way to a new need to exploit through management. Hunting and protection had become opposite

sides of the same coin. At least in this respect, home and empire were no longer so very different.

FOR FURTHER READING

Matt Cartmill, *A View to Death in the Morning: Hunting and Nature Through History* (Harvard University Press, 1993); John MacKenzie, *The Empire of Nature: Hunting, Conservation and British Imperialism* (University of Manchester Press, 1997); Harriet Ritvo, *The Animal Estate: The English and Other Creatures in the Victorian Age* (Harvard University Press, 1987); Frederick Courteney Selous, *A Hunter's Wanderings in Africa: Being a Narrative of Nine Years Spent Amongst the Game of the Far Interior of South Africa* (available in several paperback editions).

Harriet Ritvo is Professor of History at the Massachusetts Institute of Technology.

This article first appeared in *History Today,* January 2002, pp. 33-39. © 2002 by History Today, Ltd. Reprinted by permission.

UNIT 4

Modernism, Statism, and Total War: The Twentieth Century

Unit Selections

24. **The Divine Sarah**, Joseph A. Harriss
25. **Art Nouveau**, Stanley Meisler
26. **Searching for Gavrilo Princip**, David DeVoss
27. **How the Modern Middle East Map Came to Be Drawn**, David Fromkin
28. **Nazism in the Classroom**, Lisa Pine
29. **Pearl Harbor: The First Energy War**, Charles Maechling
30. **His Finest Hour**, John Keegan
31. **Mutable Destiny: The End of the American Century?** Donald W. White

Key Points to Consider

- Why is Sarah Bernhardt called the first superstar?

- What are some of the attributes of Art Nouveau? How did it influence the art world?

- How is Gavrilo Princip seen today? Why were his actions to have world wide reprocussions?

- How did the British reshape the Middle East after World War I?

- Describe school reform in Germany under the Nazis.

- Why did Japan view the United States unfavorably?

- Why is Winston Churchill one of the most famous statesmen in British history?

- Is the United States still seen as the greatest world power of the millennium? Why or why not?

 **Links: www.dushkin.com/online/**
These sites are annotated in the World Wide Web pages.

History Net
http://www.thehistorynet.com/THNarchives/AmericanHistory/
Inter-American Dialogue (IAD)
http://www.iadialog.org/
ISN International Relations and Security Network
http://www.isn.ethz.ch/
Russian and East European Network Information Center/University of Texas at Austin
http://reenic.utexas.edu/reenic.html
Terrorism Research Center
http://www.terrorism.com/
World History Review/Scott Danford and Jon Larr
http://members.aol.com/sniper43/index.html

The nineteenth century ended with high hopes for the future of Western civilization. Popular novelists foresaw air travel, television, visual telephones, records, and space travel, and even the construction of a new continent in the Pacific. Technology would liberate those living in this century from most of their burdens, or so argued the futurists of the time. There were skeptics of course: Mark Twain punctured the pious hypocrisies of Westerners who presumed that their Christianity and technology demonstrated their superiority over the heathens of the non-Western world. And a few writers questioned whether humans would be any happier, even with all the material benefits of the promised future.

Even before this glittering future could be realized, turn-of-the century artists and thinkers brought forth an alternative vision of far greater originality. They set in motion a period of unprecedented cultural innovation and artistic experimentation, out of which emerged modern music, theater, literature, art, and architecture. Never before had there been so many cultural manifestos: Fauvism, Cubism, and Futurism. In "The Divine Sarah" we see the growing fame of a "superstar," while in "Art Nouveau," we see how this movement influenced art and architecture around the world. In philosophy it was the age of pragmatism, positivism, and Bergsonism. On the intellectual frontier, Alfred Binet, Ivan Pavlov, and Sigmund Freud reformulated the premises of psychology. Advanced work in experimental science concentrated on radioactivity and the atom, setting the stage for Albert Einstein's abstract theories.

Thus, in the years before World War I, the West was able to point to unrivaled accomplishments. Aristocrats and the middle class were smugly confident of the future because they were eminently satisfied with the present.

In hindsight, all this seems a great illusion. We can now see how such illusions blinded Europeans to the coming war. Millions of lives were lost in World War I, which was a showcase for the destructive forces of European technology. The war dashed the hopes of an entire generation and contributed to revolutions in Russia, Germany, and Austria. The war spurred the breakup of the Ottoman Empire, caused the collapse of the international economy, and was responsible for the emergence of totalitarian dictatorships. These events, in turn, brought on World War II.

The article by David DeVoss, "Searching for Gavrilo Princip," discusses the assassination that led to World War I. Then the essay "How the Modern Middle East Map Came to Be Drawn" traces many current problems to the international politics of the World War I settlement. The two articles, "Pearl Harbor: The First Energy War" and "His Finest Hour" recount the reasons for the Japanese war with the United States and Winston Churchill's brilliant leadership of Great Britain during the conflict. Finally, Donald W. White, in "Mutable Destiny: The End of the American Century?" questions whether the United States will be able to keep its hegemony.

The Divine Sarah

Bewitching her admirers around the world, Sarah Bernhardt dazzled audiences as she pioneered the cult of celebrity

By Joseph A. Harriss

IT WAS THE KIND OF SURREAL MOB SCENE NEW YORK RESERVES for showbiz celebs, with frenzied fans gathered at the stage door for a glimpse of the famous foreign star. When she finally appeared, late, after 29 curtain calls, they went wild. Everyone was shouting to her, reaching for her. One wild-eyed woman tore a gold brooch from her own coat and nearly knocked her down pinning it on her; another tried to snip a lock of her hair but ended up slicing an ostrich plum from her hat. (After another performance, men thrust out their arms and noisily begged her to autograph their cuffs.) A hysterical girl brandished an autograph book, then realized her pen was out of ink; she plunged her teeth into her own wrist and dipped the instrument in her blood. With the mob out of hand, the frightened star beat a retreat back to the theater. She tore off her hat, veil and chinchilla cloak, put them on her sister and sent her out to impersonate her while she slipped out by another door.

Despite her modest origins, Sarah wasn't very impressed by emperors and their ilk.

It could have been yesterday's rock star event. But it was 1880 and the star was Sarah Bernhardt, The Divine, The Eighth Wonder of the World, and the most celebrated woman of the Victorian era besides—and maybe including—Queen Victoria herself. Arguably the first international entertainment icon, The Bernhardt, as Americans called her, personified stardom carried to mythical proportions; when *Variety* ran a story on the 100 top stars of the 20th century, she was lionized as "the first superstar-diva." It is difficult today to imagine the spell she cast over admirers as various as Sigmund Freud, who purportedly kept a photograph of her in his waiting room, and philosopher William James, who called her "the most race-horsey, high-mettled human being I've ever seen." Mark Twain observed there were five kinds of actresses: bad, fair, good, great—" and then there is Sarah Bernhardt."

Her myth traveled throughout the pre-cinema, pre-television world via paintings, photographs, posters and newspaper stories. One biographer calculates that if pasted end to end, the articles about her during her 62-year career from 1861 to 1923 would stretch around the earth, while a pile of her printed photographs would reach the top of the Eiffel Tower. She promoted that myth with panache, eccentric behavior and in-your-face attitude. She made sure everyone knew that she slept in a coffin. And when a reporter exclaimed during an interview, "Why, New York didn't give Dom Pedro of Brazil such an ovation!" she purred, "Yes, but he was only an emperor."

Despite her modest origins, Madame Sarah wasn't very impressed by emperors and their ilk. Many had been at her feet— and even closer. Britain's Prince of Wales was a very dear friend indeed, and her only child was fathered by Belgian Prince Henri de Ligne. Europe's crowned heads visited her backstage, and she gave command performances in their palaces. Austrian Emperor Franz Joseph placed an antique cameo necklace around her neck, while Archduke Friedrich insisted she stay at one of his palaces while in Vienna. Italy's King Umberto gave her an exquisite Venetian fan, Spain's King Alfonso XII, a diamond brooch, France's Emperor Louis-Napoleon, a magnificent pin with the imperial initials in diamonds. In Saint Petersburg, where they ran a red carpet over the snow to the stage door, Czar Alexander III called on her after a command performance at the Winter Palace. As she was making a deep curtsy, he stopped her: "No, Madame," he ordered, "it is I who must bow to you." And so he did before his entire court.

The Divine continues to fascinate. Earlier this year a New York theater presented *The Divine Trilogy of Sarah Bernhardt*, while Connie Clark, an actress based in North Carolina, has performed her one-woman show, Sarah, tracing Bernhardt's life and career, at the Lincoln Center, universities and in Europe. Paris paid homage to her last winter with a sumptuous exhibition at the ornate old Bibliothèque Nationale, just a short walk down rue de Richelieu from the Comédie Française theater where she starred and stormed.

The show presented paintings, costumes, playbills and photographs recalling her life, loves and many of the 125 plays she acted in. "She was really the first media star of our era," says Noelle Guibert, director of the Bibliothèque Department of Theater Arts, who was the curator of the show. "She incarnated the fantasies of the Belle Epoque. She was the one everybody admired, the one to whom they attributed the wildest passions, eccentricities and perversions."

At a convent school,
her tempestuous, headstrong
behavior drove the
nuns to distraction.

Quite a symbolic load to bear for a pathologically skinny girl whom doctors expected to die before 20. Henriette-Rosine Bernard was born on October 23, 1844, in Paris, the illegitimate daughter of a Dutch-Jewish woman of dubious morals from Amsterdam and an unknown, probably French, father. She was an emotionally unstable, sickly child who seemed to run a constant temperature and frequently spat up blood. Doctors diagnosed a wasting disease like tuberculosis and prescribed snail soup for strength.

Her mother, Julie, a high-flying courtesan, had little time for her. She often left Sarah with a nanny, before sending her to a girls' school in suburban Paris, where she learned to read and write and throw memorable tantrums. After that it was a convent school in Versailles, where her tempestuous, headstrong behavior drove the nuns to distraction. Although she received

only six years or so of formal education. She tells us in her memoirs, *My Double Life*, an artful mix of fact and myth-making, that when she was 9 she adopted her spunky lifelong motto, *"Quand même,"* meaning in spite of everything. She had jumped over a wide ditch on a dare, landing painfully on her face and spraining a wrist. "I'll do it again if they dare me," the willful child screamed through tears at her mother and aunt as they doctored her. "And I'll do whatever I want all my life!" Sighed the aunt prophetically, *"Quelle enfant terrible!"*

At 15 she overheard doctors telling her mother that she had only a few years to live. Death became an obsession, and she acquired a pretty coffin so she could get used to it. (The resulting rosewood and satin model became one of the stage props in her life; countless postcard photographs of her reclining dramatically in the flower-strewn casket were sold in Europe and America.) About this time, too, the influential Duc de Morny, one of Julie's wealthy lovers and Emperor Napoleon III's half brother, advised the family to send the enfant terrible to the Conservatory of Music and Drama in Paris. When Morny got her a box seat at the Comédie Française, France's prestigious national theater, Sarah sobbed uncontrollably at the heroine's plight. That did it: the girl who would become the last of the great Romantic actresses was hooked on the theater.

She threw herself into her lessons at the conservatory, then considered the world's finest drama school, even if she later took the opportunity to mock it in her memoirs. It was solid training, but mostly a bore for Sarah, who always relied on her instincts and raw emotion for effect.

Still, it got her into the august Comédie Française—with a little pull from Morny—at the age of 17. Her first performance on August 11, 1862, was nearly a catastrophe due to a bad case of teeth-chattering stage fright, which would nag her all her life. The critics were indulgent but unimpressed. "Mademoiselle Bernhardt… is a tall, attractive young woman with a slender waist and most pleasing face," wrote one. "She carries herself well and pronounces her words with perfect clarity. That is all that can be said for the moment." In any case, the high-strung, rebellious young woman felt uncomfortable among the stuffed shirts of the French theater establishment. Within a year she was fired for slapping a leading lady who had been rude to the younger sister Sarah doted on, Régine.

Out of work except for occasional roles, Sarah turned to her mother's trade to make ends meet. It was a time when "actress" was virtually synonymous with courtesan or kept woman, and the dandies expected their favors as a right. One day, for example, the Prince de Joinville, Emperor Louis-Philippe's son, sent a cryptic note to Rachel, one of France's great leading ladies: "Where? When? How much?" She zinged back a succinct, practiced reply: "Your place. This evening. No charge."

In 1864, after a particularly bad performance in a second-rate play, Sarah took off and ended up eventually in Brussels. There she had an affair with Prince Henri de Ligne, got pregnant and gave birth to a son she named Maurice, whom she would adore and indulge for the rest of her life. If anyone had the bad taste to inquire about his paternity, she would assume a pensive pose and reply evenly that she could never make up her mind whether it was French Prime Minister Léon Gambetta, Victor Hugo or perhaps General Georges Boulanger.

Nearly two years later her slow, erratic acting start took a turn for the better when she joined Paris' Left Bank Théatre de l'Odéon. There she honed what would become her trademark technique: authentic, impassioned acting that she reveled in. Favoring improbable, wholehearted, three-hankie drama, she emerged as the consummate tragedienne, running the emotional gamut of tigerish passion, melting seduction, excruciating loss and unbearable sorrow.

Such technique compensated for being no great beauty. Her hair was hopeless, a frizzy, unruly, reddish blonde mop. She hid her low brow beneath a tumble of curls, which also had the advantage of enlarging her small eyes. And in a day when the canons of beauty called for opulent, Rubenesque women, she was not only thin, she was skeletal—"A Madonna's head stuck on a broomstick," as the writer Alexandre Dumas *fils* called her. She never needed an umbrella, boulevard wits said, as she was so skinny she could walk between the raindrops.

Brown Brothers

Bernhardt's arrival on any shore created a frenzy: disembarking at Folkstone for a tour in England, she was feted by an admiring entourage.

It was at the Odéon that a star was born on the evening of January 16, 1872, when she played the love-stricken Queen of Spain in Victor Hugo's *Ruy Blas*. Backstage visitors included the Prince of Wales, who stepped aside respectfully when the white-maned, bewhiskered author, by then a French monument, entered, dropped to one knee, kissed Sarah's hand and murmured *"Merci, merci."* Outside, a cheering crowd filled the streets, while excited students unhitched the horses from her carriage and pulled it themselves shouting "Make way for our Sarah!"

Shortly thereafter the Comédie Française invited her back. Although she was handed some important roles in the House of

Molière, she again chafed under rules that rotated leading parts, operated on strict bureaucratic seniority and permitted no stars—a stifling atmosphere for an actress with her temperament. She threw so many tantrums and slammed so many doors that the theater's exasperated director began referring to her as "Mademoiselle Révolte."

But even French bureaucracy could not prevent Madame Sarah's star quality from shining in another Hugo tragedy, *Hernani*, in which she played a Castilian noblewoman who loves the bandit Hernani and takes poison with him at the end. So moved was Hugo this time that he sent her a box with a note in it next day. "Madame," he wrote, "when the public, touched and enchanted by you, applauded, I wept. This tear that you caused me to shed is yours. I place it at your feet." The tear in question was a single perfect diamond on a gold bracelet.

Hugo loved what he termed her golden voice. Not powerful or deep, it was a highly musical voice that writers vied to describe: "As sonorous as pure crystal," wrote Alphonse Daudet, while Jules Lemaitre called it "a caress that strokes you like fingers, so pure, so tender, so harmonious."

But beyond that, the lady could really act. "Acting is all internal, but must be externalized," she said. Sarah built her characters from the inside out and embraced less stylized, more truthful acting than was generally practiced at the time. As a young woman she could transform herself into an 80-year-old crone, simulating blindness by showing only the whites of her eyes. As a 56-year-old grandmother, she could convincingly play the 20-year-old Duke of Reichstadt, Napoleon's consumptive son, dying in the last act "as angels would die if they were allowed to," said one critic. And in *Joan of Arc*, when the judge demanded her age, she invariably brought the house down when she deliberately turned to face the audience, who knew she was 65, and declared triumphantly, "Nineteen!"

Both her memory and stagecraft were the stuff of legends. She could memorize a part merely by reading it through four times, blocking out her moves as she went; after the fifth reading she had it down pat—and performed without a prompter. When playing Cleopatra, she often used a real snake for the final scene. And she captivated audiences at *La Tosca* with her stage business of placing lit candlesticks around the body of Scarpia and a crucifix on his chest after stabbing him, then slowly backing off in horror, her gown's long train trailing along the stage until the curtain fell. It was her acting that inspired Puccini to compose his opera based on the play.

She was said to smoke cigars, take boxing lessons and dress in men's clothes.

Inevitably, the time came for her to decide whether to stay in safe repertory at the national theater with its stilted acting style or try an independent career. She resigned from the Comédie

Studiously cultivating her image, Bernhardt, who had been a sickly child, appropriated an obsession with death as one aspect of her persona. Rumored to sleep in a coffin, she also capitalized on a reputation for brooding intensity, as the image (right) suggests.

Française in 1880, formed her own troupe and headed to London's Gaiety Theater to begin her life as an international star. It was the first stop on foreign tours that would, over the next 40 years, take her throughout Europe, from Britain to Greece and Spain to Russia, and to North and South America.

After London, where rumors were rife—she was said to hold a witches' Sabbath certain nights, smoke cigars in the morning, take boxing lessons, even dress in men's clothes—Sarah sailed for New York for a six-month tour. She landed on October 27, 1880, amid all the fanfare her canny impresario for the tour, Edward Jarrett, could muster with spicy advance publicity, perhaps the first deliberate campaign to create an international star. The public was dying to learn more about The Bernhardt.

> *"I adore this country, she said while visiting America, "where women reign."*

Her first New York performance, *Adrienne Lecouvreur* at Booth's Theater, was declared off-limits to children because it dealt with an unmarried actress's affair with a rakish aristocrat. Despite, or perhaps because of, that, she played to a packed house that broke into roaring applause after Adrienne died in the final scene, and went on for 27 curtain calls. It was at Booth's that same month of November 1880 that she created her signature role, Marguerite Gauthier in *La Dame aux Camélias* by

Dumas *fils*, that for the next 43 years she would play more than 3,000 times all over the world. On a later U.S. tour, railway magnate William Henry Vanderbilt attended every one of her New York performances of *Camille*, weeping openly into a large handkerchief. When Sarah returned to France, he gave it to her as a souvenir.

Then it was on to Boston. Proud of its open-minded appreciation of culture, the city welcomed her more warmly than New York. The critics were ecstatic: "Before such perfection, analysis is impossible," wrote one. Sarah returned the feeling. "Boston belongs to women," she declared. "They are in the majority there, they are intelligently puritan, and gracefully independent." The tour comprised 156 appearances in 50 cities and towns from Albany and Pittsburgh to Detroit. After Chicago, she boarded the Sarah Bernhardt Special and rode in her own private Palace Car with walls of inlaid wood, brass gas lamps, Turkish carpeting, lounge area with sofas, piano and potted palms. The dining room table seated ten and was laid with linen and china with her *Quand Même* crest. Two cooks prepared meals. (On another tour, in Louisiana, she bought a small alligator she named Ali-Gaga, which make itself comfortable beneath the bedcovers at night. It finally died, they say, from too much champagne.)

Americans fell in love with Sarah, and vice versa. "I adore this country, where women reign," she said. In at least eight more tours—four billed as "The Farewell Tour of Mme. Sarah Bernhardt"—she crisscrossed the country. She did *Camille* in huge tents in Missouri and Texas, cornstalk stubble tearing the dresses of women spectators. At one Texas stop a cowboy rode

Thousands of mourners thronged the streets of Paris to pay their final respects to the legendary actress, who died on March 26, 1923.

up and asked for a seat. None was available until he pulled his six-shooter. Entering the tent he drawled in passing, "By the way, what does this gal do, sing or dance?"

This was an interesting change of pace for "that anxious, strange, morbid being named Sarah Bernhardt"—her own description. At home in her Paris town house on Boulevard Péreire, her furnishings included a skull on her desk and a skeleton named Lazarus, plus the famous coffin in which she often studied her roles and, gossips said, received her lovers. She liked to welcome other visitors dressed in a long white gown and reclining on a cushion-strewn divan on a platform, canopied with Oriental hangings supported by velvet-covered spears. She kept a menagerie that at various times included her enormous wolfhound Osman, a friendly lynx on a leash, a baby tigress named Minette, and a tame lion, until the beast started smelling too bad. Visitors never knew what to expect. When Alexandre Dumas *fils* called one day to show Sarah a new play he had just written, a pet puma calmly devoured his straw hat.

None of which deterred her devoted admirers, known as *sarahdoteurs*, from flocking to her. Her court, as she called them collectively, ranged from writers like Hugo, Zola, Dumas, Flaubert and Oscar Wilde, who wrote the play *Salome* especially for her, to statesmen like Gambetta, the Prince of Wales and Theodore Roosevelt. She could be very funny, mimicking some of them wickedly, and regaling them with catty remarks. Of an actress who tried to play the male lead she had made her own in *L'Aiglon*, she said, "The poor dear isn't man enough to make us forget she's a woman, and not woman enough to be appealing."

That wasn't her problem. Sarah played some 25 male parts, from Prince Charming to Cyrano de Bergerac, Judas and

Hamlet. She liked men's roles, she said, because they were generally more tormented and intellectual than women's.

> *When Dreyfus was unjustly sentenced, she helped persuade Zola to write "J'Accuse."*

Certainly she had courage enough for several men. When Army Captain Alfred Dreyfus, who was Jewish, was unjustly sentenced to Devil's Island in 1894 on trumped-up, anti-Semitic charges of treason, Sarah took his side against most French popular opinion. Though many of her friends and her son, Maurice, stopped talking to her, she helped persuade Emile Zola to write his famous "J'Accuse" article that turned the tide in Dreyfus' favor. And when spreading gangrene struck her right leg in 1915, she pleaded with two doctors to amputate it, threatening to shoot herself in the knee if they refused. (She had endured painful problems with her knee for years.) They declined because she was 71 and suffered from chronic uremia. Finally a surgeon agreed, and she hummed the "Marseillaise" as she was wheeled down the hospital corridor. Later, she tried an artificial leg but found it too cumbersome. Also refusing to use a wheelchair, she opted for a specially designed litter chair in Louis XV-style with gilt carving, and was carried around like a Byzantine princess. She altered her stage business so that actors were gathered around her, seated, and kept on acting. For ovations she stood on one leg, held on to a piece of furniture, and gestured with one arm.

Shortly after the amputation, she visited the WWI front lines near Verdun to perform for French troops in mess tents, hospital wards, open marketplaces and ramshackle barns. Propped in a shabby armchair, she recited a patriotic piece to war-dazed men fresh from the trenches. When she ended with a rousing *"Aux armes!"* they rose cheering and sobbing.

Despite failing health, Sarah flung herself into silent movies, making eight in her waning years, including her biggest hit, *Queen Elizabeth*. She was shooting a film on location in her town house for an American producer in the spring of 1923 when she collapsed. She died in the arms of Maurice on March 26 at the age of 78. That evening, all Paris theaters observed two minutes of silence. Parisians lined the streets as her funeral procession wound its way to Père Lachaise cemetery, where Molière and admirers Marcel Proust and Oscar Wilde were buried. There she was interred in the rosewood coffin. In contrast to the famous cemetery's ornate tombs with handsome sculptures and long inscriptions, only two words were deemed worthy to decorate the simple granite tomb of The Divine: Sarah Bernhardt.

Joseph A. Harriss, a frequent contributor, is based in Paris.

From *Smithsonian* magazine, August 2001, pp. 68-76. © 2001 by Joseph A. Harriss.

Art Nouveau

BY STANLEY MEISLER

As the 20th century neared, more than a hundred years ago, artists and intellectuals and merchants throughout Europe and in the United States tried to whip art into new shapes so it would keep pace with the ever-changing modern world. This frenzy to throw off the stultifying past and become modern, excited architects, painters, sculptors, illustrators, jewelers, potters, furniture makers, glassblowers, metalworkers, writers, dealers and shopkeepers. Since they believe they were creating everything anew, their style is best known today as Art Nouveau, French for "new art."

The new art, popular from the early 1890s to the eve of World War I, took many different paths and drew inspiration from many different sources—Japanese, Chinese, and Islamic art, Celtic and Viking revivals, 18th-century rococo furniture, the British Arts and Crafts Movement and literary trends such as symbolism. At its most typical, the highly decorative and ornamental style was lavish with arabesques and whiplash curves, botanical and zoological forms, portraits of seductive women and a decadent symbolism. At their best, Art Nouveau artists worked in several disciplines—architects designing armoires as well as buildings, for example, and furniture makers designing jewelry as well as armoires. Harmony was their ideal, so that a room's paintings, wallpaper and furniture would all fit together. Some of the ornamentation was so excessive that it seems kitsch now, but much of Art Nouveau is still delicate, beautiful, dynamic and free.

A number of cities emerged as busy workshops for the new creativity, including Paris, Nancy, Brussels, Barcelona, Glasgow, Vienna, Munich, Turin, New York and Chicago. Giants dominated the style: the Scottish architect Charles Rennie Mackintosh, the Austrian painter Gustav Klimt, the French architect Hector Guimard, the Czech illustrator Alphonse Mucha, the Belgian architect and interior designer Victor Horta, the Spanish architect Antoni Gaudí and the German-born dealer Siegfried Bing. The style had a host of different names a hundred years ago: Secession in Vienna, Jugendstil in Germany, Stile Liberty in Italy, Modernismo in Barcelona and most famously, the one that stuck, Art Nouveau in France.

The style had enormous popularity at its height but always provoked detractors as well. Designer Walter Crane, a leader of the British Arts and Crafts Movement, called Art Nouveau "a strange decorative disease." British sculptor Alfred Gilbert sneered that it was "absolute nonsense" and belonged to "the young lady's seminary." A French critic derided it as "the art of vegetarians." And for much of the 20th century, champions of Pablo Picasso and Henri Matisse and modern art treated Art Nouveau with contempt.

VICTORIA & ALBERT PICTURE LIBRARY, LONDON

Although British Arts and Crafts designer Walter Crane created works such as this swan wallpaper (1875) that anticipated Art Nouveau, he railed against the style's decadence and hedonism.

In recent decades, however, there has been renewed, almost nostalgic, interest in the styles that came before the age of modern art, and Art Nouveau has benefited from the attention.

Deemed the first fully mature Art Nouveau image, Aubrey Beardsley's 1893 illustration was inspired by Oscar Wilde's play Salome.

In April, London's Victoria and Albert Museum opened the largest exhibition of Art Nouveau ever assembled. The show, expanded even more, comes to the National Gallery of Art in Washington on October 8 and remains on view there through January 28, 2001. A reduced exhibition then goes on to the Tokyo Metropolitan Art Museum in April 2001 for its final stop. Not since the Paris Exposition Universelle of 1900 has Art Nouveau been on display before so many people.

The show in Washington, which is sponsored by Daimler-Chrysler, will feature some spectacular masterpieces. A cast-iron entrance wrought by Guimard for the Métropolitain, the

Paris subway, with lampposts like giant tendrils and grillwork twisting in audacious curves, will be on view. So will the ladies' lunchroom that Mackintosh designed for Glasgow's Ingram Street tearoom, complete with high, straight-back chairs, gleaming silver-and-white walls and a mural of the languid figures of women, created by Mackintosh's wife, Margaret Macdonald. Turin designer Agostino Lauro's double parlor for an Italian villa, with curved mirrors, hand-carved woodwork and the same green-gold floral-patterned silk moiré adorning both the furniture and the walls, has been installed as well. On a much smaller scale, French jeweler René Lalique's *Dragonfly Woman*, a corsage ornament in the form of a nude woman with the lower body and diaphanous wings of a dragonfly, all crafted in gold, enamel and precious stones, is also on display.

It is fitting that the Victoria and Albert mount an Art Nouveau show of such magnitude and quality. "In the 19th century, the Victoria and Albert, which was then known as the South Kensington Museum, was virtually the only real decorative art museum in the world," says the V&A's Paul Greenhalgh, curator of the exhibition and editor of the accompanying catalog. Many Art Nouveau artists, he says, came there to look at designs and gather ideas.

The museum, in fact, purchased a large selection of the Art Nouveau works displayed at the 1900 Paris Exposition. When the museum exhibited them soon afterward, however, there was an outcry by detractors, some of them prestigious leaders of the British art establishment. The museum gave in and shipped all the pieces to the satellite venue in east London. When the building was transformed into the Victoria and Albert's Bethnal Green Museum of Childhood, the works of Art Nouveau were arrayed alongside a trove of toys and dollhouses. It was not until the 1980s that the V&A recuperated the Paris Exposition purchases for its main building.

Art Nouveau owed much of its early popularity to marketing, and Siegfried Bing, a dealer in Paris, served as guru, merchant and public relations flack for the movement. Bing came from a German mercantile family that had imported French porcelain and glass for many years. After attending school in Hamburg, he joined the Paris branch of the family business and eventually embarked on his own in France.

Bing found it "an astonishing anachronism" that so much of contemporary decoration was copied from previous centuries. Insisting that decorative arts deserved a standing as high as fine arts, he persuaded young painters to try their hands at textile and furniture design. He preached that a room should have a harmonious style and not look like an agglomeration of bric-a-brac and disparate furniture.

At first, Bing acted primarily as a merchant for artists. But finding that his shop had become a hodge-podge of unrelated items, he solved the problem by organizing his own workshops, becoming a partner in artistic creation by, as he put it, "having the articles made under my personal direction, and securing the assistance of such artists as seem best disposed to carry out my ideas."

In a celebrated commission, Bing purchased designs from colorist painters such as Pierre Bonnard and Henri de Toulouse-Lautrec for Louis Comfort Tiffany to transform into stained-

CALOUSTE GULBENKIAN MUSEUM, LISBON; MUSEE D'ORSAY, PARIS

René Lalique's *Dragonfly Woman* (top) was exhibited at the 1900 Paris Exposition. The Topaz-studded "Apparitions" brooch (above) was designed by Eugène Samuel Grasset for Maison Vever jewelers.

glass windows at his New York studios. Bing displayed these windows when he opened a new gallery, L'Art Nouveau, at 22 rue de Provence in Paris. He was so influential by then that the style swiftly assumed the mercantile name. Bing conceived of his enterprise as an international marketplace, but this concept upset some critics who accused him of hurting French culture and artisans by lavishing so much attention on foreigners like Tiffany and Belgian architect Henry van de Velde.

French novelist Edmond de Goncourt wrote in his journal, "Are we to be *denationalized*, conquered morally in a conquest worse than real war?… No! This cannot be the new furniture of France! No! No!" Designer Charles Genuys admonished that "we cannot violate our Latin and Gaulish nature by capitulating to the Saxons."

Bing was stung by the accusations. Although born in Hamburg, he was a recipient of the French Legion of Honor and re-garded himself as a French patriot. But he retreated in the face of the criticism. When the Bing pavilion opened at the Paris Exposition of 1900, it exhibited art almost entirely by French artists or foreign-born colleagues who had adopted France as their home.

Bing was not the only merchant specializing in the sale of Art Nouveau. His British counterpart was Arthur Lasenby Liberty, whose shop on Regent Street in London sold fabrics, silver, pewter, jewelry and furniture. Liberty's exports to Italy were so well-publicized that Art Nouveau was known there as the *Stile Liberty*, or Liberty Style.

For France, the architect and designer Hector Guimard epitomized Art Nouveau more than any other artist. His 141 Metro entrances, after all, graced the landscape of Paris. Even today, 86 still stand, all now classified as French historic monuments. His Castel Béranger, a large apartment building completed in 1898 when he was just 31, is an obligatory stop on the itinerary of any Art Nouveau aficionado who comes to Paris.

Guimard looked on nature as the model for his curves and twists and exuberant botanical forms. "Beauty appears to us in perpetual variety," he said. "Forms are engendered from movements which are never alike.… Let us bend before… the examples of the great architect of the universe." This idealization of nature led him into sinuous and sensuous forms, infused with femininity.

Guimard attracted a good deal of notice when the Castel Béranger won a prize from the city of Paris for the best façade created that year. A self-promoter, he rented an apartment in the building and organized guided tours of the premises. He even published 24 postcards advertising what he called the "Guimard Style." The artist Paul Signac was also a tenant. Soon after he moved in, he wrote a friend, "Come soon, our blue staircase will amuse you."

Most architects proposed little stone buildings resembling railroad stations as entrances to the new subway system that opened in time for the 1900 Exposition. But Guimard's design of cast-iron gates and grilles—in myriad modular combinations—struck the fancy of officials looking for a modern motif. The Spanish Surrealist Salvador Dalí, who extolled Guimard long after Art Nouveau fell out of favor, insisted that "those divine entrances" led one to "descend into the region of the subconscious.…"

Guimard, whose wife was American and Jewish, took refuge in New York before the outbreak of World War II and died there in relative obscurity in 1942. When an admirer tried in vain to prevent the destruction of a Guimard building in Sèvres in the late 1960s, the novelist André Malraux, President Charles de Gaulle's minister of culture, told him, "You like that stuff?… Everyone to his own nasty taste." Despite Malraux's derision, a swelling movement of artists and intellectuals had already emerged determined to safeguard and restore the works and reputation of Guimard.

The career of Czech-born Alphonse Maria Mucha illustrates the range of the best Art Nouveau artists. Working for a Paris printer, he was the only illustrator available in the shop in 1894 when the great actress Sarah Bernhardt ordered a poster advertising her in the play *Gismonda*. That chance commission made

ART ON FILE/CORBIS

The dragonfly, a popular Art Nouveau motif, takes flight in Hector Guimard's entrance to the Porte Dauphine station of the Paris Métro.

him an instant celebrity. Bernhardt was so pleased with his design that she signed him to a six-year contract to produce more posters for her. He would also design theatrical sets for her plays and jewelry for her to wear onstage.

News of the Bernhardt commission prompted others to seek him out, and Mucha was soon swamped with orders to create posters, lithographs, murals, magazine covers, book illustrations, theater programs, restaurant menus, carpets, fabrics, furniture and jewelry. Although Mucha's drawings of "the Divine Sarah" portrayed her as dignified, almost regal, he created erotic, exotic, heavy-lidded women with luxurious hair for his other commissions. In one poster, Mucha, anticipating modern advertising, hawked Job cigarette paper through a seductive woman with cascading hair that tangled below her waist like vines in a forest.

In 1900–1901, Mucha designed a shop on the rue Royale for the jeweler Georges Fouquet. The store, which was closed in 1923 and later reassembled in the Carnavalet Museum in Paris, is practically a primer of Art Nouveau, a fantasy of all the symbols of the style. A bronze frieze of a slightly draped woman with heavy jewelry dominates a façade that also displays ten stained-glass portraits of women. The interior features sculp-

tures of peacocks, fish and nude women, carved furniture, floral designs and wallpaper patterned with strange insects.

The heyday for Art Nouveau came with the Paris Exposition of 1900. The fair, which attracted 48 million visitors and included exhibitions from 40 nations, stretched alongside both banks of the Seine from the Eiffel Tower to the new Alexandre III bridge. Art Nouveau works could be found throughout the pavilions. The lavish main entrance—the Porte Binet—incorporated many Art Nouveau themes. And so did the wonderful Pavillon Bleu restaurant on the Seine. Bing's own pavilion—L'Art Nouveau Bing—featured six rooms designed and decorated by three different artists. Some 35 Art Nouveau pieces from the 1900 fair, including important works by the master Paris jeweler René Lalique and Nancy furniture maker Louis Majorelle, will be featured in the exhibition at the National Gallery of Art.

Loïe Fuller, an American dancer who starred at the Folies Bergère, also had her own pavilion, its Art Nouveau façade rippling with curves. Shimmering under the colored lights of electricity, a novel source of energy in those days, Fuller twirled her billowing, diaphanous robes to metamorphose herself into birds, butterflies, flowers and some less recognizable forms of Art Nouveau. A short video, played continuously at both the Victoria and Albert and the National Gallery of Art, shows her swooping like a bird and then accelerating into a tornado of curving motion. The celebrated dancer Isadora Duncan praised Fuller for dancing with all the "magic of Merlin." Artists were entranced by Fuller's movements and used her as a model for posters, sculpture and lamps.

Despite all the hoopla in Paris, Art Nouveau was hardly a French exclusive. Bing, in fact, credited Belgium, where architects Henry van de Velde and Victor Horta worked, as "the cradle of this species of art." Van de Velde championed the idea of creating harmonious rooms, while Horta changed the face of the new bourgeois neighborhoods of Brussels. Although conservative King Leopold II refused to commission Horta for any public works, rich Belgians sought him as architect for their private homes.

The Art Nouveau phenomenon spread across Europe and spanned the Atlantic as artists and craftsmen exchanged ideas and techniques through travel, international expositions and a growing number of art magazines. Moreover, the urge to break with the past, to feel new, to feel modern, struck artists everywhere from Helsinki to Chicago.

The new look took on different shapes in different cities. In Barcelona, the buildings of Antoni Gaudí were so ornate and curvaceous that they seemed to pulse with life. In Glasgow, however, the Art Nouveau of Charles Rennie Mackintosh (SMITHSONIAN, January 1997) was far more subtle, his wonderful buildings and furniture made exciting by soft touches of curve, color and asymmetry.

Sometimes the style took different directions even in the same city. In Vienna, Gustav Klimt was surely the most decorative of Art Nouveau painters, his portraits of femmes fatales bathed in a mosaic of gold and brilliant color. Yet designer Josef Hoffmann, allied with Klimt, designed silver products so geometric and functional that their decoration seems secondary.

Although Chicago architects Louis Sullivan and Frank Lloyd Wright worked in the style, the most prominent Art Nouveau personage in the United States was Louis Comfort Tiffany, son of jeweler Charles Lewis Tiffany, who founded New York's renowned Tiffany & Co. Louis was a painter, decorator and designer who profited from his father's connections and from the appetite of the new, wealthy American industrial elite for the latest fashions in arts and crafts. As a young man, he and his associates received commissions to decorate the Connecticut home of Mark Twain and the Red and Blue rooms of the White House under President Chester A. Arthur. Louis Tiffany was best known, however, as the creator of exquisite glass. Like many of his European cohorts, he loved lavish color, admired Middle Eastern and other exotic ceramics, and pored over books about insects and flowers in his search for subjects for design. He developed new methods for mixing an amazing variety of colors and for rendering glass iridescent. "I have reached the point," he said, "where it is possible to produce any color and any luster that may be required."

Tiffany became as much an entrepreneur as an artist, employing scores in his workshops on Long Island. He was known as a high-handed boss who tolerated no lapses in the quality of the work from his crews of specialists and apprentices. The host of Tiffany pieces in the current exhibition includes what was regarded as his masterpiece at the 1900 Paris Exposition—a tri-panel glass screen decorated in an intense, color-rich tangle of vines, vegetables and fruit.

Art Nouveau emerged at a time when writers, following new neurological theory, believed that the tensions of modern urban life weakened the body but sharpened the senses. This belief spawned a movement of writers with a penchant for describing intense sensitivity. Members of the movement became known as the decadents. A French novel, *A Rebours (Against Nature)* by Joris-Karl Huysmans, the story of an aesthete searching for exotic pleasures, was hailed as "the breviary" of the decadent movement. The English writer Oscar Wilde, closely allied to Art Nouveau, used the Huysmans novel as a device in a plot of his own decadent novel, *The Picture of Dorian Gray*. The heightened sensitivity of the decadents led their literary movement close to Art Nouveau and its sensual imagery.

One aspect of that closeness was the obsession of many writers and artists with female sexuality. An extraordinary number of erotic inkwells, candlesticks, lamps and figurines—most small and inexpensive—entered middle-class homes as Art Nouveau. The zeal of the artists sometimes went too far. In 1896 the furniture maker Rupert Carabin produced a wooden chair that features the sculpture of a trussed-up nude woman clinging to its back.

This obsession led to anxiety about femmes fatales—evil, usually exotic women who manipulated their charms to destroy men. Salome—the princess famed for her seductive dancing and for ordering the decapitation of John the Baptist—was one of the most popular. British artist Aubrey Beardsley, who was reputed to own a collection of the "finest and most explicitly erotic Japanese prints in London," created a series of illustrations based on Oscar Wilde's French dramatization of the story. One panel, a supreme achievement of Art Nouveau design, with tensile lines and mannered arabesques, shows a determined Salome with serpentine hair clutching the head of John the Baptist while mocking him with the boast that she has just kissed him on the mouth.

After the first decade of the 20th century, Art Nouveau began to experience a loss of favor. By 1914 it was moribund, barely selling at all. "The speed with which it died is amazing," says exhibition curator Greenhalgh. A growing uneasiness over the association with decadence and erotica was a factor in the decline. But, perhaps more important, the style was also hurt by the intensification of nationalist feelings that tended to deride Art Nouveau as too international, by a growing distaste for conspicuous consumption, by a nascent preference for geometric abstraction over nature in design, and by a reaction against Art Nouveau's love of decoration.

Adolf Loos, an influential Vienna architect, won numerous converts to his plea for purity. "The man of our time who daubs the walls with erotic symbols to satisfy an inner urge is a criminal or a degenerate," he wrote in 1908. "The evolution of culture is synonymous with the removal of ornament from objects of daily use."

All in all, Art Nouveau was simply not modern enough. As a teenager, Picasso spent a good deal of his time at Els Quatre Gats, the tavern that served as a center of Art Nouveau in Barcelona. He listened to the advice of the city's leading Catalan painters and tried to follow their style. But in 1900, at the age of 19, he turned his back on Els Quatre Gats and left for Paris to create what he would regard as true modern art.

For Picasso and other pioneers of 20th-century art, Art Nouveau had not broken far enough from the styles of the 19th century. The views of such modernists prevailed during the next few decades. But the ideological battle need not concern us anymore. No matter where it stands in art history, Art Nouveau a hundred years later strikes us as pleasing, often refreshing, sometimes worthy of awe and always kind of fun.

Frequent contributor Stanley Meisler has written for these pages on the cities of Glasgow and Vienna and on Scottish architect Charles Rennie Mackintosh.

From *Smithsonian* magazine, October 2000, pp. 74-87. © 2000 by Stanley Meisler.

Searching for Gavrilo Princip

*Eighty-six years ago the Serbian teenager shot an archduke
and set Europe on the road to World War I. Today he is all but forgotten*

By David DeVoss

THE WANING LIGHT OF AUTUMN FLOWED THROUGH THE double-paned windows, enveloped the silvery mane of the aging historian, then puddled softly atop a pile of sepia prints strewn across his desk. "This is a picture of the monument Austria erected to the memory of Franz Ferdinand after the assassination," said Sarajevo municipal councilman Borislav Spasojevic, carefully extracting a hand-painted postcard from the stack of fraying images. "Of course, it's no longer there," he smiled. "It was taken down about the time the museum commemorating Gavrilo Princip and the Young Bosnia movement opened across the street. Now that's gone, too, replaced by…" Spasojevic sighed, allowing his silence to complete the thought.

"Sarajevo is the vortex of an accursed meridian that witnessed the death of three empires," he concluded with a wave of his hand. "But you'll find few tangible reminders here of the event that changed the world."

I had arrived in Bosnia several months before, knowing little about Sarajevo except that it had hosted the 1984 Winter Olympics and had withstood a devastating 1992–95 siege involving Bosnian Serb besiegers and Bosnian Muslim defenders in which 10,000 citizens had died before the defenders, with help from Western Europe and the United States, prevailed over their mainly Serb enemies. War with forces from neighboring Croatia had further devastated the region. After excruciating negotiations, Bosnia and Herzegovina had been created out of part of what had been multiethnic Yugoslavia, with now mainly Muslim Sarajevo as its principal city and the remaining Serbs a beleaguered minority.

I also knew that these ethnic passions were nothing new in the Balkans, where such conflicts have been the rule for centuries. Sarajevo was the place where, on June 28, 1914, a 19-year-old Serb nationalist named Gavrilo Princip shot Austrian arch-duke Franz Ferdinand, heir to the throne of the Austro-Hungarian Empire, then suzerain of all of what would later become Yugoslavia.

CORBIS/BETTMANN

Immediately after the assassination of Franz Ferdinand and his wife, Sophie (above), police arrest Ferdinand Behr, a bystander who assisted gunman Gavrilo Princip.

"It will be difficult to find people willing to talk candidly about Gavrilo Princip."

One of my first priorities upon arriving in Sarajevo was to find the famous corner where the assassination had occurred, but after several false starts, I realized that Gavrilo Princip, a national hero prior to Yugoslavia's early 1990s' disintegration into warring factions, was now considered a criminal terrorist by Bosnia. Not only was the Princip museum closed but all traces of its name had been sandblasted from the exterior. Gone, too, were the concrete-embedded footprints marking the spot where Princip stood when he fired the fatal bullets. Even finding the site of the assassination was difficult, since officials had changed street names and removed all historical markers pertaining to the event. "The assassination is a very sensitive topic," advised Sarajevo University professor Kemal Bakarsic. "It will be difficult to find people willing to talk candidly about Gavrilo Princip."

The assassination was one of the defining moments of the 20th century. One month after Franz Ferdinand's death, Austria declared war on Serbia after the Serbs rejected an impossible Austrian ultimatum. The announcement prompted Russia's Czar Nicholas II to come to the aid of his fellow Slavs in Serbia. Two days later, Germany's Kaiser Wilhelm sent a "Dear Niki" memo to Moscow imploring him to recall his troops. If war breaks out, German diplomat Arthur Zimmerman told a worried British ambassador, it will be the fault of "this damned system of alliances… the curse of modern times."

But Europe's iron dice already had started to roll. When Russian ally France ordered a general mobilization the following day, Germany rallied to Austria's defense and declared war on Russia. Forty-eight hours later, Berlin declared war on France and set its troops into Belgium. This forced Britain, bound by treaty to defend Belgian neutrality, into the war and prompted anti-Russian Turkey to side with Austria and Germany.

The ensuing Great War cost the lives of 8.6 million combatants and 6.5 million civilians. By the end of 1918, more than a generation of Europe's best lay dead in the trenches. The Austrian Empire was in shambles, the Ottoman Turks had retreated to Anatolia and the last of the ruling Romanovs of Russia lay buried in an Ekaterinburg grave.

As I walked out of the faded colonial building where Spasojevic's office was located, the old man's last words echoed like a melancholy refrain: "In the Balkans, history often is destroyed, or hidden away pending further interpretation."

The muddy Miljacka River runs through the center of Sarajevo like a crimson scar. It was here on the quay, alongside a strand of belle epoque buildings, that the archduke and his Czech wife, Sophie Chotek von Chotkowa und Wognin, died. The question historians never have answered successfully, however, is why the royal couple tempted fate by coming to Sarajevo at this time. Yes, Franz Ferdinand was Inspector General

of the Austrian Army, and yes, he had been asked by Bosnia's colonial governor, Gen. Oskar Potiorek, to review a military exercise.

But why invite the Habsburg heir to the empire's most rebellious province? Especially when only the month before, Serbian Prime Minister Nikola Pasic had asked his minister in Vienna to warn Austria about he possibility of an assassination attempt. Even Franz Ferdinand's closest advisers said the trip was needlessly provocative. After all, June 28 was St. Vitus Day, Vidovdan, the Orthodox holiday during which Serbs paused to commemorate their 1389 defeat by the Ottoman Turks at Kosovo and celebrate the memory of Serb nobleman Milos Obilic, who, following the battle, crept into the sultan's tent and stabbed him to death before being hacked to bits by the Ottoman guards.

It had taken Serbia almost 500 years to regain full independence from the Turks, who left an enduring legacy in the Balkan's Muslim population. Freshly victorious in two Balkan wars, Serbia was on the rise. And all of the resentment engendered by centuries of Muslim occupation what directed at Vienna, seat of the Austro-Hungarian rulers, seen by Serbs as but the latest oppressors. Yet, despite the apparent danger, Franz Ferdinand accepted the invitation to visit the turbulent region German chancellor Otto von Bismarck had earlier proclaimed not worth "the bones of a single Pomeranian grenadier."

THE HABSBURG'S UNRULY EMPIRE

THE EARLY 20TH CENTURY WAS NOT A GOOD TIME FOR authority figures. During the first 13 years of the new century there had been some 40 political assassinations around the world.

Of all Europe's rulers, none were more vulnerable than the Habsburgs. Started by a minor German count who was elected Holy Roman Emperor in 1273, the family had ruled in Central Europe for more than six centuries. During that time, it had twice driven back Turkish invasions of Central Europe. The Holy Roman Empire had become the Austrian Empire, encompassing eight nationalities, 17 provinces, 20 parliamentary bodies and a variety of cultures that extended more than eight degrees of latitude across the map of Europe. But under the leadership of Emperor Franz Josef, the empire had suffered reverses and faced internal threats.

In 1867 Franz Josef saved the empire with a compromise, proposing that Austria and Hungary become separate sovereign states under one ruler who would be called Emperor of Austria and King of Hungary.

The real threat to Austrian hegemony in the region, however, came not from rivalries among the Central European and Balkan states but from dozens of secret societies, the most notorious of which was the Black Hand. A Serbian nationalist cult, the group was led by Maj. Dragutin Dimitrijevic, a rogue nationalist nicknamed Apis after the bull-god of ancient Egypt. Dimitrijevic developed a talent for assassination in 1903 when he helped plan and execute the murder of Serbia's King Alexander Obrenovic and Queen Draga. Now he was prepared to

Gavrilo Princip sits in the center of the first row in this photograph of the trial of the assasination plotters. Princip told the court he was sorry only for the death of Sophie.

strike again, but instead of employing disgruntled army officers, this time his assassins would be idealistic schoolboys.

For decades the mountains of Bosnia had been a breeding ground for discontent. Serb peasants there were bound by a feudal system that forced them to surrender one-third of their harvest to Bosnian Muslim landlords. Abandoned to their poverty, Bosnia's embittered Serbs turned inward, seeking inspiration from the heroic songs of wandering balladeers called *guslas* and instruction from nationalistic Orthodox priests.

Young men flocked to secret societies. Drawn to Serbia in hopes of finding ways to support its causes in the Balkans, many found their way to the Black Hand. The group eventually recruited six Bosnians, one of them Gavrilo Princip, and sent them back home across the Drina River to Sarajevo, armed with bombs and revolvers.

On the morning of June 28, Franz Ferdinand and Sophie arrived early by train from the resort town of Ilidza, where they had spent the night in an ersatz Tyrolean spa called the Hotel Bosna. As they climbed into the Graef und Stift touring car that would carry them to Sarajevo's city hall, both were in a good mood.

Although Sophie's family, the Choteks, were one of the oldest aristocratic families in Bohemia, they were considered commoners under the Habsburg Family Law. After repeated entreaties, Franz Josef agreed in 1900 to allow the couple to marry, but only after Franz Ferdinand formally agreed to a morganatic union that would prevent Sophie from becoming Empress of Austria and forever bar their children from the throne. According to the terms of the renunciation, Sophie could not sit beside her husband in a court carriage, appear at his side in the

royal box at the opera or be buried in the Habsburg family crypt. Even after 14 years of marriage and three children, she ranked below the youngest archduchess when in Vienna. But outside Austria, in lands administered by the military, things were different. On this glorious summer day in Sarajevo, the Duchess of Hohenberg finally would receive all of the imperial honors due the wife of the heir apparent.

But first the royal couple had to pass through the gauntlet of six zealous assassins. Their car was only a third of the way down Appel Quay when Nedeljko Cabrinovic threw the first grenade. But the archduke's chauffeur sped up, and instead of landing in the car, the grenade bounced off and exploded under the trailing vehicle, wounding about 20 people. The archduke's car roared past Gavrilo Princip toward the faux Moorish city hall.

Transformed later into the national library, Sarajevo's old city hall today stands gutted and silent, a ghostly victim of Serb incendiary bombs fired in the spring of 1992. Behind its graffiti-covered walls lie the cinders of 700,000 books. But when the royal couple pulled in front of the crenellated structure 86 years ago, the municipal officials were oblivious to the attempted assassination. Sarajevo's Lord Mayor greeted Franz Ferdinand effusively with a prepared text. "Our hearts are full of happiness on the occasion of the most gracious visit with which your Highnesses have deigned to honor the capital of our land...."

"Herr Bürgermeister," the archduke interrupted, "what is the good of your speeches? I come to Sarajevo on a friendly visit and someone throws a bomb at me. This is outrageous."

The archduke's outrage should have been directed at Gen. Oskar Potiorek, who had taken almost no precautions. Despite the rumblings of trouble, only 120 policemen were on duty that day.

Instead of asking Franz Ferdinand and his wife to remain inside the city hall until soldiers could arrive to escort them to safety, Potiorek's solution to the lapse in security was to change the motorcade's prearranged route. Instead of winding through the narrow streets of the Bascarsija Turkish quarter, he proposed the royal couple return the way they came, along the Quay road, a broader, straighter street where the car could travel more rapidly.

DEATH COMES FOR THE ARCHDUKE

AS THE ROYAL PARTY GOT BACK IN THE CAR, THE SITUATION seemed under control. Grenade thrower Cabrinovic was in custody. Four of the other would-be assassins, several of whom had no stomach for killing, had abandoned their posts. Only Gavrilo Princip remained. But he was positioned around a corner, along the route that had been published in the morning's papers.

Flanked by curious bystanders, the procession returned along the river, but instead of speeding through the Bascarsija intersection, the cars turned right. Potiorek had forgotten to tell the chauffeurs of the change in plans. When he realized what was happening, Potiorek ordered Franz Ferdinand's car to halt and back up. But the archduke now was only three steps from Princip, and while the driver fumbled with the car's cumbersome gears, Princip, the man considered too timid to be given a bomb, pulled a .38 Browning pistol from his pocket and stepped forward.

"I was only 11 when Gavrilo shot the archduke, but I knew his girlfriend."

The two men who faced each other were emblematic of the age; one a disdainful aristocrat with an inverted hussar's mustache and plumed hat, the other a romantic teenage nationalist hoping to gain immortality. Princip fired two shots. The first tore through the side of the car and penetrated Sophie's corset. The second pierced the neck of Franz Ferdinand's powder-blue tunic, severing the jugular vein before lodging against his spine.

What kind of man was Gavrilo Princip? The corner where the attack occurred reveals no clues. But four blocks away, up a grimy stairway in a small apartment behind the shuttered Serb Orthodox Cathedral, lives a woman with memories of the past.

"I was only 11 when Gavrilo shot the archduke, but I knew his girlfriend Jelena Milisic when we were both teachers at Sarajevo's primer gymnasium (academic high school) in 1946," smiles 97-year-old Lubica Tuta. "Jelena and the art history teacher, Borislav Mihacevic, were Young Bosnia revolutionaries with Gavrilo. Boro used to tease Jelena about spending the night with Gavrilo in the park across the river from where the attack occurred. Gavrilo desperately wanted to make love, but Jelena said no. Even when he told her he probably would die the

following morning, she wouldn't relent. Boro said Gavrilo was so angry the morning of June 28 that he would have shot God himself."

Today, despite two world wars, a half-century of socialism and a bloody siege lasting more than a thousand days, downtown Sarajevo still has the look of a small Austrian town. The bond between Vienna and its former colony remains strong, in part because for nearly a century every deserving Bosnian student could apply for a university scholarship in Austria. There even is talk of restoring the monument to Franz Ferdinand and Sophie that was demolished at the end of World War I. Until that day comes, however, Sarajevo's Austrian artifacts will stay locked in the basement of the National Art Gallery.

"Politicians believe these works are controversial, so we keep them hidden away," says gallery director Seid Hasanefendic, as he descends a narrow stairway into the clammy bowels of the building and unlocks a heavy door. Edging past jumbles of artifacts, his breath misting in the chill, he finally arrives at another door, which opens into a small chamber where the busts of forgotten monarchs peer through discolored tarpaulins.

In the corner is a life-size statue of Franz Josef, his imperious glare stone-cold and covered with dust. Resting on a stack of old newspapers is all that remains of Austria's assassination monument: a bas-relief bronze plaque bearing the profiles of Franz Ferdinand and Sophie.

"The Yugoslav Army declared war on history when it began shelling Sarajevo in 1992," says Hasanefendic. "They destroyed the national library and hit this building with 50 bombs, but we survived. The irony is that our politicians now are afraid to exhibit these faded symbols of power."

Outside the gallery still swathed in protective scaffolding, I walked across Zelenih Beretki Street to the public square where students from the nearby law faculty were enjoying the afternoon sun and tiny cups of Turkish coffee. Was it possible that the history of Gavrilo Princip and the event that sparked World War I was not lost or destroyed, but merely hidden away? I had heard stories of what transpired late in the summer of 1992 when Serb snipers and artillery began pounding Sarajevo. As the death toll mounted, citizens frustrated by their helplessness began attacking symbols of the former Yugoslavia. First on their list was the Princip museum. Though many items were stolen or smashed, the bulk of the collection was saved. I was told, by a courageous curator named Bajro Gec, who literally lived inside the battered museum for more than two years, protecting with his life the priceless photographs and period costumes from vandals and thieves.

But where was Gec? Finding a person can be difficult in Sarajevo, which has no money for telephone directories and a municipal government that considers everything an official secret. Fortunately, Austrian ambassador Valentin Insko had met Gec when the embassy had inquired about restoring the Franz Ferdinand memorial. "Try the Jewish Museum," Insko advised. "You may find him there."

Located on the western edge of Bascarsija, the Jewish Museum, now known as the Museum of Sarajevo, does not appear as a museum on any city map. Built as a synagogue in the 16th century, the building has no identifying markings and turns away any tourist who might wander across its cobbled courtyard to bang on the rested metal door. "How can we open to the public when we have no money?" asked museum director Mevlida Serdarevic, with a hint of desperation.

"I can show you where the Princip collection is located, but only Bajro has the key to get inside," she says, walking down a wooden stairway into a vaulted chamber in which an enormous book containing the names of every Sarajevo Jew killed during World War II hangs suspended by a chain from the ceiling. Our arrival prompts a chorus of coughs from six people who sit shivering at their desks. "Every employee here has the flu, but the cold is good for the antiques because it keeps away the bugs," she explains. Walking down another flight of stairs, we arrive in what appears to be Europe's basement, a room filled with gilded sabers, Orthodox iconography, broken spinning wheels and oil portraits of Turkish pashas. It's as if every decade of the past century has deposited its fading grandeur here before embracing the next new fad.

HIDDEN HISTORY

"THE PRINCIP EXHIBITS ARE OVER THERE, BUT WE MUSTN'T go closer without Bajro Gec," cautions Serdarevic. Why doesn't the director of a museum have access to all its exhibits, I wonder? "Can you imagine the bravery it took to transfer these items amid the chaos of a city under siege?" she responds. "Bajro Gec saved the history of Gavrilo Princip, and now it is his to show."

While waiting for Gec to return. I walked down Sarajevo's main boulevard, Marsala Tita, looking at the coffee bars and cake shops that were full even in the middle of the afternoon. There is no better metaphor for the Balkan's historical ambivalence than Marsala Tita. A century ago the street was called Cemalusa, after a Turkish feudal landlord. After World War I, when Bosnia was incorporated into the Yugoslavian monarchy, the name changed again to King Alexander Street. During the Nazi occupation, it was christened Adolf Hitler Street. When communist partisans finally liberated the city, the tree-lined avenue was renamed after their leader, Josip Broz Tito.

It was Tito who turned Gavrilo Princip into a national icon. In Gavrilo's anticolonialism, communist hagiographers detected the first stirrings of socialism. In 1953 the government opened the Princip museum in Sarajevo. Eleven years later it proclaimed the family's refurbished peasant shack a national landmark. If Bosnian Muslims or Croats objected to the deification of an Orthodox Serb, they wisely kept silent.

When I return to the shuttered museum, Bajro Gec escorts me down to the basement, where two large wooden trunks secured by enormous padlocks sit beneath barred windows. After opening the locks with an iron key, he slowly lifts one of the lids as the hinges shriek in protest. "Here are the clothes Princip wore when he was arrested," says Gec, holding up a black wool suit with tarnished metal buttons. Layered deeper in the trunk are Austrian military uniforms, a beaded corselette belonging to Princip's mother, Maria, and a dress identical to the one Sophie Chotek selected for St. Vitus Day. Strewn throughout the pile of

musty clothes are old shoes, tattered newspaper articles and black-and-white photographs curling with age in which young conspirators affect regal poses while staring stiffly at the camera.

The most famous photograph shows Princip and his fellow revolutionaries at their trial, staring indifferently at their inquisitors. There were 25 defendants in all. At the end of the trial the presiding judge asked all of the accused to stand up if they felt sorry for their act. All stood except Princip. When asked why he did not rise, Princip responded that he was sorry for the children who had lost their parents, and he was especially sorry for killing Duchess Sophie. The bullet that hit her was intended for Gen. Potiorek, he explained. "As far as suggestions are concerned that somebody talked us into committing the assassination that is not true," Princip said. "The idea for the assassination grew among us and we realized it. We loved our people."

Five days later the judges returned with their verdicts. Nine of the accused were set free, five were sentenced to be hanged, while the remainder received prison terms ranging from three years to life. Since Princip was 19 at the time of the assassination, he could not be hanged under Austrian law. He was sentenced to 20 years at hard labor with the proviso that every June 28 he remain in a darkened cell without food or a mattress.

PROUD TO BE A PRINCIP

"POLITICIANS WANT TO FORGET PRINCIP BECAUSE HE WAS A Serb," says Gec. "I've always thought of Sarajevo as the Jerusalem of Europe, a place where different cultures can come together. But if we refuse to recognize our history and refuse to restore our monuments, it will be difficult to keep Sarajevo a multinational city."

A more immediate problem for Gec, however, is the rapid disintegration of the items he has been able to salvage. "The temperature and humidity make preservation almost impossible. Our staff managed to save these items from Belgrade artillery, but now we're losing them to mildew."

Not all of the history from 1914 has been lost or locked away. The Hotel Bosna where Franz Ferdinand and his wife spent their last night has survived two wars and the breakup of Yugoslavia, albeit in a form no Habsburg would recognize. Encircled by razor wire, microwave dishes and sandbag revetments, the former royal residence now serves as headquarters for the NATO-led forces in Bosnia. The building groans under the weight of too much history.

The respect that eluded the archduke and duchess in life also escaped them in death. Because Sophie was not a Habsburg, the funeral service in Vienna was perfunctory. Only the three children of the imperial family sent flowers. To minimize public expressions of sympathy, Franz Josef's chamberlain ordered their coffins transported only at night, and he would have succeeded in having them buried separately had not Franz Ferdinand left specific instructions that he was to be buried alongside his wife at their family home in Artstetten.

But Franz Ferdinand's death was more enviable than the life that faced Gavrilo Princip. He was taken to Theresienstadt, an old Bohemian fortress north of Prague that had been converted into a military prison and later would serve as a Jewish concentration camp during World War II. Chained with shackles weighing 22 pounds, the 145-pound prisoner was kept in solitary confinement in an unheated cell. Tuberculosis consumed him, and on April 28, 1918, Princip died weighing 88 pounds.

Fearing his bones might become relics, Princip's Austrian jailers took the body in secret to an unmarked grave, but a Czech soldier assigned to the burial detail made a map, and in 1920 Princip and the other "Heroes of Vidovdan" were disinterred and brought to Sarajevo, where they were buried together beneath a chapel "built to commemorate for eternity our Serb Heroes" at St. Mark's Cemetery.

For the Heroes of Vidovdan, however, eternity ended with the breakup of Yugoslavia. St. Mark's today is in practice ignored by Sarajevo officialdom. Visitors are discouraged by a locked gate, weed-choked pathways and packs of scrofulous dogs that feed on the heads of sheep thrown at the chapel by butchers at a nearby market.

Shortly before his departure to Theresienstadt, Princip was told that the war he had started, to free all South Slavs, was, in fact, consuming them. Although Belgrade had fallen to Austrian troops, he remained positive. "Serbia may be invaded but not conquered," he told one of his German guards. "Serbia will one day create Yugoslavia, mother of all South Slavs."

Today Yugoslavia is a country in name only. Slovenia, Croatia and Macedonia are independent states. The province of Kosovo in a UN protectorate and Bosnia is, in fact if not officially, divided into two entities—one, Serb, the other Muslim—each with its own parliament, police and army. The Grahovo Valley home where Gavrilo grew up lies in ruins, destroyed by Croat troops in 1995, four months before the Dayton Peace Accords ended the war in Bosnia.

No longer are bridges, barracks and schools named after Gavrilo Princip. But his memory still is revered by Petar Princip, 61, the family's last direct descendant in Bosnia, who lives with his wife, Dusanka, in the Serb city of Banja Luka. Permanently dressed in black for their son Danilo, who died fighting the Croats, the Princips have turned their apartment into a shrine, of sorts, dominated by a portrait of Gavrilo at age 18.

"People say he was a crazy terrorist, but Gavrilo was a schoolboy from an educated family," says Petar, a botanist who harvests herbs from the forest. "Mine was a respected family," he adds, as his wife lights a candle beneath the large portrait of Gavrilo. "My cousin was the liberator of the Slav people. But now I've lost my home, my son and the respect I once enjoyed. I'm proud to be a Princip, but I'm also sad to be part of a forgotten history."

Los Angeles journalist David DeVoss lived in Bosnia for more than a year.

From *Smithsonian* magazine, August 2000, pp. 42-53. © 2000 by David DeVoss.

How the Modern Middle East Map Came to be Drawn

When the Ottoman Empire collapsed in 1918, the British created new borders (and rulers) to keep the peace and protect their interests.

David Fromkin

The dictator of Iraq claimed—falsely—that until 1914 Kuwait had been administered from Iraq, that historically Kuwait was a part of Iraq, that the separation of Kuwait from Iraq was an arbitrary decision of Great Britain's after World War I. The year was 1961; the Iraqi dictator was Abdul-Karim Qasim; and the dispatch of British troops averted a threatened invasion.

Iraq, claiming that it had never recognized the British-drawn frontier with Kuwait, demanded full access to the Persian Gulf and when Kuwait failed to agree, Iraqi tanks and infantry attacked Kuwait. The year was 1973; the Iraqi dictator was Ahmad Hasan al-Bakr; when other Arab states came to Kuwait's support, a deal was struck, Kuwait made a payment of money to Iraq, and the troops withdrew.

August 2, 1990. At 2 A.M. Iraqi forces swept across the Kuwaiti frontier. Iraq's dictator, Saddam Hussein, declared that the frontier between Iraq and Kuwait was invalid, a creation of the British after World War I, and that Kuwait really belonged to Iraq.

It was, of course, true, as one Iraqi dictator after another claimed, that the exact Iraq-Kuwait frontier was a line drawn on an empty map by a British civil servant in the early 1920s. But Kuwait began to emerge as an independent entity in the early 1700s—two centuries before Britain invented Iraq. Moreover, most other fron-

tiers between states of the Middle East were also creations of the British (or the French). The map of the Arab Middle East was drawn by the victorious Allies when they took over these lands from the Ottoman Empire after World War I. By proposing to nullify that map, Saddam Hussein at a minimum was trying to turn the clock back by almost a century.

A hundred years ago, when Ottoman governors in Basra were futilely attempting to assert authority over the autonomous sheikdom of Kuwait, most of the Arabic-speaking Middle East was at least nominally part of the Ottoman Empire. It had been so for hundreds of years and would remain so until the end of World War I.

The Ottomans, a dynasty, not a nationality, were originally a band of Turkish warriors who first galloped onto the stage of history in the 13th century. By the early 20th century the Ottoman Empire, which once had stretched to the gates of Vienna, was shrinking rapidly, though it still ruled perhaps 20 million to 25 million people in the Middle East and elsewhere, comprising perhaps a dozen or more different nationalities. It was a ramshackle Muslim empire, held together by the glue of Islam, and the lot of its non-Muslim population (perhaps 5 million) was often unhappy and sometimes tragic.

In the year 1900, if you traveled from the United States to the Middle East, you

might have landed in Egypt, part of the Ottoman Empire in name but in fact governed by British "advisers." The Egyptian Army was commanded by an English general, and the real ruler of the country was the British Agent and Consul-General—a position to which the crusty Horatio Herbert Kitchener was appointed in 1911.

The center of your social life in all likelihood would have been the British enclave in Cairo, which possessed (wrote one of Lord Kitchener's aides) "all the narrowness and provincialism of an English garrison town." The social schedule of British officials and their families revolved around the balls given at each of the leading hotels in turn, six nights out of seven, and before dark, around the Turf Club and the Sporting Club on the island of El Gezira. Throughout Egypt, Turkish officials, Turkish police and a Turkish army were conspicuous by their absence. Outside British confines you found yourself not in a Turkish-speaking country but in an Arabic-speaking one. Following the advice of the *Baedeker*, you'd likely engage a dragoman—a translator and guide—of whom there were about 90 in Cairo ("all more or less intelligent and able, but scarcely a half of the number are trustworthy").

On leaving Egypt, if you turned north through the Holy Land and the Levant toward Anatolia, you finally would have encountered the reality of Ottoman gov-

For years the real ruler of Egypt was Lord Kitchener, a general, whose main concern was for the Suez Canal.

ernment, however corrupt and ineffi-cient, though many cities—Jerusalem (mostly Jewish), Damascus (mostly Arab) and Smyrna, now 1zmir (mostly Greek)—were not at all Turkish in char-acter or population.

Heading south by steamer down the Red Sea and around the enormous Ara-bian Peninsula was a very different mat-ter. Nominally Ottoman, Arabia was in large part a.vast, ungoverned desert wil-derness through which roamed bedouin tribes knowing no law but their own. In those days Abdul Aziz ibn Saud, the youthful scion of deposed lords of most of the peninsula, was living in exile, dreaming of a return to reclaim his rights and establish his dominion. In the port towns on the Persian Gulf, ruling sheiks paid lip service to Ottoman rule but in fact their sheikdoms were protectorates of Great Britain. Not long after you passed Kuwait (see map) you reached Basra, in what is now Iraq, up a river formed by the union of the great Tigris and Euphrates.

A muddy, unhealthy port of heteroge-neous population, Basra was then the capital of a province, largely Shiite Arab,

ruled by an Ottoman governor. Well north of it, celebrated for archaeological sites like Babylon and Nippur, which drew tourists, lay Baghdad, then a heavily Jewish city (along with Jerusa-lem, one of the two great Jewish cities of Asia). Baghdad was the administrative center of an Ottoman province that was in large part Sunnl Arab. Farther north still was a third Ottoman province, with a large population of Kurds. Taken to-gether, the three roughly equaled the present area of Iraq.

Ottoman rule in some parts of the Middle East clearly was more imaginary than real. And even in those portions of the empire that Turkish governors did govern, the population was often too di-verse to be governed effectively by a sin-gle regime. Yet the hold of the Turkish sultan on the empire's peoples lingered on. Indeed, had World War I not inter-vened, the Ottoman Empire might well have lasted many decades more.

In its origins, the war that would change the map of the Middle East had nothing to do with that region. How the Ottoman Empire came to be involved in the war at all—and lost it—and how the triumphant Allies found themselves in a position to redesign the Middle Eastern lands the Turks had ruled, is one of the most fascinating stories of the 20th cen-tury, rich in consequences that we are still struggling with today.

The story begins with one man, a tiny, vain, strutting man addicted to dramatic gestures and uniforms. He was Enver Pa-sha, and he mistook himself for a sort of Napoleon. Of modest origins, Enver, as a junior officer in the Ottoman Army, joined the Young Turks, a secret society that was plotting against the Ottoman re-gime. In 1913, Enver led a Young Turk raiding party that overthrew the govern-ment and killed the Minister of War. In 1914, at the age of 31, he became the Ot-toman Minister of War himself, married the niece of the sultan and moved into a palace.

As a new political figure Enver scored a major, instant success. The Young Turks for years had urgently sought a European ally that would prom-ise to protect the Ottoman Empire against other European powers. Britain, France and Russia had each been ap-

Though he was blamed for Gallipoli, Winston Churchill was put in charge of reorganizing the entire Middle East.

proached and had refused; but on August 1, 1914, just as Germany was about to in-vade Belgium to begin World War I, En-ver wangled a secret treaty with the kaiser pledging to protect the Ottoman domains.

Unaware of Enver's coup, and with war added to the equation, Britain and France began wooing Turkey too, while the Turks played off one side against the other. By autumn the German Army's plan to knock France out of the war in six weeks had failed. Needing help, Ger-many urged the Ottoman Empire to join the war by attacking Russia.

Though Enver's colleagues in the Turkish government were opposed to war, Enver had a different idea. To him the time seemed ripe: in the first month of the war German armies overwhelm-ingly turned back a Russian attack on East Prussia, and a collapse of the czar's armies appeared imminent. Seeing a chance to share in the spoils of a likely German victory over Russia, Enver en-tered into a private conspiracy with the German admiral commanding the pow-erful warship *Goeben* and its companion vessel, the *Breslau*, which had taken ref-uge in Turkish waters at the outset of hostilities.

During the last week of October, En-ver secretly arranged for the *Goeben* and the *Breslau* to escape into the Black Sea and steam toward Russia. Flying the Ot-

British camel unit jogs down the Jordan Valley; Prince Faisal and T. E. Lawrence often used camels in guerrilla raids on Turks.

toman flag, the Germans then opened fire on the Russian coast. Thinking themselves attacked by Turks, the Russians declared war. Russia's allies, Britain and France, thus found themselves at war with the Ottoman Empire too. By needlessly plunging the empire into war, Enver had put everything in the Middle East up for grabs. In that sense, he was the father of the modern Middle East. Had Enver never existed, the Turkish flag might even yet be flying—if only in some confederal way—over Beirut and Damascus, Baghdad and Jerusalem.

Great Britain had propped up the Ottoman Empire for generations as a buffer against Russian expansionism. Now with Russia as Britain's shaky ally, once the war had been won and the Ottomans overthrown, the Allies would be able to reshape the entire Middle East. It would be one of those magic moments in history when fresh starts beckon and dreams become realities.

"What is to prevent the Jews having Palestine and restoring a real Judaea?" asked H. G. Wells, the British novelist, essayist and prophet of a rational future for mankind. The Greeks, the French and the Italians also had claims to Middle East territory. And naturally, in Cairo,

Lord Kitchener's aides soon began to contemplate a future plan for an Arab world to be ruled by Egypt, which in turn would continue to be controlled by themselves.

At the time, the Allies already had their hands full with war against Germany on the Western Front. They resolved not to be distracted by the Middle East until later. The issues and ambitions there were too divisive. Hardly had the Ottoman Empire entered the war, however, when Enver stirred the pot again. He took personal command of the Ottoman Third Army on the Caucasus frontier and, in the dead of winter, launched a foolhardy attack against fortified positions on high ground. His offensive was hopeless, since it was both amateurishly planned and executed, but the czars generals panicked anyway. The Russian government begged Lord Kitchener (now serving in London as Secretary of State for War) to stage a more or less instant diversionary action. The result was the Allied attack on the Dardanelles, the strait that eventually leads to Constantinople (now Istanbul).

Enver soon lost about 86,000 of his 100,000 men; the few, bloodied survivors straggled back through icy moun-

tain passes. A German observer noted that Enver's army had "suffered a disaster which for rapidity and completeness is without parallel in military history." But nobody in the Russian government or high command bothered to tell the British that mounting a Dardanelles naval attack was no longer necessary. So on the morning of February 19, 1915, British ships fired the opening shots in what became a tragic campaign.

Initially, the British Navy seemed poised to take Constantinople, and Russia panicked again. what if the British, having occupied Constantinople, were to hold onto it? The 50 percent of Russia's export trade flowing through the strait would then do so only with British permission. Czar Nicholas II demanded immediate assurance that Constantinople would be Russia's in the postwar world. Fearing Russia might withdraw from the war, Britain and France agreed. In return, Russia offered to support British and French claims in other parts of the Middle East.

With that in mind, on April 8, 1915, the British Prime Minister appointed a committee to define Britain's postwar goals in the Middle East. It was a committee dominated by Lord Kitchener

After the final surrender of the Turks, on October 31, 1918, the question was: How to administer the remains of the Ottoman Empire?

through his personal representative, 36-year-old Sir Mark Sykes, one of many remarkable characters, including Winston Churchill and T. E. Lawrence, to be involved in the remaking (and remapping) of the Middle East.

A restless soul who had moved from school to school as a child, Sykes left college without graduating, and thereafter never liked to stay long in one spot. A Tory Member of Parliament, before the war he had traveled widely in Asiatic Turkey, publishing accounts of his journeys. Sykes' views tended to be passionate but changeable, and his talent for clever exaggeration sometimes carried over into his politics.

As a traditional Tory he had regarded the sultan's domains as a useful buffer protecting Britain's road to India against Britain's imperial rivals, the czar chief among them. Only 15 months earlier, Sykes was warning the House of Commons that "the disappearance of the Ottoman Empire must be the first step towards the disappearance of our own." Yet between 1915 and 1919, he busily planned the dismantling of the Ottoman Empire.

The Allied attack on the Dardanelles ended with Gallipoli, a disaster told and retold in books and films. Neither that defeat, nor the darkest days of 1916–17, when it looked for a while as though the Allies might lose the war, stopped British planning about how to cut up the Turkish Middle East. Steadily but secretly Sykes worked on. As the fight to overthrow the Ottoman Empire grew more intense, the elements he had to take into account grew more complex.

It was clear that the British needed to maintain control over the Suez Canal, and all the rest of the route to their prized colonial possession, India. They needed to keep the Russians and Germans and Italians and French in check. Especially the French, who had claims on Syria. But with millions of men committed to trench warfare in Europe, they could not drain off forces for the Middle East. Instead, units of the British Indian Army along with other Commonwealth forces attacked in the east in what are now Iraq and Iran, occupying Basra, Baghdad and eventually Mosul. Meanwhile, Allied liaison officers, including notably T. E. Lawrence, began encouraging the small-ish group of Arabian tribesmen follow-

ing Emir (later King) Hussein of the Hejaz, who had rebelled against the Turks, to fight a guerrilla campaign against Turkish forces.

Throughout 1917, in and near the Hejaz area of Arabia (see map), the Arabs attacked the railway line that supported Turkish troops in Medina. The "Arab Revolt" had little military effect on the outcome of the war, yet the fighting brought to the fore, as British clients and potential Arab leaders, not only Hussein of the Hejaz, but two of his sons, Faisal and Abdullah. Both were deadly rivals of Ibn Saud, who by then had become a rising power in Arabia and a client of the British too.

British officials in Cairo deluded themselves and others into believing that the whole of the Arabic-speaking half of the Ottoman Empire might rise up and come over to the Allied side. When the time came, the Arab world did not follow the lead of Hussein, Abdullah and Faisal. But Arab aspirations and British gratitude began to loom large in British, and Arab, plans for the future. Sykes now felt he had to take Arab ambitions into account in his future planning, though he neglected those of Ibn Saud (father of to-

Early planning for postwar Middle East fell to Sir Mark Sykes, whose work grew in complexity as rival Allied and Arab claims evolved.

day's Saudi king), who also deserved well of Britain.

By 1917 Sykes was also convinced that it was vital for the British war effort to win Jewish support against Germany, and that pledging support for Zionism could win it. That year his efforts and those of others resulted in the publication of a statement by Arthur James Balfour, the British Foreign Secretary, expressing Britain's support for the establishment of a Jewish national home in Palestine.

The year 1917 proved to be a turning point. In the wake of its revolution Russia pulled out of the war, but the entrance by the United States on the Allied side insured the Allies a victory—if they could hold on long enough for U.S. troops to arrive in force. In the Middle East, as British India consolidated its hold on areas that are now part of Iraq, Gen. Edmund Allenby's Egyptian-based British army began fighting its way north from Suez to Damascus. Lawrence and a force of Arab raiders captured the Red Sea port of Aqaba (near the point where Israel and Jordan now meet). Then, still other Arabs, with Faisal in command, moved north to harass the Turkish flank.

By October 1918, Allenby had taken Syria and Lebanon, and was poised to invade what is now Turkey But there was no need to do so, because on October 31 the Ottoman Empire surrendered.

As the Peace Conference convened in Paris, in February 1919, Sykes, who had been rethinking Britain's design for the Middle East, suddenly fell ill and died. At first there was nobody to take his place as the British government's overall Middle East planner. Prime Minister David Lloyd George took personal charge in many Middle East matters. But more and more, as the months went by, Winston Churchill had begun to play a major role, gradually superseding the others.

Prime Minister Lloyd George (right) sought full control of the Middle East.

Accordingly, early that year the ambitious 45-year-old politician was asked by the Prime Minister to serve as both War Minister and Air Minister. ("Of course," Lloyd George wrote Churchill, "there will be but one salary!") Maintaining the peace in the captured—and now occupied—Arab Middle East was among Churchill's new responsibilities.

Cheerful, controversial and belligerent, Churchill was not yet the revered figure who would so inspire his countrymen and the world in 1940. Haunted by the specter of a brilliant father, he had won fame and high office early, but was widely distrusted, in part for having switched political parties. Churchill's foresighted administration of the Admiralty in the summer of 1914 won universal praise, but then the botched Dardanelles campaign, perhaps unfairly, was blamed on him. As a Conservative newspaper put it, "we have watched his brilliant and erratic course in the confident expectation that sooner or later he would make a mess of anything he undertook." In making Churchill minister of both War and Air in 1919, Lloyd George was giving his protege' a try at a political comeback.

By the end of the war, everyone was so used to the bickering among the Allies about who was going to get what in the postwar Middle East that the alternative—nobody taking anything—simply

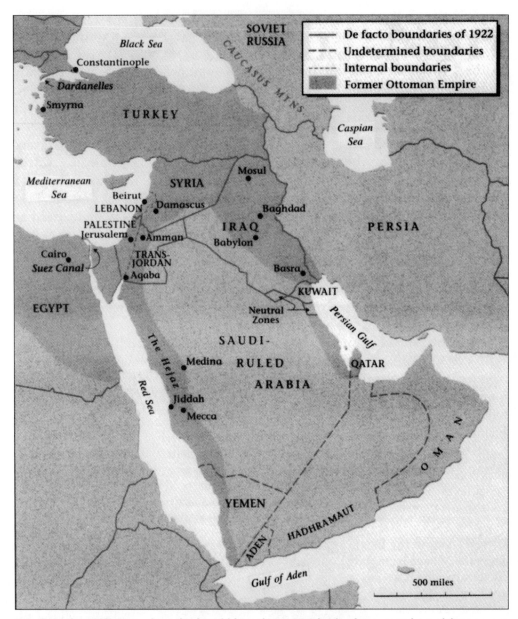

Map shows the Middle East redrawn by the British as of 1922. Iraq has just been created out of three more or less incompatible Ottoman provinces. Part of Palestine has become Transjordan (today's Jordan), which is still ruled by one of Abdullah's descendants.

didn't enter into the equation. Churchill was perhaps the only statesman to consider that possibility. He foresaw that many problems would arise from trying to impose a new political design on so troubled a region, and thought it unwise to make the attempt. Churchill argued, in fact, for simply retaining a reformed version of the Ottoman Empire. Nobody took him seriously.

After the war, a British army of a million men, the only cohesive military force in the region, briefly occupied the Middle East. Even as his real work began, however, Churchill was confronted

with demands that the army, exhausted from years of war, be demobilized. He understood what meeting those demands meant. Relying on that army, Prime Minister Lloyd George had decided to keep the whole Arab Middle East under British influence; in the words he once used about Palestine: "We shall be there by conquest and shall remain." Now Churchill repeatedly warned that once British troops were withdrawn, Britain would not be able to impose its terms.

Lloyd George had predicted that it would take about a week to agree on the terms of peace to be imposed on the de-

feated Ottoman Empire. Instead it took nearly two years. By then, in Churchill's words, the British army of occupation had long since "melted away," with the dire consequences he predicted.

In Egypt, demonstrations, strikes and riots broke out. In Arabia, Ibn Saud, though himself a British client, defeated and threatened to destroy Britain's protégé Hussein. In Turkey, the defeated Enver had long since fled the country to find refuge in Berlin. From there he journeyed to Russia, assumed leadership of Bukhara (in what is now the Uzbek Republic of the USSR) in its struggle for independence from Moscow, and was killed in battle against the Red Army of the Soviet Union in 1922. Turkish nationalists under the great Ottoman general Mustafa Kemal (later known as Kemal Ataturk) rebelled against the Allied-imposed treaty and later proclaimed the national state that is modern Turkey

In Palestine, Arabs rioted against Jews. In what is now Saddam Hussein's Iraq, armed revolts by the tribes, sparked in the first instance by the imposition of taxes, caused thousands of casualties. "How much longer," the outraged London *Times* asked, "are valuable lives to be sacrificed in the vain endeavour to impose upon the Arab population an elaborate and expensive administration which they never asked for and do not want?"

By the end of 1920, Lloyd George's Middle East policy was under attack from all sides. Churchill, who had warned all along that peacetime Britain, in the grip of an economic collapse, had neither the money, the troops, nor the will to coerce the Middle East, was proved right—and placed even more directly in charge. On New Year's Day 1921 he was appointed Colonial Secretary, and soon began to expand his powers, consolidating within his new department responsibility for all Britain's domains in Arabic-speaking Asia.

He assembled his staff by combing the government for its ablest and most experienced officials. The one offbeat appointment was T. E. Lawrence. A young American journalist and promoter named Lowell Thomas, roaming the Middle East in search of a story, had found Lawrence dressed in Arab robes, and proceeded to make him world-famous as "Lawrence of Arabia." A complex personality, Lawrence was chronically insubordinate, but Churchill admired all the wonderful stories he'd heard of Lawrence's wartime exploits.

Seeking to forge a working consensus among his staff in London and his men in the field, Churchill invited them all to a conference that opened in Cairo on March 12, 1921. During the ten-day session held in the Semiramis Hotel, about 40 experts were in attendance. "Everybody Middle East is here," wrote Lawrence.

Egypt was not on the agenda. Its fate was being settled separately by its new British proconsul, Lord Allenby. In 1922 he established it as an independent kingdom, still largely subject to British control under terms of a unilateral proclamation that neither Egypt's politicians nor its new king, Fuad, accepted.

All Britain's other wartime conquests—the lands now called Israel, the West Bank, Jordan and Iraq—were very much on the agenda, while the fate of Syria and Lebanon, which Britain had also conquered, was on everybody's mind. In the immediate aftermath of the war, it was control of Syria that had caused the most problems, as Lloyd George tried to keep it for Britain by placing it under the rule of Lawrence's comrade-in-arms, Prince Faisal, son of Hussein. After Syria declared its independence, the French fought back. Occupying all of Syria-Lebanon, they drove Faisal into exile. The French also devised a new frontier for Lebanon that invited eventual disaster, as would become evident in the 1970s and '80s. They refused to see that the Muslim population was deeply hostile to their rule.

Churchill, meanwhile, was confronted by constant Arab disturbances in Palestine. West of the Jordan River, where the Jewish population lived, Arabs fought against Jewish immigration, claiming—wrongly, as the future was to show—that the country was too barren to support more than its existing 600,000 inhabitants. Churchill rejected that view, and dealt with the Arab objections to a Jewish homeland by keeping—though redefining—Britain's commitment to Zionism. As he saw it, there was to be a Jewish homeland in Palestine, but other homelands could exist there as well.

The 75 percent of Palestine east of the Jordan River (Transjordan, as it was called, until it became Jordan in 1950) was lawless. Lacking the troops to police it and wanting to avert additional causes of strife, Churchill decided to forbid Jews from settling there, temporarily at least.

Fittingly while still War and Air Minister, Churchill had devised a strategy for controlling the Middle East with a minimum number of British troops by using an economical combination of airpower

and armored cars. But it would take time for the necessary units to be put in place. Meanwhile tribal fighting had to be contained somehow. As the Cairo conference met, news arrived that Abdullah, Faisal's brother, claiming to need "a change of air for his health," had left Arabia with a retinue of bedouin warriors and entered Transjordan. The British feared that Abdullah would attack French Syria and so give the French an excuse to invade Transjordan, as a first step toward taking over all Palestine.

As a temporary expedient Churchill appointed Abdullah as governor of a Transjordan to be administratively detached from the rest of Palestine. He charged him with keeping order by his prestige and with his own bedouin followers—at least until Britain's aircraft and armored cars were in place. This provisional solution has lasted for seven decades and so have the borders of Transjordan, now ruled over by Abdullah's grandson, Hussein, the Hashemite King of Jordan.

The appointment of Abdullah seemed to accomplish several objectives at once. It went part way toward paying what Lawrence and others told Churchill was Britain's wartime debt to the family of King Hussein, though Hussein himself was beyond help. Too stubborn to accept British advice, he was losing the battle for Arabia to his blood rival, Ibn Saud. Meanwhile Prince Faisal, Britain's preferred Arab ruler, remained in idle exile.

Other chief items on the Cairo agenda were the Ottoman territories running from the Persian Gulf to Turkey along the border of Persia, which make up present-day Iraq. Including what were suspected—but not proved—to be vast oil reserves, at a time when the value of oil was beginning to be understood, these territories had been the scene of the bloodiest postwar Arab uprisings against British rule. They caused so many difficulties of every sort that Churchill flirted with the idea of abandoning them entirely, but Lloyd George would have none of it. If the British left, the Prime Minister warned, in a year or two they might find that they had "handed over to the French and Americans some of the richest oil fields in the world."

As a matter of convenience, the British administered this troubled region as a unit, though it was composed of the three separate Ottoman provinces—Mosul, Baghdad and Basra, with their incompatible Kurdish, Assyrian Christian, Jewish, Sunnl Muslim, and Shiite populations. In making it into a country, Churchill and his colleagues found it convenient to continue treating it as a single unit. (One British planner was warned by an American missionary, "You are flying in the face of four millenniums of history…") The country was called Iraq—"the well-rooted country"—in order to give it a name that was Arabic. Faisal was placed on the throne by the British, and like his brother Abdullah in Transjordan, he was supposed to keep Iraq quiet until the British were ready to police it with aircraft and armored cars.

One of the leftover problems in 1921 was just how to protect Transjordan's new governor, Abdullah, and Iraq's new king, Faisal, against the fierce warriors of Ibn Saud. In August 1922 Ibn Saud's camel-cavalry forces invading Transjordan were stopped outside Amman by British airplanes and armored cars. Earlier that year, the British forced Ibn Saud to accept a settlement aimed at protecting Iraq. With this in mind, the British drew a frontier line that awarded Iraq a substantial amount of territory claimed by Ibn Saud for Arabia: all the land (in what is now Iraq) west of the Euphrates River, all the way to the Syrian frontier. To compensate Ibn Saud's kingdom (later known as Saudi Arabia) the British transferred to it rights to two-thirds of the territory of Kuwait, which had been essentially independent for about two centuries. These were valuable grazing lands, in which oil might exist too.

It is this frontier line between Iraq, Kuwait and Arabia, drawn by a British civil servant in 1922 to protect Iraq at the expense of Kuwait, that Iraq's Saddam Hussein denounced as invalid when he invaded.

In 1922, Churchill succeeded in mapping out the Arab Middle East along lines suitable to the needs of the British civilian and military administrations. T.E. Lawrence would later brag that he, Churchill and a few others had designed the modern Middle East over dinner. Seventy years later, in the tense deliberations and confrontations of half the world over the same area, the question is whether the peoples of the Middle East are willing or able to continue living with that design.

Lawyer Historian David Fromkin is the author of a prizewinning book entitled A Peace to End All Peace.

Nazism in the Classroom

Lisa Pine *looks at how lessons in the classroom were perverted in the service of the Third Reich.*

Whilst most governments seek, or have sought, to imbue their nation's youth with correct values and ideals, those regimes of an authoritarian nature have attempted to do so with greater thoroughness—in part, to create a consensus for their rule and ideology. This is clearly demonstrated, for example, by the way in which Mussolini's regime reformed the education system in Italy, introduced state textbooks and set up youth organisations in order to instil Italian youth with Fascist ideology.

In Austria, too, the clerico-fascist regime of 1934–38 attempted to inculcate its beliefs in Austrian youth by similar means. But perhaps the most striking example of this type of youth manipulation through ideological 'education' was the Nazi regime, which introduced sweeping reforms into the German school system reinforced by the activities of its youth groups, the Hitler Youth and the League of German Girls. It went so far as to utilise school textbooks as propaganda tools, with which to disseminate its ideology.

The socialisation of youth was already a prominent part of educational activity during the nineteenth century, when the publishers of children's literature and textbooks clearly recognised that they could be used to shape a child's view of the world by disseminating social values. Story books, as well as history books, were used to diffuse positive social values, but also more negatively to disseminate racist values by means of stereotyping, with such tales as *The Story of Little Black Sambo* (1899). Racial ste-

reotyping in school books was based upon distorted generalisations, as well as pseudo-scientific and religious justifications, and was reinforced by the use of vivid descriptions and illustrations. This kind of indoctrination was seized upon eagerly by the Nazi government.

The Nazi *Weltanschauung* or 'world view' served as the basis of all educational activity in the Third Reich and became an instrument of justification and legitimisation for the actions of the regime. The concepts of racial superiority, 'national community' and leadership stood at the centre of the Nazi *Weltanschauung*, and were directly applied to principles of education which was no longer aimed at benefiting the individual, but instead, was directed towards the creation of an entire generation of German youth that would be strong, prepared for sacrifice, and willing to undertake its responsibilities towards the 'national community', a notion based upon mass emotion, not rationality. As such, children were pedagogic objects, subjected to the arbitrariness of the system.

In *Mein Kampf* Hitler had already laid out his ideas about education and what it should entail. He claimed that the highest task of education was to consist of the preservation, care and development of the best racial elements. Education, in the Nazi state, was understood in terms of racial selection, so that only the élite would reproduce. This was, of course, reflected in all policy, not just educational policy. Young 'Aryan' children had to be made aware of the differences between people who fitted into the 'na-

tional community' and those who did not. In Hitler's words: 'No boy and no girl must leave school without having been led to an ultimate realisation of the necessity and essence of blood purity'.

In December 1934, Wilhelm Frick, the Minister of the Interior, announced that 'the political task of the school is the education of youth in the service of nation and state in the National Socialist spirit'. Similarly, according to Bernhard Rust, the Minister of Education, the purpose of school textbooks was to achieve 'the ideological education of young German people, so as to develop them into fit members of the national community... ready to serve and to sacrifice'.

To this end strict censorship was imposed upon the publishing industry. Certain titles 'blacklisted' by Josef Goebbels, the Minister of Propaganda, were removed from circulation as 'alien' or 'decadent' literature. Censorship was implemented by Philipp Bouhler, the Director of the Party Censorship Office, in conjunction with Bernhard Rust at the Ministry of Education. At first, publishers often reprinted pre-Nazi schoolbooks, with only slight amendments, such as the insertion of swastika flags and Party slogans. However, by the late 1930s, when new writing and illustrations serving the regime became more widely available in greater quantities, school textbooks were employed more blatantly to represent Nazi ideals. Old textbooks were replaced by new editions which incorporated the central tenets of Nazi ideology. These were written by authors approved by the Ministry of Education and the National Socialist Teachers' Association. Whilst some of these were by named authors, others were anonymous. For example, many primers and readers were compiled and edited by 'an expert team of German educators'.

The lack of subtlety of approach in the regime's unashamed utilisation of schoolbooks for propaganda purposes revealed itself, for example, in primers, where the first page consisted of the words 'Heil Hitler', with children portrayed raising their arms in the Hitler salute. A picture of Hitler usually appeared on the frontispiece, sometimes alone, but more usually showing him with a child or group of children.

Primers contained numerous stories and poems about Hitler, who was portrayed as an omniscient, generous and benevolent man. One such piece entitled 'A Happy Day' from the *German Reader for Elementary Schools* (1936) describes the mounting excitement of school children in their anticipation of a visit by Hitler to their village.

Nazi symbols were often used in conjunction with domestic themes in order to make them familiar and more accessible to small children. An illustrated story, in a primary school reader entitled *My First Book* (1935), shows children helping their mother decorate their home with a swastika flag, roses and a painting of a swastika. Here, a political message was delivered through familiar, familial channels of consciousness. Another story in the *German Reader for Elementary Schools* (1938) about unemployment and its effects on family life was also used to political effect. It tells of a distressed mother whose husband is unemployed. The family are experiencing severe financial hardship, and can afford only potato soup for dinner, instead of meat. The father has been shot in the foot during the First World War and has not worked since. In this story, the Nazi regime rescues the family from the clutches of poverty and misery, by specifically helping the war-wounded man. The story ends with the father returning home triumphantly one day, with the news that he has a job starting the next day, working with 200 others on the construction of a new bridge. This brings

tremendous joy to the family and meat back to their dinner table.

The theme of young children 'helping the *Führer*' appears in numerous textbooks from 1939 onwards, when the government was clearly concerned about shortages of raw materials and the war effort. One story tells of a boy who collects old materials for recycling from his home and the homes of his relatives. Another, in a book entitled *Happy Beginnings* (1939), with an illustration of a family sitting around the dinner table, deals with the *Eintopf*. This was the 'one-pot' dish that German families were encouraged to eat instead of their usual meal on one Sunday of each month, in order to save money which was instead to be donated to the needs of the state. In this story, one of the children tells her parents that she used to think that the *Eintopf* meant that there was a large pot outside the town hall, and that all the people went there to eat. Her brother laughs at her, but their father admonishes him, saying that the girl at least now understood what the *Führer* meant. There is a knock at the door and the collector appears. One of the children is told to go and fetch the money, and to give double that day, as it is the father's birthday. This story explained the political significance of the *Eintopf*, using the family context to instil the message.

In *Fables for Lower Saxony* (1939), a mother asks her daughters to fetch potatoes from the cellar in baskets to fill up a sack for the Winter Relief Organisation, whose motto was 'no one shall go hungry, no one shall freeze'. They bring up three baskets of potatoes and ask if this is enough. Their mother tells them to bring up another basket, as the sack is not yet full, emphasising that they should be pleased to make sacrifices for the Winter Relief Organisation and, hence, the state.

The Nazi idealisation of the mother features heavily in the textbooks of the period. There were ordinary stories of children preparing a special treat for their mother's birthday or for Mother's Day, aimed at young children, but in reading books for older children, depictions of the mother could be found under the subheading of 'heroes of everyday life'. This sense of the mother being raised to a heroic position was one that the regime

clearly wished to instil in children. For example, one schoolbook includes a play for Mother's Day, in which four councillors are portrayed, contemplating ways to relieve the mother of her many burdens and duties. Just as they are considering the possibility of finding someone to help the mother, a woman appears at the door. The councillors ask her if she is a wife and mother, to which she replies that she is. They then ask her if she takes care of her family, to which she answers that she does—from dawn to dusk. However, when the suggestion is made that some assistance might lighten her burden, she firmly rejects the idea, claiming that mothers love their domain and are happy to toil from early in the morning until late at night for their families. After she goes, the councillors conclude their session by deciding that 'mothers do not want to be relieved' of their tasks and duties.

Bucolic life, untainted by the depravities of urbanisation was accorded a special significance during the Third Reich. The Nazi 'Blood and Soil' doctrine defined the strength of the nation in terms of an idealisation of peasant values and the sacredness of the German soil. The regime excoriated many aspects of life in the big cities, not least the tendency of young couples to limit the size of their families. Urbanisation leading to the 'death of the nation' was a recurrent theme.

This comes across especially strongly in certain textbooks, such as *Country Folk and Agricultural Work* (1939), aimed specifically at pupils in rural areas, to demonstrate to them their own importance and value in maintaining a healthy nation. The rural family was portrayed as the 'archetype of a true family'. Textbooks went to great lengths to show that what was regarded as a family in the big cities, was often not a true family, but a distorted image of one. A husband and wife living in a city, without children, but with domestic pets instead, could be described at best as a 'household', but not as a 'family'.

Another aspect of rural family life that was deemed positive by the Nazi regime was the inclusion of the grandparents in the home. In this extended family, both the grandmother and grandfather had their roles and duties to perform. The other advantages of emphasising their presence was to make children more aware of their ancestry.

All this related back to the issue of German blood. Much use was made of genealogy and family trees to establish purity of race. On this theme, there were texts entitled, for instance, 'You and Your Ancestors', which asked pupils: 'Do you know what kind of blood runs through your veins? Do you know your father and your mother, and have you yet seen the ancestry of your forefathers?' One writer of such a text claimed to have traced his own family tree back to around 1500, and to therefore know what blood type flowed through his veins. The presentation of ancestral knowledge in an exciting and colourful manner highlighted its importance, encouraging pupils to take an interest in their own ancestry and to consider the fact that one day they themselves would be the ancestors of a future family—as branches of a family tree would continue to grow. In addition to the pupils' books, there were a number of aids to teachers which suggested ways in which these issues could and should be taught. Another approach used, apart from actively involving children in their own ancestry, was the inclusion of numerous poems and stories about heredity, blood and kinship.

The main benefit to be derived from genealogical activities was awareness, both of an individual's own traits, and, more importantly, of his membership of the 'blood community' of the German nation. Of course, the ramifications of this went much further, by suggesting that those of non-German blood, or who could not definitively prove to be of German blood, were 'inferior'. Fundamentally, the purpose of such texts was to highlight the sense of continuity between children, their parents, their grandparents, their great-grandparents and so on. They emphasised the idea of blood flowing from the past, to the present and the future, pulsing in the veins of a family generation after generation. One book sought to demonstrate the inheritance and transmission of family characteristics through the generations by considering the composer Johann Sebastian Bach. It illustrated Bach's family tree, in order to show that in his family there

were no fewer than thirty-four 'musically competent' people, of whom approximately half were 'outstandingly gifted'. This particular example was part of a comprehensive chapter dealing with heredity, race and family. Within this context, blood was the most important symbol, for 'German blood' was the guarantee of the future of the nation.

The Nazi preoccupation with 'the order of nature' formed the basis of a number of texts. For example, in one story, a husband and wife decide to exchange roles. The husband takes over the cooking, whilst the wife goes out into the fields to do his work. After a disastrous day for the man—who previously thought his wife had the easy option in staying at home and cooking—he tells her that it is better 'not to reverse the order of nature'. The implications of this are crystal clear in relation to Nazi ideology.

In a similar vein—but more related to Nazi pseudo-scientific racial thought—was a fable appearing in the *German Reader for Secondary Schools* (1942), whose substance was as follows: A cuckoo meets a nightingale in the street. The cuckoo wants to sing as beautifully as the nightingale, but claims that he cannot do so because he was not taught to sing when he was young. The nightingale laughs and says that nightingales do not *learn* to sing, but are *born* with the ability to sing. The cuckoo, nevertheless, believes that if only he could find the right teacher, his offspring will be able to sing as beautifully as the nightingale. His wife has a clever idea. She decides to lay an egg in the nest of a hedge sparrow. When the mother hedge sparrow returns to her nest, she is surprised to see the strange egg, but decides to take care of it as if it were her own. When the eggs hatch, a young cuckoo emerges among the fledgling sparrows. He is nourished and cared for in exactly the same way as them, but he does not grow into a hedge sparrow. In fact, the older he grows, the more noticeable his differences become. When he tries to sing, he cannot. Despite growing up in the nest of a hedge sparrow, he grows up to be a true cuckoo.

This story was used to pose the questions: 'What is more important? The race from which one stems, or the nest in which one grows up?' The issues raised

in this fable are particularly significant, reflecting both the debate about inherited versus acquired characteristics, and the rudiments of Nazi racial ideology.

Racism and anti-Semitism also permeated biology and 'racial science' textbooks which aimed to point out to children the distinctions between the 'Aryan' race and 'inferior' races, for example, by means of craniology. There were also readers, such as *The Poisonous Mushroom* (1938), in which a whole array of anti-Semitic imagery was used, with caricatures, graphic illustrations and vivid descriptions of Jews as hideous, hook-nosed seducers of 'Aryan' women, Christ-slayers and money-grabbing usurers. 'The Jew' was portrayed as 'the Devil in human form'. In many secondary school books, anti-Semitic quotations by Hitler and other Nazi leaders were interspersed with folklore and nationalist literature. This type of racial indoctrination was, of course, just one small part of the Nazis' attempt to create popular consensus for their anti-Semitic policies culminating in the 'Final Solution'.

History lessons were a way of exciting children's sense of national pride and concern about the continued existence of the German state and nation, and about future glories to match—or even to exceed—those of the nation's great heroic past. History was to be looked at 'with the eyes of blood' and its primary function was to serve the 'political, intellectual and spiritual mobilisation of the nation'. Nazi history textbooks often dealt with German history only. Great rulers of Germany's past, such as Frederick the Great, were used to stress heroic leadership, ceaseless service to the state, military successes, and, of course, parallels to Hitler.

The ultimate triumphs of Nazism were given considerable priority in the history textbooks of the period, such as *Nation and Leader: German History for Schools* (1943). The issues of care and protection of the race found their way into history textbooks quite extensively too. Themes such as 'national renewal' were not uncommon in the history books of the Nazi era. Historical atlases showed Germany's greatness in her most historically important and expansive periods, and especially in the Third Reich.

Arithmetic books of the Nazi era also indoctrinated children by pervading the curriculum in a well-established tradition, echoing the religious bodies of the early nineteenth century, which based numerical tasks upon biblical content, and curricula in capitalist societies in the late nineteenth and early twentieth centuries, with textbook calculations based upon stocks and shares and profit-making. The Nazis used arithmetic exercises to propagate their racial and political ideas. The following example, from a standard 1941 textbook is overtly loaded with discrimination against the 'hereditarily ill'. Pupils were given the information that:

Every day, the state spends RM 6 on one cripple; RM 4 1/4 on one mentally-ill person; RM 5 1/2 on one deaf and dumb person; RM 5 3/5 on one feeble-minded person; RM 3 1/2 on one alcoholic; RM 4 4/5 on one pupil in care; RM 2 1/20 on one pupil at a special school; and RM 9/20 on one pupil at a normal school.

Using this, pupils were to answer questions such as 'What total cost do one cripple and one feeble-minded person create, if one takes a lifespan of forty-five years for each?' and 'Calculate the expenditure of the state for one pupil in a special school and one pupil in an ordinary school over eight years, and state the amount of higher cost engendered by the special school pupil'. This was typical of the way in which data regarding state expenditure on 'hereditarily ill' or 'inferior' people was used in 'education'. The implications of such exercises are patent.

The Nazi regime was not original in its desire to indoctrinate children from an early age and to use school textbooks for this purpose. However, it did so in conjunction with the rest of its policies and with its own specific motivations in mind. Its concern was to create a racially 'pure' 'national community', in which the development of the individual was of little or no importance. That the Nazi regime used school textbooks so widely and blatantly for the dissemination of its ideology, shows distinctly the lengths to which it was willing to go in order to influence the society it sought to create.

FOR FURTHER READING:

L. Pine, 'The dissemination of Nazi ideology and family values through school textbooks', *History of Education* (1996), vol. 25, No. 1, 91–109; W. Marsden, 'Rooting racism into the educational experience of childhood and youth in the nineteenth- and twentieth-centuries', *History of Education* (1990), vol. 19, No. 4, 333–353; C. Kamenetsky, *Children's Literature in Nazi Germany* (Ohio University Press, 1984); G. Blackburn, *Education in the Third Reich: Race and History in Nazi Textbooks* (State University of New York Press, 1985); M. Burleigh and W. Wippermann, *The Racial State: Germany 1933–1945* (Cambridge University Press, 1991).

Lisa Pine is Lecturer in Modern History at the University of Luton and author of Nazi Family Policy, 1933–1945 *(Berg, 1997).*

Pearl Harbor: The First Energy War

Charles Maechling *sees the US oil embargo against Japan as the direct origin of the decision to attack the United States in December 1941*

DECEMBER 7TH, 1941—in the words of President Franklin Roosevelt's stirring war message to Congress, '… a date that will live in infamy'—marks the devastating Japanese naval air raid on Pearl Harbor, Hawaii, that sank or crippled the US battle fleet and plunged the United States into the Second World War.

In the summer of 1941, Japan had been at war on the mainland of Asia for four years. After amputating Manchuria from China in 1932, it had begun a full-sale and brutal invasion of China itself. A Japanese army of over a million now occupied the principal Chinese cities and large stretches of the interior. The Nationalist government of Chiang Kai-shek still, however, refused to sue for peace in spite of the loss of so much territory, and the drain of Japanese manpower and supplies continued unabated.

Japan's dependence on outside sources for petroleum products was similar in 1941 to what it is today.

Just as today, Japan in 1941 was heavily dependent on outside sources for the minerals, petroleum and other raw materials needed to fuel its economy. The aim of Japan's programme of conquest, therefore, was to convert China into an economic vassal, the first step in carving out a continental economic system—the Greater East Asia Co-Prosperity Sphere, also to embrace Korea, Indo-China, Malaya, and Indonesia. The plan was to insulate the region from world-wide depression by allowing raw materials to flow into Japan for conversion into manufactured goods for the limitless Chinese market, thereby ensuring freedom from Western economic domination.

Japan's limited energy resources was the plan's Achilles' heel. Despite minimal civilian petrol consumption, and a largely unmechanised army, Japan's oil consumption since 1931 had climbed steadily from a level—unbelievably low by modern standards—of about 21 million barrels a year to over 32 million barrels in 1941. (Japan's current annual consumption is about three billion barrels.) The most imperative defence requirement was to ensure ample reserve stocks for the powerful and growing Imperial Navy, and to this end Japan had accumulated a stockpile of around 54 million barrels with 29 million reserved for the Navy.

In 1941, Japan's dependence on outside sources for petroleum products was similar to what it is today. 90 per cent of the country's needs were made up by imports which in the late 1930s varied from a low figure of 30.6 million barrels in 1938 to 37.1 million in 1940, the excess going into the stockpile. But there was one enormous difference from today—before the Second World War, the vast reserves of Saudi Arabia and the Middle East had yet to be developed, and 85 per cent of Japan's imports came from one monolithic supplier. Japan's private OPEC was the United States of America, then the world's leading exporter. And by 1941 relations with the United States had deteriorated to the verge of war.

It had not always been so. The United States had opened Japan up to the outside world in the nineteenth century. President Theodore Roosevelt had been responsible for securing a favourable settlement for Japan after the Russo-Japanese War of 1905, and Japan had been a *de facto* ally in the First World War. Despite resentment over restrictive US immigration laws, among the educated classes there was a considerable reservoir of good will for the United States, now Japan's most important

A Japanese tank makes heavy weather of the attack on Xuzhou in June 1938; on this occasion a Nationalist fightback stalled the Japanese advance.

trading partner, and vast admiration for American education and technological achievements.

But since the 'Manchurian incident' and the Japanese creation of Manchukuo in 1932, the United States had been the principal opponent of Japanese expansion in Asia. Under the Stimson Doctrine, the United States had refused to recognise the puppet regime in Manchukuo and regarded the programme for a Greater East Asia Co-Prosperity Sphere with hostility and moral disapproval—attitudes reinforced by the atrocities perpetrated by the Japanese army in China. Isolationist sentiment and the constraints imposed by recently enacted neutrality legislation not only barred the FDR administration from giving military assistance to threatened foreign countries, but inhibited any form of economic sanctions against aggressor nations. Moreover, President Roosevelt was under pressure from Britain and his own cabinet to avoid any kind of military confrontation in the Pacific that might detract from aid to the Allies and divert public attention away from Hitler.

The US Navy was even more cautious. Successive chiefs of naval operations had warned the President that until the 1934 building programme was completed, and bases in the Philippines, the Central Pacific and Hawaii reinforced, any military confrontation with Japan would find the navy at a grave disadvantage. It had neither the carrier air strength nor the auxiliary supply vessels to fight its way through the Japanese-mandated Marshall and Caroline Islands, bristling with air bases, to confront the formidable Japanese navy in its home waters.

The reluctance of the admirals became even more pronounced after the German submarine campaign in the Atlantic got under way. Destroyers of the Pacific Fleet, essential to protecting heavy ships from submarine attack, were now being transferred to the Atlantic for patrol and convoy escort duty. A recent commander of the fleet, the redoubtable Admiral James O. Richardson, had been replaced for pouring cold water on the President's fantasy of running a cruiser patrol line across the Pacific from Hawaii, and for insisting that the fleet be withdrawn to its West Coast bases because of the vulnerability of Pearl Harbor. Once the decision was made to give the lifeline to Britain top priority, a temporising stance in the Pacific was inevitable.

In July 1940, however, the passage of the Export Control Act gave the President an excuse to retaliate against Japanese expansion without appearing to be punitive. When in September 1940 the Japanese army moved into northern Indo-China, Roosevelt could cite US defence needs under the Act as justification for imposing an embargo on the export of scrap iron and steel. Shortly thereafter he prohibited the exportation of aviation fuel and lubricants to all but Great Britain and the Western Hemisphere countries. But the flow of oil and regular petrol to Japan continued without interruption, and its oil imports in 1940 only dropped to 23 million barrels from 26 million the year before.

Life is better under the Japanese: this propaganda leaflet was distributed in China in 1938 or 1939.

Meanwhile Japanese foreign policy had been undergoing a reappraisal through a convoluted and agonising process. The Japanese military—or more properly the army high command—had, since the Manchurian takeover, exercised a baleful influence over foreign policy which on several occasions (most famously in the February 26th Incident of 1936) led fanatical young officers to assassinate elderly and conservative cabinet ministers who were considered 'unworthy' of Japan's imperial destiny. The army high command risked loss of face, and even disgrace in the eyes of the Emperor and the people, the longer the war in China was permitted to drag on. The high command therefore became the principal proponent of closer ties with Germany and Italy and an aggressive move south to achieve the cherished dream of self-sufficiency.

On the other side, strong forces were at work in support of a policy of moderation. These included the nobility, the business and financial leadership, even the Imperial Navy. Though dismayed and resentful over American attitudes, these circles had a more healthy respect for American industrial might and global influence than the insular army, and dreaded the unforeseeable consequences of war with the US. The unrelenting disapproval of America to Japan's programme for Asia was upsetting but could be tolerated as long as the oil supply remained intact. Compared to the long-standing geographical, historical and economic bonds that linked Japan to the United States, the new ties with its allies of expediency, Germany and Italy, seemed artificial and flimsy.

Before a clear-cut policy could emerge, however, these differences had to be thrashed out within the imperial circle. Although crudely styled 'fascist' by the American press and politicians, and lumped in with Germany and Italy as a grinning partner in iniquity, Japan and its political system had little in common with European dictatorships. Except for the predominant influence exercised by the military caste, which was deemed to incarnate the samurai virtues, Japanese pre-war society, and especially its decision-making process, was almost morbidly traditional.

Under a layer of parliamentary formalities, vital questions concerning the future of the empire were decided by a painful process of soul-searching and mutual consultation between leaders of the principal power groups. The resulting consensus, couched in the euphemistic and abstract syle unique to Japanese culture, was then submitted to the Emperor for a kind of mystical endorsement at an elaborate ritual called a 'Throne Conference'.

Predictably, this system often produced policy compromises that embodied fatal contradictions. Typical was the decision reached in the summer of 1940 to install a civilian premier of impeccably conservative stripe, Prince Konoye. He was prepared to acquiesce in the army's programme for further conquest of the Asian mainland while at the same time making an effort to reach an accommodation with the United States. But when Konoye gave the army a limited mandate to obtain bases in French Indo-China, and in September 1940 signed a defensive alliance with Germany and Italy known as the Tripartite Pact, he made it extraordinarily difficult for Roosevelt and Secretary of State Cordell Hull to make meaningful concessions in negotiations without being labelled appeasers.

Japan next took steps to reduce its oil dependence on the United States. Civilian consumption of petrol was cut from 6–7 million barrels annually to 1.6 million. By diversifying supply it managed by the end of 1940 to reduce the proportion of oil imports from the United States to 60 per cent. But the disruption of the oil market by competing demands of neutral and warring powers alike, combined with the inaccessibility of remaining

Steaming forward: a Japanese destroyer, December 1941.

sources, made a search for alternatives essential. For years Japan had cast a covetous eye on the oil reserves of the Dutch East Indies, and in June 1940, after the German occupation of The Netherlands, demanded assurances from the Dutch colonial government in Batavia, now cut off from the mother country, that exports of oil and minerals to Japan be maintained at pre-war levels. In September 1940 the Konoye government despatched a large mission to Batavia with 'proposals' for access to raw materials on a greatly increased scale, with oil to be given top priority.

Japan demanded a guarantee of 40 per cent of the annual oil production of the Dutch East Indies.

Before the outbreak of the war, Japanese imports from the Indies had been running at about 4.5 million barrels annually. Japan now demanded a guarantee of 22 million barrels, which would have represented about 40 per cent of the annual production of the Indies (55 million barrels)—a figure almost exactly equal to Japan's oil dependence on the United States. However, the Dutch colonial administrators, although well aware of the Indies' vulnerability, displayed characteristic toughness and ob-

stinacy. They protracted the negotiations over three months, and when finally in November they agreed to an increase, the Japanese were granted only 14.5 million barrels annually; even this amount was made subject to the concurrence of the oil companies and hedged about with escape clauses.

In the winter of 1940–41, American attention increasingly focused on the plight of Britain whose trans-Atlantic lifeline was suffering catastrophic losses from the German submarine campaign. In April 1941, Germany invaded Yugoslavia and Greece and inflicted heavy defeats on the British in Crete and North Africa. President Roosevelt extended the US neutrality zone in the Atlantic and the degree of convoy protection further to the east. In May he proclaimed augmented submarine tracking and convoy protection in the zone and transferred fleet units from the Pacific to the Atlantic; a national emergency was declared. In Washington, support for Britain was now given indisputable priority.

Meanwhile, in Tokyo the policy pendulum oscillated. A new Japanese ambassador, Admiral Kichisaburo Nomura, known to be friendly to the United States, was sent to Washington with a fresh set of tentative proposals. They offered a freeze on Japanese military operations in China and initiation of negotiations with Chiang Kai-shek, who still exercised a precarious sway over its unoccupied provinces. In return, Japan asked for a lifting of embargoes on critical materials, resumption of normal trade with the United States, US assistance in restoring the flow of raw materials from South East Asia, and exertion of influ-

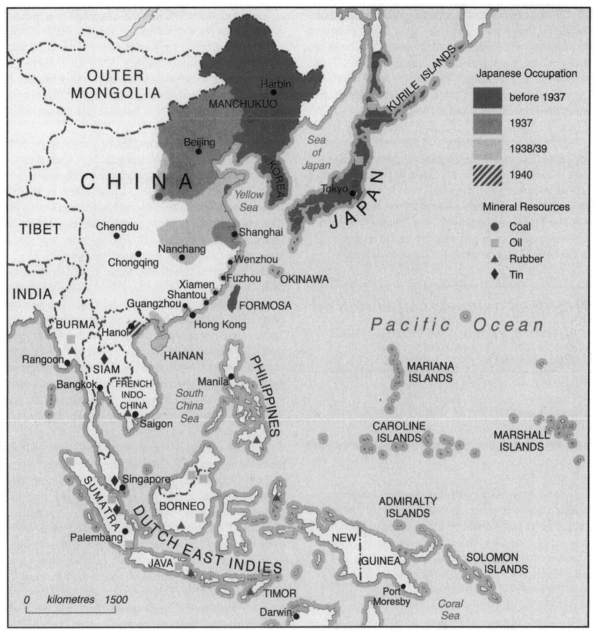

BRIDGEMAN ART LIBRARY/VATICAN MUSEUMS & GALLERIES

Japan's advance into Manchuria in the early 1930s, then into China and South-East Asia, was based in part on a relentless search for raw materials that were not available at home.

ence on Chiang Kai-shek to open peace negotiations with Japan. Secretary Hull agreed to discuss these proposals, but after fifty secret meetings with Nomura, no basis for agreement could be found. Hull declined to be drawn into specifics and countered with a demand for agreement in principle on four points before negotiations could begin—Japan was to pledge respect for the territorial integrity of all nations, non-interference in other nations' internal affairs, equality of commercial opportunity, and a commitment to peaceful change of the status quo. Japan viewed these formulations as a lawyer's device to raise obstacles to negotiating trade-offs, and the talks ended in temporary stalemate.

At the same time, new factors hardened each nation's position. In April 1941 Japan and Russia signed a surprise non-aggression pact, and in June Germany invaded the Soviet Union. These developments signified to the Japanese high command that at long last the Soviet threat along the Manchurian border had been neutralised. Also in June the United States suspended petroleum exports to Japan from East Coast and Gulf ports. The Japanese establishment went into conclave and in July, at another Throne Conference, the army high command, with the concurrence of Prince Konoye, proposed to the Emperor that the empire now had no choice but to resume the march southwards. The Emperor seemed to assent, and planning was ordered for invasion of Malaysia, the Philippines, the Dutch East Indies and Hong Kong, combined with preparations for war with the United States, Britain and the Netherlands. But no specific deadlines were set and negotiations were to continue.

163

On July 24th, the Japanese army, with the reluctant acquiescence of the Vichy government in France, occupied key positions throughout Indo-China. And on July 26th, President Roosevelt ordered the freezing of all Japanese assets in the United States and the placing of all petroleum exports to Japan under embargo subject to licence. The British and Dutch governments quickly followed suit. To this day the record is unclear as to whether the President realised the full implications of his actions. Some memoirs of his entourage indicate that he intended to use the licensing authority as a diplomatic weapon—a tap to be turned on or off for bargaining purposes. But the freeze made it almost impossible for Japan to continue paying cash for oil as before. In any case, this was a victory for the hardliners in the administration—Secretary of War Stimson, Secretary of the Treasury Morgenthau, and Secretary of the Interior Ickes—who had been pressing for an oil embargo for months in the belief that it would force Japan to its knees.

The freezing of its assets and the US oil embargo were greeted in Japan with shock and dismay.

It soon became apparent that in such a political climate, no licences would be issued and none ever was. Japan was now thrown back on her stockpile. To quote the historian Herbert Feis:

> There was no way, no uncontrolled source of supply, from which Japan could get as much as it would have to use… Ton by ton, it could be foreseen, Japan would have to empty the tanks which had been filled with such zealous foresight… From now on the clock and the oil gauge stood side by side. Each fall in the level brought the hour of decision closer.

For the American military, the timing of the President's action represented a setback. The navy in particular had repeatedly stressed US inferiority in the Pacific—it was outnumbered in aircraft carriers by ten to three—and the army had urged delay until air and ground forces in the Philippines could be strengthened. From Tokyo, Ambassador Joseph E. Grew had once more cautioned that if pushed to the wall it was in the Japanese character to react violently and without warning. But President Roosevelt believed that although he was running a risk, it was one that did not close off his options or entail serious consequences for the United States. He was reassured in this belief by the virtual unanimity of his advisers that if war came it would be far away, a Japanese move against Malaysia and the Dutch East Indies; the safety of the United States was not an issue.

The freezing of its assets and the oil embargo were greeted in Japan with shock and dismay. Records published after the war reveal an atmosphere of desperation. By August 1941 there was only a twelve-month supply of oil left for the army and eighteen months for the navy. A Throne Conference called early in September set war planning in motion, and in October a hardline cabinet headed by war minister General Hideki Tojo replaced the discredited ministry of Prince Konoye who had set his hopes on a secret summit meeting with President Roosevelt. A final Throne Conference on November 5th committed a still ambivalent emperor to war unless a last-minute diplomatic solution could be found.

Japan's final effort consisted of proposals embodying new concessions, carried to Washington by a special envoy, Saburo Kurusu, who henceforth participated with Admiral Nomura in negotiations. These agreed to immediate Japanese withdrawal from Indo-China, renunciation of further expansion in Asia, and ultimate withdrawal from China after conclusion of a peace treaty with Chiang Kai-shek. It also made clear that Japan was prepared to treat the Tripartite Pact as a nullity.

But like previous efforts, these proposals foundered on the rock of irreconcilable conflict. Japan would not totally withdraw from the Asian mainland and revert to a pinched and impoverished existence in its overcrowded islands. The United States could not accept a compromise that left Japan in possession of any part of China. However, a three-months moratorium, a *modus vivendi*, leaving all forces in place, was left on the table. But on November 26th, after Japan occupied more positions in Indo-China, Secretary Hull stunned the Japanese envoys with a blunt reversion to earlier demands, including complete Japanese withdrawal from all of China.

Throughout these events, President Roosevelt and a close circle of top advisers—the secretaries of State, War and Navy, and the Chief of Staff of the Army and Chief of Naval Operations—had been following every twist and turn of Japanese policy through cable and radio intercepts. American cryptographers had broken the Japanese diplomatic code, and thereafter, these decoded messages to Japan's overseas posts, styled MAGIC, were on Secretary Hull's desk within a few hours of receipt and translation. But although the President and his advisers knew of Japan's desperation, and intention to take drastic military measures if negotiations broke down, they did not know where and when the blow was most likely to fall. The Japanese army and navy codes were still unbroken, and while the indicators from troop movements pointed to Malaysia, the Dutch East Indies and possibly the Philippines, and to the critical dates of the weekends of December 1st and December 7th, there was no indication of an attack on the United States or its possessions.

Nonetheless, to cover all contingencies, on November 27th the war and navy departments in Washington despatched a general war warning to the commanders of the US Pacific Fleet in Pearl Harbor and the army's Hawaiian department, and to General MacArthur and the commander of the US Asiatic Fleet in Manila. Not a hint of impending war was given to Congress, the press, or the American public.

The Japanese air raid on Pearl Harbor, which killed over 3,000 American soldiers, sailors and airmen, and destroyed or disabled six battleships and most of the military aircraft on the ground, lives in American legend as the country's greatest wartime disaster. But for Japan, the attack turned out to be a military and political disaster of much greater magnitude. The Pacific Fleet's aircraft carriers—the true capital ships of the coming war—were elsewhere on the morning of December 7th. In the teeth of all the evidence of American naval inferiority in the Pacific, the commander of the Japanese navy, Admiral Yamamoto, had clung to the doctrine that before his main objectives could be achieved, an enemy 'fleet in being' on his flank had first to be destroyed. Instead of confronting President Roosevelt with the dilemma of persuading a refractory Congress to declare war in defence of the British and Dutch colonial empires, while leaving the Nazi menace unresolved, he brought a unified America headlong into war.

Even after eight official investigations, lengthy Congressional hearings, and voluminous literature of memoirs and other first-hand accounts, historians continue to debate reasons for the debacle and American lack of preparation. Revisionist works continue to appear that allege that in one way or another President Roosevelt provoked the attack, the most recent focusing on intercepts that should have triggered immediate alarm in Washington. One fact that now appears indisputable is that throughout the crisis, the Hawaiian commanders, Admiral Kimmel and General Short, were denied vital information, though whether by design, rigid chains of command, or fear of revealing even the existence of MAGIC, has never been established.

One lesson that does stand out is that while oil was not the sole cause of the deterioration of relations, once employed as a diplomatic weapon, it made hostilities inevitable. The United States recklessly cut the energy lifeline of a powerful adversary without due regard for the predictably explosive consequences. When the victim struck back, he blundered badly and unleashed forces of incalculable magnitude that we still live with today.

For Further Reading

Herbert Feis, *The Road to Pearl Harbor* (Princeton University Press, 1950); Gordon Prange, *Pearl Harbor: The Verdict of History* (McGraw Hill, 1986); Edward L. Beach, *Scapegoat* (Naval Institute Press, 1995); John Costello, *Days of Infamy* (Pocket Books, 1994); Robert J. C. Butow, *Tojo and the Coming of War* (Stanford University Press, 1961); Roberta Wohlstetter, *Pearl Harbor-Warning and Decision* (Morrow, 1963).

Charles Maechling, Jr. *is a retired naval officer, diplomat and international lawyer.*

This article first appeared in *History Today,* December 2000, pp. 41-47. © 2000 by History Today, Ltd. Reprinted by permission.

His Finest Hour

With courage and sheer will, Churchill rallied a nation and turned back Hitler's tyranny

By John Keegan

Sixty years ago this month, in May 1940, Western civilization was threatened with defeat. Liberty, the principle on which it rests, was menaced by a man who despised freedom. Adolf Hitler, the dictator of Nazi Germany, had conquered Western Europe. He challenged Britain, the last outpost of resistance, to submit. He believed Britain would, and with good reason. Its Army was beaten, its Navy and Air Force were under attack by the all-conquering German Luftwaffe. He believed no one would oppose his demands.

He was wrong. One man would and did. Winston Churchill, recently appointed prime minister, defied Hitler. He rejected surrender. He insisted that Britain could fight on. In a series of magnificent speeches, appealing to his people's courage and historic greatness, he carried Britain with him. The country rallied to his call, held steady under a concentrated air bombardment, manned the beaches Hitler planned to invade, and took strength in the struggle of "the Few," Britain's fighter pilots, in their eventually victorious battle against Hitler's air power. By the end of the year, by the narrowest of margins, Britain had survived. Hitler's war plan was flawed, never to recover, and the Western world lived to fight another day. Western civilization had found a new hero in crisis, whose example would lead it to eventual triumph.

Most of the 20th century's men of power were the antithesis of Churchill. They ruled by standards the opposite of those to which Churchill held. Churchill believed in liberty, the rule of law, and the rights of the individual. They rejected such standards. Lenin, Stalin, Hitler, Mao Zedong elevated power itself into a value in its own right. Truth, for Lenin, was a bourgeois concept, to be manipulated for revolutionary ends. Stalin despised truth, taking pleasure in forcing revolutionary idealists to deny their beliefs and confess to crimes of which they were not guilty. Hitler went further. He propagated the idea of the big lie that, if large enough, became undeniable. Mao encouraged a Cultural Revolution that vilified his civilization's historic culture and encouraged the ignorant to humiliate the learned and wise. In Bolshevik Russia, Nazi Germany, and Maoist China, civilization itself was threatened with death.

Two titans. Indeed, civilization might well have gone under in the years of the great dictators. That it did not was because of its defenders, men of principle who were also men of courage. Foremost among them were two titans of the Anglo-Saxon world, Franklin Delano Roosevelt and Winston Churchill. That they were Anglo-Saxons was no coincidence. Both derived their moral purpose from the Anglo-Saxon tradition of respect for the rule of law and freedom of the individual. Each could champion that tradition because the sea protected his country from the landbound enemies of liberty. Roosevelt's America was protected by the vast expanse of the Atlantic Ocean, Churchill's England by the English Channel. The channel is a puny bastion by comparison with the Atlantic. It was Churchill's will, buttressed by the power of the Royal Navy and Royal Air Force, that made the channel an insurmountable obstacle to Hitler's attack on liberty.

In terms of moral stature, there is little to choose between the two men. Roosevelt was a great American, consistently true to the principles on which the great republic was founded. Churchill was a great Englishman, committed with an equivalent passion to the Anglo-Saxon idea of liberty that had inspired America's founding fathers. There was this difference. The challenge of dictatorship came later to the United States than to Britain. It also came as an indirect threat. Hitler could never have invaded America. He might, following his military triumph in northwest Europe in the summer of 1940, all too easily have invaded Britain. A weaker man than Churchill might have capitulated to the threat. His refusal to contemplate surrender elevates him to a status unique among champions of freedom. Churchill was the Western world's last great hero.

Who was Churchill? The son of a prominent parliamentarian, Lord Randolph Churchill, and his beautiful American wife, Jennie Jerome, daughter of the proprietor of the *New York Times*, Winston was born into the purple of British society. His grandfather was Duke of Marlborough, a title conferred on his great ancestor, victor of the 18th-century War of the Spanish Succession—Queen

Anne's War to Americans—and the place of his birth, in 1874, was Blenheim Palace, given to the first duke by a grateful nation as a trophy of generalship.

The young Winston wanted for nothing by way of privilege and connections. Unfortunately, he wanted for money. His father, a younger son, was profligate with the wealth he inherited. Jennie was extravagant with her American income. After Lord Randolph's early death, Winston was left to make his way in the world. He yearned to follow his father into politics. Without money, however, a political career was closed to him.

He had, moreover, been a failure at school. Headstrong and wayward, careers with prospects—business, the law—were thus closed to him. He took the only option open to a penniless youth of his class. He joined the Army.

Not without difficulty. Even the comparatively simple Army exams defeated Winston at his first two attempts. He passed into the Royal Military College only on his third try, which would have been his last attempt. His grades qualified him only for the cavalry, which did not look for brains. In 1895, he joined the 4th Hussars. In 1896 he went with his regiment to India.

Soldiering may have been a career of last resort. Winston embraced it enthusiastically. He was deeply conscious of his descent from Queen Anne's great general. He also had a passionate and adventurous nature. While a junior lieutenant he used his leave to visit the fighting in Cuba between Spain and the rebels. In India he used his connections to go as a war correspondent to the Northwest Frontier; in 1898 he again went as a correspondent to the Sudan, which Britain was recapturing from the Mahdi, an inspirational Islamic leader; and in 1899 he went, again as a correspondent, to the Boer War in South Africa.

Along the way, Churchill discovered a talent. He could write. The gift did not come without effort. In his hot Indian barracks he had spent his afternoons reading the English classics Gibbon, Macaulay—and imitating their style. It was an unusual occupation for a young cavalry officer, particularly one who enjoyed the practice of his profession. Churchill was bored by routine but loved

action. He was physically fearless and had no hesitation in killing Queen Victoria's enemies. On the Northwest Frontier, he had clashed at close quarters with rival tribesmen. In the Sudan he had ridden in the British Army's last great cavalry charge. In South Africa he had fought in several battles and made a daring escape from Boer captivity.

But bravery in action did not, he early recognized, win cash returns. Vivid journalism did. By his 25th year he had made himself not only one of the most successful war correspondents of his age but also a bestselling author. His books on Indian tribal warfare, the recapture of the Sudan, and the Boer War sold in thousands, both in Britain and America, and he added to his literary income by well-paid lecturing. In 1900, with the money accumulated by writing, he was independent enough to stand for a parliamentary seat and win.

His literary success had not made him popular. Senior soldiers resented the way he had used family influence to escape from regimental duty. In the political world he was thought bumptious and self-promoting. Churchill did not care. He knew he was brave. Having proved that fact to his own satisfaction, he felt liberated to pursue his fundamental ambition, which was to achieve in politics the position he believed his father had been denied. Churchill adulated his father. The admiration was not returned. Lord Randolph regarded his son as a disappointment and often told him so. Despite the rebuffs suffered at his father's hands, Churchill took up Lord Randolph's pet cause—"Tory Democracy," which sought to align the Conservative Party of property owners with the interests of the working man. At the outset of his parliamentary career, Churchill spoke of "taking up the banner he had found lying on a stricken field," and, as an act of piety, he later wrote his father's biography. But the banner of Tory Democracy found so few followers that Churchill soon despaired of his father's party. In 1904 he left the Conservatives and joined the Liberals. "Crossing the floor" was a foolhardy act for a young parliamentarian. He thereby made himself the enemy of all of his former col-

leagues without any certainty of finding new friends on the other side.

The reformer. Such were his gifts of oratory, however, that Churchill escaped the floor crosser's common lot. In 1905 he was promoted to ministerial rank, only an under secretaryship but at the Colonial Office, whose work interested him. In that office he returned self-government to the Boers, whom he greatly admired. In 1908 he made a real leap, joining the cabinet as president of the Board of Trade. His responsibilities included social policy, and he was able to introduce a series of measures that benefited the working man, including unemployment pay and the creation of a job placement service. By 1910, when he became home secretary (a cabinet-level position similar to minister of the interior), he made a reputation as a radical social reformer, doing in the Liberal Party what he had hoped to achieve as a Tory Democrat.

Had he been kept in the social ministries, he would have built on the reputation. In 1911, however, he was made first lord of the admiralty at the height of Britain's competition with Germany in a costly naval race. Churchill loved the Royal Navy and fought successfully to win it the funds it needed. When the crisis came in July 1914, the fleet greatly outnumbered Germany's and was ready for war. Churchill sought every chance to bring it into action, actually leading a division of sailors turned soldiers in the defense of Antwerp during the German advance into Belgium. Soon afterward came the opportunity to use the Navy's battleships in the sort of decisive campaign he craved to direct. With the war in France stalemated, Churchill successfully argued that a diversionary effort should be made against Turkey, Germany's ally, by seizing the Dardanelles, the sea route from the Mediterranean to the Black Sea.

The campaign proved a failure from the start. The fleet was repulsed in March 1915, when it tried to bombard its way through the Dardanelles. When troops were landed the following month, they were quickly confined to shallow footholds on the Gallipoli Peninsula. By the year's end, casualties had risen to hundreds of thousands, and no progress had been made. In January 1916 Gallipoli was evacuated. By then Churchill was a discredited man. He had resigned political office and rejoined the Army in a junior rank, commanding a battalion in the trenches.

The reactionary. He was the only politician of his stature to serve in the trenches, and the gesture—which put him often in great danger—restored something of his reputation. In 1917 he became minister of munitions, in 1919 war minister. In the war's aftermath his responsibilities involved him in the Allied intervention against Russian Bolsheviks and in the negotiations of Irish independence. In none of his posts could he show himself at his best, however, and his political career in the 1920s took a downward path. In 1924 he fell out with the Liberal leadership over economic policy and returned to the Conservatives. As chancellor of the exchequer in 1925 he helped to precipitate the general strike of 1926 against the resulting financial stringency. He was henceforth regarded as a social reactionary by the working man he had championed when a young Liberal. He soon after acquired a reactionary name in imperial policy also. The freedom he had been eager to grant the Boers he thought inapplicable in India, and over that issue he left the Conservatives' upper ranks. By 1932 he was a lonely man. Hated by the Liberals and the new Labor Party, isolated in his own Conservative Party, he sat on the back benches of the House of Commons, frustrated and increasingly embittered.

He had consolations. His wife, the former Clementine Hozier, was one. She was a woman of strong character whom Churchill had married in 1908. Clemmie never lost faith in him. Their children also brought much pleasure. Writing, above all, filled the gap left by the collapse of his political career. Ever short of money, Churchill worked hard as a journalist to cover the costs of his ample way of life. He also found time out of office to complete his most substantial literary work, a life of his great ancestor, the first Duke of Marlborough.

Even as he brooded on the back benches, however, Churchill was identifying a new cause. He had thus far had four lives, as a soldier, as an author, as a

social reformer, and as a minister at the center of events. He now embarked on a fifth, as a Cassandra of Britain's present danger. Russian Communism had outraged his libertarian beliefs in the early Bolshevik years. In Hitler, whose rise to power began in 1933, he recognized a new enemy of liberty and one whose policies directly menaced his own country. The foreign policy of the government from which he stood aloof was one of appeasement. Anxious to protect Britain's fragile economy in the aftermath of the Great Depression, it preferred to palliate Hitler's demands rather than spend money on the rearmament that would have allowed it to oppose them. Year after year, between 1933 and 1938, Churchill warned of Germany's growing military might. He found support among experts in government who surreptitiously supplied him with the facts to authenticate his warnings. Official government persisted in denying their truth.

War is declared. Then, in 1938, the facts could no longer be denied. Hitler browbeat Czechoslovakia into surrendering much of its territory. He peremptorily incorporated Austria into Greater Germany. Neville Chamberlain's administration accepted that rearmament must now take precedence over sound economic management. France, too, bit the bullet of preparation for war, if war should come. When Hitler's aggressive diplomacy was directed against Poland, Britain and France issued guarantees to protect its integrity. Hitler chose to disbelieve their worth. He deluded himself. Two days after the Wehrmacht invaded Polish territory on Sept. 1, 1939, Britain and France declared hostilities against Germany. The Second World War had begun.

The Second World War was to be the consummation of Churchill's lifelong preparation for heroic leadership. He had proved his abilities as a soldier, as an administrator, as a publicist, as a statesman, as a master of the written and spoken word, and as a philosopher of democracy. In the circumstances of climactic conflict between the principles of good and evil, all the difficulties of his eventful life were to be overlaid by a magnifi-

cent display of command in national crisis.

Hitler almost won the Second World War. By July 1940 he had conquered Poland, Belgium, the Netherlands, and France, beaten their armies, and expelled the British Army from the Continent. He stood poised to conquer Britain also. On his strategic agenda, once Britain was invaded, stood the conquest of the Balkans and then the Soviet Union. He looked forward to being the master of Europe, perhaps of the world.

So certain was Hitler of victory that, during September 1940, he delayed the invasion of Britain in the expectation of Churchill's suing for peace. His expectation was false. There had been a moment, in late May, when Churchill was tempted to negotiate. Once it became clear that the Royal Navy could rescue the Army from Dunkirk he put that temptation behind him. Britain would fight. Its Army might be in ruins, but its Navy was intact, and so was its Air Force. To invade Britain, Hitler must first destroy the Royal Air Force so that he could sink the Royal Navy. Only then could his invasion fleet cross the English Channel. Churchill convinced himself that his Air Force would defeat the Germans in a Battle of Britain. In midsummer 1940 he set out to convince the British people also.

As war leader, Churchill was to display vital qualities: courage, boldness, intellect, cunning, and charisma all founded on deep moral purpose. His courage, and the charisma his courage created, were shown first in the series of great speeches he made to Parliament and the people in the invasion summer of 1940. On May 19, just over a week after Chamberlain resigned, Churchill broadcast to the nation: "I speak to you for the first time as prime minister," he began. He went on to describe how the Allied front was collapsing before the German attack, calling the moment "a solemn hour for the life of our country, of our empire, of our Allies, and, above all, of the cause of freedom." Further details of the crisis followed. He concluded, "We have differed and quarreled in the past, but now one bond unites us all—to wage war until victory is won, and never to surrender ourselves to servitude and shame, whatever the cost and agony may be.... Conquer we must—conquer we shall."

On May 13 he had already told the House of Commons that he could offer only "blood, toil, tears, and sweat" but went on, "You ask: What is our aim? I can answer in one word: Victory. It is victory. Victory at all costs. Victory in spite of all terror, victory, however long and hard the road may be." On June 4 he made to the Commons the same declaration in words that were to become the most famous he ever uttered.

"We shall not flag or fail," he said. "We shall go on to the end.... We shall defend our island, whatever the cost may be. We shall fight on the landing-grounds; we shall fight in the fields and in the streets.... We shall never surrender." The effect was electrifying. A taut and anxious House put aside its fears and rose to cheer him to the rafters. His words, soon transmitted to the people, also electrified them. They caught a mood of popular disbelief that so great a nation should stand in such sudden danger and transformed it into one of dogged defiance. It was from this moment that began what philosopher Isaiah Berlin identified as the imposition of Churchill's "will and imagination on his countrymen" so that they "approached his ideals, and began to see themselves as he saw them."

There had always been a strong element of the populist in Churchill. From his father he had inherited the watchword "Trust the people," and it was because of his democratic ideals that he had, as a young statesman, thrown himself so enthusiastically into legislating for the welfare of the working man. In his later posts it was the welfare of his country as a whole that had come to concern him, and his fellow politicians' laxity of purpose in defending its interests that had dispirited him and alienated him from government. Now, in the supreme crisis of his country's life, he found the voice once more to speak to his people's hearts, to encourage and to inspire. In another great speech to the Commons on June 18, the day of the French capitulation to Hitler, he appealed directly to their sense of greatness. "If we can stand up to Hitler, all Europe may be free, and

the life of the world may move forward into broad, sunlit uplands. But if we fail, then the whole world, including the United States, including all that we have known and cared for, will sink into the abyss of a new Dark Age. Let us therefore brace ourselves to our duties and so bear ourselves that if Britain and its Commonwealth last for a thousand years, many will say, 'This was their finest hour.' "

Britain's year of 1940 would have been the finest hour of any nation. The British, under the threat of invasion and starvation by the U-boats too, heavily bombed in their cities, without allies, without any prospect of salvation at all, wholly exemplified how a finest hour should be lived. They dug the dead and the living from the rubble, manned their beaches, tightened their belts, and watched spellbound the aerobatics overhead of Fighter Command's fighting—and eventually winning—the Battle of Britain. Above all, they lent their ears to Churchill's great oratory. Speech by speech, they were taught by him to shrug off danger, glory in "standing alone," and determine to wait out isolation until the turn of events brought hope of better days.

Churchill's courage, and the charisma he won by it, was matched by his extraordinary boldness in adversity. A lesser man would have husbanded every resource to defend his homeland under the threat of invasion. Under such threat, Churchill nevertheless sought means to strike back. Identifying Hitler's ally, the Italian dictator, Benito Mussolini, as a weak link in the Axis system, Churchill stripped the home islands of troops to reinforce Britain's Army in the Middle East, where, in December 1940, it inflicted a humiliating defeat on the garrison of Italy's overseas empire. The setback caused Hitler to send Field Marshal Erwin Rommel to Mussolini's aid and, when Churchill next detached troops to aid Greece as well, to complicate his plans for the invasion of Russia by launching an offensive into the Balkans. Hitler's Russian timetable never recovered.

Churchill's boldness, based on the weakest of capabilities, thus won huge advantages. His real strategic priority,

throughout the months of "standing alone," had, however, been to bring the United States into the war against Hitler on Britain's side. America was indeed Britain's last best hope. In June 1941, Hitler attacked the Soviet Union but, in a few weeks, Stalin's lot was even worse than Churchill's. German troops stood deep inside Russian territory, and the Red Army was falling to pieces. Churchill had offered Stalin a British alliance, but it was aid from the weak to the weak. Only America could reverse the balance for either.

Churchill's intellect had told him so from the inception of the disaster of 1940. A master of strategic analysis, he saw that Britain's numerical and economic inferiority to Hitler's Fortress Europe could only be offset by massive American assistance. He was also aware that an America at peace, barely recovering from the depths of the Great Depression, could be brought to intervene only step by step. It was there his cunning showed. Half American as he was, and long intimate with his mother's homeland, he recognized the strength of American suspicions of Britain's imperial position. He understood that President Roosevelt's profession of commitment to common democratic ideals and repugnance of European dictatorship was balanced by calculations of national interest and domestic policy. Where a less subtle man might have blustered and demanded, Churchill cajoled and flattered. All his efforts at establishing a "special relationship" were made by indirect appeal, through artistry and symbolism.

Five pledges. At Argentia Bay in August 1941, where Roosevelt arrived on the USS Augusta and Churchill on the HMS Prince of Wales—to be sunk five months later off Malaya by the Japanese—the prime minister extracted from the president five pledges: to give "massive aid" to Russia; to enlarge American convoys to Britain; to strengthen convoy escorts; to send American bombers to join the Royal Air Force; and to patrol the western Atlantic against U-boats. The two statesmen also agreed on a commitment to world democracy later to be known as the Atlantic Charter. It was a heartening encounter, of which Churchill made the most at home. The results still fell short of what Britain needed: a full-blooded American alliance.

That was brought him in the weeks after Dec. 7, 1941, when the Japanese Combined Fleet attacked Pearl Harbor. "So we have won after all," Churchill confided to himself that evening. His hopes ran ahead of events. Pearl Harbor merely opened a Japanese-American war. It was Hitler's megalomaniacal decision on December 11 to declare war on the United States that made America Britain's ally. Even then Churchill had much careful diplomacy to complete before he could be sure that the weight of the American war effort would be concentrated in Europe rather than in the Pacific. In the opening months of 1942 the American people's ire was directed against Japan, not Germany. Even though Roosevelt shared Churchill's judgment that Germany was the more dangerous enemy, America's generals and admirals had to be convinced of the correctness of "Germany first" as a strategy. The admirals never fully accepted it. The generals were brought to do so only by reasoned argument. Then, paradoxically, they had to be restrained. George Marshall, Roosevelt's great chief of staff, and Dwight Eisenhower, future supreme Allied commander and president, pushed in mid-1942 for an attack on Hitler's Fortress Europe at the earliest possible moment. Their impetuosity aroused Churchill's caution. Strong though his gambling instinct was, his memory of the Dardanelles disaster, the greatest setback of his career, remained with him. He was terrified by the prospect of a beaten Allied army falling back into the sea. His relief at Marshall's and Eisenhower's recognition of the prematurity of their plans was evident to all.

His caution would persist throughout 1943. It is from that year that the waning of his powers of leadership dates. He was approaching his 70th year and failing in health. He suffered a mild heart attack and other illnesses. He was confronted by a vote of confidence in the Commons, where sufficient of his old enemies re-mained to reproach him for the military disasters at Singapore and Tobruk. Roosevelt stood by him. "What can we do to help?" the president had asked after the fall of Tobruk in June 1942. Other Americans were less patient. They pressed for action from which Churchill increasingly appeared to shrink. The Russians were even more exigent.

Left out. Stalin took to deriding British halfheartedness, eventually to mocking Churchill to his face. At the three-power Tehran conference of November 1943, Stalin taunted Churchill to declare a final date for the invasion of Europe. Roosevelt lent Churchill no support. It was the beginning of a new, Russo-American special relationship, from which Churchill felt excluded. He was becoming an old man. His glory days were over.

There was to be a recovery. On May 8, 1945, the day of Germany's surrender, he made a speech to the London crowds in which he found his old voice and repaid the people for all he had asked of them in the dark days of 1940. "God bless you all," he trumpeted. "This is your victory. Everyone, man or woman, has done their best. Neither the long years nor the dangers, nor the fierce attacks of the enemy, have in any way weakened the independent resolve of the British nation. God bless you all." He, however, was not to be repaid for his lionlike wartime courage. His reputation as a young social reformer was long forgotten. The reputation given him by his Liberal and Labor opponents as a reactionary was not. In July 1945 the electorate voted against the Conservatives by a landslide. Churchill ceased to be prime minister, not to return to office for six years.

When he did resume the premiership in 1951, his powers had left him and his administration of government was an embarrassment. His resignation, forced by illness in 1955, was greeted with relief even by his closest friends and family. Yet the years since 1945 had not been without achievement. He had writ-ten a great history of the Second World War, which won him the Nobel Prize for Literature. He had become a European statesman, welcomed and honored in all the European countries that, in 1940, he had promised to liberate from Nazi tyranny and lived to see free again. He had become a hero in the United States, his mother's homeland, where he remains today the object of a cult status he does not enjoy in his own country. He had, above all, become the standard-bearer of a new crusade against a new tyranny, that of Stalinism. At Fulton, Mo., on March 5, 1946, he had warned against the descent of an "Iron Curtain" cutting off Eastern and Central Europe from the free world. The development reminded him, he said, of the appeasement years of the '30s, and he urged America and his own country not to become "divided and falter in their duty" lest "catastrophe overwhelm us all."

The Fulton speech, now so celebrated, aroused strong hostility at the time, both in America and Britain. It nevertheless laid the basis for the West's democratic resistance to the spread of communist dictatorship that, culminating in the fall of the Berlin Wall in 1989, at last restored the world to the condition of freedom that had been Churchill's central ideal and for which he had struggled all his life. "I asked," he answered his critics after the Fulton speech, "for fraternal association—free, voluntary. I have no doubt it will come to pass, as surely as the sun will rise tomorrow."

Churchill's sun, at the beginning of the third millennium, has risen and, if it should seem to shine fitfully at times and places, is nevertheless the light of the world. No other citizen of the last century of the second millennium, the worst in history, deserved better to be recognized as a hero to mankind.

Sir John Keegan, defense editor of the Daily Telegraph *and a contributing editor of* U.S. News, *is author of 20 books of military history. He is at work on a biography of Churchill for Viking Press.*

Mutable Destiny

The End of the American Century?

By Donald W. White

In 1918, when the European powers were in the last throes of the Great War, Oswald Spengler published The Decline of the West in which he argued that the continental bastion of world power since 1500 was in decline. At the time, his claim seemed fantastic. A long spell of successful world hegemony had dazzled Europeans into thinking that they were exempt from the possibility of following the paths of the failed civilizations of history. It was true that the war brought an end to the German, Austro-Hungarian, and Ottoman Empires, but the Western European powers of Great Britain, France, the Netherlands, and Belgium emerged from the war with empires of greater land area than ever before—dominating some two-thirds of the world's land surface. Spengler espoused a theory that every culture passes through a life-cycle similar to that of a human being: a culture is born, grows to vigorous youth, becomes complacent in middle age, and ages until it declines and fades away. He conceived a colorful metaphor and was prescient that the European world order and the empires that enforced it were doomed. All these empires, indeed, are no more, as the recent return of Hong Kong by the United Kingdom to China reminds us. Yet Spengler's theory does not enable one to predetermine history or, in particular, to know the fate of the United States. Societies, unlike living organisms, have no biological code, and no historical law guarantees their demise. What individuals and societies believe

and do matters in the continuity of history; each generation, ultimately, creates its own history.

When the United States was still approaching the zenith of its power, in 1914, the publisher Henry Luce wrote his well-known essay, "The American Century," presenting to Americans a shining symbol of national preeminence and helping them take their bearings in a world where American power would loom large. Though rival writers followed with alternative characterizations of the century, suggesting "The Century of the Common Man," "The People's Century," or "The Democratic Century," the American Century received lasting attention. Many presidents, philosophers, historians, and journalists have employed the expansive imagery of the phrase, including Bill Clinton—the last US president of the twentieth century—in his second inaugural address as he described how the United States became the world's mightiest industrial power, won great victories in two world wars, and waged a successful global Cold War.

The notion of the American Century represented the policy implication that the United States should act as a preeminent power—what Luce called the most vital nation in the world—exemplifying its values of capitalist free enterprise, cultural exchange, humanitarian foreign aid, political freedom, equality of opportunity, and self-reliance. This century was, of course, never entirely American—many non-American peo-

ples shared the world during this timespan—but for America, the twentieth century was an era of preeminence like that of Alexander the Great's Hellenistic Empire of the fourth century BC, the Roman Empire of the first century, the Chinese and Mongol Empire of the thirteenth century, or the British Empire of the nineteenth century. The American Century idea resembled Rome's Pax Romana or Britain's "White Man's Burden," and it expressed similar expectations and hubris. In the twilight of the closing century, we may take a broad view of the United States as a world power, examining the nation's remarkable rise to preeminence, its recent relative decline, and its prospects on the eve of a new century.

THE DAWN OF DOMINANCE

Historians debate exactly when the United States became a world power, but a common idealized explanation is that it was almost exactly one hundred years ago when, on a May morning in 1898, Admiral George Dewey's warships steamed triumphantly into Manila Bay to defeat the Spanish fleet, winning a decisive victory in the ten-week Spanish-American War. While any rise to geopolitical preeminence is a process rather than an event, the victory prompted President William McKinley to pronounce the United States a world power, but he had other evidence as well. Already in

1880, Americans produced 28.6 percent of the world's industrial output, and the United States had surpassed Britain as the world's largest industrial nation. The United States was also developing a favorable balance of trade by exporting manufactures, along with agricultural produce and natural resources. It began to build a first-class steel and steam navy. Additionally, the United States joined European nations in amassing a far-flung empire, from Puerto Rico to the Philippines to the Panama Canal Zone. As the historian Frederick Jackson Turner observed, the closing of the American frontier was turning Americans away from their preoccupation with the North American continent and driving them to conquer new lands abroad.

By the outbreak of the First World War, the United States had truly become a Great Power. The country presented formidable economic competition to Europe, accounting for over 35 percent of the world's industrial production and suddenly overtaking Great Britain as the center of global finance. By the end of the war, the United States had built up a navy that rivaled the size of the British Navy, the world's largest. Material power, however, did not imply the internationalism espoused by President Woodrow Wilson. Rejecting lasting political involvement in world affairs, Americans as a whole shunned participation in the League of Nations and sought to return to so-called normalcy.

After the close of the Second World War, the United States came to dominate the world scene as a superpower. Although its supremacy was challenged by the Soviet Union, the United States was nevertheless an entity of enormous, unprecedented power and reach. It was a unified, continental nation, so rich in natural resources that it produced almost two-thirds of the world's oil and controlled the world petroleum market. The United States had a large population, expanded by immigrants and their descendants, that ascribed to an ethic of hard work and persistence, and no nation could match America in the educational level and technical skill of its work force. The United States led the world in scientific and technological innovation in everything from transistors, air conditioning, and televisions to atomic energy. Furthermore, the US economy produced an estimated 50 percent of world GDP: one country was producing about as much as the rest of the world combined, a level of relative economic production unprecedented in the modern world since Britain had led the Industrial Revolution. Americans possessed 70 percent of the world's automobiles, 83 percent of its aircraft, 50 percent of its telephones, and 45 percent of its radios. The American standard of living was the highest in the world, twice as high as that of developed nations such as Great Britain when measured in per capita income. In addition, the US military in 1945 consisted of a navy larger than the rest of the world's navies combined, the largest air force, the best-equipped army, and a nuclear capability of unmatched destructive capacity.

But beyond this powerful combination of material strengths, the United States enjoyed a unique consensus among its people. Americans emerged from the biggest war in world history in triumph over fascism and in leadership of the Allies. American leaders talked about the nation's power and the responsibility it conferred on the people because their failure to accept that responsibility after the earlier world war had been disastrous. The people in general believed in their nation, supporting its leaders and their international policies. This unity encompassed both the left and the right, it was largely bipartisan, and it was defined by intellectuals in many fields. This national consensus effected a great transformation in outlook—that the United States should no longer be isolated from the world, but deeply involved in it.

This new perspective continued during the expansion of a world role that was one of the extraordinary occurrences in history. America's world role became manifested in a post-war alliance system that enveloped the globe from the Western Hemisphere to Western Europe to the Middle East and on to Southeast Asia, Australia, New Zealand, and Japan. At its height in the 1950s and early 1960s, the alliance system incorporated distant and scattered old empires, newly independent states, and peoples of different religions, races, and ethnicities in diverse regions from tropical to arctic. The alliances by no means constituted a traditional empire, but within their frontiers, the United States was the great center of trade, the world's banker nation, and the provider of the key international currency, the dollar. The American people shared their fortune by distributing charitable aid abroad in unprecedented quantities through programs such as the Marshall Plan and the Peace Corps. Food, clothing, movies, machinery, and science made the American name known everywhere. US military power was pledged to defend allied states, which eventually required foreign strategic outposts, naval ports and fleets, air bases, and missile launch cites.

THE ONSET OF DOUBT

The focus of this massive international activity was confronting expansive communism, an effort which embroiled the United States in costly Cold War crises from Berlin to South Vietnam. In 1975, Daniel Bell of Harvard University declared that the "American Century lasted scarcely 30 years.... It foundered on the shoals of Vietnam." He was equally harsh in his criticism of failed US policy: "There is no longer a Manifest Destiny or mission. We have not been immune to the corruption of power. We have not been the exception." Was Bell premature in his declaration of the end of the American Century?

The US failure to resolve the Vietnam War challenged the notion of US supremacy and prompted many to question whether the nation could sustain its superpower status. The United States employed massive force in Vietnam—dropping more tons of bombs on Vietnam than it did in every theater of the Second World War—but North Vietnam and the Viet Cong survived and triumphed. In the end, the United States lost a war for the first time in its history, and it lost the war as a superpower to a small peasant country, one President Lyndon Johnson had characterized as a fourth-rate power.

But America's time of troubles did not end with the final US evacuation from Vietnam in the spring of 1975. Before the end of the war, the United States had developed a deep trade deficit. After chalking up annual trade surpluses beginning in the 1890s and unprecedented surpluses after the Second World War, US trade was in the red in 1971. Since then, the country has sustained yearly trade deficits. This deficit was in the kinds of goods that Americans once exported to the world: not only in natural resources like oil and gas, but in machinery, automobiles, telecommunications, clothes, and iron and steel goods. The United States also began to buy more than it sold from most regions of the world, including Canada and Mexico, Germany and Western Europe, Japan, China and East Asia, and eventually Russia, Eastern Europe, and the former Soviet republics.

The trade deficit weakened confidence in the dollar, which was devalued against other currencies in 1971 and headed into a long-term decline against the German mark and the Japanese yen. The trade and currency crises preceded the United States becoming a debtor nation. The United States had been a creditor since early in the century, and, after the Second World War, it developed capital resources far beyond those of any other country, but by 1985, the United States was a debtor again, and it remains the biggest debtor nation in history. US overseas investment dwindled and foreign investment increased at home, with corporations, real estate, financial institutions, and government securities being swallowed up by wealthy foreign buyers. Symbolizing this new indebtedness, Japanese companies purchased notable American landmarks in the 1980s such as Columbia Studios in Hollywood, CBS Records, and New York's Rockefeller Center.

It is significant that, after rising over the course of American history, the US share of world output began to fall steadily. By the 1970s, it had fallen to 30 percent of world GDP, and by the 1990s, to 20 percent or less—less than half of what it had been at its peak and less than it was at the time of the Spanish-American War, when the United States first emerged as a world power.

America's decline from preeminent military and economic power after the Vietnam War corresponded to a breakup of the old consensus regarding its international role. Adherents to the old social consensus held to patriotic notions of American power and the glory of global exertion, while New Left protesters and the counterculture vehemently rejected the assumptions of the American Century as immoral and exploitative. Politically, the nation changed form having a patriotic trust in government, its leaders, and its foreign policies to a skepticism which was exasperated by President Johnson's deception during the buildup in Vietnam and by the Watergate scandal that brought down the Nixon White House. Economically, the nation evolved away from an orientation of production toward one of consumption, both in maintaining consumer lifestyles and in waging or preparing for war. Socially, the national popular consensus surrendered to divisions among groups of diverse ideologies, ethnicities, and parties who, in seeking to overcome past injustices of segregation or oppression, came to focus on what separated them rather than on what united them.

DECLINE OR STABILITY

Disagreement over whether America will rise to greater heights of power or is in decline reflects the difficulty of comprehending these biggest of historical questions. Perhaps, as some historians suggest, it is impossible to perceive an event as large as the rise or decline of a preeminent power while it is happening. It is easier to gauge relatively short-term spans of political or business cycles to determine how a society is faring because the conditions of prosperity and employment are more immediate to individual circumstances.

Debate over American decline was rekindled by the historian Paul Kennedy of Yale University, who published *The Rise and Fall of the Great Powers* in 1987. Kennedy believed that America's role as a world power was declining and would continue to decline. His book engaged in prophecy or future history, projecting the future of the great powers to the year 2000 based on their past since 1500. Joseph Nye of Harvard University, however, in his 1990 book *Bound to Lead*, argued that America, with plenty of resources to assure its global leadership, was still by far the dominant world power and that this dominance should continue to grow.

In evaluating these arguments, one should bear in mind that relative decline is different from absolute decline. The case for absolute decline is a hard one to prove: the United States remains a continental nation, blessed with resources, and the home of new immigrants like those who have invigorated the country throughout its history. The United States remains the world's greatest military power, it still has the world's largest economy, and it represents a prime example of democratic government. Finally, America did win the Cold War.

Since the 1970s, the US share of world economic activity has declined significantly, have stagnated for a generation, and American expectations have diminished.

But since the 1970s, the US share of world economic activity has declined significantly, have stagnated for a generation, and American expectations have diminished. Perhaps it is not meaningful to compare America today with the soaring heights it once achieved after the Second World War: its position then was extraordinary, in part a function of the ruin of the other powers. Though Americans may look back on the immediate postwar years with some emotion or pride, we might be reluctant to accept those times as a benchmark against which we can measure our present condition. But to fail to recognize the significance of those times would be like ignoring the *Pax Romana* or Britain's Victorian Age because they were once extraordinary times.

Another argument can be made that the United States has revived in power in the 1990s, economically, militarily, and culturally. Although no one would argue that America is as powerful relative to the rest of the world as it was in the 1950s, it still appears to be a leader in the new international economy and remains a vital example of democracy. In addition, though Japan and Germany seemed invulnerable ten years ago, and the United States seemed an indebted and unproductive giant, Japan and Germany have recently experienced recession or sluggish growth with high unemployment.

Japan remains the world's biggest creditor and most successful trader, while the United States continues to suffer towering trade deficits and remains the world's greatest debtor. As a debtor, the United States finds it difficult to afford the accouterments of global leadership—foreign aid, prodigious embassy staffs, information agency installations, and military presence.

The reserves of US military strength that had vastly increased throughout the cold war remain available for use in the 1990s, but the United States has experienced constraints in maintaining an enormous defense establishment to support troops in foreign bases, a global navy and air force, and an extensive nuclear arsenal. Although the United States has abandoned bases from the Philippines to Germany and has cut military spending substantially, the partial dismantling of this military, particularly the nuclear arsenal, is a positive and natural development after the Cold War.

In the exchange of culture, the United States still dominates with the popularity of American habits, clothing, and fads—Marlboro cigarettes, McDonald's burgers, T-shirts and NFL jerseys, Hollywood movies, and television (not the sets, which the United States has practically stopped manufacturing, but the prime-time programming, from the classic I Love Lucy to Baywatch).

So why the sense of loss? Perhaps America's current sense of drift is a product not of American failure but of success: America overcame devastating economic downturns and went on to defeat both fascism and communism. America stands, it follows, on the eve of the twenty-first century with no great crusades left.

But complacency can mask social divisions over real international issues and over America's world view. There is a lost consensus over America's role in the world. What does America stand for in the post-Cold War world? For what does it seek to be known? By its status as sole remaining military superpower? By its industry and trade? By its art, music, and popular culture? The end of the Cold War opens great opportunities for peace, growth, and general welfare, but it has not ended war or eliminated international conflict over issues of economic competition, poverty, the environment, immigration, and nationality. America's future prospects depend on a new consensus, but a consensus for what?

BACK IN THE SADDLE

When Henry Luce concluded his essay declaring that the twentieth century was American, he was careful to write that this was only a first American Century, leaving open the expectation for more. Is American preeminence at an end?

Great empires of history *do* decline and *have* declined, as Spengler showed, but no law of history allows accurate predictions of when or how these declines take place: at the end of the American Revolution in 1783, many Britons bemoaned the condition of their empire, which seemed to have entered a period of decline after its triumph in the Seven Years War in 1763. In Parliament, Edmund Burke declared after the British defeat at Yorktown that Britain had lost "her empire on the ocean, her boasted, grand, and substantial superiority which made the world bend before her!" Along with the loss of trade and of "happiness at home," the war had reduced Britain from "the most flourishing empire in the world to one of the most unenviable powers on the face of the globe." Lord George Germanine, Lord North's Minister of War, maintained that "from the instant when American independence should be acknowledged, the British empire was ruined." How wrong these doomsayers were. Britain went on to expand its industry and its trade into every region and to spread the English language and system of law, becoming the global superpower of the nineteenth century—until its eventual decline in the twentieth century.

Every one of the hegemonic empires of the past has eventually declined or fallen into oblivion. The Egyptian, Persian, Greek, Roman, Chinese, and British Empires have vanished. That thought is daunting, but decline is not the immutable law of history that Spengler thought it was. The United States has not ceased to be a world power. It has declined in power from a position of preeminence and is not about to take up again the role of a preeminent power with its costs and burdens. It simply cannot afford a role of this global scope as a debtor nation, although this condition can be reversed. There does not now appear to be any call for a Russian, Chinese, German, or Japanese Century, and the United States could emerge in the leadership vacuum.

The United States can remain a leader by rebuilding within. It should seek to reemphasize the health of its democracy and the productive capability of its society as the primary objectives of nationhood.

The United States has within its power the ability to harness resources once lavished on consumption and military preparedness for productive purposes, and, to the extent that the United States has carried out this reconversion, it has slowed its relative decline. Within a thriving society, founded on equal opportunity for all people, the challenges of poverty, unemployment, welfare costs, and even affirmative action can best be addressed. Martin Luther King's 1968 book, *Where Do We Go From Here?* posed two alternative paths for human history in its subtitle: "Chaos or Community?" Political equality has been achieved, he wrote; economic opportunity for all has not. He did not foresee the economic downturn that followed the prosperity of the postwar years, but he looked for an economy that would bring benefits to majority and minority alike, for one can not truly prosper without the other. The question he asked and the vision he presented are just as relevant today.

Yet rebuilding within is not enough. The United States has to be engaged fully in the world as it becomes increasingly interdependent. More dependent on foreign technology, materials, and capital than ever before, the United States has to reconcile its own values and interests with those of developed nations as well as rising powers like China, India, Indonesia, and Brazil. The United States certainly can no longer afford to choose between internationalism and isolationism, for the latter is no longer a realistic option. The United States, rather, must determine what kind of internationalism it will practice. One compelling option would be for the United States to use international organizations such as the United Nations as essential instruments of policy and to throw its weight behind them. Therein lie the mechanisms for peacemaking and for sharing the burdens the United States had once borne alone in its preeminence. The example of a leading power putting its full support behind cosmopolitan internationalism might have enormous, though not immediately apparent, benefits for the United States and other countries. Despite the argument that working within a multilateral framework would display weakness, the cultivation of meaningful international cooperation may leave the United States in a stronger position in terms of its material strength, internal cohesion, and international legitimacy.

Historians who point to a recent American decline are correct, but prophecies of America's impending demise as a leading force in the world remain untested and unproved.

Those who point to a recent American decline are correct, but prophecies of America's impending demise as a leading force in the world remain untested and unproved. The United States has declined from the position of preeminent power it had reached in the middle years of the twentieth century. Future historians may well record that this extraordinary era of American preeminence was when the United States had its greatest influence on the world's peoples, nations, and history. The American Century—the era of American preeminence—may be ending, but not the history of America in the world, which remains for Americans and their international partners to make. The goals and ideals that will guide the United States through the next century of its history may be the nation's founding principles themselves. Frederick Jackson Turner once wrote, "Other nations have been rich and prosperous and powerful. But the United States has believed that it had an original contribution to make to the history of society by the production of a self-determining, self-restrained, intelligent democracy." The power of that moral example of America may be the most enduring meaning of America in the world.

DONALD W. WHITE teaches history at NYU and is author of *The American Century: The Rise and Decline of the US as a World Power*

UNIT 5

Conclusion: The New Millennium and the Human Perspective

Unit Selections

32. **A Brief History of Relativity**, Stephen Hawking
33. **Malaria Kills One Child Every 30 Seconds**, Donovan Webster
34. **The Big Meltdown**, Eugene Linden
35. **Jungles of the Mind: The Invention of the 'Tropical Rain Forest'**, Philip Stott
36. **Why Don't They Like Us?** Stanley Hoffmann
37. **Folly & Failure in the Balkans**, Tom Gallagher
38. **The Poor and the Rich**, *The Economist*
39. **Reform for Russia: Forging a New Domestic Policy**, Boris Nemtsov
40. **'The Barbarians Have Not Come'**, Peter Waldron

Key Points to Consider

• Discuss the contributions of Albert Einstein, who was chosen *Time*'s "Man of the Twentieth Century."

• Why is the warming of the Arctic region important for the future? Why are the views about rain forests not always accurate?

• What are some of the problems between the West and Islam? What are some of the solutions?

• Although there have been many problems, what are some of the signs of progress in civilization?

 **Links: www.dushkin.com/online/**
These sites are annotated in the World Wide Web pages.

Center for Middle Eastern Students/University of Texas/
http://menic.utexas.edu/menic/religion.html

Europa: European Union
http://europa.eu.int/

InterAction
http://www.interaction.pair.com/advocacy/

The North-South Institute
http://www.nsi-ins.ca/ensi/index.html

Organization for Economic Co-operation and Development/FDI Statistics
http://www.oecd.org/daf/statistics.htm

U.S. Agency for International Development
http://www.info.usaid.gov/

Virtual Seminar in Global Political Economy/Global Cities & Social Movements
http://csf.colorado.edu/gpe/gpe95b/resources.html

World Bank
http://www.worldbank.org/

World Wide Web Virtual Library: International Affairs Resources
http://www.etown.edu/vl/

Looking at the future, from the vantage point of the recent Millennium celebrations, the West contemplates the twenty-first century. This time the prospects for disillusionment seem slight, for there is little optimism about the current or future prospects of Western civilization. Indeed, with the development and spread of nuclear weapons in the non-Western world, we are forced to consider the possibility that our civilization might destroy itself in an instant, as evidenced by the terrifying events of September 11, 2002. Of course, like our ancestors a century ago, we can point to continued progress, particularly in science and technology.

Our ambivalence about technology is paralleled by our growing recognition that we can no longer depend upon an unlimited upward spiral of economic growth, as seen in the recent erratic swings of the stock markets around the world. In the course of the last century other visions have eluded us, including the hope that we could create a just and equal society through drastic and rapid social reorganization. Most of the great revolutionary promises of the age have not been met. Nor do we see that elimination of repressive social and moral taboos will produce an era of freedom and self-realization. By now most areas of human conduct have been demystified (and trivialized); confusion rather than liberation seems to be the immediate result. Finally, modernism, that great artistic and intellectual movement of the century's early years, has exhausted itself. For decades avant-garde experimentation had challenged established styles and structures in art, music, architecture, and literature, creating an ever-changing "tradition of the new," to borrow Harold Rosenberg's phrase. Avant-gardism presumed the existence of cultural norms to be tested, but now we find ourselves in the so-called postmodern condition, "a kind of unregulated marketplace of realities, in which all manner of belief systems are offered for public consumption." Old beliefs and new are in a continuous process of redefinition.

These developments have contributed to an uncommon degree of self-consciousness in our culture. Seldom in any era have people been so apprehensive about the future of civilization and the prospects for humanity. The articles in this concluding section convey some current optimistic or pessimistic concerns. "A Brief History of Relativity" looks forward to progress as do the articles, "Reform for Russia," and "The Barbarians Have Not Come," while "Malaria Kills One Child Every 30 Seconds," and "The Big Meltdown" describe a bleak future, whether from the Last Judgment, disease, or the environment. "Why Don't They Like Us?" and "Folly & Failure in the Balkans" focus on widespread tribalization, a trend that pits culture against culture, religion against religion, and ethnic group against ethnic group. The unequal distribution of the world's wealth can also sow seeds of conflict as seen in "The Poor and the Rich," which attempts to explain why some nations are richer than others.

A Brief History Of Relativity

What is it? How does it work? Why does it change everything?
An easy primer by the world's most famous living physicist

By Stephen Hawking

Toward the end of the 19th century scientists believed they were close to a complete description of the universe. They imagined that space was filled everywhere by a continuous medium called the ether. Light rays and radio signals were waves in this ether just as sound is pressure waves in air. All that was needed to complete the theory was careful measurements of the elastic properties of the ether; once they had those nailed down, everything else would fall into place.

Soon, however, discrepancies with the idea of an all-pervading ether began to appear. You would expect light to travel at a fixed speed through the ether. So if you were traveling in the same direction as the light, you would expect that its speed would appear to be lower, and if you were traveling in the opposite direction to the light, that its speed would appear to be higher. Yet a series of experiments failed to find any evidence for differences in speed due to motion through the ether.

The most careful and accurate of these experiments was carried out by Albert Michelson and Edward Morley at the Case Institute in Cleveland, Ohio, in 1887. They compared the speed of light in two beams at right angles to each other. As the earth rotates on its axis and orbits the sun, they reasoned, it will move through the ether, and the speed of light in these two beams should diverge. But Michelson and Morley found no daily or yearly differences between the two beams of light. It was as if light always traveled at the same speed relative to you, no matter how you were moving.

The Irish physicist George FitzGerald and the Dutch physicist Hendrik Lorentz were the first to suggest that bodies moving through the ether would contract and that clocks would slow. This shrinking and slowing would be such that everyone would measure the same speed for light no matter how they were moving with respect to the ether, which FitzGerald and Lorentz regarded as a real substance.

But it was a young clerk named Albert Einstein, working in the Swiss Patent Office in Bern, who cut through the ether and solved the speed-of-light problem once and for all. In June 1905 he wrote one of three papers that would establish him as one of the world's leading scientists—and in the process start two conceptual revolutions that changed our understanding of time, space and reality.

In that 1905 paper, Einstein pointed out that because you could not detect whether or not you were moving through the ether, the whole notion of an ether was redundant. Instead, Einstein started from the postulate that the laws of science should appear the same to all freely moving observers. In particular, observers should all measure the same speed for light, no matter how they were moving.

*Space and time,
he discovered,
were as pliable as
rubber bands*

This required abandoning the idea that there is a universal quantity called time that all clocks measure. Instead, everyone would have his own personal time. The clocks of two people would agree if they were at rest with respect to each other but not if they were moving. This has been confirmed by a number of experiments, including one in which an extremely accurate timepiece was flown around the world and then compared with one that had stayed in place. If you wanted to live longer, you could keep flying to the east so the speed of the plane added to the earth's rotation. However, the tiny fraction of a second you gained would be more than offset by eating airline meals.

Einstein's postulate that the laws of nature should appear the same to all freely moving observers was the foundation of the theory of relativity, so called because it implies that only relative motion is important. Its beauty and simplicity were convincing to many scientists and philosophers. But there remained a lot of opposition. Einstein had overthrown two of the Absolutes (with a capital A) of 19th century science: Absolute Rest as represented by the ether, and Absolute or Universal Time that all clocks would measure. Did this imply, people asked, that there were no absolute moral standards, that everything was relative?

This unease continued through the 1920s and '30s. When Einstein was awarded the Nobel Prize in 1921, the citation was for important—but by Einstein's standards comparatively minor—work also carried out in 1905. There was no mention of relativity, which was considered too controversial. I still get two or three letters a week telling me Einstein was wrong. Nevertheless, the theory of relativity is now completely accepted by the scientific community, and its predictions have been verified in countless applications.

A very important consequence of relativity is the relation between mass and energy. Einstein's postulate that the speed of light should appear the same to everyone implied that nothing could be moving faster than light. What happens is that as energy is used to accelerate a particle or a spaceship, the object's mass increases, making it harder to accelerate any more. To accelerate the particle to the speed of light is impossible because it would take an infinite amount of energy. The equivalence of mass and energy is summed up in Einstein's famous equation $E=mc^2$, probably the only physics equation to have recognition on the street.

Among the consequences of this law is that if the nucleus of a uranium atom fissions (splits) into two nuclei with slightly less total mass, a tremendous amount of energy is released. In 1939, with World War II looming, a group of scientists who realized the implications of this persuaded Einstein to overcome his pacifist scruples and write a letter to President Roosevelt urging the U.S. to start a program of nuclear research. This led to the Manhattan Project and the atom bomb that exploded over Hiroshima in 1945. Some people blame the atom bomb on Einstein because he discovered the relation between mass and energy. But that's like blaming Newton for the gravity that causes airplanes to crash. Einstein took no part in the Manhattan Project and was horrified by the explosion.

Although the theory of relativity fit well with the laws that govern electricity and magnetism, it wasn't compatible with Newton's law of gravity. This law said that if you changed the distribution of matter in one region of space, the change in the gravitational field would be felt instantaneously everywhere else in the universe. Not only would this mean you could send signals faster than light (something that was forbidden by relativity), but it also required the Absolute or Universal Time that relativity had abolished in favor of personal or relativistic time.

Gravity, he said, could change the curvature of space-time

Einstein was aware of this difficulty in 1907, while he was still at the patent office in Bern, but didn't begin to think seriously about the problem until he was at the German University in Prague in 1911. He realized that there is a close relationship between acceleration and a gravitational field. Someone in a closed box cannot tell whether he is sitting at rest in the earth's gravitational field or being accelerated by a rocket in free space. (This being before the age of *Star Trek*, Einstein thought of people in elevators rather than spaceships. But you cannot accelerate or fall freely very far in an elevator before disaster strikes.)

If the earth were flat, one could equally well say that the apple fell on Newton's head because of gravity or that Newton's head hit the apple because he and the surface of the earth were accelerating upward. This equivalence between acceleration and gravity didn't seem to work for a round earth, however; people on the other side of the world would have to be accelerating in the opposite direction but staying at a constant distance from us.

On his return to Zurich in 1912 Einstein had a brainstorm. He realized that the equivalence of gravity and acceleration could work if there was some give-and-take in the geometry of reality. What if space-time—an entity Einstein invented to incorporate the three familiar dimensions of space with a fourth dimension, time—was curved, and not flat, as had been assumed? His idea was that mass and energy would warp space-time in some manner yet to be determined. Objects like apples or planets would try to move in straight lines through space-time, but their paths would appear to be bent by a gravitational field because space-time is curved.

With the help of his friend Marcel Grossmann, Einstein studied the theory of curved spaces and surfaces that had been developed by Bernhard Riemann as a piece of abstract mathematics, without any thought that it would be relevant to the real world. In 1913, Einstein and Grossmann wrote a paper in which they put forward the idea that what we think of as gravitational forces are just an expression of the fact that space-time is curved. However, because of a mistake by Einstein (who was quite human and fallible), they weren't able to find the equations that related the curvature of space-time to the mass and energy in it.

Einstein continued to work on the problem in Berlin, undisturbed by domestic matters and largely unaffected by the war, until he finally found the right equations, in November 1915. Einstein had discussed his ideas with the mathematician David Hilbert during a visit to the University of Gottingen in the summer of 1915, and Hilbert independently found the same equations a few days before Einstein. Nevertheless, as Hilbert admitted, the credit for the new theory belonged to Einstein. It was his idea to relate gravity to the warping of space-time. It is a tribute to the civilized state of Germany in this period that such scien-

special relativity

Einstein's 1905 theory claims that light moves through a vacuum at a constant speed relative to any observer, no matter what the observer's motion—with bizarre consequences

relativity and time

A moving clock runs slower than a stationary one from the perspective of a stationary observer

1 A man riding a moving train is timing a light beam that travels from ceiling to floor and back again. From his point of view, the light moves straight down and straight up.

Light

Distance light pulse travels

The observer riding the train thinks the light bulb and mirror are standing still

Mirror

2 From trackside, Einstein sees man, bulb and mirror moving sideways: the light traces a diagonal path. From Einstein's viewpoint, the light goes farther. But since lightspeed is always the same, the event must take more time by his clock.

Distance light pulse travels, as seen by Einstein, is farther

The observer watching the train thinks the light bulb and mirror are moving

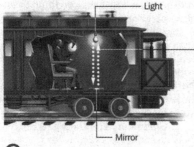

More time has elapsed

relativity and length

A moving object appears to shrink in the direction of motion, as seen by a stationary observer

1 The man now observes a light beam that travels the length of the train car. Knowing the speed of light and the travel time of the light beam, he can calculate the length of the train.

Distance light pulse travels, as seen by observer on train

The observer on the train sees only the motion of the light beam

2 Einstein is not moving, so the rear of the train is moving forward from his point of view to meet the beam of light: for him, the beam travels a shorter distance. Because the speed of light is always the same, he will calculate the train's length as shorter—even after he allows for his faster-ticking clock. As the train approaches the speed of light, its length shrinks to nearly zero.

Distance light pulse travels, as seen by Einstein

Someone watching from outside sees the light beam moving but with the motion of the train added

SOURCES: *WORLD BOOK ENCYCLOPEDIA: EINSTEIN FOR BEGINNERS*

---

tific discussions and exchanges could go on undisturbed even in wartime. What a contrast to 20 years later!

The new theory of curved space-time was called general relativity to distinguish it from the original theory without gravity, which was now known as special relativity. It was confirmed in spectacular fashion in 1919, when a British expedition to West Africa observed a slight shift in the position of stars near the sun during an eclipse. Their light, as Einstein had predicted, was bent as it passed the sun. Here was direct evidence that space and time are warped, the

greatest change in our perception of the arena in which we live since Euclid wrote his *Elements* about 300 B.C.

Einstein's general theory of relativity transformed space and time from a passive background in which events take place to active participants in the dynamics of the cosmos. This led to a great problem that is still at the forefront of physics at the end of the 20th century. The universe is full of matter, and matter warps space-time so that bodies fall together. Einstein found that his equations didn't have a solution that described a universe that was unchanging in time.

Rather than give up a static and everlasting universe, which he and most other people believed in at that time, he fudged the equations by adding a term called the cosmological constant, which warped space-time the other way so that bodies move apart. The repulsive effect of the cosmological constant would balance the attractive effect of matter and allow for a universe that lasts for all time.

This turned out to be one of the great missed opportunities of theoretical physics. If Einstein had stuck with his original equations, he could have predicted that the universe must be either expand-

general relativity

In 1915 Einstein broadened his special theory of relativity to include gravity. In general relativity, light always takes the shortest possible route from one point to another

the equivalence of gravity and acceleration

Without external clues, it's impossible to tell if you're being pulled downward by gravity or accelerating upward. Your legs will feel the same pressure; a ball will fall precisely the same way

The realization that gravity and acceleration are equivalent was a key insight that eventually allowed Einstein to construct his theory of general relativity.

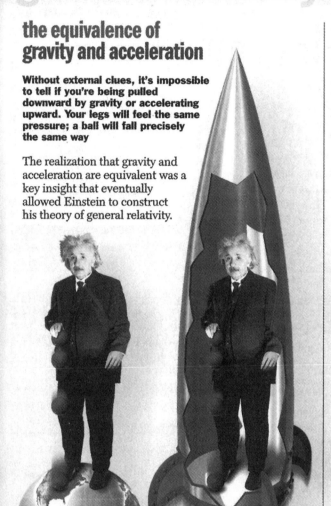

relativity and gravity

According to relativity, gravity is not a force; it's a warping of space-time (which is an amalgam of time and space) that happens in the presence of mass. The warping is analogous to the bending of a rubber sheet when a weight is placed on it

1 When starlight passes near a massive body, such as the sun, the shortest route is a curved line that follows the curvature of space-time. Thus, the starlight appears to be coming from a different point than its actual origin. The observation of this effect in 1919 convinced physicists that Einstein's strange theory was right.

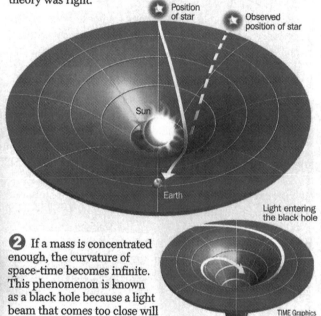

Position of star

Observed position of star

Sun

Earth

Light entering the black hole

2 If a mass is concentrated enough, the curvature of space-time becomes infinite. This phenomenon is known as a black hole because a light beam that comes too close will never escape.

TIME Graphics by Ed Gabel and Joe Lertola

ing or contracting. As it was, the possibility of a time-dependent universe wasn't taken seriously until observations were made in the 1920s with the 100-in. telescope on Mount Wilson. These revealed that the farther other galaxies are from us, the faster they are moving away. In other words, the universe is expanding and the distance between any two galaxies is steadily increasing with time. Einstein later called the cosmological constant the greatest mistake of his life.

General relativity completely changed the discussion of the origin and fate of the universe. A static universe could have existed forever or could have been created in its present form at some time in the past. On the other hand, if galaxies are moving apart today, they must have been closer together in the past. About 15 billion years ago, they would all have been on top of one another and their density would have been infinite. According to the general theory, this Big Bang was the beginning of the universe and of time itself. So maybe Einstein deserves to be the person of a longer period than just the past 100 years.

General relativity also predicts that time comes to a stop inside black holes, regions of space-time that are so warped that light cannot escape them. But both the beginning and the end of time are places where the equations of general relativity fall apart. Thus the theory cannot predict what should emerge from the Big Bang. Some see this as an indication of God's freedom to start the universe off any way God wanted. Others (myself included) feel that the beginning of the universe should be governed by the same laws that hold at all other times. We have made some progress toward this goal, but we don't yet have a complete understanding of the origin of the universe.

The reason general relativity broke down at the Big Bang was that it was not compatible with quantum theory, the other great conceptual revolution of the early 20th century. The first step toward quantum theory came in 1900, when Max Planck, working in Berlin, discovered that the radiation from a body that was glowing red hot could be explained if light came only in packets of a certain size, called quanta. It was as if radiation were packaged like sugar; you cannot buy an arbitrary amount of loose sugar in a supermarket but can only buy it in 1-lb. bags. In one of his groundbreaking papers written in 1905, when he was still at the patent office, Einstein showed that Planck's quantum hypothesis could explain what is called the photoelectric effect, the way certain metals give off electrons when light falls on them. This is the basis of modern light detectors and television cameras, and it was for this work that Einstein was awarded the 1921 Nobel Prize in Physics.

Einstein continued to work on the quantum idea into the 1920s but was deeply disturbed by the work of Werner Heisenberg in Copenhagen, Paul Dirac in Cambridge and Erwin Schrödinger in Zurich, who developed a new picture of reality called quantum mechanics. No longer did tiny particles have a definite position and speed. On the contrary, the more accurately you determined the particle's position, the less accurately you could determine its speed, and vice versa.

Einstein was horrified by this random, unpredictable element in the basic laws and never fully accepted quantum mechanics. His feelings were expressed in his famous God-does-not-play-dice dictum. Most other scientists, however, accepted the validity of the new quantum laws because they showed excellent agreement with observations and because they seemed to explain a whole range of previously unaccounted-for phenomena. They are the basis of modern developments in chemistry, molecular biology and electronics and the foundation of the technology that has transformed the world in the past half-century.

When the Nazis came to power in Germany in 1933, Einstein left the country and renounced his German citizenship. He spent the last 22 years of his life at the Institute for Advanced Study in Princeton, N.J. The Nazis launched a campaign against "Jewish science" and the many German scientists who were Jews (their exodus is part of the reason Germany was not able to build an atom bomb). Einstein and relativity were principal targets for this campaign. When told of publication of the book *One Hundred Authors Against Einstein*, he replied, Why 100? If I were wrong, one would have been enough.

After World War II, he urged the Allies to set up a world government to control the atom bomb. He was offered the presidency of the new state of Israel in 1952 but turned it down. "Politics is for the moment," he once wrote, "while… an equation is for eternity." The equations of general relativity are his best epitaph and memorial.

They should last as long as the universe. The world has changed far more in the past 100 years than in any other century in history. The reason is not political or economic but technological—technologies that flowed directly from advances in basic science. Clearly, no scientist better represents those advances than Albert Einstein: TIME's Person of the Century.

Professor Hawking, author of A Brief History of Time, *occupies the Cambridge mathematics chair once held by Isaac Newton.*

Malaria kills one child every 30 seconds

A new pandemic imperils half the world. Scientists think they know
what has to be done, but the disease continues to outsmart them

By Donovan Webster

The problem arrives at sunset. Every evening, as twilight blankets the tropical world, the air grows thick with disease on the wing. It's happening around me right now as I sit on the porch of a shack in Armopa, a tiny outpost deep in the Indonesian jungle.

The sun slipped below the horizon 30 minutes ago, and in the gathering dark, danger rises from Armopa's swampy earth like an income tide. From daylight hiding places in the humid shadows, the mosquitoes have come out, zeroing in on any flesh they can find. They begin biting my bare feet, then move up my ankles. Within minutes, dozens of them are on the back of my neck. Some, no doubt, are carrying one of the malaria-causing species of *Plasmodium*, single-celled parasites that are transported by mosquito from human to human, leaving deadly infections in their wake.

According to the World Health Organization, malaria infects up to 500 million people each year.

I lift my feet from the porch's planked floor, resting them on a rail above the malarial flood. Beyond the porch, Armopa's stilt huts are illuminated by flickering cooking fires. Armopa is a region in Irian Jaya, Indonesia's state on the island of New Guinea. Much of the area is made up of new villages—grids of dirt paths, irrigation canals and garden plots—that exist because of a government "transmigration" policy. Mile-square clearings have been bulldozed into the jungle and populated by the landless and unemployed of Indonesia's other, more crowded islands.

To my left, seated beneath a bare lightbulb and sipping a lukewarm soda, is J. Kevin Baird, a 42-year-old commander in the U.S. Navy. An athletic man dressed in khaki shorts and a T-shirt, Baird has a thatch of wavy dark hair and a precisely trimmed mustache. He, too, has lifted his feet above the biting tide. "Here they come," he says, slapping a mosquito on his leg.

Baird has a Ph.D. in parasitology and is the malaria program director at NAMRU-2, the Naval Medical Research Unit in Jakarta. As director, he is charged with helping the Navy develop new says to fight malaria—which, according to the World Health Organization (WHO), infects up to 500 million people a year and kills as many as 2.7 million, including at least one child every 30 seconds. Baird believes it is only a matter of time before scientists develop a vaccine that stops malaria in its tracks. For the present, he and NAMRU-2 are overseeing field trials for new anti-malaria drugs. As malaria has, in recent years, become resurgent around the world, effective treatments are more necessary than ever. And malaria-heavy Armopa, with its fresh crop of farmers creating new lives from this spongy ground, is the perfect place to test new remedies.

NAMRU-2 has been operating out of Jakarta for 30 years, and in Irian Jaya for nearly 20. In cooperation with the Indonesian government, the research unit tests new drugs and diagnostic methods, and studies human immune response and the natural history of malaria—while treating many residents in the course of their studies. In addition to their work in Armopa, NAMRU-2 has researchers in the central highlands of Irian

Jaya, studying possible causes of the malarial epidemics that arose there in the wake of El Niño.

A patient and persistent man, Baird has gotten malaria seven times in 12 years. "It's an incredibly resourceful parasite," he says, taking another swig of soda. "It's devious, and in an environment like this, it's everywhere." He slaps another mosquito. Navy studies in these jungles, Baird says, show that even if a person employs bed nets and window screens, he or she will still receive roughly one infectious bite a week. "Of course," he adds, "there are parts of Africa where you get one infectious bite every day."

In the lightbulb's glow, I examine a mosquito on my wrist. The bug focuses on my sunburned hide, dips its head and drives its needle-nose into my flesh. If I had not started taking the antimalarial drug doxycycline before I left the States, this could be my "infectious event." Or maybe another of the bites I'll get tonight will be the one. After all, I'm a prime target. I've been here five days.

Until recently, many in the United States and other Western countries may have remained blithely unaware of the persistence of malaria as a global killer. For the most part, in Northern, industrialized countries, the disease was essentially eradicated by the middle of this century. But recent cases appearing in New York, California, Texas, Michigan and New Jersey (not to mention that other mosquito-borne killer, West Nile virus) have raised interest and concern. Malaria researchers worldwide hope it will also raise awareness of the global impact of the disease, and of a drug-resistant malaria pandemic that imperils nearly 40 percent of the world's population. It's an epidemic that, in recent years, has had as high a global casualty rate as AIDS. Until the recent surge in AIDS deaths in Africa, in fact, the malaria casualty rate was significantly higher than that of AIDS.

The cause of the malaria crisis is threefold. First, malaria quickly develops resistance to any new drug it encounters. "Resistance is a common outcome with all antimicrobial drugs," says Dr. David Brandling-Bennett, deputy director of the Pan American Health Organization. "As soon as you administer any antimicrobial heavily, the organism targeted will show resistance. At that moment, you have to either administer the drug at levels that completely eradicate the organism, or drug-resistant strains of the organism will remain and predominate. It's survival of the fittest."

The second factor in the resurgence of malaria is a recent rise in global development. In many emerging nations, tropical frontiers along what has been called the "Malaria Belt" have undergone increased logging, mining, irrigated farming and road- and town-building. As more and more jungles and swamps are disrupted, the pools of water left behind become perfect environments for incubating anopheline mosquitoes, the carriers of malaria. And as more people flock to these areas, creating new hosts for the disease as well as new victims, malaria rates soar. Often, as is the case in much of the malaria-ridden world, there are inadequate public health services in place.

The third factor in the worldwide malaria epidemic is the lack of safe, effective and affordable insecticides. DDT—a pesticide with both a long history of effective use in mosquito con-

trol and a devastating effect on food chains—has been the center of an international debate, as the United Nations moves toward passing a global ban that may or may not include an exemption for malaria control. Many scientists point out that when restricted to limited, indoor use, DDT is not particularly dangerous to the environment. Others are concerned, however, that DDT meant for malaria control could easily be diverted to agriculture. And so the debate continues. In the meantime, an annual household spraying with the next-most-effective class of pesticides, pyrethroids, costs at least nine times as much as with DDT—and many poor nations, facing outside pressures to avoid DDT, are now going without insecticide treatment altogether.

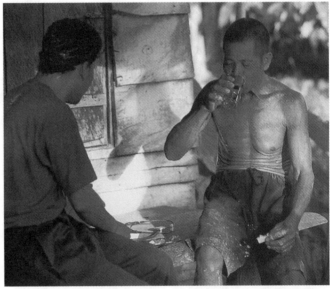

PHOTOGRAPH BY MICHAEL FREEMAN

The U.S. Navy has conducted research on malaria in Irian Jaya for nearly 20 years. In the Irianese outpost of Armopa (above), a subject in a drug study takes his pill.

As far as Kevin Baird is concerned, while dousing houses with insecticide is effective, defeating malaria involves much more. "Developing new drugs and controlling mosquito breeding areas are equally important," he says.

It's 7:30 in the morning, and Baird wants me to see his drug-testing program. But first, as we walk along one of Armopa's swampy gardens, he points to the ground, where a shoeless human footprint has been pressed into the dark mud. "One good rain and that footprint fills with water," he says. "Then, in no time, that stagnant water is incubating mosquito larvae." In little more than a week, the larvae become adults. After the females fly off in search of "blood meals" that help their own eggs develop, some will pick up plasmodia from malaria-infected human hosts. Subsequently, they will transport those microbes and infect countless other people.

I'm now introduced to Totok, a 20-year-old Indonesian health-care worker. He and Dr. Judy Ling—a physician overseeing the clinical aspects of the study—are going to show me how a NAMRU-2 study is done. As we stroll up the central street of one Armopa village, beneath an already hot sun, Totok checks his satchel full of plastic bags. Some of the bags contain one of the study's test drugs—called Malarone and made by the international pharmaceutical giant Glaxo Wellcome—while others contain identical-looking sugar tablets packaged the same way. Subjects get either the drug, which is supposed to destroy the malaria parasite before it bloom in the blood-stream, or the placebo, which does nothing. (Elsewhere, other subjects receive the drug primaquine, which is already used in the United States and other countries as a malaria treatment, but is being tested here for use as a preventive.)

PHOTOGRAPHY BY MICHAEL FREEMAN

In the central highlands of Irian Jaya, where traditional homes are built on steep hills, malaria rates are usually low.

A study like this involves 300 to 400 subjects, with the identities of who gets drugs and who receives the placebo known only to off-site test regulators. Precautions are taken to make sure no subject is pregnant, has malaria, or suffers from any other serious illness or systemic problem.

Totok turns off the main road up a dirt track called Street #8. The path is lined with wooden stilt huts with shuttered windows and corrugated steel roofs. Fronting each house is a small garden: lemongrass, peppers, flowers and spices. Behind some of the houses are small rice paddies, diked to keep the water moving.

Dr. Ling tells me that roughly 3,000 people—about 700 families—live in this village. As I turn to look across the area, tidy houses sit in every direction. Beyond the streets and houses, a thick tapestry of rain forest rises. Occasionally, prehistoric-looking birds called hornbills cross the sky, their feathers making a rustily mechanical *creeek* at each wingbeat.

We follow Totok up the road. Every day, he and a platoon of healthcare workers visit every subject in the study: they inquire about each subject's health, administer a biscuit (to help digestion) and a pill, witness each subject literally swallow the pill, then get each to sign a document stating they have taken the pill at a prescribed time.

Totok stops at one of the stilt huts on Street #8. It's the home of Sujatin, a transmigrant from the island of Java. A petite woman with mocha-colored skin and dark hair, she's dressed in shorts and a Dallas Cowboys T-shirt. She invites us into her small front room and tells Totok she feels well.

"I enjoy being in the study," Sujatin tells me as she takes her pill with a sip of water. She signs the documents. "It keeps me from having malaria. My husband works as a logger in the jungles. He's gone for weeks at a time—so he can't be in the study, and he gets malaria. It is a terrible thing to have. Sweating. Very bad headaches. High, high fever. You vomit. You are so weak… when malaria comes every few days, you feel like you want to die."

Totok makes note of the time on Sujatin's document, and we move on, walking along the streets, dispensing Malarone or its placebo for the next 90 minutes. As we go, Dr. Ling says that six cases of malaria have been presented so far during the study. She believes all six will turn out to have been people who were given the placebo, though not until the study results are tabulated will anyone know for certain. And, of course, once someone in the study gets malaria, they are placed on proven antimalarial drugs.

For Dr. Ling and Totok, daily rounds like this are the rule during the six months it takes to complete this part of the study. When this test is finished, the NAMRU-2 team will start over, testing yet another antimalarial drug.

After seeing perhaps 20 test subjects, we return to Armopa's medical unit, our clothing soaked in sweat. Totok's satchel is empty; his paperwork complete. He drops the paperwork off with a pair of lab clerks for incorporation in the study's database. In another office, Kevin Baird is combing through data files, searching for typos, trying to stay cool in the morning's spiking heat.

"These projects have their rivetingly boring moments," Baird says, wiping sweat from his brow. "But you have to stay on top of things. If something were to happen, it could throw the entire study into question." If any of the study's protocols were shown to have been breached, the blame would fall on Baird alone. He'd never be allowed to run a drug trial again. "That fast"—Baird snaps his fingers—"my career in this field would be over."

Baird and the rest of the Armopa team have far more to contend with than test protocols. Much of Indonesia is in turmoil these days. In Irian Jaya, a rebel group is agitating for independence from the central government. The government has lately begun phasing out the transmigration program, which most native Irianese have long opposed, but the phaseout has less to do with Irianese opinion than simple lack of funds. And even if transmigration had continued, the villages in Armopa are now fully occupied. With no more new migration to Armopa, Baird and NAMRU-2 are finding other study sites in which to continue their work, including recently settled palm-oil plantations near the city of Jayapura.

Baird and his colleagues are hardly the first to try to understand malaria, a disease that has been afflicting mankind since long before the dawn of recorded history. The early Egyptians are thought to have suffered from it, and Hippocrates, the ancient Greek physician, wrote of its fevers some 2,400 years ago. While various cultures have developed treatments for the disease's symptoms over the centuries—including the bark of the South American cinchona tree, which contains quinine—it wasn't until the end of the 19th century that scientists discovered that malaria was caused by the *Plasmodium* parasite and transmitted by mosquitoes.

In 1955 WHO declared a global war on malaria, launching an eradication campaign that included free DDT spraying of houses in afflicted areas and the development of new drugs. The program succeeded in some areas but produced little change in the overall number of malaria cases. It was officially declared a failure in 1976. Two years ago WHO decided to try again, this time in concert with UNICEF, the United Nations Development Programme, and the World Bank. The aim is to cut malaria deaths in half worldwide within the next decade by raising awareness, providing antimalarial treatments, from drugs to insecticide-treated netting, and helping to identify hotbeds of malaria incubation.

Through WHO's Roll Back Malaria program, and the efforts of other groups and consortiums around the world, interest in malaria research has grown considerably. Some scientists are encouraged by recent progress on a genetically modified, malaria-resistant mosquito. Others are pinning their hopes for a silver bullet on the development of a malaria vaccine.

Dr. Stephen Hoffman, Kevin Baird's boss at the Naval Medical Research Center in Silver Spring, Maryland, is working on a DNA-based vaccine that will attack the parasite at an early stage, before symptoms emerge. In those individuals for whom the vaccine is not 100 percent effective, it will also limit the surviving parasites' reproduction so that the infection is less severe.

While hopeful that his and other vaccines will be ready in 7 to 15 years, Dr. Hoffman explains the difficulty in developing them. "First of all, plasmodia have about 6,000 genes in their DNA, compared to viruses like small-pox or measles, which have less than 30. The organism has built-in redundancy, so it can more readily escape attack. Second, if you take, say, a 6-year-old child from sub-Saharan Africa who has malaria, he may have as many as five different strains existing at once within him. And you have to have a vaccine that attacks all five. Lastly, the parasite matures and circulates in different forms inside the human body, hiding inside existing cells until it's ready

to attack, So you have to create multiple vaccines, in effect, that are each stage-specific, and then combine them."

The species of *Plasmodium* that cause malaria begin as sporozoites, or malaria seeds, that can live in the salivary glands of female anopheline mosquitoes, of which there are at least 60 species worldwide. As an infected female anopheline takes human blood, sporozoites migrate into the human's bloodstream. The malarial seeds quickly seek out the liver, where they burrow inside cells. Though they can remain dormant for years, sporozoites usually multiply furiously over a period of less than four weeks, ripening into merozoites. When a liver cell fills to capacity, it ruptures, spilling thousands of merozoites into the bloodstream, where they penetrate red blood cells and multiply once again. In 48 to 72 hours, the red cells burst, releasing yet another bloom of merozoites in search of still more host cells. This is when the unfortunate victim begins to suffer from headaches, muscle and joint pain, sweat-drenching fevers and teeth-rattling chills.

Today, there are dozens of species of *Plasmodium* around the world, four of which infect humans. The most widespread of the four is called *Plasmodium vivax;* the deadliest is called *P. falciparum*. Together, these two account for nearly all of the world's malaria.

Vivax gets its name from the lively way its merozoites vibrate inside red blood cells when scientists examine them live under microscopes. As the heartiest malarial strain, it also thrives in nontropical environments and has managed to withstand barrages of antimalarial drugs.

Still, of the nearly three million people who die of malaria every year, relatively few have vivax. The vast majority have falciparum, which thrives in hot, moist environments, such as sub-Saharan Africa and Southeast Asia, and is named for the scimitar shape the parasite gives the red blood cells it invades. Beyond causing the anemia all malaria sufferers endure, falciparum also occludes blood flow through capillaries in vital organs, which often leads to death.

To prevent malaria, two basic families of drugs are now in use. The first, called "suppressives," eradicates malaria in the bloodstream. This group—which includes quinine, mefloquine and chloroquine, as well as such antibiotics as doxycycline and tetracycline—must be taken before and after visiting malarial zones to make sure all liver-stage cells have hatched and been destroyed.

A second family of drugs, called "causals," destroys the liver-stage merozoites before the parasite reaches the bloodstream. Travelers using one of these need take it only during periods of exposure to potentially infected mosquitoes. Currently just one causal drug, primaquine, can be prescribed in the United States, and it is licensed for use as a treatment, not as a preventive. Malarone, one of the drugs being evaluated by Baird and NAMRU-2 in Armopa during my visit, has since been licensed in the United States as a suppressive, and has also shown causal activity against falciparum malaria.

The availability of more effective new drugs is one important weapon in the war on malaria. Others are the old standbys—spraying houses with DDT, which many experts believe must be allowed as an exception to any ban; the use of insecticide-treated bed nets; and the systematic elimination of the standing water that mosquitoes need to breed. In most places, these weapons must be used in concert, while in others one may be enough to turn the tide.

"In 1969, Timika had 600 people," Wignall tells me. "Today, there are more than 75,000."

Which is where Dr. Steve Wignall comes in. Wignall retired as a Navy captain in 1996 and went to work as an adviser on public health for P. T. Freeport Indonesia, the Indonesian arm of Freeport-McMoRan Copper & Gold of New Orleans. P. T. Freeport Indonesia mines the world's third-largest copper reserves and largest gold reserves, both in a mountain that, at almost 14,000 feet, forms part of the "spine" of Irian Jaya. Although the firm has been accused by watchdog groups of committing environmental and human rights abuses, its malaria control program is clearly a case of enlightened self-interest, benefiting everyone involved.

At the elevation of the mines, mosquitoes and malaria are nonexistent. But in the mid-1980s, expansion of the mine operations led Freeport to relocate many of its offices and employees' homes to the town of Timika, 50 miles south of the mine and 13,000 feet lower in elevation.

Wignall, a tall, avuncular Southerner wearing blue jeans and a button-down shirt, relates all this after picking me up at Timika's airport. "In 1969, Timika had 600 people," he says. "Today, there are more than 75,000. We estimate at least 80 new people a month arrive looking for work."

With around 30 feet of rain annually and nonstop construction in order to house the human inflow, Timika should rate as one of the world's malarial hothouses. But thanks to a $3 million-a-year public-health program paid for and administered by Freeport, it doesn't. "Back in the 1980s, malaria was present in 85 percent of the people in the area," Wignall says, steering along well-tended drainage canals. "Today, we usually have a rate of 7 or 8 percent. We think most who are infected are new transmigrants—people not yet integrated into our public-health program. Still, our goal is to get the incidence of malaria here down to zero."

Wignall drops me off at P. T. Freeport Indonesia's malaria-control offices, where an Australian biologist named Peter Ebsworth is waiting to show me around. Gray-bearded and friendly, Ebsworth says Freeport's goal is to defeat malaria by controlling its source: mosquitoes. "Freeport has set a high standard for keeping the huge amounts of rain that fall here moving. That way, anopheline mosquitoes don't have an opportunity to breed."

Everywhere Ebsworth takes me, the earth has been gently graded toward the drainage ditches, concrete-lined trenches and catch basins that spirit the water toward the sea, 28 miles farther to the south. Freeport's executive suburb of Kuala Kencana is a marvel of tiered gardens and tilted earth. Its encircling forests have been tiered, as well. As Ebsworth is proud to point out, there is no mosquito breeding in Kuala Kencana—or anywhere nearby. "We've made sure that people understand the danger of standing water outdoors," he says. "As a result, any mosquitoes we find here have almost always flown in from the outside."

Freeport actually pays workers to spend their nights attempting to catch mosquitoes. It also has its own mosquito abatement teams: dozens of men who spend days crossing the perhaps 400-square-mile area of Timika, Kuala Kencana and the outlying transmigration towns, where they sample ditches, jungle creeks and roadside channels with dip nets in search of mosquito larvae.

At the end of my three-day visit to Timika, Steve Wignall drives me back to the airport. "The money Freeport is spending here is what's keeping malaria at bay. But push is going to come to shove," he says, referring to the population growth. "We're not the government. Eventually, hard choices about who gets public-health and mosquito-control programs and who doesn't will have to be made."

According to Harvard economist Jeffrey Sachs, malaria costs impoverished countries billions of dollars in lost wages, business and tourism annually—more than $20 billion in sub-Saharan Africa alone. Aid of at least $1 billion per year, he suggests, might make all the difference—in reducing suffering and saving economies—if applied to research, prevention and treatment. Says Kevin Baird: "WHO estimates that more than $56 billion a year is spent on health research—but less than 10 percent is directed toward malaria and the other diseases that affect more than 80 percent of the world's population. Most of the money—which comes primarily from rich nations—goes toward problems that directly affect the citizens of those nations. And that includes everything from cancer research to developing Viagra and baldness treatments."

That might change if those of use who dwell in affluence had to confront, firsthand, the suffering malaria causes elsewhere. It will be a long time before I forget the man I saw in a Jayapura hospital's malaria ward. Gaunt, pallid and unconscious, he had been suffering for months from an attack of falciparum. The crimson liquid in the catheter bag beside his bed was the patient's urine, stained by hemoglobin released from exploded red blood cells. "His water has gone black," a physician told me. "Not a good sign."

I stared at the patient, imagining a bloom of microscopic malarial parasites spreading through his bloodstream, searching out fresh red blood cells to invade. In a war that spans the ages, his body was the latest battleground.

Author Donovan Webster and photographer Michael Freeman are both frequent contributors to SMITHSONIAN.

The Big Meltdown

As the temperature rises in the Arctic, it sends a chill around the planet

By Eugene Linden, Churchill

Here's a tip for anyone trying to figure out when and whether global warming might arrive and what changes it will bring: hop a plane to the Arctic and look down. You'll see that climatic changes are already reworking the far-north landscape. In the past two decades, average annual temperatures have climbed as much as 7°F in Alaska, Siberia and parts of Canada. Sea ice is 40% thinner and covers 6% less area than in 1980. Permafrost—permanently frozen subsoil—is proving less permanent. And even polar tourists are returning with less than chilling tales, one of which was heard around the world last week.

Back from a cruise to the North Pole aboard the Russian icebreaker *Yamal*, tourists told the New York *Times* that a mile-wide lake had opened up at 90° north, with gulls fluttering overhead, and they had the pictures to prove it. The newspaper declared that such an opening in polar ice was possibly a first in 50 million years, though that claim was dismissed by scientists who nonetheless see other serious signs of Arctic warming (*see box*).

On a less cosmic level, Mike Macri, who runs nature tours in Churchill, on the western shores of Hudson Bay in Canada's Manitoba province, has had to rewrite his brochures. The old ones encouraged tourists to arrive at Churchill in mid-June to see beluga whales, which migrate up the mouth of the Churchill River following the spring ice breakup.

The new brochure encourages visitors to arrive as early as May.

The ice also forms as much as two weeks later in the autumn than it used to in Hudson Bay, creating a bewildering situation for some of the local wildlife. Polar bears that ordinarily emerge from their summer dens and walk north up Cape Churchill before proceeding directly onto the ice now arrive at their customary departure point and find open water. Unable to move forward, the bears turn left and continue walking right into town, arriving emaciated and hungry. To reduce unscheduled encounters between townspeople and the carnivores, natural-resource officer Wade Roberts and his deputies tranquilize the bears with a dart gun, temporarily house them in a concrete-and-steel bear "jail" and move them 10 miles north. In years with a late freeze—most years since the late 1970s—the number of bears captured in or near town sometimes doubles, to more than 100.

Humans are feeling the heat too. In Alaska, melting permafrost (occasionally hastened by construction) has produced "roller coaster" roads, power lines tilted at crazy angles and houses sinking up to their window sashes as the ground liquefies. In parts of the wilderness, the signal is more clear: wetlands, ponds and grasslands have replaced forests, and moose have moved in as caribou have moved out. On the Mackenzie River delta in Canada's Northwest Territories, Arctic-savvy Inuit inhabitants have watched with dismay as warming ground

melted the traditional freezers they cut into the permafrost for food storage. Permafrost provides stiffening for the coastline in much of the north; where thawing has occurred, wave action has caused severe erosion. Some coastal Inuit villages are virtually marooned as the ground crumbles all around them. And as the ice retreats farther from the coast, Inuit hunters are finding that prey like walrus has moved out of reach of their boats.

These isolated dramas play out far from the mid-latitudes of the planet, where the vast majority of people live, but they could soon have serious implications for all of us. What is really at risk in the Arctic is part of the thermostat of the earth itself. The difference in temperatures between the tropics and the poles drives the global climate system. The excess heat that collects in the tropics is dissipated at the poles, about half of it through what has been nicknamed the ocean conveyor, a vast deepwater current equivalent to 100 Amazon Rivers. Much of the rest of the heat is conveyed as energy in the storms that move north from the tropics. If the poles continue to warm faster than the tropics, the vigor of this planetary circulatory system may diminish, radically altering prevailing winds, ocean currents and rainfall patterns. One consequence: grain production in the breadbaskets of the U.S. and Canada could be in jeopardy if rainfall becomes less steady and predictable. Already, severe and unpredictable storms across the northern hemisphere may be a sign that the global system is changing.

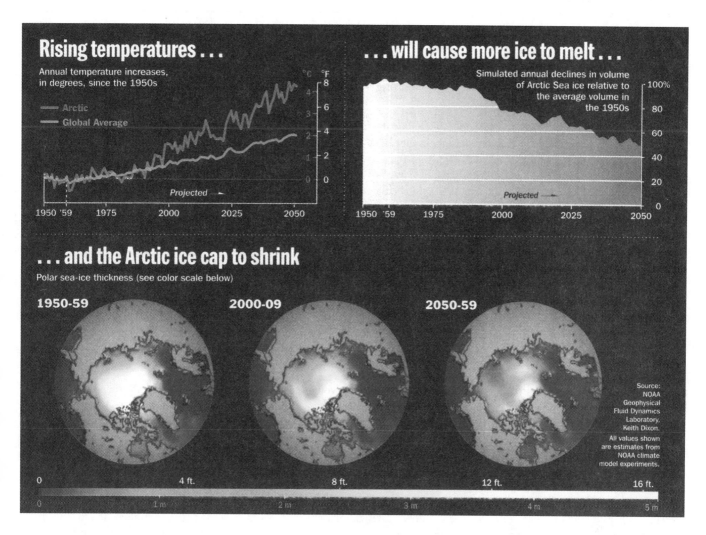

Rising temperatures . . .

Annual temperature increases,
in degrees, since the 1950s

— Arctic
— Global Average

Projected →

1950 '59   1975   2000   2025   2050

. . . will cause more ice to melt . . .

Simulated annual declines in volume
of Arctic Sea ice relative to
the average volume in
the 1950s

100%
80
60
40
20
0

Projected →

1950 '59   1975   2000   2025   2050

. . . and the Arctic ice cap to shrink

Polar sea-ice thickness (see color scale below)

1950-59   2000-09   2050-59

Source:
NOAA
Geophysical
Fluid Dynamics
Laboratory,
Keith Dixon.

All values shown
are estimates from
NOAA climate
model experiments.

0   4 ft.   8 ft.   12 ft.   16 ft.

0   1 m   2 m   3 m   4 m   5 m

Even greater climate change could be on the way. Growing numbers of scientists fear that the warming trend will so disrupt ocean circulation patterns that the Gulf Stream, the current that warms large parts of the northern hemisphere, could temporarily shut down. If that happens, global warming would, ironically, produce global cooling—and bring on a deep freeze.

Such a calamity could be self-inflicted. Many scientists believe that the current warming is related to the increased burning of fossil fuels, such as gasoline and coal, which overloads the atmosphere with carbon dioxide and other greenhouse gases. That's why 160 countries signed the 1997 Kyoto Protocol, which requires industrial nations to reduce their greenhouse emissions to an average of 5.2% below 1990 levels between the years 2008 and 2012. But even that weak treaty remains controversial, and governments have made little

progress toward implementing the pact. The U.S. Senate hasn't even considered ratifying it. Opponents seize on the possibility that the warming we're seeing may not be our doing but just part of the natural variation in climate.

Partly in response to this deadlock, NASA climatologist James Hansen last week unveiled an alternative strategy. Instead of pursuing the politically unpopular goal of drastically reducing consumption of fossil fuels, he suggests going after other greenhouse gases, such as methane, which he thinks has accounted for as much warming as carbon dioxide in the past century, even though it is present in the atmosphere in much smaller quantities.

W ITHOUT ACTION, MAJOR CHANGES appear inevitable. Should surface water temperatures in the high Arctic rise just a few degrees, the sea ice could disappear

entirely, but even a partial melting could devastate the northern hemisphere's climate. A combination of melting ice, increased precipitation and runoff from melting glaciers on land could leave a layer of buoyant freshwater floating atop the denser salt water, at a point in the North Atlantic where water ordinarily cools and sinks. The lighter freshwater wouldn't sink, interrupting the vertical circulation at a crucial point in the cycling of heat through the ocean—as if you're grabbing a conveyor belt and slowing it down.

S O HOW WOULD THAT PRODUCE cooling? Ordinarily the conveyor is propelled by the pull created by masses of water sinking in the North Atlantic. When this pull diminishes, the movement of warm water north in the Gulf Stream could slow or stall, driving down

POLAR NOTES

The Hole at 90° N

For the tourists and their scientific guides aboard the Russian icebreaker *Yamal*, it was an astonishing sight. Just as they approached the North Pole, they spotted a mile-wide hole in the ice. "It was totally unexpected," Harvard oceanographer James McCarthy, one of the scientists on board, later told the New York *Times*. Paleontologist Malcolm McKenna, of New York City's American Museum of Natural History, said, "I don't know if anybody in history ever got to 90° north to be greeted by water, not ice." Even more surprising, they saw ivory gulls soaring blithely overhead. The *Times* itself commented that the last time anyone could be certain the pole was awash in water was more than 50 million years ago.

Telling evidence of global warming, right? Not necessarily, climatologists quickly pointed out. Thanks to wind and waves, without any help at all from rising temperatures, fissures often form in the polar ice, especially in the warmer summer months.

"In fact," says Claire Parkinson of NASA's Goddard Space FlightCenter, whose satellites have long kept an eye on the polar ice cap, "it happens many, many times every year." Sometimes the openings can be hundreds of miles long, explains the Jet Propulsion Lab's Ronald Kwok, another Arctic observer.

Even so, the scientists did not dispute the many other signs of warming in the Arctic. It's just that one opening in the ice, even at the pole itself, doesn't mean a polar meltdown. But what about those ivory gulls? Aren't they pretty rare birds in a locale known more for fauna like polar bears? Not really, explains the Audubon Society's John Bianchi, who points out that the tough gulls are regular inhabitants of the Arctic Ocean. "If you've got open water at the pole or anywhere else up there," he says, "you're going to find these birds, because that's where they eat."

—By Frederic Golden. Reported by Sora Song/New York

temperatures in Europe and North America, and possibly elsewhere.

It has happened before. Roughly 12,000 years ago, at the end of the last Ice Age, a natural warming sent freshwater from melting glaciers flowing out of the St. Lawrence River into the North Atlantic, all but shutting down the Gulf Stream and plunging Europe into a 1,300-year deep freeze. The more that becomes known about this period, named the Younger Dryas (after a tundra plant), the more scientists fear that the rapid melting of sea ice could cause the same catastrophe again. Only next time, writes geophysicist Penn State's Richard Alley in a forthcoming book, *Two-Mile Time Machine*, the effects would be much greater, "dropping northern temperatures and spreading droughts far larger than the changes that have affected humans through recorded history." Would this be "the end of humanity?" he asks rhetorically. "No," he replies. "An uncomfortable time for humanity? Very."

A sudden chill would shorten growing seasons, and the resulting changes in precipitation could be even more damaging. Colder air is dryer air, and Alley points out that during the Younger Dryas, the monsoon weakened in Asia and the Sahara expanded. Harvey Weiss, a Yale archaeologist who has studied the role of climate in human history, notes that it's not changes in temperature that bring down civilizations but changes in precipitation.

Protecting civilization is the goal of the Kyoto Protocol, but the treaty allows 12 more years for implementation, on the assumption that climate change will be gradual. That assumption looks shaky. Studies of deep underground ice layers in Greenland, which reveal a record of climate changes over hundreds of thousands of years, show that major climate shifts, like the onset of the Younger Dryas, can come very abruptly—within a few decades.

It probably won't be possible to avoid some climate change this century, up or down—and there's still a chance that the earth's systems will compensate for any that occurs—but the possibility that climate turns rapidly and unpredictably should spur us into doing whatever is practical to turn from fossil fuels—fast. If done right it can be a boon. Energy conservation usually increases profits. In developing nations it's often cheaper to use alternatives like wind power to electrify new areas.

At the entrance to the Churchill Northern Studies Centre, a base for investigations of regional climate change, a rusting rocket is a mute reminder of the complex's earlier life as part of defenses against Soviet nuclear attack. That threat never materialized, and now, belatedly, scientists venture from the base to study a threat that has materialized but against which no adequate defense has been mounted. Despite the danger that climate change poses, the resources currently devoted to studying this problem—and combatting it—are inconsequential compared with the trillions spent during the cold war. Twenty years from now, we may wonder how we could have miscalculated which threat represented the greater peril.

Jungles of the Mind

The invention of the 'tropical rain forest'

***Philip Stott** unravels the emergence of myths about the tropical rain forests.*

ONE OF THE EARLIEST European accounts of the tropical world is found in the famous letter, dated February 1493, of Christopher Columbus (1451–1506) describing his first voyage of 1492–93. This was published in Spanish in Barcelona in April 1493 by Pedro Posa, with a Latin version appearing a little later. His account helped to establish a number of European myths about the tropics that still flourish today.

Columbus offered an image of great fecundity and diversity, yet did not *see* 'vegetation' as such, but rather 'a great variety of trees stretching up to the stars'. Using a modern colloquialism, we might say he couldn't see the forest for the trees. Columbus described the islands of the Caribbean as intensely 'fertile' and 'distinguished by various qualities', the palm trees numerous and far excelling 'ours in height and beauty, just as all the other trees, herbs, and fruit do'. His focus was on *individual* plants and organisms, and on their extraordinary variety of forms and functions.

Columbus's letter was a classic example of what James Krasner has called (1992) 'a disordered and fragmented visual field'. The notion of tropical 'vege-

tation', which is a prerequisite for the idea of the 'tropical rain forest', today an emblematic icon of the 'environment in danger', had not yet been invented in the European mindset. Europeans would not, in fact, see the tropics 'organismically' (holistically) for another three centuries.

Columbus's 'fractured seeing' is exemplified in the sections of his 'Letter' dealing with Hispana (now Hispaniola) and the island of Juana. In these, he described the plants he encountered as 'different' or exotic—and in this we might say he was adopting an 'orientalist' view of the exotic 'Other', in the sense espoused by Edward Said, whose *Orientalism* (1979) comprises a complex discourse on power, domination and hegemony with regard to the relationships between the West (Occident) and the Rest (Orient). Yet Columbus balanced this with careful analogies with the home country:

> trees... the leaves of which I believe are never shed, for I saw them as green and flourishing as they are usually in Spain in the month of May.

Indeed, until the late-nineteenth century, European observers of the tropics saw little but a riot of individuality, or alternatively a gloomy area of highly generalised 'forest'. However, one word, 'jungle', did enter the English language in the mid-eighteenth century. This word derived from Indian origins and would change its meaning radically in European hands to become an important 'organismic' construct.

A very early reference to 'jungle' appears in *The Journals of Major James Rennell, first Surveyor General of India, written for the information of the Governors of Bengal during his surveys of the Ganges and Brahmaputra Rivers 1764–1767:*

> We find the depths of Water from 34 to 8 Cubits (in ye dry Season), the Banks being mostly covered with Jungle we have very troublesome work to survey them.

Rennell here seems to have been equating the word 'jungle' with some sort of scrubby riverside vegetation. As he approached the Sunderbans, the great coastal plain on the Bay of Bengal, he ap-

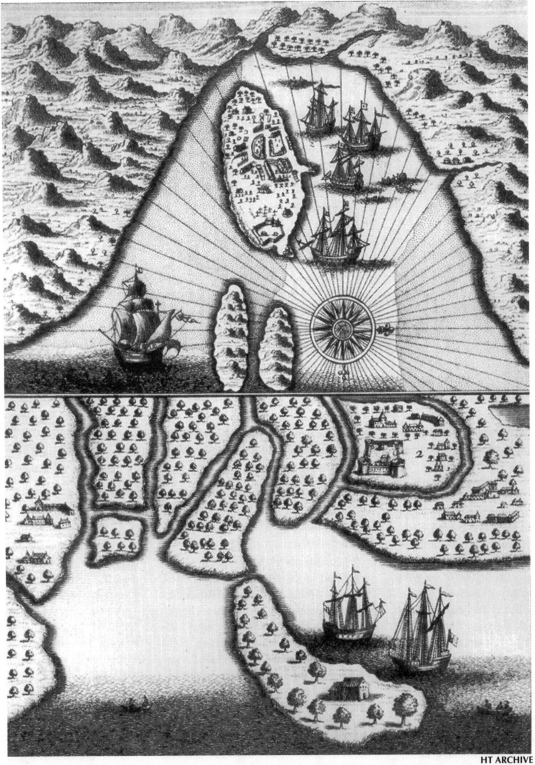

Madagascar and the East African coast, from *Histoire des Découvertes et Conquestes des Portugais,* by J.F. Lafitau (1733). The forests here are seen as neat rows of individual trees.

peared to distinguish 'jungly' vegetation from what he called 'woody' vegetation, by which he most probably meant mangroves and mangrove swamps that are influenced by the inflow of saline water from the sea. He later observed that there

are many 'Tygers' in the 'Jungle'. His use of the word, therefore, does not equate with 'forest' in a modern sense.

'Jungle' is derived from a Hindi and Marathi word, *jangal*, which, in turn, comes from a Sanskrit word (*jangala*)

for 'dry', 'dryland', 'wilderness', or even 'desert'. The fundamental meaning is thus 'wasteland', or *forêt* in the Norman French sense—that is, 'uncultivated and unenclosed land'. The word first entered English parlance to mean any uncultivated area noted for its tumble of long grasses, underwood, and thick vegetation. It later became transformed, so that by the twentieth century it had largely lost its Anglo-Indian connotations and referred instead to high forest and to the wild wood proper. This remarkable lexical change was well caught by Guy Madoc, who joined the Federated Malay States (FMS) Police in 1930. When interviewed for radio, Madoc continued to employ the romantic, exotic, and orientalist 'myths' that so characterised the writing of Columbus:

When we got beyond the rubber estates and saw the wilderness of the jungle, that, I think, is really what got me—that first impression of the jungle as a mysterious and impenetrable place.

Hundreds of miles of jungle over rolling mountains, exciting torrents coming down through the jungle, and when the torrents levelled out into smooth river, green *padi*-fields and little Malay *kampongs*, dotted around in the shade of fruit trees and coconut trees. It was all I had imagined of rural Malaya.

The transfer of meaning from dry open scrub to high forest may well have been assisted by the colonial expansion of Britain from India to Southeast Asia and to the Far East, the Malay Archipelago being far more heavily forested than the Indian sub-continent. Moreover, where the margins of the forest there have been affected by cutting and burning, they tend to exhibit an impenetrable mix of vegetation, with many climbers and lianas, very reminiscent of the original meaning of *jangal*. Most Europeans would have only seen such forest margins, so that the word would feel entirely appropriate, an amalgamation in the mind of 'jungle' and 'tangle'. Even today, 'jungle' conjures up a brightly-coloured Disney-like image, or Hollywood 'film set', of riotous climbers and creepers, with Tarzan and his chimp swinging from tree to tree. Hence also modern examples such as the trade mark 'Jungle Gym', for a climbing frame used by children.

By contrast, the undisturbed inner forest is dark, dull green, and remarkably empty. It is thus salutary to remember that the modern idea of impenetrable virgin 'jungle' was probably derived from forests that had been cut and burnt by humans. The resulting mass of vegetation later encouraged the formation of many analogous negative phrases, such as 'concrete jungle', a place of intense competition, or ruthless struggle for survival, and the 'blackboard jungle' for inner-city schools. In US slang, these connotations also gave rise, in the Depression, to the use of the word 'jungle' to mean a gathering place of the unemployed. 'Jungle' is not, and never has been (except in the most popular of meanings), equivalent to 'tropical rain forest.'

The idea of 'tropical rain forest' had to be created in the European mind *before* it could be seen on the ground. The term itself was invented in 1898, although the idea had been prefigured in the writings of the German naturalist and polymath, Alexander von Humboldt (1769–1859). As the historian David Arnold argues, Humboldt, through his *Personal Narrative of Travels to the Equinoctial Regions of the Americas* (1824–25), 'helped invent the tropics both as a field for systematic scientific enquiry and a realm of aesthetic appreciation.' However, it would take nearly a century before his 'Romantic belief in the fundamental unity of the natural world' (the Cosmos) and his ideas of 'organic richness' would give rise to the *tropischer Regenwald*, 'tropical rain forest', proper.

By the mid-nineteenth century, explorers, following Humboldt, were at last beginning to think in terms of 'forests', although the language employed remained remarkably simplistic and general. The engineer and naturalist, Thomas Belt (1832–78), for example, in *The Naturalist in Nicaragua* (1874), a work that Darwin called '… the best of all natural history journals which have ever been published', confined his descriptors to phrases such as 'great forest', 'black forest' and 'gloomy forest.' In South America, there were also the 'Atlantic forest' and the *selva*, a word derived from Portuguese and Spanish, but originally from the Latin, *silva* ('forest'). Yet Belt still had no precise 'scientific' linguistic entity to employ.

This gap was finally filled by pioneer plant geographer and ecologist Andreas Franz Wilhelm Schimper (1856–1901) in his founding work on synecology (the ecology of living organisms and the environment grouped together) entitled *Planzengeographie auf physiologischer Grundlage* (1898; translated into English in 1903 as *Plant-Geography upon a Physiological Basis*). Schimper at last gave a precise linguistic entity 'tropical rain forest' definition and content:

evergreen, hygrophilous [water-loving] in character, at least thirty metres high, rich in thick stemmed lianes and woody as well as herbaceous epiphytes.

Like Humboldt, Schimper was deeply imbued with both German romanticism and a Teutonic sense of the *Wald* (forest). He too saw the world organismically, and he sought to identify all the 'organic entities' that were adapted to the land and to the prevailing climate. To him, 'tropical rain forest' was such an organism, a named functioning biome or vegetation unit. And because it was *Wald*, to his mind it was one of the most significant. In similar fashion, in *Politische Geographie* (1897), the human geographer and natural scientist Friedrich Ratzel (1844–1904) regarded the political state as another type of organism attached to the land. Such holistic ideas would eventually lead to the development in 1935, by Sir Arthur George Tansley (1871–1955), of the concept of the 'ecosystem', to the holistic views of the South African statesman, soldier and botanist, Jan Smuts, and, much later, to more fanciful constructs, such as James E. Lovelock's 'Gaia hypothesis', in which the whole Earth is regarded as a living organism.

A linguistic analyst would describe Schimper as a 'segregationist', for whom communication pre-supposes signs and signs are the prerequisites of communication. In this approach 'tropical rain forest' does not exist as an unequivocally defined 'object', but from 1898 when Schimper's definition offered a linguistic sign, people could learn what such an entity might comprise, and 'see' this organismic construction in the landscape. By contrast Darwin—and Columbus before him—was, in linguistic terms, an 'integrationist', for whom signs are the direct product of observation. Put more simply, in 1898 there was a marked change from 'seeing' a riot of individuals to 'knowing' or learning an organismic entity.

Darwin was the quintessential observer, so much so that he was utterly befuddled by the 'brilliancy' (his word) of the tropical world. The geographer Luciana L. Martins, writing in the *Singapore Journal of Tropical Geography* (2000), captures this well when she says:

> ... what most puzzled Darwin was the profusion of associations that rushed into his mind. Rather than being concerned with limits and categorisation of species, Darwin sought evidence of relations and transformation. In contrast to Humboldt, Darwin's encounter with tropical landscapes offered few possibilities for quiet contemplation.

In essence Darwin, like Columbus, possessed Krasner's 'disordered and fragmented visual field', and did not see 'tropical rain forest', but rather a vast and perplexing diversity of nature. Despite, therefore, Darwin's synthesis of the revolutionary and integrating idea of 'evolution' in *On the Origin of Species* (1859), during the second voyage of the *Beagle*—which he described as 'the most important event in my life'—he still 'saw' the landscapes of the tropics in a manner that differed little from Columbus and those who had gone before him.

The organismic approach was not only a key to changing a 'fractured view' of the world; it was also an essential prerequisite for the development of both modern 'scientific' ecology and social environmentalism. Yet, when the word 'ecology' was coined in 1866 by the German zoologist and philosopher, Ernst Haeckel (1834–1919), he gave it a distinctly 'autecological' definition: the focus was still clearly on the individual plant or animal. Haeckel thus retained the 'fractured vision' of Darwin, with

whom he frequently corresponded. Ten years later Haeckel's definition of ecology had changed radically under the influence of Humboldt and of German Romanticism into a more organismic and synecological one, in which the totality of plants and animals at any given location is viewed as a whole in relationship both to their environment and to each other. The idea of 'vegetation units' was created which, in turn, would lead to the work of Schimper, to the concepts of *tropischer Regenwald*, ecosystem and the biosphere, and ultimately to Lovelock's 'Gaia'.

Interestingly, the organismic approach to ecology finds strong precursors in the writings of two key American pioneer environmentalists, Henry David Thoreau (1817–62) and George Perkins Marsh (1801–82). In their respective masterpieces, *Walden* (1854) and *Man and Nature* (1864), the idea of synecology had been sensed, if not yet named, and both writers, the one in Massachusetts, the other from Vermont, had been influenced by German philosophy through East Coast Transcendentalism. Some scholars have even claimed that Thoreau was the first to have employed the word ecology, although, on more careful study, this appears not to have been the case.

Schimper's 'tropical rain forest' thus was the first 'scientific' or 'ecological' diagnosis of the construction. Unfortunately, there are now hundreds of such 'scientific' constructions, all varying in complexity and coverage, and, in consequence, creating linguistic and taxonomic confusion. By the 1970s, the problem had become so severe that an umbrella term was invented by the Food and Agriculture Organisation (FAO) of the United Nations, 'tropical moist forests' (TMFs). This construct embraces a whole range of Schimperian inventions, such as the seasonal 'monsoon forest' and 'savanna forest'. Inevitably, it caused yet more confusion, and most modern statistics of tropical deforestation tend to refer to this broad entity of TMF rather than to the older 'tropical rain forest', as defined much more narrowly by Schimper.

Many of the organismic notions now found in 'Green' literature such as

HT ARCHIVE

H.M. Stanley, *In Darkest Africa* (1890), commented on the amount of decaying vegetation to be found in the depths of the forests of Africa.

Friends of the Earth (FOE) and Greenpeace pamphlets owe much of their mythical content to twentieth-century embellishments of the original Germanic idea of *Wald*. The first of these was a direct product of the organismic view itself, namely an attempt to provide 'vegetation units', and later 'ecosystems', with their own life stories. Between 1910 and 1940, two ecologists, the one American, Frederick E. Clements (1870–1945), and the other British, Sir Arthur George Tansley (1871–1955), expanded the organismic idea through their concept of 'ecological succession': that is the succession of forms through which vegetation must 'grow' to achieve its maximum, optimum, state of adulthood. In this theory, they developed the idea of 'the climax formation' which, in the words of Clements, represents '... the adult organism, of which all initial and medial stages are but stages of development.' 'Tropical rain forest' was seen as a classic example of such a climax, and this 'adult organism', or tropical optimum, was deemed to be in balance and harmony with its environment.

In the theory of succession, climate was all-powerful, especially for Clements. The climax formation of the 'tropical rain forest', for example, was seen as in balance with a long-prevailing humid tropical climate. It is amazing that, as late as 1936 and in the face of a welter of evidence concerning climatic instability, Clements could still write that:

> … stabilisation is the universal tendency of all vegetation under the *ruling* [my italics] climate… and… climaxes are characterised by a high degree of stability when reckoned in thousands or even millions of years.

Thus, he presented 'tropical rain forest' as the primaeval, undisturbed, climatic climax and optimum of the tropical world, a veritable 'cathedral of the wild'. Of course, to disturb the ancient harmony of this last surviving Eden, this remnant of a 'Golden Age', was the ultimate human sin. For Clements, 'man [*sic*] alone can destroy the stability of the climax during the long period of control by its climate….' This had to some extent been foreshadowed by George Perkins Marsh in *Man and Nature* (1864), where he wrote: 'Man [*sic*] is everywhere a disturbing agent. Wherever he plants his foot, the harmonies of nature are turned to discords.' However, Marsh, unlike Clements, did not subscribe to the view that 'Nature' should, or could, be left alone, or that 'undisturbed wilderness' was all that mattered.

Thus, German Romanticism, and its organismic view of the world, could now focus on the process of criminalising human actions with regard to its very own environmental construct, its very own utopia. The modern 'tropical rain forest' of the Green movement was nearly complete, and its construction was reinforced in 1952 by the publication of Paul Richards's fundamental Schimperian and successional text, *The Tropical Rain Forest: an Ecological Study*, a book that remained a standard work until very recently. A much-delayed second edition was issued in 1996.

By 1960, the 'tropical rain forest' had at last been invented. It was, in Edward Said's terms, an orientalist exotic 'Other', a European myth with elements dating back to Columbus. It was also the home of profuse biodiversity, as described by Charles Darwin, and of Michel de Montaigne's 'cannibals' and Jean-Jacques Rousseau's 'noble savage.' It was the linguistic sign of Schimper and, later, of Paul Richards. But above all, it was a German Romantic myth, with a deep emphasis on its role in achieving equilibrium, balance, and harmony; it was the optimum vegetation for its region of the Earth, primaeval and ancient, the last Eden, vulnerable only to the sullying greed and sinfulness of humankind. It was also Germanic and Massachusetts *Wald;* the hunting horns of Carl Maria von Weber's *Der Freischütz* could be heard blaring across the world. Moreover, such an *ur-wald* must be saved at all costs. In the words of the environmental historian Anna Bramwell, 'tropical rain forest,' like environmentalism itself, became the 'Northern White Empire's last burden and may be its last crusade.'

Today, the 'tropical rain forest' has grown into a hegemonic myth that sometimes can exclude all others from international debate. Yet there were, and are, many other ways of seeing and describing these 'tropical rain forests'. The French geographer Pierre Gourou, for example, presented a markedly different tropical entity in his magisterial survey, *Les pays tropicaux* (1947). David Arnold writes that, in Gourou, '… there is scarcely a trace of the Edenic: poverty and pathogenicity are all pervading. The tropical world is full of "horrors", a region where climate and disease are "terrible foes" to mankind.' Likewise Lucian Febvre, the founding geographer of the Annales School, denounced the Germanic creation of the 'tropics' as an 'over-idealistic geography', in which the soils were not fecund and in which virtually everything was inimical to humans. For him, the tropical rain forest was no wooded Eden; it 'was a desert, covered with verdure'. After all, both Europe and North America had developed and become rich precisely because they had cleared their forests, even in Germany,

the very heart of the cult of the *Wald* itself, in England, Massachusetts, and Vermont. Ironically, these are untypical regions of the world in that their 'forest' is indeed a 'climax' of sorts, if only a recent one since the ice sheets had retreated from the land just 16,000 years ago.

Baloo, Bagheera and their 'Little Brother' in Kipling's *Jungle Book*, a pioneering myth of humans in harmony with tropical nature.

It is intriguing to think how 'ecology' might have developed differently, if its roots had lain, not in the *Wald* of Germany, but in the open *veld* of southern Africa, or in the Mediterranean scrub of California, or in the deserts of Arabia, or, above all, in the seas and oceans, the dominant cover of the Earth. Forests are an exception in the world at large, and, even today, despite the human 'disturbance' so deprecated by Clements and Greenpeace, there are far more forests and trees than existed at the end of the last Ice Age, including in the tropics. It comes as a shock to many people to learn that most 'tropical rain forests' are less than 12,000 years old.

Yet, along with the giant panda and the whale, the 'tropical rain forest', Schimper's 1898 invention, has become an icon for all 'Green' movements, for environmentalists, for Deep Ecologists, and for New Age folk throughout Europe and North America. They are regarded as the ultimate organismic entity, 'the lungs of the world' (though this image is nonsense, lungs taking in oxygen and giving out carbon dioxide, the reverse of the action of photosynthesis!). To the older European myths have been added a whole gamut of such so-called 'scientific' myths to help to ensure that 'tropical rain forests' are seen as essential to us all, wherever we live and whatever we do.

It comes as a shock to many people that most 'tropical rain forests' are less than 12,000 years old.

But how acceptable is this Northern neo-colonial myth, which has been exported worldwide through both empire and education? How far does it mirror the reality of an ever-changing tropical world? How far is it dangerously constraining development in the poorer countries of the South? Superficially, it may seem a moral myth, and one widely embraced by the new 'citizen scientists' of the North; yet it is still a myth that helps the North to exercise power over the lands of the South. The myth is thus a fine example of the prevalence, persistence and perils of *idées fixes* in environmental history and debate.

In essence, 'tropical rain forests' do not exist as an object; like 'beauty' and 'liberty', they are in the eye of the beholder, where they are created, and re-created, to suit each new generation and age, each new power structure. In the near future, there will surely be 'virtual rain forests', far from anything envisioned by Columbus, Darwin, Schimper, or even Greenpeace. And with inexorable climate change, who knows how the 'real' world will look in a thousand years time?

FOR FURTHER READING

David Arnold, *The Problem of Nature: Environment, Culture and European Expansion.* (Blackwell, 1996); D. Botting, *Humboldt and the Cosmos* (Sphere Books, 1973); Anna Bramwell, *The Fading of the Greens* (Yale UP, 1994); E. Cittadino, *Nature as the Laboratory: Darwinian Plant Ecology in the German Empire, 1880–1900* (Cambridge UP, 1990); 'Constructing the Tropics', *Singapore Journal of Tropical Geography, Special Issue*, Volume 21 (1), March 2000; James Fairhead and Melissa Leach, *Reframing Deforestation: Global Analysis and Local Realities* (Routledge, 1998); James Krasner, *The Entangled Eye: Visual Perception and Representation of Nature in Post-Darwinian Narrative* (Oxford UP, 1992); Philip Stott, *Tropical Rain Forest: a Political Ecology of Hegemonic Mythmaking* (Coronet Books, 1999); Philip Stott and Sian Sullivan (eds.), *Political Ecology: Science, Myth and Power* (Arnold and Oxford UP, 2000); Tim Whitmore, *An Introduction to Tropical Rain Forests* (Clarendon Press, 1990).

Philip Stott is Professor of Biogeography in the School of Oriental and African Studies (SOAS), University of London.

This article first appeared in *History Today*, May 2001, pp. 38-44. © 2001 by History Today, Ltd. Reprinted by permission.

Why Don't They Like Us?

How America Has Become the Object of Much of the Planet's Genuine Grievances—and Displaced Discontents

BY STANLEY HOFFMANN

It wasn't its innocence that the United States lost on September 11, 2001. It was its naïveté. Americans have tended to believe that in the eyes of others the United States has lived up to the boastful clichés propagated during the Cold War (especially under Ronald Reagan) and during the Clinton administration. We were seen, we thought, as the champions of freedom against fascism and communism, as the advocates of decolonization, economic development, and social progress, as the technical innovators whose mastery of technology, science, and advanced education was going to unify the world.

Some officials and academics explained that U.S. hegemony was the best thing for a troubled world and unlike past hegemonies would last—not only because there were no challengers strong enough to steal the crown but, above all, because we were benign rulers who threatened no one.

But we have avoided looking at the hegemon's clay feet, at what might neutralize our vaunted soft power and undermine our hard power. Like swarming insects exposed when a fallen tree is lifted, millions who dislike or distrust the hegemon have suddenly appeared after September 11, much to our horror and disbelief. America became a great power after World War II, when we faced a rival that seemed to stand for everything we had been fighting against—tyranny, terror, brainwashing—and we thought that our international reputation would benefit from our standing for liberty and stability (as it still does in much of Eastern Europe). We were not sufficiently marinated in history to know that, through the ages, nobody—or almost nobody—has ever loved a hegemon.

Past hegemons, from Rome to Great Britain, tended to be quite realistic about this. They wanted to be obeyed or, as in the case of France, admired. They rarely wanted to be loved. But as a combination of high-noon sheriff and proselytizing missionary, the United States expects gratitude and affection. It was bound to be disappointed; gratitude is not an emotion that one associates with the behavior of states.

THE NEW WORLD DISORDER

This is an old story. Two sets of factors make the current twist a new one. First, the so-called Westphalian world has collapsed. The world of sovereign states, the universe of Hans Morgenthau's and Henry Kissinger's Realism, is no longer. The unpopularity of the hegemonic power has been heightened to incandescence by two aspects of this collapse. One is the irruption of the public, the masses, in international affairs. Foreign policy is no longer, as Raymond Aron had written in *Peace and War*, the closed domain of the soldier and the diplomat. Domestic publics—along with their interest groups, religious organizations, and ideological chapels—either dictate or constrain the imperatives and preferences that the governments fight for. This puts the hegemon in a difficult position: It often must work with governments that represent but a small percentage of a country's people—but if it fishes for public support abroad, it risks alienating leaders whose cooperation it needs. The United States paid heavily for not having had enough contacts with the opposition to the shah of Iran in the 1970s. It discovers today that there is an abyss in Pakistan, Saudi Arabia, Egypt, and Indonesia between our official allies and the populace in these countries. Diplomacy in a world where the masses, so to speak, stayed indoors, was a much easier game.

The collapse of the barrier between domestic and foreign affairs in the state system is now accompanied by a disease that attacks the state system itself. Many of the "states" that are members of the United Nations are pseudo-states with shaky or shabby institutions, no basic consensus on values or on procedures among their heterogeneous components, and no sense of national identity. Thus the hegemon—in addition to suffering the hostility of the government in certain countries (like Cuba, Iraq, and North Korea) and of the public in others (like, in varying degrees, Pakistan, Egypt, and even France)—can now easily become both the target of factions fighting one another in disintegrating countries and the pawn in their quarrels (which range over such increasingly borderless issues as drug trafficking, arms trading, money laundering, and other criminal enterprises). In addition, today's hegemon suffers from the volatility and turbulence of a global system in which ethnic, religious, and ideological sympathies have become transnational and in which groups and individuals uncontrolled by states can act on their own. The world of the nineteenth century, when hegemons could impose their order, their institutions, has been supplanted by the world of the twenty-first century: Where once there was order, there is now often a vacuum.

What makes the American Empire especially vulnerable is its historically unique combination of assets and liabilities. One has to go back to the Roman Empire to find a comparable set of resources. Britain, France, and Spain had to operate in multipolar systems; the United States is the only superpower.

But if America's means are vast, the limits of its power are also considerable. The United States, unlike Rome, cannot simply impose its will by force or through satellite states. Small "rogue" states can defy the hegemon (remember Vietnam?). And chaos can easily result from the large new role of nonstate actors. Meanwhile, the reluctance of Americans to take on the Herculean tasks of policing, "nation building," democratizing autocracies, and providing environmental protection and economic growth for billions of human beings stokes both resentment and hostility, especially among those who discover that one can count on American presence and leadership only when America's material interests are gravely threatened. (It is not surprising that the "defense of the national interest" approach of Realism was developed for a multipolar world. In an empire, as well as in a bipolar system, almost anything can be described as a vital interest, since even peripheral disorder can unravel the superpower's eminence.) Moreover, the complexities of America's process for making foreign-policy decisions can produce disappointments abroad when policies that the international community counted on—such as the Kyoto Protocol and the International Criminal Court—are thwarted. Also, the fickleness of U.S. foreign-policy making in arenas like the Balkans has convinced many American enemies that this country is basically incapable of pursuing long-term policies consistently.

NONE OF THIS MEANS, OF COURSE, THAT THE UNITED STATES has no friends in the world. Europeans have not forgotten the liberating role played by Americans in the war against Hitler and in the Cold War. Israel remembers how President Harry Truman sided with the founders of the Zionist state; nor has it forgotten all the help the United States has given it since then. The democratizations of postwar Germany and Japan were huge successes. The Marshall Plan and the Point Four Program were revolutionary initiatives. The decisions to resist aggression in Korea and in Kuwait demonstrated a commendable farsightedness.

But Americans have a tendency to overlook the dark sides of their course (except on the protesting left, which is thus constantly accused of being un-American), perhaps because they perceive international affairs in terms of crusades between good and evil, endeavors that entail formidable pressures for unanimity. It is not surprising that the decade following the Gulf War was marked both by nostalgia for the clear days of the Cold War and by a lot of floundering and hesitating in a world without an overwhelming foe.

STRAINS OF ANTI-AMERICANISM

The main criticisms of American behavior have mostly been around for a long time. When we look at anti-Americanism today, we must first distinguish between those who attack the United States for what it does, or fails to do, and those who attack it for what it is. (Some, like the Islamic fundamentalists and terrorists, attack it for both reasons.) Perhaps the principal criticism is of the contrast between our ideology of universal liberalism and policies that have all too often consisted of supporting and sometimes installing singularly authoritarian and repressive regimes. (One reason why these policies often elicited more reproaches than Soviet control over satellites was that, as time went by, Stalinism became more and more cynical and thus the gap between words and deeds became far less wide than in the United States. One no longer expected much from Moscow.) The list of places where America failed at times to live up to its proclaimed ideals is long: Guatemala, Panama, El Salvador, Chile, Santo Domingo in 1965, the Greece of the colonels, Pakistan, the Philippines of Ferdinand Marcos, Indonesia after 1965, the shah's Iran, Saudi Arabia, Zaire, and, of course, South Vietnam. Enemies of these regimes were shocked by U.S. support for them—and even those whom we supported were disappointed, or worse, when America's cost-benefit analysis changed and we dropped our erstwhile allies. This Machiavellian scheming behind a Wilsonian facade has alienated many clients, as well as potential friends, and bred strains of anti-Americanism around the world.

A second grievance concerns America's frequent unilateralism and the difficult relationship between the United States and the United Nations. For many countries, the United Nations is, for all its flaws, the essential agency of cooperation and the protector of its members' sovereignty. The way U.S. diplomacy has "insulted" the UN system—sometimes by ignoring it and sometimes by rudely imposing its views and policies on it—has been costly in terms of foreign support.

Third, the United States' sorry record in international development has recently become a source of dissatisfaction abroad. Not only have America's financial contributions for narrowing the gap between the rich and the poor declined since the end of the Cold War, but American-dominated institutions such as the International Monetary Fund and the World Bank have often dictated financial policies that turned out to be disastrous for developing countries—most notably, before and during the Asian economic crisis of the mid-1990s.

Finally, there is the issue of American support of Israel. Much of the world—and not only the Arab world—considers America's Israel policy to be biased. Despite occasional American attempts at evenhandedness, the world sees that the Palestinians remain under occupation, Israeli settlements continue to expand, and individual acts of Arab terrorism—acts that Yasir Arafat can't completely control—are condemned more harshly than the killings of Palestinians by the Israeli army or by Israeli-sanctioned assassination squads. It is interesting to note that Israel, the smaller and dependent power, has been more successful in circumscribing the United States' freedom to maneuver diplomatically in the region than the United States has been at getting Israel to enforce the UN resolutions adopted after the 1967 war (which called for the withdrawal of Israeli forces from then-occupied territories, solving the refugee crisis, and establishing inviolate territorial zones for all states in the region). Many in the Arab world, and some outside, use this state of affairs to stoke paranoia of the "Jewish lobby" in the United States.

ANTIGLOBALISM AND ANTI-AMERICANISM

Those who attack specific American policies are often more ambivalent than hostile. They often envy the qualities and institutions that have helped the United States grow rich, powerful, and influential.

The real United States haters are those whose anti-Americanism is provoked by dislike of America's values, institutions, and society—and their enormous impact abroad. Many who despise America see us as representing the vanguard of globalization—even as they themselves use globalization to promote their hatred. The Islamic fundamentalists of al-Qaeda—like Iran's Ayatollah Khomeini 20 years ago—make excellent use of the communication technologies that are so essential to the spread of global trade and economic influence.

We must be careful here, for there are distinctions among the antiglobalist strains that fuel anti-Americanism. To some of our detractors, the most eloquent spokesman is bin Laden, for whom America and the globalization it promotes relentlessly through free trade and institutions under its control represent evil. To them, American-fueled globalism symbolizes the domination of the Christian-Jewish infidels or the triumph of pure secularism: They look at the United States and see a society of materialism, moral laxity, corruption in all its forms, fierce selfishness, and so on. (The charges are familiar to us because we know them as an exacerbated form of right-wing anti-Americanism in nineteenth- and twentieth-century Europe.) But there are also those who, while accepting the inevitability of globalization and seem eager to benefit from it, are incensed by the contrast between America's promises and the realities of American life. Looking at the United States and the countries we support, they see insufficient social protection, vast pockets of poverty amidst plenty, racial discrimination, the large role of money in politics, the domination of the elites—and they call us hypocrites. (And these charges, too, are familiar, because they are an exacerbated version of the left-wing anti-Americanism still powerful in Western Europe.)

On the one hand, those who see themselves as underdogs of the world condemn the United States for being an evil force because its dynamism makes it naturally and endlessly imperialistic—a behemoth that imposes its culture (often seen as debased), its democracy (often seen as flawed), and its conception of individual human rights (often seen as a threat to more communitarian and more socially concerned approaches) on other societies. The United States is perceived as a bully ready to use all means, including overwhelming force, against those

who resist it: Hence, Hiroshima, the horrors of Vietnam, the rage against Iraq, the war on Afghanistan.

On the other hand, the underdogs draw hope from their conviction that the giant has a heel like Achilles'. They view America as a society that cannot tolerate high casualties and prolonged sacrifices and discomforts, one whose impatience with protracted and undecisive conflicts should encourage its victims to be patient and relentless in their challenges and assaults. They look at American foreign policy as one that is often incapable of overcoming obstacles and of sticking to a course that is fraught with high risks—as with the conflict with Iraq's Saddam Hussein at the end of the Gulf War; as in the flight from Lebanon after the terrorist attacks of 1982; as in Somalia in 1993; as in the attempts to strike back at bin Laden in the Clinton years.

Thus America stands condemned not because our enemies necessarily hate our freedoms but because they resent what they fear are our Darwinian aspects, and often because they deplore what they see as the softness at our core. Those who, on our side, note and celebrate America's power of attraction, its openness to immigrants and refugees, the uniqueness of a society based on common principles rather than on ethnicity or on an old culture, are not wrong. But many of the foreign students, for instance, who fall in love with the gifts of American education return home, where the attraction often fades. Those who stay sometimes feel that the price they have to pay in order to assimilate and be accepted is too high.

WHAT BRED BIN LADEN

This long catalog of grievances obviously needs to be picked apart. The complaints vary in intensity; different cultures, countries, and parties emphasize different flaws, and the criticism is often wildly excessive and unfair. But we are not dealing here with purely rational arguments; we are dealing with emotional responses to the omnipresence of a hegemon, to the sense that many people outside this country have that the United States dominates their lives.

Complaints are often contradictory: Consider "America has neglected us, or dropped us" versus "America's attentions corrupt our culture." The result can be a gestalt of resentment that strikes Americans as absurd: We are damned, for instance, both for failing to intervene to protect Muslims in the Balkans and for using force to do so.

But the extraordinary array of roles that America plays in the world—along with its boastful attitude and, especially recently, its cavalier unilateralism—ensures that many wrongs caused by local regimes and societies will be blamed on the United States. We even end up being seen as responsible not only for anything bad that our "protectorates" do—it is no coincidence that many of the September 11 terrorists came from America's protégés, Saudi Arabia and Egypt—but for what our allies do, as when Arabs incensed by racism and joblessness in France take up bin Laden's cause, or when Muslims talk about American violence against the Palestinians. Bin Laden's extraordinary appeal and prestige in the Muslim world do not mean that his apocalyptic nihilism (to use Michael Ignatieff's term) is fully endorsed by all those who chant his name. Yet to many, he plays the role of a bloody Robin Hood, inflicting pain and humiliation on the superpower that they believe torments them.

Bin Laden fills the need for people who, rightly or not, feel collectively humiliated and individually in despair to attach themselves to a savior. They may in fact avert their eyes from the most unsavory of his deeds. This need on the part of the poor and dispossessed to connect their own feeble lot to a charismatic and single-minded leader was at the core of fascism and of communism. After the failure of pan-Arabism, the fiasco of nationalism, the dashed hopes of democratization, and the fall of Soviet communism, many young people in the Muslim world who might have once turned to these visions for succor turned instead to Islamic fundamentalism and terrorism.

One almost always finds the same psychological dynamics at work in such behavior: the search for simple explanations—and what is simpler and more inflammatory than the machinations of the Jews and the evils of America—and a highly selective approach to history. Islamic fundamentalists remember the promises made by the British to the Arabs in World War I and the imposition of British and French imperialism after 1918 rather than the support the United States gave to anticolonialists in French North Africa in the late 1940s and in the 1950s. They remember British opposition to and American reluctance toward intervention in Bosnia before Srebrenica, but they forget about NATO's actions to save Bosnian Muslims in 1995, to help Albanians in Kosovo in 1999, and to preserve and improve Albanians' rights in Macedonia in 2001. Such distortions are manufactured and maintained by the controlled media and schools of totalitarian regimes, and through the religious schools, conspiracy mills, and propaganda of fundamentalism.

WHAT CAN BE DONE?

Americans can do very little about the most extreme and violent forms of anti-American hatred—but they can try to limit its spread by addressing grievances that are justified. There are a number of ways to do this:

- First—and most difficult—drastically reorient U.S. policy in the Palestinian-Israeli conflict.
- Second, replace the ideologically market-based trickle-down economics that permeate American-led development institutions today with a kind of social safety net. (Even *New York*

Times columnist Thomas Friedman, that ur-celebrator of the global market, believes that such a safety net is indispensable.)
- Third, prod our allies and protégés to democratize their regimes, and stop condoning violations of essential rights (an approach that can only, in the long run, breed more terrorists and anti-Americans).
- Fourth, return to internationalist policies, pay greater attention to the representatives of the developing world, and make fairness prevail over arrogance.
- Finally, focus more sharply on the needs and frustrations of the people suffering in undemocratic societies than on the authoritarian regimes that govern them.

America's self-image today is derived more from what Reinhold Niebuhr would have called pride than from reality, and this exacerbates the clash between how we see ourselves and foreign perceptions and misperceptions of the United States. If we want to affect those external perceptions (and that will be very difficult to do in extreme cases), we need to readjust our self-image. This means reinvigorating our curiosity about the outside world, even though our media have tended to downgrade foreign coverage since the Cold War. And it means listening carefully to views that we may find outrageous, both for the kernel of truth that may be present in them and for the stark realities (of fear, poverty, hunger, and social hopelessness) that may account for the excesses of these views.

Terrorism aimed at the innocent is, of course, intolerable. Safety precautions and the difficult task of eradicating the threat are not enough. If we want to limit terrorism's appeal, we must keep our eyes and ears open to conditions abroad, revise our perceptions of ourselves, and alter our world image through our actions. There is nothing un-American about this. We should not meet the Manichaeanism of our foes with a Manichaeanism of self-righteousness. Indeed, self-examination and self-criticism have been the not-so-secret weapons of America's historical success. Those who demand that we close ranks not only against murderers but also against shocking opinions and emotions, against dissenters at home and critics abroad, do a disservice to America.

STANLEY HOFFMANN *is the Paul and Catherine Buttenwieser University Professor at Harvard University.*

Folly & Failure in the Balkans

Tom Gallagher examines the sorry story of ethnic conflict in the Balkans, and concludes that foreign interference has needlessly fanned the flames of nationalism.

Bismarck's opinion that the Balkans were not worth the bones of a single Pomeranian grenadier has long been heeded by hard-headed statesmen from Disraeli to Kissinger who warned against active involvement in the region. A sense of fatalism about the ability of local leaders and their populations to aspire to good government and 'civilised' conduct has long coloured Western policy towards south-east Europe.

But the statements and actions of powerful Western leaders in the recent war over Kosovo suggested that a break with past traditions may be occurring. Madeleine Albright, the US Secretary of State, declared to Congress in May that 'the Continent cannot be whole and free as long as its south-east corner is wracked by ethnic tensions and threatened with conflict'. With maps of the region by his side, President Clinton went on television to show the American people where Kosovo was and why the peace of Europe depended on securing justice for deported Kosovo refugees. Britain's prime minister Tony Blair delighted Albanian refugees by promising that they would all be able to return to their homes. Other leaders promised a new Marshall Plan for the region in order to integrate it economically with the rest of Europe.

A look at the role of the great powers in the Balkans over the last two hundred years shows that such clear statements of principles are uncharacteristic. States-

men have been reluctant to act as peacemakers in the region, at least for extended periods. Altruistic gestures towards oppressed peoples have been overtaken by the need to preserve a balance of power between states whose interests collide in the region.

The Balkan peninsula is a region where civilisations and social systems have collided and merged for thousands of years. For over four hundred years, the Ottoman Empire headed by a Muslim sultan in Constantinople controlled most of the Balkans. The Ottomans taxed their subject peoples heavily and conscripted their young men to fight in frequent wars. But the west European obsession with ensuring that the religion of the people matched that of the ruler was not shared. The Orthodox Christian Church and the Jews enjoyed freedom of worship. They were allowed to maintain their own courts and judges, applying their own laws to their communities in a whole range of civil matters. Forcible conversions to Islam were rare. But among certain peoples, particularly the Slavs of Bosnia and the Albanians, large-scale conversions took place, not least because of the opportunities for upward mobility in the Ottoman bureaucracy or the military provided for Muslims.

The autonomy enjoyed by the Orthodox Church preserved cultural values pre-dating Islam, particularly memories of the Byzantine Empire which had lasted until 1453. This sense of religious

and historical separation would provide the seedbed for nationalism when the Ottoman empire decayed. A Byzantine heritage was also preserved by influential Greek families, known as the *phanariots*, who administered parts of the Empire on behalf of the Sultan.

The Orthodox Church was a supranational body that was non-national in its doctrines and outlook. Sometimes the harshness of church courts and the exactions of the *phanariots* made ordinary Greeks view the Turks as less onerous oppressors. During the seventeenth century Greek peasants in the Peloponnese welcomed the return of the Turks after periods of Venetian rule marked by heavy taxation and forcible conversion to Catholicism.

Memories of the sacking of Constantinople in 1204 by Crusaders who looted and massacred, desecrating churches and fatally weakening the Byzantine empire, created long-term enmity between western and eastern Christianity. Today in Greece these images of western treachery and barbarism enable opinion formers to appeal for solidarity with fellow Orthodox Serbs and condemn what is seen as Nato aggression first in Bosnia and later in Kosovo.

Two hundred years ago, as the Ottoman empire became enfeebled and corrupt, it was the West which appeared to offer the path to modernisation and renewed greatness for local Christian leaders and especially restless intellectuals in the Balkans.

In 1807 the Serbs were the first South Slav people to establish their independence. This achievement encouraged the view among Serb rulers that they were entitled to play the leading role in creating a union of South Slav peoples. When Yugoslavia emerged in 1918, the domineering attitude of the Serb leadership provoked resentment among other peoples, particularly the Croats, who, because of their experience of Austrian Habsburg rule from Vienna, had acquired different governmental traditions and expectations.

Before their current demonisation, the Serbs had long enjoyed a vogue in Europe because of their martial sacrifices in the cause of political freedom as well as the beauty of their poetry. Writers from Goethe and Walter Scott to Rebecca West expressed their admiration for the lyric beauty of Serbian popular songs, while Jacob Grimm ranked Serb poetry alongside that of Homer.

Intellectuals were encouraged to explore the past and invent glorious historical pedigrees.

The romantic nationalism pioneered by the German philosopher Herder found a ready audience among restless intellectuals in Eastern Europe. With its emphasis on the unique value of every ethnic group and on each group's 'natural right' to carve out a national home of its own, romantic nationalism was able to undermine the multi-cultural traditions of the Eastern world. When Herder hailed the Slavs as 'the coming leaders of Europe', intellectuals were encouraged to explore the past and all-too-often invent glorious historical pedigrees meant to give reborn nations the inalienable right to enjoy contemporary greatness. If this meant dominating territories shared by more than one ethnic group, then many nationalists justified such a course even if it meant that they were imitating the imperialists whose rule they were seeking to throw off.

The prospects of cultural nationalism were transformed by the French Revolution and Napoleon's humiliation of dynastic empires. The revolution against the traditional political order legitimised a West European concept of nationalism allowing a people to identify with a territory on which they were entitled to establish a state and government of their own.

The appeal of romantic nationalism for European public opinion was first revealed by the Greek War of Independence in the 1820s. Acts of cruelty were committed on both sides but it was the Ottoman atrocities against the Greeks that moved the liberal European conscience. The Ottoman massacre of Greeks on the island of Chios in 1822, immortalised in Delacroix's painting, enabled European public opinion to overrule governments that might have wished to limit Greek ambitions. It was not just Byron, but Shelley, Goethe and Schiller who unleashed a storm of enthusiasm for Philhellenism that cautious governments found hard to stem. In 1824, a series of privately financed loans, which in effect made the City of London the financier of the revolution, proved critical in ensuring Greek success.

One hundred and fifty years later, philhellenism was still a strong enough force to ensure that Greece entered the European Union even though there were nagging doubts about her real commitment to a post-nationalist agenda based upon European integration. In the 1980s and early 1990s Greece would earn the reputation of being arguably the most nationalistic of the Balkan states, under the populist premier Andreas Papandreou. Persistent interference by outside powers in its internal affairs had produced a culture of suspicion and complaint which helped nationalism to flourish.

After Greek independence was achieved in 1832, Great Power interference combined with local factionalism to weaken the prospects of effective government. Russia and Britain in particular had conflicting interests and ambitions in the Balkans. As a multi-national empire in its own right, Russia was hostile to the pretensions of European small state nationalism. But the tsars claimed to be the legitimate successors to the Or-

thodox Empire at Byzantium and the defenders of east European Christendom.

In 1774 Catherine the Great of Russia extracted from the sultan the right to appoint consuls in the Ottoman empire who could make representations on behalf of its Christian subjects. Between 1787 and 1792, Russia fought a war with Turkey whose aim was to partition the Ottoman empire and establish Russian control of Constantinople and the Bosphorus Straits. For the first time Britain became aware of conflicting British and Russian interests in the Near East. The realisation gave birth to long-standing international tensions as two rival European powers sought to fill the vacuum left by the retreating Ottoman empire on their own terms.

Britain feared that its imperial possessions in India would be threatened if Russia became a Mediterranean power. Thus the Foreign Office became associated with the policy of propping up the Ottoman empire, or at least preventing its slow decline becoming a rapid collapse that might overturn a precarious balance of power.

An anti-Russian coalition headed by Britain waged war in the Crimea in 1853–54 to foil the tsar's bid to partition the Ottoman empire. Thus the only general European conflict in the hundred years between 1815 and 1914 was due to the Eastern Question. An independent Romania emerged afterwards under the sponsorship of France. The victors in the Crimean War chose to sponsor Romania to prevent Russia controlling the mouth of the Danube. The Romanians claimed Latin ancestry and could act as a bulwark preventing a union of South Slav peoples which Britain feared would enable Russia to clinch its ambitions in the eastern Mediterranean.

Thus the precedent was established for map changes in the Balkans in order to satisfy a precarious balance of power rather than to suit the wishes of the local inhabitants. Emerging peoples threw in their fortunes with a Great Power in the hope that they could achieve their territorial goals. Prospects of co-operation between the Balkan peoples diminished as outside powers were prepared to sponsor rival nationalisms for short-term goals. In 1876 the power of events in the Balkans to galvanise international opinion was shown by the reaction in Britain to massacres perpetrated by Turkish forces against Christian Slavs in Bulgaria. William Gladstone, the leader of the Liberal opposition, published his pamphlet *The Bulgarian Horrors and the Question of the East* in September 1876 and by the end of that month it had sold 200,000 copies. He demanded that prime minister Disraeli use Britain's authority to compel the sultan to grant freedom to the Christian Bulgarians.

Gladstone had earlier earned the gratitude of the Greeks when, after serving as governor of the Ionian Islands, he had persuaded the House of Commons to place them under Greek rule. He wished British policy in the Balkans to be guided by moral criteria, challenging the doctrine set down by Palmerston in 1848 when he argued that

the furtherance of British interests should be the only object of a British Foreign Secretary… [and] that it is in Britain's interest to preserve the balance of power in international affairs.

In 1994, when addressing the House of Commons for the first time as foreign secretary, Malcolm Rifkind repeated the words of Palmerston and said that they would be his motto. Britain was then under fire for pursuing a policy of minimal engagement in the war in Bosnia. Its refusal to support the lifting of the arms embargo which would have enabled the Muslim-led government to defend itself against its Serb adversaries was widely criticised. The government's most vociferous critic was Gladstone's descendant as Liberal leader, Paddy Ashdown, who visited the Bosnian war zone on numerous occasions and argued that Britain was lowering standards of behaviour in the region by refusing to countenance forceful action against Serbs who had subjected the city of Sarajevo to a three-year siege and 'ethnically cleansed' many other areas populated by Muslims. Gladstone's 'Midlothian campaign' of public speaking on the Bulgarian crisis contained the advocacy of the underdog and the condemnation of aggressors which was to become a hallmark of Bal-

kan crises in the 1990s. Intellectuals, churchmen and ordinary citizens, moved or repelled by Gladstone's rhetoric, entered the fray. The poet Swinburne, who wrote in 1877 that 'the Turks are no worse than other oppressors around the world,' had his counterparts among leading playwrights and television personalities in the late 1990s who argued that there were many Kosovos around the world for whom Nato refused to act.

In 1877 Tennyson's sonnet hailing tiny Montenegro which had repulsed the Ottomans centuries earlier as 'a rough rock-throne of freedom' got much attention. It was accompanied by a long article about Montenegran history written by Gladstone, no other British leader identifying himself so completely with a Balkan cause until Tony Blair's emotional tours of Albanian refugee camps in May 1999. But Gladstone's campaign failed to move his great rival Disraeli. War with Russia appeared imminent in 1877 when, after a Russian victory at the siege of Plevna, Constantinople seemed to lie at its feet. Britain feared an enlarged Bulgaria would become an extension of Russia and an international conference was held in Berlin in 1878 to arbitrate the dispute.

The diplomatic carve-up of the region that ensued under the cynical guidance of Bismarck ruled out the creation of a viable pattern of states as the Ottoman empire was gradually forced out of Europe. Decisions were made about Macedonia, Bulgaria and Bosnia which would return to disturb the peace of Europe in subsequent decades. Rather than sponsoring a Balkan confederation or large ethnically mixed states where minority rights were protected by international guarantees, the European powers left two South Slav states with unsatisfied national programmes who would clash in wars over the next sixty years: Serbia and Bulgaria. Territory was annexed by the powers to which they had but the flimsiest claim: Bessarabia was taken by Russia despite its mainly Romanian population; while Bosnia had been occupied by Austria-Hungary in 1876. The biggest losers were the region's Muslim peoples, several million of whom were driven out of Serbia, Bulgaria and Bosnia, due to the absence of a powerful protector.

The rise of nationalism in the Balkans had arguably left the region as vulnerable to foreign penetration as it had been before. But communities which had been slow to acquire a national identity, such as the Albanians, quickly asserted their own national claims so as not to be overwhelmed by competitors. In Constantinople, western-style nationalism was adopted by modernising sections of the Turkish elite to stave off the complete dissolution of their state. One early result was the persecution of minorities deemed to be acting on behalf of Russia, the first of a series of horrific massacres being perpetrated against the Christian Armenians in 1896. These culminated under the cover of the First World War in 1915, when as many as a million Armenians were massacred or died in forced evacuations of their territory.

The powers had sponsored small, unstable and weak states, each based on the idea of nationality.

In a bid to protect trading routes, secure military objectives, or establish client states, the powers had sponsored small, unstable and weak states, each based on the idea of nationality. The Balkan states usually had conflicting territorial claims as well as ethnic minorities that had to be assimilated or driven out. They formed unstable local alliances, sought backing from outside powers in order to guarantee security or satisfy national ambitions and, in turn, were used by these powers for their own strategic advantage.

The term 'Balkanisation' has acquired world notoriety to describe the problems arising from such a fragmentation of political power. Two Balkan wars in 1912 and 1913, as Turkey was forced to give up most of its Balkan possessions, degenerated into a bloody scramble for territory among rival states. International arbitration guaranteed an independent Albania in 1913. But the capacity of the Balkans to trigger a wider conflict was shown by the way the great powers went to war following the assassination of the heir to the Austrian throne, Archduke Franz-Ferdinand, in Sarajevo on June 28th, 1914, by local pro-Serb nationalists.

At Versailles in 1919 the victorious Allied states rejected the precedent of the Congress of Berlin and instead sponsored territorially powerful states in the Balkans: Romania, Yugoslavia, and Greece. A new European order based on the national self-determination of peoples and operating under the aegis of the League of Nations was meant to guarantee the peace. But the self-determination principle often only applied where it weakened enemy states such as Austria-Hungary and it was disregarded where its consequences proved unfavourable to the victors. Thus Italy acquired the South Tyrol and parts of the Dalmatian coast where non-Italians predominated. Meanwhile, Yugoslavia excluded the Albanians of Kosovo. The burning of villages in the 1920s followed by the confiscation of land from Albanians in the 1930s, unless they had Yugoslav documents to prove ownership, was a foretaste of future deportations.

The League of Nations lacked the powers to protect minorities in states where insecure majorities which had gained territory as a result of the outcome of a European war often gave subject peoples the grim choice of assimilation or exclusion. Turkey's success in foiling an effort sponsored by the Allies to create a Greater Greece in parts of Asia Minor encouraged other defeated powers to defy Versailles Europe. In 1922 the deportation of 1.3 million Greeks from Asia Minor to Greece and 800,000 Turks in the opposite direction created an ominous precedent.

The mutual hostility which poisoned relations between the East European states encouraged the effective withdrawal of Britain and France from the whole region in the 1930s. The ascendancy of Germany was only challenged in 1939 by Britain and France as the threat to the balance of power became too great to ignore. But the eventual defeat of Nazi Germany only resulted in a swop of tyrannical rulers. In October 1944 Churchill concluded his famous 'Percentages Agreement' with Stalin which assigned the Soviet Union a dominant role in Bulgaria and Romania, and an equal stake for both powers in Yugoslavia, with Britain enjoying a majority stake in Greece. Despite his great services to the cause of freedom, Churchill was prepared to abandon more countries to a tyrannical fate than Chamberlain actually did at Munich in 1938.

During the Cold War, the West identified with bids by countries like Poland and Czechoslovakia to throw off the Soviet yoke. Lech Walesa and Vaclav Havel were seen as the champions of liberty-loving peoples that had been cruelly severed from the West, their natural home. However, the emphasis in the Balkans was in backing a strong leader or strong regional power capable of keeping 'ancient ethnic hatreds' in check and preserving a balance of power that would prevent the superpowers coming to blows there.

Thus Marshal Josip Broz Tito, the architect of Communist Yugoslavia, became a recipient of Western financial and diplomatic support after he broke with Stalin in 1948. Tito was probably the most enlightened Communist ruler the world has ever seen. But he still ran a police state and Western creditors poured money into Yugoslavia without linking aid to gradual democratisation. Milovan Djilas who went from being Tito's loyal lieutenant to his chief critic, was warning in the 1950s that social democracy and the social market were crucial requirements to prevent the internal tensions which festered under one-party rule, but his long imprisonments produced relatively little concern in the West.

During the last decades of the Cold War the West was even prepared to back Romania's Nicolae Ceausescu, an unsavoury Communist despot, in the mistaken belief that he was a weak link in the chain of Soviet power. But it is not just from the Communist Balkans that the evidence showing a Western preference for authoritarian leaders over democratically-elected ones comes.

After the defeat of the Communists in the 1944–49 Greek civil war, the United States was the main power behind right-wing forces determined to prevent the centre-left opposition winning office. Simultaneously, after going back on a First World War offer to Greece to cede Cyprus, with its Greek majority to Athens, Britain pursued a policy of divide-and-rule which left a bitter legacy of ethnic strife even after it conceded independence in 1960. In 1964, when the moderate left finally won office in Athens, the United States proposed to settle the Cyprus question by partition. When the Greek ambassador in Washington told Lyndon Johnson that such a plan could never be accepted, the president retorted:

> F___ your parliament and your constitution. America is an elephant, Cyprus is a flea. If these two fellows continue itching the elephant, they may just get whacked by the elephant's trunk, whacked good.... If your prime minster gives me talk about democracy, parliament and constitution, he, his parliament, and his constitution, may not last very long.

The US Central Intelligence Agency was implicated in the 1967 military coup which extinguished Greek democracy for seven years, just as it was in the attempted overthrow in 1974 of Archbishop Makarios, the leader of Cyprus, which led to a Turkish occupation and partition of the island.

The liking for improvised, short-term solutions to complex problems that ignore the wishes of local populations and are enforced by tyrannical leaders characterised the major powers' approach to the Balkans before and after 1945. It produced some of the biggest American and British blunders of the Cold War and has left two well-armed Balkan states, Greece and Turkey, which several times have almost gone to war.

Similarly, the penchant for diplomatic quick-fixes epitomised the West's engagement with Yugoslavia as it dissolved into fratricidal conflict in the 1990s. A new note was apparently struck in the Kosovo conflict in the spring of 1999 as Nato committed itself to undoing the effects of ethnic violence perpetrated on over a million Kosovar Albanians. Nato leaders also promised to abandon the view that the Balkans are a non-European zone of disorder and recurring hatreds by integrating the region with the economic and security structures that brought peace to western Europe after 1945. Time will tell whether these expensive pledges, made in the heat of war, will be redeemed by those who made them or their successors.

The lazy statecraft of external-policy makers has turned the Balkans into a European danger zone. Unless a new approach based on conflict prevention and permitting ill-used Balkan peoples to en-joy the same opportunities as the West emerges from the war in Kosovo, there is every likelihood that Balkan wars and crises will be a feature of the new millennium as they were of the old.

FOR FURTHER READING

Barbara Jelavich, *History of the Balkans* (two volumes; Cambridge University Press 1995); *Unfinished Peace: Report of The International Commission on the Balkans* (Aspen Institute/ Carnegie Endowment For International Peace, 1996); Tim Judah, *The Serbs: History, Myth and the Destruction of Yugoslavia* (Yale University Press, 1997); C.M. Woodhouse, *Modern Greece, A Short History* (Faber 1998). Noel Malcolm, *Kosovo: A Short History* (Macmillan 1998).

Tom Gallagher is Professor of Ethnic Peace and Conflict at Bradford University. His Europe's Turbulent South-East is to be published in 2000 by Harwood.

The Poor and the Rich

In recent years, researchers have moved closer to answering the most important question in economics: why are some countries richer than others?

Understanding growth is surely the most urgent task in economics. Across the world, poverty remains the single greatest cause of misery; and the surest remedy for poverty is economic growth. It is true that growth can create problems of its own (congestion and pollution, for instance), which may preoccupy many people in rich countries. But such ills pale in comparison with the harm caused by the economic backwardness of poor countries—that is, of the larger part of the world. The cost of this backwardness, measured in wasted lives and needless suffering, is truly vast.

To its shame, economics neglected the study of growth for many years. Theorists and empirical researchers alike chose to concentrate on other fields, notably on macroeconomic policy. Until the 1980s, with a few exceptions, the best brains in economics preferred not to focus on the most vital issue of all. But over the past ten years or so, this has changed. Stars such as Robert Lucas of the University of Chicago, who last year won the Nobel prize in economics, have started to concentrate on growth. As he says of the subject, "the consequences for human welfare... are simply staggering. Once one starts to think about them, it is hard to think of anything else."

Early economists certainly thought about them. Adam Smith's classic 1776 book was, after all, called an "Inquiry into the Nature of Causes of the Wealth of Nations". Many building-blocks for understanding growth derive from him. Smith reckoned that the engine of growth was to be found in the division of labour, in the accumulation of capital and in technological progress. He emphasised the importance of a stable legal framework, within which the invisible hand of the market could function, and he explained how an open trading system would allow poorer countries to catch up with richer ones. In the early 19th century, David Ricardo formalised another concept crucial for understanding growth— the notion of diminishing returns. He showed how additional investment in land tended to yield an ever lower return, implying that growth would eventually come to a halt—though trade could stave this off for a while.

The foundations of modern growth theory were laid in the 1950s by Robert Solow and Trevor Swan. Their models describe an economy of perfect competition, whose output grows in response to large inputs of capital (ie, physical assets of all kinds) and labour. This economy obeys the law of diminishing returns: each new bit of capital (given a fixed labour supply) yields a slightly lower return than the one before.

Together, these assumptions give the neoclassical growth model, as it is called, two crucial implications. First, as the stock of capital expands, growth slows, and eventually halts: to keep growing, the economy must benefit from continual infusions of technological progress. Yet this is a force that the model itself makes no attempt to explain: in the jargon, technological progress is, in the neoclassical theory, "exogenous" (ie, it arises outside the model). The second implication is that poorer countries should grow faster than rich ones. The reason is diminishing returns: since poor countries start with less capital, they should reap higher returns from each slice of new investment.

THEORY INTO PRACTICE

Do these theoretical implications accord with the real world? The short answer is no. The left-hand side of the chart on the next page shows average growth rates since 1870 of 16 rich countries for which good long-term data exist. Growth has indeed slowed since 1970. Even so, modern growth rates are well above their earlier long-run average. This appears to contradict the first implication, that growth will slow over time. It may be that an acceleration of technological progress accounts from this, but this should hardly console a neoclassical theorist, because it would mean that the main driving force of growth lies beyond the scope of growth theory.

What about the second implication—are poor countries catching up? The right-hand side of the chart plots, for 118 countries, growth rates between 1960 and 1985 against their initial 1960 level of GDP per person. If poor countries were catching up, the plots on the chart should follow a downward-sloping pattern: countries that were poorer in 1960 should have higher growth rates. They do not. Indeed, if there is any discernible pattern in the mass of dots, it is the opposite: poorer countries have tended to grow more slowly.

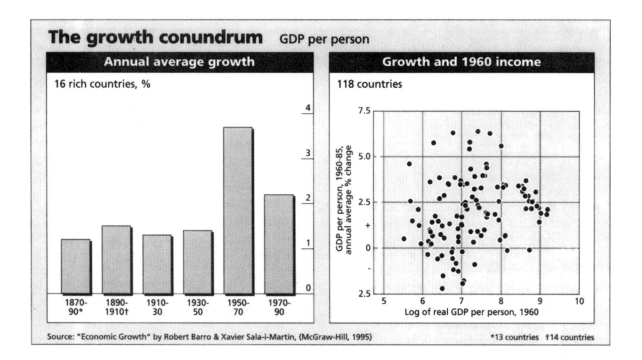

The growth conundrum — GDP per person

Annual average growth — 16 rich countries, %

Growth and 1960 income — 118 countries

GDP per person, 1960-85, annual average % change vs. Log of real GDP per person, 1960

Source: "Economic Growth" by Robert Barro & Xavier Sala-i-Martin, (McGraw-Hill, 1995)   *13 countries †14 countries

Having arrived at neoclassical growth theory, however, economics by and large forgot about the subject. It had a model that was theoretically plausible, but did not seem to fit the facts. How best to proceed was unclear. Then, after a pause of 30 years, along came "new growth theory".

This new school has questioned, among other things, the law of diminishing returns in the neoclassical model. If each extra bit of capital does not, in fact, yield a lower return than its predecessor, growth can continue indefinitely, even without technological progress. A seminal paper was published in 1986 by Paul Romer (see references at the end). It showed that if you broaden the idea of capital to include human capital (that is, the knowledge and skills embodied in the workforce), the law of diminishing returns may not apply. Suppose, for example, that a firm which invests in a new piece of equipment also learns how to use it more efficiently. Or suppose it becomes more innovative as a by-product of accumulating capital. In either case, there can be increasing, not decreasing, returns to investment.

In this and other ways, new growth theorists can explain how growth might persist in the absence of technological progress. But, they have gone on to ask, why assume away such progress? A sec-

ond strand of new growth theory seeks to put technological progress explicitly into the model (making it "endogenous", in the jargon). This has obliged theorists to ask questions about innovation. Why, for instance, do companies invest in research and development? How do the innovations of one company affect the rest of the economy?

A further divergence from the neoclassical view follows. As a general rule, a firm will not bother to innovate unless it thinks it can steal a march on the competition and, for a while at least, earn higher profits. But this account is inconsistent with the neoclassical model's simplifying assumption of perfect competition, which rules out any "abnormal" profits. So the new growth theorists drop that assumption and suppose instead that competition is imperfect. Attention then shifts to the conditions under which firms will innovate most productively: how much protection should intellectual-property law give to an innovator, for instance? In this way, and not before time, technological progress has begun to occupy a central place in economists' thinking about growth.

In the latest resurgence of interest in growth theory, however, the original neoclassical approach has enjoyed something of a revival. Some economists are questioning whether the "new" theories

really add much. For instance, the new theory emphasises human capital; arguably, this merely calls for a more subtle measure of labour than the ones used by early neoclassical theorists. More generally, it is argued that if factors of production (capital and labour) are properly measured and quality-adjusted, the neoclassical approach yields everything of value in the new theory, without its distracting bells and whistles. So it often proves in economics: the mainstream first takes affront at new ideas, then reluctantly draws on them, and eventually claims to have thought of them first.

THE MISSING LINK

To non-economists, however, both approaches seem curiously lacking in one crucial respect. Whereas in popular debate about growth, government policy is usually the main issue, in both neoclassical and new growth theory discussion of policy takes place largely off-stage. To the extent that government policy affects investment, for instance, either could trace out the effects on growth—but the connection between policy and growth is tenuous and indirect. Each approach may take a strong view about the role of diminishing returns, but both remain frustratingly uncommitted about the role of government.

An upsurge of empirical work on growth is helping to fill this hole—and, as a by-product, shedding further light on the relative merits of the new and neoclassical theories. The nuts and bolts of this work are huge statistical analyses. Vast sets of data now exist, containing information for more than 100 countries between 1960 and 1990 on growth rates, inflation rates, fertility rates, school enrollment, government spending, estimates of how good the rule of law is, and so on. Great effort has been devoted to analysing these numbers.

One key finding is "conditional convergence", a term coined by Robert Barro, a pioneer of the new empirical growth studies. His research has found that if one holds constant such factors as a country's fertility rate, its human capital (proxied by various measures of educational attainment) and its government policies (proxied by the share of current government spending in GDP), poorer countries tend to grow faster than richer ones. So the basic insight of the neoclassical growth model is, in fact, correct. But since, in reality, other factors are not constant (countries do not have the same level of human capital or the same government policies), absolute convergence does not hold.

Whether this is a depressing result for poor countries depends on what determines the "conditional" nature of the catch-up process. Are slow-growing countries held back by government policies that can be changed easily and quickly? Or are more fundamental forces at work?

Most empirical evidence points to the primacy of government choices. Countries that have pursued broadly free-market policies—in particular, trade liberalisation and the maintenance of secure property rights—have raised their growth rates. In a recent paper, Jeffrey Sachs and Andrew Warner divided a sample of 111 countries into "open" and "closed". The "open" economies showed strikingly faster growth and convergence than the "closed" ones. Smaller government also helps. Robert Barro, among others, has found that higher government spending tends to be associated with slower growth.

Human capital—education and skills—has also been found to matter. Various statistical analyses have shown that countries with lots of human capital relative to their physical capital are likely to grow faster than those with less. Many economists argue that this was a factor in East Asia's success: in the early 1960s the Asian tigers had relatively well-educated workforces and low levels of physical capital.

A more difficult issue is the importance of savings and investment. One implication of the neoclassical theory is that higher investment should mean faster growth (at least for a while). The empirical studies suggest that high investment is indeed associated with fast growth. But they also show that investment is not enough by itself. In fact the causality may run in the opposite direction: higher growth may, in a virtuous circle, encourage higher saving and investment. This makes sense: communist countries, for instance, had extraordinarily high investment but, burdened with bad policies in other respects, they failed to turn this into high growth.

The number-crunching continues; new growth-influencing variables keep being added to the list. High inflation is bad for growth; political stability counts; the results on democracy are mixed; and so on. The emerging conclusion is that the poorest countries can indeed catch up, and that their chances of doing so are maximised by policies that give a greater role to competition and incentives, at home and abroad.

But surely, you might think, this hides a contradiction? The new growth theory suggests that correct government policies can permanently raise growth rates. Empirical cross-country analysis, however, seems to show that less government is better—a conclusion that appeals to many neoclassical theorists. This tension is especially pronounced for the East Asian tigers. Advocates of free market point to East Asia's trade liberalisation in the 1960s, and its history of low government spending, as keys to the Asian miracle. Interventionists point to subsidies and other policies designed to promote investment.

Reflecting the present spirit of rapprochement between the growth models,

it is now widely argued that this contradiction is more apparent than real. Work by Alwyn Young, popularised by Paul Krugman, has shown that much of the Asian tiger's success can be explained by the neoclassical model. It resulted from a rapid accumulation of capital (through high investment) and labour (through population growth and increased labour-force participation). On this view, there is nothing particularly miraculous about Asian growth: it is an example of "catch-up". Equally, however, the outlines of East Asian success fit the new growth model. Endogenous growth theory says that government policy to increase human capital or foster the right kinds of investment in physical capital can permanently raise economic growth.

The question is which aspect of East Asian policies was more important—which, up to a point, is the same as asking which growth model works best. Although debate continues, the evidence is less strong that micro-level encouragement of particular kinds of investment was crucial in Asia. Some economists dissent from that judgment, but they are a minority. Most agree that broader policies of encouraging education, opening the economy to foreign technologies, promoting trade and keeping taxes low mattered more.

ONE MORE HEAVE

There is no doubt that the neoclassical model of the 1950s, subsequently enhanced, together with the theories pioneered by Mr Romer, have greatly advanced economists' understanding of growth. Yet the earlier doubt remains. Both models, in their purest versions, treat the role of government only indirectly. The new empirical work on conditional convergence has set out to put this right. The fact remains that in the earlier theoretical debate between the neoclassical and the new schools, the question that matters most—what should governments do to promote growth?—was often forgotten.

A new paper by Mancur Olson makes this point in an intriguing way. The starting-point for today's empirical work is a striking fact: the world's fastest-growing economies are a small subgroup of exceptional performers among the poor countries. Viewed in the earlier theoretical perspective, this is actually rather awkward. Mr Romer's theories would lead you to expect that the richest economies would be the fastest growers: they are not. The basic neoclassical theory suggests that the poorest countries, on the whole, should do better than the richest: they do not. Neither approach, taken at face value, explains the most striking fact about growth in the world today.

Mr Olson argues that the simplest versions of both theories miss a crucial point. Both assume that, given the resources and technology at their disposal, countries are doing as well as they can. Despite their differences, both are theories about how changes in available resources affect output—that is, both implicitly assume that, if resources do not change, output cannot either. But suppose that poor countries simply waste lots of resources. Then the best way for them to achieve spectacular growth is not to set about accumulating more of the right kind of resources—but to waste less of those they already have.

Marshalling the evidence, Mr Olson shows that slow-growing poor countries are indeed hopelessly failing to make good use of their resources. Take labour, for instance. If poor countries were using labour as well as they could, large emigrations of labour from poor to rich countries (from Haiti to the United States, for instance) ought to raise the productivity of workers left behind (because each worker now has more capital, land and other resources to work with). But emigration does not have this effect.

Data on what happens to migrants in their new homes are likewise inconsistent with the two growth theories. Immigrants' incomes rise by far more than access to more capital and other resources would imply. It follows that labour (including its human capital, entrepreneurial spirit, cultural traits and the rest) was being squandered in its country of origin. When workers move, their incomes rise partly because there is more capital to work with—but also by a further large margin, which must represent the wastage incurred before. Mr Olson adduces similar evidence to show that capital and knowledge are being massively squandered in many poor countries.

This offers a rationale for the pattern of growth around the world—a rationale that, consistent with the recent work on conditional convergence, places economic policies and institutions at the very centre. According to this view, it is putting it mildly to say that catch-up is possible: the economic opportunities for poor countries are, as the tigers have shown, phenomenal. The problem is not so much a lack of resources, but an inability to use existing resources well. It is surely uncontroversial to say that this is the right way to judge the performance of communist countries (those exemplars of negative value-added) before 1989. Mr Olson's contention is that most of today's poor countries are making mistakes of an essentially similar kind.

The question still remains: what are the right policies? One must turn again to the empirical evidence. That seems a frustrating answer because, suggestive though recent work on conditional convergence may be, such findings will always be contested. Citizens of the world who sensibly keep an eye on what economists are up to can at least take pleasure in this: the profession has chosen for once to have one of its most vigorous debates about the right subject.

Main Papers Cited

"Increasing Returns and Long-Run Growth". By Paul Romer. Journal of Political Economy, 1986.

"Economic Reform and the Process of Global Integration". By Jeffrey Sachs and Andrew Warner. Brookings Papers on Economic Activity, 1995.

"The Tyranny of Numbers: Confronting the Statistical Realities of the East Asian Experience". By Alwyn Young. NBER working paper 4680, 1994.

"Big Bills Left on the Sidewalk: Why Some Nations Are Rich, and Others Poor". By Mancur Olson. Journal of Economic Perspectives, forthcoming.

Reform for Russia

Forging a New Domestic Policy

Boris Nemtsov

How has Russian arrived where it is today? In what direction is it headed? To answer the first question, we must return to where change began. Mikhail Gorbachev half-hearted reforms of the 1980s opened the way for further democratization and led to improved relations with the developed countries of the world, but they also led to economic chaos. It is easy to overrate Gorbachev's political reforms and forget the ensuing economic troubles.

Nevertheless, the steps toward political maturity made since Gorbachev's time have been dramatic. In mid-1991, at the time of the Russian Federation's first free presidential elections, only two parties were legally registered in the Soviet Union: the Communist Party of the Soviet Union (CPSU) and Vladimir Zhirinovsky's Liberal Democratic Party (LDP, later transformed into the Liberal Democratic Party of Russia, or LDPR). The latter was perceived by the party nomenklatura as a lackey opposition. The electoral system in place during the legislative elections in the USSR and the RSFSR (the Russian Soviet Federated Socialist Republic) was not democratic. Not only was pluralism absent, but the deputies from civic organizations granted seats in the Soviet parliament as a democratic measure under perestroika were nonetheless co-opted by the CPSU line. A free press already existed, but as before, the government owned Russia's main newspapers. Public demonstrations were restricted, and government TV stations were plagued by censorship.

The economic situation was extremely grave. The consolidated government budget deficit for 1991 reached 30 percent, and hyperinflation loomed large. Besides increasing the state's foreign debt, the government was also taking over the monetary assets of citizens and enterprises that had always been held in Sherbank (the Soviet Union's lone savings institution) and Vnesheconombank (the Soviet foreign-exchange agent). In the cities, people stood in line for hours to buy sugar, soap, cigarettes, and vodka. Setting up legitimate businesses through administrative channels was a bureaucratic nightmare; authorization to engage in export-import operations could be obtained only through case-by-case decisions by the cabinet, and licenses to open banks were also contingent on case-by-case decisions by the State Bank of the USSR (the Soviet Union's central bank). The penal code of the Russian republic contained articles that penalized private entrepreneurship, "speculation," (in this case, simply normal private-trade transactions) and currency operations. At the same time, whole ministries and enterprises were being privatized for free or for just kopecks. Their directors simply obtained formerly public property for themselves through juridical machinations.

CAUSE FOR "MODERATE OPTIMISM"

Where is Russia now, a decade later? A full-fledged democratic system functions. Though this does not mean that only deserving individuals are in power, the people have at least been able to elect their leaders. A multi-party system has developed, and the press enjoys fundamental freedoms. Russia has a constitution built on the basic values of the civilized world that posits the supremacy of human rights and guarantees property rights, separation of powers, and civil liberties. Yes, our constitutional space does have a bleeding wound—Chechnya, where laws have ceased to function. But we must be honest—war alters normal civic conditions. And this time, it was the Chechen extremists who started the war by attacking Russian territory in pursuit of plunder.

The foundation of a market economy has also been built in Russia. Prices are freely determined, the ruble has become a convertible currency, and banks can open and engage in foreign-trade operations without individual permission from the government. Privatization has taken place—a lion's share of Russia's GDP is now produced by the private sector. The labor market has also changed. More than half of the working-age population is employed in the service sector. A civil code, which regulates private legal relations, has been passed. Today, all of these developments may seem obvious and hardly worth mentioning. Yet only ten years ago, none of them existed.

Russia will likely take one of three paths in the next few years. The "optimistic" scenario, in my view, will see accelerated liberal reforms of the economy and the supplanting of arbitrary legal regulations. Unfortunately, Russia now seems unlikely to follow this path. Although societal opposition to liberal reforms has weakened somewhat, the electorate's demand for such reforms is insufficient to bring about major change. Moreover, the inclination of Russia's leadership toward political change has been inversely proportional to the price of oil, which is now relatively high.

The "pessimistic" possibility, wholesale reversal of economic reforms together with the germs of the rule of law, would require a return not only to a command economy, but also to mass terror. This variant would be quite short-lived due to the relatively high costs for the government of such a dramatic and turbulent change, and thus it is also less likely.

The "moderately optimistic" scenario involves conservatism and moderately reactionary shifts. Some political and constitutional freedoms may be restricted. Some economic freedoms, as on financial assets abroad, may be curtailed as well, while others (like those on land trades, the activity of foreign companies, and guarantees for the unity of economic space) may be expanded. This path, which appears the most likely of all, could lead to economic stagnation. Nevertheless, even curtailed rights can produce positive results if they are perceived as long-term rules of the game—a legal framework that encourages consistency. Indeed, Russia needs time for legal precedents in rights protection to accumulate.

RUSSIAN VOTERS— NOT SO FICKLE?

How has the Russian voter responded to ten years of dramatic change? One of the first scholars who tried to model and formally analyze the behavior of the Russian voter was my late colleague A. A. Sobyanin. He was the first to suggest that Russians' electoral preferences are stable—contradicting the theories of many outside observers, who assume that Russia is a "unique historical case." K. Truevtzev's model of "electoral niches" is entirely based on this hypothesis.

Voting patterns in Russia's post-Soviet presidential elections also suggest

electoral stability. In the first round of the 1996 election, Boris Yeltsin received the votes of the democrats (minus Yabloko's seven percent), the centrists, and a portion of the voters who usually support non-political parties of the "Beer Lovers" type. In the second round, Yeltsin played to various groups when he scored his victory with the votes of centrists, democrats, and a percentage of the patriots. Alexander Lebed and Vladimir Zhirinovsky shared the "patriots'" votes (in total about 20 percent). Gennady Zyuganov received his consistent 32 percent for the communists. The apparent tendency of vote concentration toward the leading party in each category also should be interpreted as a sign of "rational" and therefore more predictable voter behavior.

LEGAL QUANDARIES

Industrial revolutions in the West created a demand for inviolable guarantees of individual rights, freedom of speech and conscience, and property rights, including intellectual-property rights. Progress in the post-industrial era is unthinkable without the reliable protection of these basic rights. Unfortunately, in Russia today these rights are not even guaranteed to the extent they were in late 18th-century England. One of the reasons for this lag is the ineffectiveness of the judicial system.

In 1991, Russia's new democratic government rejected a radical overhaul of judicial institutions and instead guaranteed job stability to the alumni of socialist-era law schools. These specialists are schooled in an archaic concept of law and have an outdated conception of state powers and prerogatives. To these stalwarts of the old system, a call from the regional committee or the governor can be "legal" grounds for a court decision. The law schools where Communist Party civil servants studied for years continue to prepare a new generation of judges and prosecutors to replace the current one. It is unlikely that the new generation of law experts will want to or be able to adjust to the new rules of Russian law. Moreover, the Russian judiciary has been granted self-regulation, which often leads to the sieving out of those

judges who actually make decisions in line with the Constitution. A sensible response is to legalize a "precedent principle" in law, as some legal experts have suggested. Law-enforcement organizations and the best lawyers and prosecutors would incur the costs of considering multiple applications in order to arrive at legal decisions.

The need to decrease the influence of federal-governmental institutions on the courts is more obvious, absolutely urgent, and technically simple. The creation of court districts that do not overlap with the administrative-territorial units of the Russian Federation would go a long way in this regard.

Before rushing to revise Russia's constitution with amendments and additions, we should first learn to apply it. In the long run, it is important to strengthen the following constitutional rule regarding governmental organs and personnel: "all that is not directly permitted is forbidden." This would prevent state officials from manipulating hazily defined powers for extragovernmental purposes. It would also be prudent to limit the president's constitutional right to dismiss the government. It is logical that this procedure, as well as the appointment of the prime minister, should involve consultation with parliament. In addition, constitutionally strengthened parliamentary oversight would make government organs more transparent to the public.

In the arena of economic transparency, in order to stop the regular violation of shareholders' rights, Russia needs to amend its laws on joint-stock companies and securities. These laws should include direct and unambiguous references to the corresponding articles of the Penal Code and the Code for Shareholder's Rights (KoAP), which deal with violations of the rights of shareholders and participants in securities markets. Today, violating securities law is hardly risky, even when the courts arrive at a just decision.

The ability of the Russian government and its officials to manipulate their positions of power in ways that damage the economy should be restricted. The adoption of the liberal bill "On Nationalization, " though killed by the first Duma, would eliminate nationalization of private assets if passed. This bill would be a strong positive sign of improvement in the Russian investment climate. Improved anti-trust laws would also be instrumental in fighting the unfair fringe benefits enjoyed by various officials. These laws would help abolish the most insidious type of monopoly—those protected by government regulations that create artificial barriers to competition. Anti-trust laws would give the entrepreneur a crowbar with which to break the administrative "padlocks" of licensing and accreditation. The anti-trust laws should in particular help break down the artificial barriers that surround the electricity market. We should not rely only on Anatoly Chubais's wisdom and sense of responsibility, because we cannot expect him to lead the United Energy Service forever. Anti-trust regulations can also bolster the energy industry, helping independent oil-extractors break onto the market.

The media and information market must be made more accessible as well. Without a universal and compulsory periodical lottery for the rights to TV-channel frequencies we not only lose huge sums of money, but also deprive the country from the best guarantee of freedom of speech and information.

AN ECONOMIC TOP-TEN LIST

The current situation appears sufficiently favorable to the implementation of economic reforms. There is political stability, and the main political forces have converged somewhat in their stances. The government is relatively popular, and the new president, Vladimir Putin, enjoys the public's confidence. The budget is balanced and the social obligations of the state are realistically laid out. Moreover, public expectations of the government's role in social welfare have been dropping steeply.

The following are criteria for the completion of the first stage of economic reform in Russia and the beginning of the second stage: (1) start of a significant foreign direct investment (FDI) flow; (2) annual inflation below 20 percent; (3) real annual interest rates below 8–10 percent; (4) a 20-percent increase in the

ruble's real exchange rate; (5) commencement of dedollarization of the internal market to make savings in rubles more attractive than savings in foreign currency; (6) the emergence of at least a few stable non-government commercial banks and foreign credit organizations; (7) increased monetization of Russia's GDP to at least 20 percent; (8) a stop to increases in real and nominal arrears and liquidation of budget arrears; (9) a substantial increase in the currency reserve; (10) regulation of the foreign debt.

These should be the government's short-term economic goals. They will be achieved only if the government is not foolishly seduced into over-regulation. In past cases, the government has cited the chimerical "fight against capital flight" as a pretext for strengthening currency regulations and intensifying control over foreign economic activity.

Also worrying is the tendency to allocate advance payments to groups with strong lobbying positions. Orders from the military-industrial complex and defense expenditures are both up (even excepting emergency expenditures for the Chechnya campaign from the calculation). The international community of developed democratic states could stimulate Russia to terminate such economically irresponsible ventures.

Nonetheless, the Western public's campaign to paint Russia as a country of organized crime and corruption is damaging. It is as misinformed yet deleteriously effective as the analogous campaign carried out against the United States during the Soviet era. Such a campaign influences politics, and politics affects investment-risk estimates, which in turn chart the investment climate in Russia. When measures of the investment climate worsen, Russian capital flight to the United States accelerates.

The Russian state has developed a multi-level system of corruption. Russia's government apparatus and its huge oligarchic businesses have both become parasites, robbing millions of now-destitute people and entrepreneurial, industrious citizens. The privileges of Gazprom (Russia's state-owned natural-gas monopoly) and Sibneft (an integrated oil giant) effectively tap the pockets of unpaid pensioners and the taxes of entrepre-

neurs. The residence-permit system and cellular-phone licensing and regulation (Putin recently reformed the latter) translated into thousands of rubles of illegal income for rank-and-file policemen. That a complicated system of preferential treatment for some and extortion for others exists is not accidental. It is a purposive policy, supported not only by individual corrupt bureaucrats but also by wide layers of the population involved in "government-related business." This practice revolves around the robbing of the ordinary citizen and entrepreneur. A storeowner in Moscow for example—the capital of "bureaucratic capitalism"—may be inspected by more than 20 different organizations with the "right" to check on him.

The weakness of political institutions has allowed many governors and republic leaders to reinvent themselves as "feudal princes" in a fragmented political environment.

REINING IN THE REGIONS

The Constitution of the Russian Federation clearly allocates authority between the federal, regional, and municipal levels of government. However, the weakness of political institutions has allowed many governors and especially republic leaders to reinvent themselves as "feudal princes," implementing in a fragmented political environment only those aspects of the "Russian truth" that they like.

When I worked in the government of the Russian Federation, we often ran into regional-level obstacles. Communal-housing reform was hindered, and our plan to transfer budgetary funds for servicing by the treasury rather than by authorized banks was sabotaged. Moreover, over the critical months of the spring and summer of 1998, many governors in practice supported the "rail war" (in which disgruntled unpaid coal miners blockaded parts of Russia's rail system)

VOTER SUPPORT FOR RUSSIAN POLITICAL PARTIES BY CATEGORY

percentage of votes cast

—1995—

32.2%	**COMMUNISTS–**
	Communist Part of the Russian Federation (KPRF), Power to the People, Working Russia for the USSR, Agrarian Party of Russia
19.0	**PATRIOTS–**
	Derzhava (State), For the Motherland, Govorukhin's Bloc, National Republican party for Russia, Congress of Russian Communities, Liberal Democratic Party of Russia (LDPR)—Zhirinovski
22.7	**CENTRISTS–**
	Transformation of the Fatherland, Duma-96, Tikhonov-Tupolev-Tikhonov, ROD, Interethnic Union, Stable Russia, border Generation, My Fatherland, Women of Russia, Our Home is Russia, 89 Regions, PRES, Trade Union and Industrialists—Union of Labor, PST (Fedorov)
15.7	**DEMOCRATS–**
	Federal Democratic Movement, Common Cause, Pamfilova-Gurov-Lisenki, Yabloko, Forward Russia, Democratic Choice of Russia, Social Democrats, party of Economic Freedom, Christian Democratic Union

—1999—

29.9	**COMMUNISTS–**
	KPRF, Communists-Workers of Russia-For the Soviet Union, All-Russian Political Movement in Support of the Army, "Peace, Labor, May," Stalinist Bloc, Party of Peace and Unity, All-Russian Political Party of the People, Spiritual Legacy
7.0	**PATRIOTS–**
	Zhirinovsky's Bloc, Congress of Russian Communities: Boldyrev's Movement, Russian Socialist Party, Movement of the Patriotic Forces—Russian Cause
36.7	**CENTRISTS–**
	Unity, Fatherland-All Russia
16.4	**DEMOCRATS–**
	Union of Right-Forces, Yabloko, Our Home is Russia, For Civil Dignity, Conservative Movement of Russia.

and thus condoned criminal action. The employees of the federal executive institutions whose job was to monitor law enforcement (including the Internal Affairs Bureau, the Federal Security Service, the State Tax Service, the Federal Tax-Police Service, the federal prosecutor's office, and the judiciary), had become the governors' lackeys. With such levers in hand, the governors could highjack the electoral process and thus guarantee their incumbency.

That is what spurred the idea to abolish the elective component of the governor's institution. The Russian ruling class has realized the need to safeguard the territorial, economic, and legal unity of Russia, and steps in this direction will certainly be taken. But I do not think that in order to achieve this goal we will give up elections of the Russian regional leaders. The current members of both the upper and the lower houses of parliament do not support this idea. The executive branch could better protect Russia's in-

tegrity by strengthening control over law enforcement in the regions.

In the meantime, authoritarian regimes that persecute people with dissenting opinions have emerged in certain regions. Some regional governments have gravely violated the federal constitution and laws, joined forces with federal representatives, suppressed the media, and weakened or destroyed local self-governance (as in Tatarstan, Bashkortostan, Kabardino-Balkaria, Ingushetia). Some have coalesced with criminal business ventures or built a system of privileges for corporate figures.

In order to secure the loyalty of regional leaders and protect its economic and legal unity, Russia needs a cadre policy in the structures subject to federal control and independent from the governor. Take away the pliant police force and tax inspectors from any governor and he will no longer manage to pressure an "inconvenient" commercial structure or protect a close associate in his "fiefdom."

Local self-government in the Russian Federation is, as a rule, merely an addendum to the executive power at the respective level. This is due to very low rates of voter participation at the municipal level. Many voters seem to feel that the further removed the official (president, minister, governor), the more he can do for them personally. The government could make an effort to give municipal governments more authority so that people feel that order in the state starts from order in one's home, one's street, and one's municipality. This strengthening should extend to governors: at present, local self-government is the governor's natural opponent.

Local self-government should get involved in communal-housing reform, a sphere currently monopolized by former Soviet housing agencies that are too expensive for most citizens. Current limitations on who can participate in the renovation of communal-housing apartments prevent competition that would drive down prices. Government subsidies for housing, which currently comprise up to a third of many regional budgets, also artificially drive up the cost of housing. If the housing market were freed up, then the funds currently used to subsidize could be given to destitute citizens rather than to organizations.

As reforms implemented in the communal housing sphere in the Baltics show, paying for what really is consumed turns out to be more profitable than paying according to administratively overestimated rates of consumption calculated by an interested institution.

Moreover, experience shows that citizens who can are willing to spend money to acquire additional apartment space, so long as the price corresponds to what they are getting—a condition that the market fosters.

When the communist system of the USSR was collapsing, many citizens naively supposed that prosperity would arrive immediately. The Western public was similarly deluded, counting on the former Soviet states to build quickly the institutions of civil society, political democracy, and a market economy. The absence of such institutions after ten years of reform was taken to reflect the pervasive bad will of the "Russian mafia," Russia's voters, and others.

In fact, Russia just has to travel the road that the developed countries have already followed for a century. We hope that we will manage to travel more quickly, and the speed that we have demonstrated over the last decade gives us reason to hope.

BORIS NEMTSOV is Russian State Duma Vice-Speaker (Right Forces Union).

From *Harvard International Review,* Summer 2000, pp. 16-21. © 2000 by Harvard International Review.

'The Barbarians Have Not Come'

*As we approach the true end of the century, **Peter Waldron** argues that those who describe Europe's experience of the last hundred years as bleak and dark are missing part of the story.*

THE DYING YEARS of the twentieth century have not been kind to its memory. Historians and commentators almost universally judged the period an unmitigated disaster for Europe and the wider world. 'The most terrible century in Western history' in the words of the polyglot philosopher Isaiah Berlin; 'the most violent century in human history'—the novelist William Golding; 'a century of massacres and wars'—the French scientist Rene Dumont, while historian Mark Mazower titled his recent book on the twentieth century, *Dark Continent*. I want to argue, however, that this gloomy view of the last hundred years is misleading and fails to take into account the huge advances that have benefited the lives of ordinary people in this time.

It is, though, undeniable that Europe in the twentieth century witnessed many horrors. War engulfed the entire continent twice, between 1914 and 1918 and in the six years after 1939. There were localised conflicts, especially in the Balkans in 1912–13 and again in the 1990s. Civil war tore into individual countries: most memorably in Spain in the 1930s, but also in Ireland in 1922–23, in Finland and Russia in the aftermath of the Bolshevik revolution and in Greece between 1947 and 1949.

The wars of the twentieth century were of a ferocity that set them apart from previous conflicts. The last general war in Europe before 1914 had been the Napoleonic campaigns at the very beginning of the nineteenth century, but since then rapid industrialisation had brought with it the development of lethal new weapons that could kill and maim with great effectiveness. The rapid repeating rifle, machine gun and heavy artillery were all to make the First World War wholly different in nature from any preceding conflict.

---

46 million Europeans found themselves uprooted from their homes between 1939 and 1948.

The number killed and wounded as a result of war between 1900 and 2000 far exceeded that in any other century. More than 8 million died during the First World War. This toll, though, pales into insignificance beside the price exacted by the Second World War. Perhaps as many as 40 million Europeans died in the six years 1939 to 1945. In contrast to previous conflicts, more than half of those killed were civilians. The two world wars were 'total wars', reaching deeply into civilian society. The wider population came under direct military attack. Total war required the mobilisation of the civilian population to produce the munitions and equipment needed for such intense fighting. Civilians worked longer and harder than before, and food was rationed. War ceased to be a male preserve: women were drawn in through the need for labour in both factory and field to replace men conscripted to fight.

The consequences of war were dramatic, especially in compelling people to migrate from their homeland. Fighting between Greeks and Turks led to more than 1.5 million becoming refugees after 1922, as Greek Muslims were deported to Turkey and Orthodox Christian Turks were shipped to Greece, even though in both cases the refugees had little in common with their new homes. The Bolshevik revolution of 1917 produced a wave of emigration as more than 1 million stalwarts of the old regime left Russia for foreign shores. In Eastern Europe the creation of new states after the First World War produced a backlash, especially against Germans, who found themselves unwelcome in areas where they had formerly held sway. Nearly 500,000 Spaniards fled north into France when Franco triumphed at the end of the Spanish Civil War in 1939. And after the Second World War more than 11 million Europeans were formally classified as Displaced Persons. But this huge number was less than one quarter of the total 46 million who found themselves uprooted from their homes in the decade between 1939 and 1948.

Statistics can be compelling by the sheer force of their numbers, but it is equally illuminating to disaggregate some of these millions of individual experiences. Take the case of a little Polish girl aged just four when war broke out in 1939. Deported with her parents and sisters to the Soviet Union, more than fifty years later she can still recall her mother burying her sisters, digging their graves with her own hands. They were sent from camp to camp, ending up in the and wastes of Central Asia and, at the end of the war, she managed to escape with her mother through the Middle East to British-occupied North Africa. Or picture an Estonian youth conscripted into the Red Army when Stalin's troops marched into Estonia in the summer of 1940, but then, as the Germans swept east in 1941, managing to desert, only to find himself conscripted for a second time, this time into the Nazi forces. As Soviet troops moved west in 1944 and 1945, he understood that any return to Estonia would be extremely dangerous, and took ship from a Baltic port not knowing where he would end up. As it happened, the ship's destination was South Wales, but to this day he has no knowledge of what happened to his parents or brothers. Both of these people ended up in Britain, making successful lives for themselves, but theirs are only two experiences taken from tens of millions in the demographic turbulence that engulfed central and eastern Europe at the end of the war.

War did profoundly affect Europe during the twentieth century, but the last conflict to involve the major European powers ended more than half a century ago. Since then Europe has been essentially at peace, and few Europeans under the age of fifty-five have had experience of armed conflict. The explanation for European peace since 1945 is, however, bound up with the nature of that last war. While the First World War was a conflict that the states involved stumbled into, the Second was explicitly ideological in character.

The 1939–45 conflict resulted from an attempt to stifle the democratic regimes of Europe and to impose the Nazi New Order across the continent, stifling nascent democracies and supplanting them with authoritarian and ideologically-based regimes. German Nazism and Italian Fascism represented one strand in this process, and the right-wing dictatorships that dominated the Iberian peninsula drew their inspiration from the same source. On the left, the regime that Lenin and Stalin instituted in the Soviet Union was also based on an ideological framework. The authoritarianism of both right and left aimed at destroying the nation-state structures that had been evolv-

ing since the sixteenth century and replacing them with supra-national authority: for Hitler the domination of Europe by a Nazi Germany, for Stalin by a Communist Russia. These twin regimes tried to impose an imperialism across Europe that had implications not just for its political structure but also for its social organisation. Slavery returned during the 1930s in the form of the Soviet *gulag*, and Hitler's regime also relied on forced labour to a substantial extent. It was not simply that the principle of slave labour became a reality, but the methods by which people were selected, institutionalised authoritarian attitudes. The Nazi regime brought explicitly racial thinking to the fore, exalting the Germans as the imperial master race and condemning other races to perpetual slavery in their construct of European society. Slavery in this context meant not just oppression but death. Hitler's Holocaust brought about the slaughter of some 6 million Jews, as well as targeting other minority groups foe attack.

Stalin's Soviet Union was hardly less cruel in its treatment of its population. The terror of the 1930s pushed millions into prison and labour camps. Stalin's motive was not racial, but the destruction once and for all of the old social structures and attitudes that had persisted beyond the 1917 revolution. Hitler's victims might have discerned some rationale—albeit a wholly repugnant one—for their fate, but for many of those killed or deported in the Soviet Union during the 1930s, there was no explanation other than Stalin's desire to inculcate terror into the population. The edicts issued from Moscow during the 1930s often simply required local officials to meet numerical targets for executions and arrests. The poet Anna Akhmatova summed it up: 'What was he arrested for?' people would ask 'What for? It's time you understood that people are arrested for nothing!' But Stalin's arbitrary terror barely survived the end of the Second World War. After his death in 1953 the Soviet Union settled into a mood of dull oppression, largely without the brutal violence that had characterised the late dictator's rule.

German and Italian Fascism were defeated through war and the Spanish and

Portuguese dictators faded away and were supplanted by democratic regimes. Stalinist Communism proved unsustainable in the end. The Soviet imperial domination of eastern Europe faced severe difficulties: in Poland, Czechoslovakia and Hungary outright opposition to the Communists was manifested on the streets in the 1950s and 1960s. In the Soviet Union itself, the Communist state disintegrated at the end of the 1980s. The people who lived under Hitler and Mussolini, Franco and Stalin were able to survive the experience. Christabel Bielenberg provides a vivid picture of a group of women she came across in the ruins of Berlin six months after the end of the war. Wearing 'drab headgear, caps and scarves and shapeless lumps of felt', they told tales of 'being driven from their homes as the Russians advanced, husbands dead or missing, children lost and then the final days and nights in Berlin, the howling shells, the seething flames'. But even in the ruins of the capital each was going about her appointed task, 'each had learned the value of team work in the survival game'. Much of the evidence about the experience of everyday folk in Stalin's Russia points to the same conclusions: times were hard both in material terms and less tangibly, but the Soviet people, as well as the Germans, proved to be survivors. In the words of a man who was twenty-five in 1939:

In spite of material difficulties… neither I nor the young people around me had any anti-Soviet feelings. We simply found in the heroic tension involved in the building of a new world an excuse for all the difficulties.

War and authoritarianism were thus repulsed across Europe, despite exacting a high price, and many who lived under these regimes were able to survive the experience. At the same time, however, more subtle and less dramatic pressures were at work. For the common people of Europe, the circumstances of everyday life at the beginning of the twentieth century were marked by more persistent and troubling problems. William Beveridge gave eloquent articulation to these difficulties in the 1940s when he wrote about the 'five giants' of want, disease, ignorance, squalor and idleness that stood in the way of post-war reconstruction. These very practical problems confronted almost every European at the beginning of the twentieth century.

At the beginning of the century only half the towns in Germany were connected to a proper water supply.

While want and squalor—poverty and filth—could be avoided by the prosperous, even they had no defence against illness. Disease was the central problem facing Europe in 1900. Rapid industrialisation across the continent during the nineteenth century and the growth of urbanisation saw the creation of cities that lacked the basic infrastructure of public health. Death rates in some parts of Europe—Estonia and Latvia, for example—increased in the decades around 1900 as the situation reached crisis point. Water supplies in many European cities still transmitted disease. At the beginning of the twentieth century only half of German towns were connected to a proper water supply and just two-thirds had a decent sewage system. The most unhealthy place in Europe was the capital of one of the Great Powers, St Petersburg in Russia. When the Russian prime minister addressed the Russian parliament in 1911 on a bill to install a sewage scheme in the city, he was embarrassed to admit that more than 100,000 people had died from a cholera epidemic in the previous year, that smallpox was still rife in the city and that, most damningly, the death rate in St Petersburg was exceeding the birth rate. While St Petersburg was a spectacularly unhealthy place, disease was a central feature of life in 1900 right across the continent.

Tuberculosis was a major killer. 37 per cent of all civilian deaths in Germany in 1914 were the result of TB and other respiratory diseases. The sanatorium that Thomas Mann depicted in his 1920s novel *The Magic Mountain* was an all too common feature of life for the well-to-do; the poor simply suffered without relief. Infant mortality was high across much of the continent: in Bulgaria it was 160 per thousand live births during the first year of life in 1900, and in France much the same. Life expectancy for a British man born in 1900 was forty-five. The health of Europeans has been transformed over the twentieth century. Advances in medical technology mean that most infectious diseases can now easily be cured. Vaccination against infection, first utilised at the end of the eighteenth century, developed slowly: only in the 1930s was an effective prophylactic against diphtheria introduced. But drug-based treatment of infectious disease is now the norm: the discovery and development of antibiotics during the 1930s and 1940s has meant that the epidemics that wiped out tens or hundreds of thousands of people are now a thing of the past. Viral infections have also been attacked through vaccination. A vaccine against polio, one of the most common killing or disabling diseases, was first produced in 1956. Drugs have also been used to deal with a wide range of other diseases: the control of kidney problems, blood pressure regulation and heart disease have all been aided by drug-related treatments.

The importance of public health has been recognised across the continent: water-borne diseases no longer kill. Infant mortality has been sharply reduced: in Bulgaria it was 14 per thousand in 1988, and in France and most of Western Europe 9 per thousand. Vaccination programmes have wiped out many of the threats to child health that persisted until well into the second half of the century. Europeans today are physically larger than they were a hundred years ago: an adult European is on average between 5 and 10 per cent taller today than in 1900. At the beginning of the twenty-first century, the most common diseases killing Europeans—heart disease and cancer—are mainly diseases of affluence. At the beginning of the last century heart disease was effectively an illness of those who could afford a high fat diet, and accounted for only 1 per cent of deaths in Germany and Britain. The changes to people's lives that have come about as a result of new medical technology have dealt effectively with one of Beveridge's five giants and, even in countries such as Russia, where conditions have deteriorated over the last decade, the warnings of renewed epidemics have not come to pass.

While actual famine made no real appearance in peacetime Europe during the twentieth century, malnutrition was common in the first part of the century. This was very much a result of poverty, of want. Poverty has not, of course, been eliminated altogether, despite signs of material prosperity. Urban poverty is more immediate and obvious, but rural want, harder to identify, is still widespread. In what has traditionally been the very poorest part of Europe, the region of Ruthenia—today split between Poland, Slovakia and Ukraine—even in the 1990s it was not an uncommon sight to see farmwork being carried out entirely by hand, without help from the most primitive agricultural machinery.

The idleness of which Beveridge spoke has also been much reduced, or at least its impact has been severely limited. At the beginning of the century, the chief causes of poverty were unemployment—idleness—and old age. Across the continent, the state has moved to ensure that neither the unemployed nor the elderly are reduced to absolute penury simply by virtue of losing a job or growing old. The first schemes of social insurance date from the 1880s when Bismarck's Germany introduced compulsory national insurance against sickness, invalidity and old age. In Britain, 1911 saw the beginning of unemployment insurance, in Denmark and Sweden old age pensions came in 1891 and 1913 respectively. In some parts of Europe, progress was much slower. France only came to adopt proper unemployment and pension provisions in the 1930s. The safety net of the welfare state has come to cover most of Europe. By 1970 more than 70 per cent of the European population—only excepting Greece, Spain and Portugal—was covered by accident, health, old-age and unemployment insurance. This evens out the tensions created by swings in the economic cycle, and means the increasing numbers of elderly can escape the poverty that many faced a century ago.

The lives of ordinary people have been hugely changed by the elimination of ignorance.

The lives of ordinary people have also been hugely changed by the elimination of ignorance. Literacy levels, the most basic outcome of education, were unimpressive across much of Europe in 1900. Imperial Russia was the most backward of the great European powers, with only 21 per cent of the population literate in 1897. Things were not much better in many of the new smaller states that came into being at the end of the First World War. Half of the population of the new Yugoslavia was classified as illiterate, along with 40 per cent of Romanians, and 30 per cent of Bulgarians and Poles. Even in the mid-1920s, only half the Greek population could read and write. The position of the more industrialised countries was slightly better: in 1900 only 5 per cent of the French were illiterate and in Britain and Germany, illiteracy had effectively vanished by the beginning of the century. But the elimination of illiteracy did not mean that a particularly high level of education had been achieved. A more exacting test was provided by evidence from the educational achievement of conscripts into the armed forces: in France in 1914, 35 per cent of recruits were classified as having 'an education which is nil or inadequate'. Even for those who had received a formal education, it seemed as if few of them remembered what they had been taught. Many French soldiers appeared to believe that Napoleon had been burnt alive on St Helena.

Schooling for most European children at the beginning of the century lasted only three or four years. Today almost no European child can escape ten years of compulsory education, while higher education—the preserve of a tiny elite in 1900—is now open to a much wider spectrum of society. There was especial progress in this field in the states of eastern Europe: in the thirty years between 1939 and 1969 the number of university students in Hungary grew sixfold; in Poland in the same period it increased from 50,000 to 250,000. In the countries of western Europe, around 30 per cent of young people are now able to enter universities. Ignorance, then, has been to a large extent suppressed.

There is one further area of dramatic change in the twentieth century. This is the transformation of the lives of women. In 1900 the civil rights of women were far inferior to those of men. This was reflected not only in their political subordination—the franchise was exclusively male in 1900 throughout Europe—but was even more evident in terms of their social and economic position. In France women could not open their own bank accounts until the 1960s. Legislation for equality in the work place was only introduced during the 1960s and 1970s (and was then only a precursor to genuine equality). Advances in medical technology have had a particular impact on women with the development of contraception enabling women to regulate their own childbearing.

Taken together, these changes to the lives of the common people of Europe are the most revolutionary of any that have affected the continent. They have been gradual, uneven and slow. There is little here of the drama of war, the passion of political revolution, few of the titanic struggles that have characterised the experience of Europe's political and social elites. Improvements in living standards, advances in medicine and greater access to education develop slowly day by day, year by year, decade by decade. There is none of the rapid pace of armed conflict, little inspiring oratory, few defining moments to these elements of Europe's history. And yet, these changes have given ordinary people today lives that our ancestors in 1900 could not have dreamed about. The material improvements are obvious but the less tangible benefits of health, education and a degree of security from appalling poverty are at least as significant.

The twentieth century was clearly one of hardship and terror for many, but we must balance this against the processes of social change that have worked their way across the continent. War and fascism have been defeated. The threat of war that reasserted itself during the Cold War of the 1960s and 1970s failed to erupt. Fascism has given way to properly constructed civil societies, and much of central and eastern Europe has come out from under the Soviet umbrella to reshape itself along democratic lines. The reasons for the endurance and rebirth of democratic systems and pluralist values are complex. The long gestation of these concepts and practices across Europe have much to do with it: society has changed gradually over many centuries, little by little embedding notions of equity and tolerance in the European psyche. During the twentieth century, Europe lost its position at the centre of international politics, so greater resources have been available to devote to social issues—especially since the end of the Second World War—and the barbarisms of disease and ignorance, of want and squalor have been tamed. In the words of the Greek poet Constantine Cavafy, 'the barbarians have not come'.

FOR FURTHER READING

George Lichtheim, *Europe in the Twentieth Century* (Weidenfeld and Nicolson, 1972); Mark Mazower, *Dark Continent: Europe's Twentieth Century* (Allen Lane, 1998); Eric Hobsbawm, *Age of Extremes: The Short Twentieth Century 1914–1991* (Michael Joseph, 1994); Michael Howard & Wm. Roger Louis, *The Oxford History of the Twentieth Century* (Oxford UP, 1998); Christabel Bielenberg *The Road Ahead* (Chatto & Windus, 1992). Two volumes deal with parts of Europe that have witnessed especially dramatic change: D.G. Kirby, *Finland in the Twentieth Century: A History and Interpretation* (Hurst & Co, 1984); J.J. Lee, *Ireland 1912–1985* (Cambridge UP, 1989).

This article is adapted from Peter Waldron's inaugural lecture as Professor of European History at the University of Sunderland.

Index

A

Abdullah, 153
Acquinas, Thomas, 23
Act of Settlement of 1701, 28
Adams, Samuel, 23
Adolphus, Gustavus, 3, 4
"aerial nitrate," 47
Albert Edward, duke of Clarence, 117
Albright, Madeleine, 201
alchemy, 44–49
Alexander the Great, 44
alkabest, as goal of alchemy, 45
Allenby, Edmund, 151, 153
anti-Americanism, 197–200
antiglobalism, anti-Americanism and, 199
Arabia, 148
Arabian Peninsula, 148
Arabs, anti-Americanism and, 198, 199
Arctic warming, climate change and, 188–190
Aristotle, 23, 44, 46, 47
Arkwright, Richard, 84–88
Army Debates of 1647–49, 25
Art Nouveau, 136–140
Ashcraft, Richard, 26
Asia, expansion in, 27–31
Atalanta Fugiens (Maier), 48
Atlantic Charter, 169
Augustus the Strong, 4
Austria, emergence of, as Great Power, 2–7

B

Baghdad, Iraq, 149
Baird, J. Kevin, 183–187
Balkans, ethnic conflict in, 201–205
Barro, Robert, 208
Basra, 147, 148
Belt, Thomas, 193
Bernhardt, Sarah, 130–135, 138–139
Bible, witchcraft beliefs in, 57
Big Bang theory, 181–182
big-game hunters, conservation and, 123–127
bin Laden, Osama, 197–200
Bing, Siegfried, 137–138
Black Hand, 142–143
Blair, Tony, 201, 203
Boer War, 167
Boerhaave, Herman, 47
Bonaparte, Napoleon, 77–81
Book of Christmas, The (Hervey), 98, 99, 100, 101
Boulton, Matthew, 52
Boyle, Robert, 26, 45, 48
bullion, 8–9
Burke, Edmund, 19, 20, 21, 69
Büsch, Otto, 90

C

canton system, in Prussia, 89–92

carol-singing, 98
"casuals," malaria drugs and, 186
Catherine the Great, empress of Russia, 72–76
Catholicism, 2
Charles II, king of England, 3
Charles XII, king of Sweden, 4
Christmas cards, 102
Christmas Carol, A (Dickens), 99–101
Christmas crackers, 102
Christmas, celebration of, in 1840s England, 97–102
Christmas trees, 99
Churchill, Winston, 149, 151–152, 153, 154; vs. Adolph Hitler, 166–170
Clements, Frederick E., 194
climate change, 188–190
Clinton, Bill, 201
Cloquhoun, Patrick, 111–112
Colbert, Jean-Baptiste, mercantilism and, 8–9
Colley, Thomas, 57–58
Columbus, Christopher, 191
Commercial Revolution, 9, 13
Commission of the Arsenal, 15–16
communism, 216
Communist Party of the Soviet Union (CPSU), 210
"conditional convergence," 208
consciousness, Descartes on, 33, 36
conscription, in Prussia, 89–92
conservation, big-game hunters and, 123–126
Contrast, The (Rowland), 77
Convention for the Preservation of Wild Animals, Birds and Fish in Africa, 126
Cooper, Anthony Ashley, 26
Crane, Walter, 136
Crimean War, 202
Crispi, Francesco, 103–107
Cromwell, Oliver, 25, 26
Cumming, Roualeyn Gordon, 123–124
cunning folk, 59

D

Darwin, Charles, 194
Darwin, Erasmus, 52–53, 54–55
DDT, malaria and, 184, 186–187
Decline of the West, The (Spengler), 171
Descartes, Rene, 32–38
Dickens, Charles, 99–101, 113
Dimitrijevic, Dragutin, 142–143
Discourse on the Method (Descartes), 33, 35, 38
diseases: malaria and, 183–187; twentieth century advances in fighting, 216
doctrine of papal infallibility, 110
Drebbel, Cornelius, 48
Druitt, Montague, 116–117, 118

E

East India Company, 18–22

ecological succession, invention of tropical rain forest and, 194–195
economics, 8–13, 51; growth theory on poor versus rich countries and, 206–209; reform in Russia and, 210, 212–214
education, in Nazi Germany, 155–158; political, in Italy, 105–106; twentieth century advances and, 218
Edward VII, king of England, 117
Egan, Pierce, 113
Egypt, 147149
Einstein, Albert, theory of relativity and, 178–182
Eisenhower, Dwight, 170
Elephants Preservation Act of 1879, 125
Elixir of Life, 45, 47
Emerald Tablet, 43–44, 47
Emile (Rousseau), 67, 69
Emmens, Stephen H., 44
English Reformation, 25
Enlightenment, 24–25, 63; British, 50–55
enrolling, system of, in Prussia, 89–92
environmental issues: Arctic warming and, 188–190; big-game hunters, conservation and, 123–127; invention of tropical rain forest and, 191–196
Essays on the Law of Nature (Locke), 26, 27
Europe: monarchism in, 77–81; twentieth century in, 215–218
Export Control Act, 161

F

farming, capitalism, 52
Feis, Herbert, 164
Fielding, Henry, 111
Fitzgerald, George, 178
Founders, of United States, 23, 24–25
France, 2–7, 9–10; Poison Affair in, 14–17; revolution in, 62–66, 67, 69, 70, 77–81
Franklin, Benjamin, in London, England, 39–43
Franklin, William, 40, 41
Franz Ferdinand, archduke of Austria-Hungary, assassination of, 141–146
Franz Josef, emperor of Austria-Hungary, 142, 143–144
Frederick William, elector of Prussia, 5, 89
Frederick William I, king of Prussia, 89
free trade, 12
Freemasons, Jack the Ripper and, 117–118
French, John, 47
Fulton speech, 170

G

Galileo, 62
Geber theory, of metals, 44, 46
genealogical awareness, in Nazi education, 156–157
German romanticism, invention of tropical rain forest and, 193–194, 195

Index

Germany, Nazism in classrooms in, 155–158

Gibbon, Edward, 50–51

Gladstone, William, 203

global warming, 188–190

Glorious Revolution of 1688, 4, 23

gold, 8–9; alchemy and, 44–49

Gorbachev, Mikhail, 210

Gourou, Pierre, 195

Grant, James, 113

Great Britain: Benjamin Franklin and, 39–43; breakup of Ottoman Empire and, 147–154; celebration of Christmas in 1840s in, 97–102; East India Company and, 18–22; emergence of, as Great Power, 2–7; Enlightenment, 50–55; slavery and, 93–96; street people in, 111–114; witchcraft in, 56–61

Great Instruction (Catherine the Great), 73, 74

Great Powers, emergence of, 2–7

Greater East Asia Co-Prosperity Sphere, 159, 160

Grossman, Marcel, 179

growth theory, poor versus rich countries and, 206–209

guillotines, 62

Guimard, Hector, 138

Gull, William, 117

H

Habsburgs, 2

Haeckel, Ernst, 194

health: malaria and, 183–187; twentieth century advances in, 216

Hermetic philosophers, 45, 47, 49

Hervey, Thomas K., 98, 99, 100, 101

Highs, Thomas, 84–85, 87

Hilbert, David, 179–180

Hitler, Adolf, 216; vs. Winston Churchill, 166–170

Hoffman, Stephen, 185

House of Commons, of Great Britain, 169, 169, 170

human capital, growth theory and, 207, 208

human rights, 67

Humboldt, Alexander von, 193

Hume, David, 51

hunger line, The (Kennedy), 114

hunters, conservation and big-game, 123–126

I

Industrial Revolution: commercial development in, 18–22; textile industry and, 84–88

insecticides, malaria and, 184, 186–187

Iran, 147

Israel, anti-Americanism and, 198

Italy, 5–6; Francesco Crispi and, 103–107

J

Jack the Ripper, 115–122

Japan, 174: U.S. oil embargo against, and World War II, 159–165

Jefferson, Thomas, 23

Johnson, Samuel, 57

Journals of Major James Rennell, first Surveyor General of India, written for the information of the Governors of Bengal during his surveys of the Ganges and Brahmaputra Rivers 1764–1767 (Rennell), 191–192

judicial system, reform in Russia and, 211–212

"jungle," 191–193

K

Kaye, John, 84–85, 87

Kennedy, Bart, 114

Kennedy, Paul, 173

Kertzer, David, 108–109

Kidnapping of Edgardo Mortara, The (Kertzer), 108–109

Kircher, Athanaius, 37–38

Kuwait, 147

L

Law, Edmund, 50

League of Nations, 204

legal system, reform in Russia and, 211–212

Letter Concerning Toleration, A (Locke), 23, 26

Liberty, Arthur, 138

Ling, Judy, 184–185

literacy levels, twentieth century advances and, 218

Lloyd, George David, 151, 152, 153

Locke, John, 23–29, 51

London and Calcutta (Mullens), 112–113

Louis XIV, king of France, 3, 4, 7; Poisons Affair and, 14–17

Louis XVI, king of France, 62, 69

M

Macpherson, David, 18

magical practitioners. *See* "cunning folk"

Maier, Michael, 48

malaria, 183–197

Malarone, 185

malnutrition, twentieth century advances in fighting, 217

Man and Nature (Marsh), 194

manufacturing, 53, 84–88

Marsh, George Perkins, 194

Marshall, George, 170

Marshall Plan, 201

Martins, Luciana L., 194

Masterman, Charles, 113–114

Mathias, Peter, 12

Maybrick, James, 119–122

McNaghten, Melville, 116, 117

Mearns, Andrew, 113

medical technology, twentieth century advances in, 216

mercantilism, 8–13, 51

metric system, invention of, 62

Meyrick, Frederick, 112

Michaelson, Albert, 178

Middle East, 147–154

migration, war in Europe and, 215–216

"monied interest," 20

Montespan, Athenais de, 15–16, 17

Morley, Edward, 178

Mortara, Edgardo, 108–109

mothers, Nazi idealization of, in education, 156

Mucha, Alphonse Maria, 138–139

Mullens, Joseph, 112–113

Murray, Margaret, 60

Muslims, anti-Americanism and, 198

N

nationalism, rise of, in Balkans, 202, 203

Naval Medical Research Unit (NAMRU-2), malaria and, 183–187

Nazism, in German classrooms during World War II, 155–158

Need, Samuel, 85, 87

Netherlands, 2–3, 4

"new growth theory," 207

Newton, Isaac, 44

Nilgiris Game and Fish Preservation Act of 1879, 125

Nine Years' War, 20

Nomura, Kichisaburo, 162

North, Dudley, 51

North's Regulating Act of 1773, 20

Nye, Joseph, 173

O

"Of the Balance of Trade" (Hume), 51

oil embargo, of United States against Japan, and World War II, 158–165

Olson, Mancuri, 208–209

On the Origin of Species (Darwin), 194

Osborne, Ruth, 57–58

Ottoman Empire, 201–202; breakup of, 147–154

Owen, Robert, 53–54

oxygen. *See* "aerial nitre"

P

paningenesis, 45

panvitalism, 45

papal infallibility, doctrine of, 110

Pasha, Enver, 148, 149, 153

Pearl Harbor, 170

Peter III, emperor of Russia, 72–73

Peter the Great, tsar of Russia, 4, 5

phanariots, 201

Phillips, Watts, 113

Philosopher's Stone, 45

philosophical inquiry, politics as tangible application of, 23

Philosophical Investigations (Wittgenstein), 32

Pius IX, Pope, 108–110

Pius XII, Pope, 108

Plant-Geography upon a Physiological Basis (Schimper), 193

Plasmodium vivax, 186

Plummer, Thomas William, 19

Poison Affair, in France, 14–17

political education, in Italy, 105–106

politics, domination of, in history books, 23

poverty: street people in seventeenth century England and, 111–114; twentieth century advances and, 217

preservation, big-game hunters and, 123–126

Price, Richard, 50

Priestly, Joseph, 47–48

Princip, Gavrilo, 141–146

privatization, in Russia, 210

Prussia, 2–7, 63; origins of militarism in, 89–92

public health: malaria and, 183–187; twentieth century advances in, 216

Q

quantum theory, 182

Quintilian, 37

R

Reign of Terror, 62, 63, 65

relativity, history of, 178–182

religion, as cause of war, 2, 3

Rennell, James, 191–192

Richard, Paul, 195

Rise and Fall of the Great Powers, The (Kennedy), 173

romantic nationalism, 202

Romer, Paul, 208, 209

Roosevelt, Franklin Delano, 160, 164, 166, 169, 170

Rousseau, Jean-Jacques, 67, 69

Rowlandson, Thomas, 77

Rules of the Direction of the Mind (Descartes), 37

Rump Parliament, 25

Russia, 2–7, 77, 148, 149, 163; Catherine the Great and, 72–76; reform of, 210–214

S

saltpeter, 47

Schimper, Andreas Franz Wilhelm, 193–194

science fiction, 50

Scottish Statute of 1563, 56

scratching, as method of breaking power of witches, 59

self-government, reform in Russia and local, 213–214

Selous, Frederick Courteney, 123–124

Sendivogius, Michael, 46–47, 48, 49

serfs, Catherine the Great and, 74

silver. *See* bullion

Singapore Journal of Tropical Geography (Martins), 194

Skepticism, 36–37

slavery: British and, 93–96; as trade, 11–12

Smalley, John, 85, 87

Smith, Adam, 20, 21, 23, 51–52

social militarism thesis, Prussia and, 90–91

Society for Bettering the Condition of the Poor, 112

Society for the Preservation of the Wild Fauna of the Empire, 126

Spain, 2, 9

Spengler, Oswald, 171

St. John, James Augustus, 59

Stalin, Joseph, 170, 216

street crime, poverty in seventeenth century England and, 111–112

Strutt, Jedidiah, 85, 87

sugar, slavery and, 94

"superstitious" beliefs, science and medicine as, 56

"suppressive," malaria drugs and, 186

Sweden, 3, 4–5

Sykes, Mark, 150–151

Syllabus of Errors, 109–110

T

Tansley, Arthur George, 194

tariffs, 12, 13

textile industry, 53; beginning of, and Industrial Revolution, 84–88

Thales, 32

Thirty Years' War of 1618–1648, 2, 3, 47

Thoreau, Henry David, 194

Tiffany, Louis Comfort, 140

torture, Catherine the Great and, 73

trade, global, 8–13

Treatise on the Elements of Nature (Drebbel), 48

tropical rain forests, invention of, 191–196

tuberculosis, twentieth century advances in, 216

Turkey, 2, 3

Two Treatises of Government (Locke), 23–29

U

unilateralism, anti-Americanism and, 198

United Nations, 198

United States: argument over relative decline of, 171–175; oil embargo against Japan by, and World War II, 159–165

V

vaccination, twentieth century advances in, 216

Vindication of the Rights of Woman (Wollstonecraft), 67, 68, 69, 71

W

Walden (Thoreau), 194

Watt, James, 86

Wealth of Nations, The (Smith), 8, 51

Wedgewood, Josiah, 53

Wignall, Steve, 187

Wilde, Oscar, 140

William III, king of Netherlands, 4

"witch doctors," 59

witch-bottle, as cure for witches' spells, 59

Witchcraft Act of 1736, 56–57

witchcraft, in eighteenth and nineteenth centuries in Great Britain, 56–60

Witch-Cult in Western Europe, The (Murray), 60

witch-swimming, as trial by water of witches in Great Britain, 57, 59

Wittgenstein, Ludwig, 32, 34

Wollstonecraft, Mary, 50, 67–71

women, rights of, 67–71, 218

World War I, 215; assassination of Franz Ferdinand and, 141–146; breakup of the Ottoman Empire and, 147–154

World War II, 168–170, 215, 216; U.S. oil embargo against Japan and, 159–165

Test Your Knowledge Form

We encourage you to photocopy and use this page as a tool to assess how the articles in *Annual Editions* expand on the information in your textbook. By reflecting on the articles you will gain enhanced text information. You can also access this useful form on a product's book support Web site at *http://www.dushkin.com/online/*.

NAME: _____ DATE: _____

TITLE AND NUMBER OF ARTICLE: _____

BRIEFLY STATE THE MAIN IDEA OF THIS ARTICLE: _____

_____

LIST THREE IMPORTANT FACTS THAT THE AUTHOR USES TO SUPPORT THE MAIN IDEA:

_____

_____

WHAT INFORMATION OR IDEAS DISCUSSED IN THIS ARTICLE ARE ALSO DISCUSSED IN YOUR TEXTBOOK OR OTHER READINGS THAT YOU HAVE DONE? LIST THE TEXTBOOK CHAPTERS AND PAGE NUMBERS:

_____

_____

LIST ANY EXAMPLES OF BIAS OR FAULTY REASONING THAT YOU FOUND IN THE ARTICLE:

_____

_____

LIST ANY NEW TERMS/CONCEPTS THAT WERE DISCUSSED IN THE ARTICLE, AND WRITE A SHORT DEFINITION: